Prisoners on Criminology

Prisoners on Criminology

Convict Life Stories and Crime Prevention

William S. Tregea

LEXINGTON BOOKS
Lanham • Boulder • New York • London

Published by Lexington Books
An imprint of The Rowman & Littlefield Publishing Group, Inc.
4501 Forbes Boulevard, Suite 200, Lanham, Maryland 20706
www.rowman.com

16 Carlisle Street, London W1D 3BT, United Kingdom

British Library Cataloguing in Publication Information Available

Library of Congress Cataloging-in-Publication Data

Tregea, William, 1944–
Prisoners on criminology : convict life stories and crime prevention / William S. Tregea.
pages cm
Includes bibliographical references and index.
ISBN 978-0-7391-4587-6 (cloth : alk. paper) — ISBN 978-0-7391-4588-3 (paper : alk.
paper) — ISBN 978-0-7391-4589-0 (electronic)
1. Prisoners—United States. 2. Crime—United States—Sociological aspects
3. Criminology—United States. 4. Criminals—Rehabilitation—United States.
5. Crime prevention—United States. I. Title.
HV9471.T74 2014
365'.6092273—dc23   2014015733

Printed in the United States of America

Contents

Preface

The author, as a Prison College and volunteer teacher for more than thirty years in Michigan and California prisons, awoke early in that prison teaching career to the fact that convicts can be thoughtful fellow human beings. Crime, law, circumstance, and punishment are one facet of the prisoners' self, but there are other sides of prisoners as human beings—human beings on the inside of a prison. This book emerges from that *inside* experience where prisoners study and write in their housing unit and take their stories to the prison school building for a prison college class or a prison volunteer class such as the author's "Social Science and Personal Writing." In that eight-week class, criminology theories were assigned and prisoners were asked to "write a story" about each topic. These prisoner stories are the basis for this book. The essays tell life stories that exemplify the many criminology theories.

These prisoner stories admit criminal intent, but often go behind the proximate legal or individualistic cause, such as: "I got fronted some dope, was given a gun, and told 'You'll need this.'" Instead, their insightful essays sketch disorganized neighborhoods—the violent, jobless "hyperghetto" of postindustrial American cities—dysfunctional families, and the culture of street crime *as a way of growing up*.

In the author's first book, coauthored with Marjorie Larmour, *The Prisoners' World: Portraits of Convicts Caught in the Incarceration Binge* (2009), we presented a background of why and how the United States has built up the world's largest prison system, and presented eighty prisoner essays and authors' narratives of what prison is like.

In this second book, *Prisoners on Criminology*, the author facilitated Michigan prisoners in writing weekly *personal stories* on various criminology readings and comparing those theories to their own lives.

Most criminology courses are based on a text with a reader. This book, *Prisoners on Criminology*, adds a graphic approach with "voices from the prisoners." This unique book includes a review of criminology theories, but also helps college and university students grasp a theory when it's exemplified in a memorable story by a prisoner.

Chapter 1, "Prisoners on Criminology," introduces prisoners' views that a great deal of their criminality came from their experiences growing up. Comparisons of individual, family, and community levels of explanation for crime led the prisoners to conclude that family and community are most important. Chapter 2, "The Making and Unmaking of the Prison State," gives an overview of the *prison binge era* as the recent thirty-five-year context for U.S. prisoners' experiences. It seeks to answer the question: Why and how did the U.S. embark on an incarceration binge to build the world's largest mass incarceration prison system? Chapter 3, "The Politics of Mass Incarceration," delves deeper into the political context in the making of such an unprecedented level of mass incarceration. Chapter 4, "Prisoners on Education," establishes that the education level of state prisoners is very low and traces out the consequences for their life stories. Each of chapters 1 through 4 has prisoner essays to example the topic.

The next four chapters present individual, family, and community pathways to crime, and explore sociological and critical criminology theories of crime. Each of chapters 5 through 8 has prisoner essays to example the topic. Chapter 5, "The Individual and Crime," reviews the individual level of crime explanation, including problems of addiction. Chapter 6, "The Family and Crime," reviews the family level of crime explanation.

Many prisoners describe how their criminality reflected "just the way it was" growing up in their neighborhoods. Chapter 7, "Community and Crime," reviews the community level of crime explanation. This "neighborhood effect" is elaborated in criminological concepts such as: subproletariat hyperghetto (Wacquant 2008); urban underclass (Anderson 2008; Wilson 1987; Wilson 1996); "ghetto poor" (Wilson 2012); or "social disorganization theory" (Sampson 2011; Agnew 2005). Social disorganization is defined as the inability of the community to enforce (through informal social control) its norms and values. In listening to the prisoners, we find it is necessary to trace the effect of socially disorganizing processes on the individual, the family, and the community.

Chapter 8, "Social Structure, Social Process, and Alternative Theory," reviews social structure explanations of criminality locating "structural strain" on individuals located in a society and its institutions, which hold out expectations of reaching cultural goals to all but provide limited institutional means to achieve these goals, leading to "innovation" in the form of street crime deviance. There are also individual stresses in a person's life (Agnew 2005) that lead to crime. This chapter also reviews social process explanations of criminality focusing on interaction with others who have a favorable attitude toward breaking the law. Social processes such as differential association (Sutherland 2005), social learning, modeling, imitation (Bandura), and identification (Glaser 2005) that lead to crime are explained. Chapter 8 also reviews alternative criminology that criticizes mainstream America as reflecting too much inequality. These power and inequality explanations of criminality include conflict theory, Marxist criminology, Left Realism, and feminist perspectives.

Chapter 9, "In-Prison Criminological Issues: Survival, Transformation, and Reentry," explores two convict movements: first, an effort by long-term prisoners to work with younger prisoners to end the culture of street crime; and, second, ex-cons who have earned PhDs and become professors pursuing convict perspectives to criminology to alter that academic world from the inside. This chapter also explores how prisoners can "become interested in other things," thus altering their life on the inside to prosocial values, and addressing their concerns about reentry and recidivism. Chapter 9 has prisoner essays on survival, transformation, and reentry.

Chapter 10, the concluding chapter, summarizes what has been learned and reviews policy issues related to crime prevention. The difficulties and opportunities of downsizing prisons are addressed with a view toward shifting resources to "justice reinvestment" in high crime urban areas.

Acknowledgments

Books are the outcome of many hours of work from the author and are improved through a network of individuals who contribute to the writing process. I acknowledge my now-deceased writing partner Marjorie Larmour for her part in coauthoring an inspiring earlier draft of this book. I also acknowledge the many hours that Michigan prisoner students put into writing their essays, including prisoner students at the Parnall and Cooper Street Correctional Facilities in Jackson, Michigan, and the Gus Harrison Correctional Facility in Adrian, Michigan. Thanks also go to Ms. Christina Bates, special activities director at the Gus Harrison Correctional Facility, and Julia Cady, Michigan Prisoner Reentry Initiative (MPRI) director at the Parnall Facility. Additional thanks go to Adrian College student Jordyn Shekell for typing up the many original, handwritten prisoner essays.

Special thanks go to Michael Sisskin and Jana Hodges-Kluck and her assistant, Eric Wrona, of Lexington Books. I also extend thanks to Stephen Richards and Jeffrey Ian Ross for their encouragement, and more generally to the *Convict Criminology* colleagues, who continue to give voice to prisoners' views. Appreciation is given in recognition to John Irwin, now deceased, for his leadership of the convict criminology movement. Appreciation is also given to Barbara Levine and Laura Sager for their support of prison educational programs as part of their leadership of Michigan's Citizen Alliance on Prisons and Public Spending (CAPPS 2008), and for ongoing practical work and hope for change (www.capps-mi.org).

The prisoner voices in this book will not be wasted if the public can move away from the expanding prison world and overuse of confinement (especially for drug crimes, but also for too-long sentences for murder and sex offenses). Prisons are the "holding pens" and revolving door for the young men (Irwin 2005) of our throw-away cities (Williamson, Imbroscio, and Alperovitz 2002). Overuse of warehouse incarceration locks up our tax dollars as social resources (Jacobsen 2005) and neglects the development of social skills and human capital of prisoners (Useem and Piehl 2008). Let's hope that prisoner voices—and those who can hear and understand—can help in the effort to move toward a set of more sensible laws, prison programming, and parole policies (CAPPS 2008); a new harm-reduction approach to drugs (Abadinsky 2008:408–18); and a community justice and justice-reinvestment approach (Clear and Cadora 2003; Austin et al. 2013) for Americans to address the problems of mass incarceration in our cities. Let's hope that the *prisoner voices* can take their place in helping to lead to a better life—not only for their sakes, but for ours.

1

Prisoners on Criminology

I am angry. I've been angry for a long time about the way jobless ghettos have emerged and festered in U.S. cities. And, I've been angry about how the African Americans in these impoverished, drug-infested inner-city neighborhoods disproportionately wind up in prison. From a critical perspective what is going on with mass incarceration in the United States is a form of convenient oppression. I have seen this develop in my lifetime.

When I was in high school in the late 1950s and early 1960s I saw racial discrimination firsthand. Over the last thirty-five years the United States has developed the world's largest prison system. Several states have begun to halt the growth of the prison population, and a handful of states have actually reduced their prison population (Austin et al. 2013). There are calls to end the disenfranchisement of African American ex-felons as part of a "new civil rights movement" (Alexander 2012). Influential criminologists have been examining high-impact neighborhoods that have single blocks costing upward of a million dollars a year in prison costs and argue to reduce prison expenses and invest the money saved in those neighborhoods (Austin et al. 2013). Are we at a "tipping point" of a new decarceration and justice reinvestment movement?

MY STORY

I arrived in Michigan from Northern California in the early summer of 1961 as a seventeen-year-old who had just finished his junior year of high school. I went to work in a Lake Michigan upstate beach resort hotel. At the end of the summer the owner of the hotel asked me to drive his car to his home city of Cincinnati. He indicated a hotel maid who lived in Cincinnati would be coming along. She was a black lady in her forties. I was a white student, new to Michigan and the Midwest, trying to finish my last year of high school at East Lansing, home of Michigan State University (MSU) where my mother worked and was a graduate student. The hotel owner had given me $50 for expenses and a credit card for gas.

The long drive was uneventful until we stopped at a restaurant in Fort Wayne, Indiana. We hadn't spent any of the $50. I wanted to eat at an expensive restaurant. My mouth watered for a nice steak dinner.

We waited in line at this fancy restaurant for the host to seat us. But a strange thing was happening. Each time a table opened up, the host led people behind us to those seats. We waited some more. When it came our turn again, the host went around us again to the next people behind us—he was bypassing us. The African American maid was poking me in the side with her elbow, indicating we were not going to be served and should leave.

I was stunned. Crushed and depressed, I trudged with the maid back to the hotel owner's Cadillac. It had been a long drive and I thought we really deserved a good meal. We wound up going to a drive-in burger and fries place down the road.

Those fries tasted terrible as we sat there in silence, eating our "meal." When we got to Cincinnati my car passenger, the maid, put me up on her living room sofa bed and, the next morning, made a nice breakfast of bacon and eggs. Her small low-income "project" apartment was warm and inviting. I returned the car to the hotel owner at his office in downtown Cincinnati. He paid for my first airplane trip ever—two legs—Cincinnati to Detroit and then to Lansing. It had been an interesting summer job and trip to Cincinnati, but the encounter at the fancy restaurant had left a bad taste in my mouth. It was 1961.

This was not to be my only experience with racism in the form of prejudice and discrimination. In the fall of 1961 I was starting my high school senior year, living in a rental room in East Lansing, and working in Lansing at a chicken and ribs fast food restaurant. I can remember a time when I was making a delivery to a small house on the near west side of Lansing—the black section of town—when an African American man with a goatee opened the door. He had a white wife and two kids. I recognized him. He was one of only a handful of African American faculty at Michigan State University. Instantly surprised, I blurted out: "What are you doing living here?" He replied that he and his family could not buy a house in East Lansing because realtors, reflecting the racism in that community, wouldn't sell to him.

Later, when I was twenty, I traveled to the big cities on the east coast in 1964 and saw the many festering inner-city neighborhoods that were developing at that time. White cops seemed to crawl all over the streets, dominating the black ghettos—there seemed to be no black police officers.

It's not that I'm against the idea of police. I'm not particularly happy about crimes of violence against persons and predation upon others property. I was mugged on that trip to New York City and have been the victim of home invasions over the years in my periods of living in low-income neighbor-hoods. But now that I've worked in the prisons, I can see the connection between the development of the festering inner cities, crime, and the build-up of the world's largest prison system. It's like a feedback loop: jobless ghetto—crime—prison—back to the same crime-ridden neighborhood on parole—then back to prison. How did this start? The short answer is—roads.

While I was not personally angry about nice, smooth roads, I saw how the U.S. highway system being built (starting with the Interstate Highway Act of 1958) was putting wide concrete highway roads with ramps through urban neighborhoods and taking the people who could afford it out to the new suburbs where the housing tracts and shopping malls grew. Some of it was "white flight," but the suburbs were the new way to live. I became aware that the jobs—the factories, the office complexes, and the "main street" stores—were moving out to malls and strip malls of the suburbs. It was also "capital flight" or disinvestment—the businesses were moving to the "edge cities" (Garreau 1991).

The central cities were left behind, abandoned, developing into high poverty neighborhoods (40 percent or more poor) and "concentrated disadvantage" poverty areas (Sampson 2011). The people in the high crime areas were poor and many of the young black males were going to prison. African Americans, 12 percent of the U.S. population, had always been overrepresented in the rural southern prison system. Blacks made up 30 percent of the U.S. prison population by the mid-1960s.

The civil rights movement of the late 1950s and 1960s culminated in the 1963 Washington Mall rally for jobs and freedom where Dr. Martin Luther King Jr. gave his "I Have a Dream" speech. All the social changes helped pressure Congress into taking action and led to the 1964 Civil Rights Act. African Americans and Latinos now had some strong laws to prevent dis-criminatory behavior in employment. Through primarily public sector jobs, blacks were starting to get a "middle class."

But the inner-city urban blacks remained, largely without good paying jobs—and many of the black, Latino, and poor white youth were alienated. They had heard of the U.S. civil rights movement. In the mid-1960s, the black inner-city youth were stirred up by the expectations of the civil rights move-ment, but in their inner-city world, their life was not getting any better (Irwin 2005). In fact, it was getting worse. They began listening to Malcolm X more than Dr. King (Haley 1964).

I felt alienated. In 1964, as a twenty-year-old Michigan State University student, I switched from a philosophy major to a sociology major, in part because social change seemed to be "where it was at" and in part because I felt like a "marginal person." I was alienated and felt marginal partly from what I had seen—the stories above—but also because I was raised as the only child of a single career mother. My independent-minded mother and I had been affected by sexism. In the 1950s, she tried to be a career woman, but lost jobs. As a twelve-year-old onward, I bounced between relatives: from my mother, to my father, to my grandparents. My mother may have made a mistake getting divorced, she was having a hard time trying to be a professional career women struggling against the headwinds of deep sexism in the workplace, and perhaps, at this point in her life, she wasn't doing such a good job as a mother. But I was proud that she had finished her master's degree in journalism at the University of California–Berkeley and had moved to East Lansing to work on a PhD at Michigan State. I stayed with other relatives; she lived a student-bohemian life.

I had worked my way through the last two years of high school, living on my own, and was familiar with jobs and housing in the low-rent part of town. I saw some of the poverty conditions. By 1965 I was working my way through Michigan State, was twenty-one, and was likely to become drafted into the unpopular war in Vietnam. In order to change things, to oppose a war, you have to get angry. I was a good student, and part of the first large U.S. generational cohort to go to college (Trout, Tregea, and Simmons 1968). But while I was alienated and angry, the U.S. economy was booming. Ordinary adult-pay jobs were easy to get. I didn't know "what I wanted to do" after the university. It seemed that working together in "The Movement" was more important than a business, professional, or academic career.

To some extent the Michigan black story was the same as the Michigan white story. Whites came north from Kentucky, Tennessee, West Virginia, western Pennsylvania, Indiana, and Ohio. Some Michigan black families also moved north from the southern states after World War II and worked at the auto factories in Detroit and Flint. Both blacks and whites had good-paying, union, manufacturing jobs. After a rough experience in the 1930s' Great Depression and the 1940s' World War II, whites, in the 1950s and 1960s were getting "good jobs with big companies," and blacks, after the Civil Rights Act of 1964, were increasing their numbers in good-paying, increasingly unionized, public sector jobs. This was a large generational cohort that had hope. But still, in 1965, most African Americans in the ghetto areas of the big cities and in the rural areas were poor.

In the spring of 1965, at MSU, the students had a "sit-in" in front of East Lansing's City Hall to support an "open housing" ordinance." My roommate, Alex, said, "Come on, come on: You've got to be a part of this." I was dubious. Working my way through MSU, I didn't want to get a police record. But, I joined in. The issue was housing discrimination: could the black middle class buy a house in East Lansing, a white bedroom-community suburb for those who worked in the capitol city of Lansing and host city for Michigan State University? Three hundred of us sat in the street, blocking traffic. I thought: "Well, there was a parade here two weeks ago that blocked the street." The fair-minded people of East Lansing voted, two weeks later, to support the "open housing ordinance." We had helped win that issue.

But, meanwhile, the poor blacks in U.S. inner cities were suffering. In the summer of 1965 a south-central Los Angeles inner city named Watts had a riot with buildings aflame. In that same year the popular leader of the black urban poor, Malcolm X, was assassinated. In 1965 the Vietnam War escalated to 525,000 American troops. I went to a "teach-in" with speakers criticizing the war, sponsored by MSU faculty. This "teach-in movement" was happening all across the nation at universities. Millions of students were beginning to become organized in "mobilizations" for nonviolent demonstrations in opposition to the Vietnam War. I was finishing my bachelor's degree at MSU and continuing to check in with the local draft board—keeping a student deferment. But the days of such deferments were numbered.

In the summer of 1967 I graduated with my bachelor's degree and entered the MSU sociology master's degree program. In that same summer of 1967 inner-city Detroit had a revolt and riots. I happened to be driving through Detroit two days after the riot on my way back from being a summer camp counselor in upstate New York. I saw the buildings along Detroit's Twelfth Street still smoldering; there were National Guard troops in the streets. When I arrived in East Lansing later that day I saw the National Guard helicopters taking off from the MSU marching band practice field, a few blocks from my rental room, to take even more guard troops to enforce the martial law that was in effect in Detroit.

Martin Luther King Jr. had, in my mind, correctly connected, in a 1967 speech, the destruction on the Vietnamese people by the persistence of the U.S. government escalating the Vietnam War and the money spent on that war to a pattern of destruction of the people in the U.S. inner cities. The needed commitment and funds for the federal government's "War on Poverty" was being sucked up by the war. It meant that the national push for "all of us to rise together in America" was dying due to the decision to engage and escalate the Vietnam War. The U.S. Congress was afraid to raise taxes to pay for an unpopular war. There was not enough money for "guns and butter" both. An underfunded war on poverty failed.

Many youth in 1967 felt angry: too much poverty, too much war, too much discrimination. And there were other issues: student power, consumer protection, environmental concerns, and a building women's movement.

To oppose the war, demonstrations were mobilized. In the fall of 1967 there was a call to "March on the Pentagon" to demonstrate against the war. Looking for a way to get to Washington, D.C., I went over to a "ride board" at MSU's student union and found a ride with three women students who were also going to the "March on the Pentagon." They pulled up in my rental house driveway in a red 1963 Plymouth slant-6 station wagon with a mattress in the back. At 6-foot-4 I chose the mattress, and one of the three women joined me. We made ourselves comfortable and became friends during the trip. In the outskirts of Washington, D.C., I was elected to register us at a motel. All four of us slept in one king size bed. The next day we marched across the Potomac Bridge with more than 100,000 people to the Pentagon and demonstrated all day.

Something similar in recent history would be the adults and youths protesting in the winter of 2011 to keep the right to public sector collective bargaining and the right to have public sector unions. These rights were being attacked, and taken away in a coordinated way, by Republican governors and Republican state legislatures in Wisconsin, Ohio, and other states. Most criminal justice students entering into criminal justice jobs will be part of a public sector union. It's one thing to negotiate a contract—it's another thing to lose the right to collective bargaining altogether. These were hard won rights. To make social change, the civil rights, antiwar, and labor movements have needed to physically place their bodies into an assembly or protest. After all, the U.S. Constitution protects under the First Amendment the right to free speech and the right to peaceably assemble to petition grievances. It's not enough to sign petitions online. In the fall of 2011 and winter of 2012 the "Occupy" movement was another example of youth mobilizing, for the 99 percent, this time around highlighting how wealth and power are concentrated in 1 percent of the population.

President John F. Kennedy, who had appeared at the University of Michigan at Ann Arbor in 1962 to announce the start of the Peace Corps, had said: "Ask not what your country can do for you, but what you can do for your country." He was assassinated in 1963. His successor, President Lyndon Johnson, pushed to do something concrete about urban poverty by members of the civil rights and labor movements, and from his own beliefs in fairness, had encouraged Congress to approve a war on poverty. The federal government was going to help "eliminate poverty" and help bring everybody up together. I was aware of white poverty and did a sociology master's thesis in 1968 on rural poverty in Michigan's Upper Peninsula.

The year 1968, however, brought a lot of these economic, war, and political issues to a breaking point. Pressured by criticism over the Vietnam War, President Johnson announced in February 1968 that he would not seek reelection. A countermovement of Republican-led conservatism won the White House that fall and battled with the American antiwar movement, switching the issues away from eliminating poverty and achieving peace and, instead, attempting to focus the nation toward a "War on Crime." The largely cultural youth movement of the 1960s and early 1970s did not translate itself into a political force. Some of the energy went thenceforth into the new social movements and identity movements—some folks largely dissipated into personal adjustments. Meanwhile a shift in criminal justice philosophy—from liberal rehabilitation to conservative punishment—was to lead to (and reflect) the growth of the world's largest prison system (Cullen and Jonson 2012; Pratt 2009).

In the early 1970s, New York's governor Nelson Rockefeller started a "War on Drugs," and this proved popular with the new conservative administration of president Ronald Reagan in the early 1980s. Starting around 1986, with the antidrug abuse legislation, U.S. rates of incarceration rose fourfold—from 125 per 100,000 to 500 per 100,000—to create the world's largest prison system.

Why had the prison population suddenly quadrupled? Had the American people become more violent and crime-prone? There *was* an increase in crime from 1986 to 1991 due to the crack epidemic. But, more important, the approach to street drugs changed from the 1950s' short-sentence "rehabilitative ideal," to the 1980s' tough-on-crime long-sentence "war on drugs." Long mandatory minimum sentences meant that more and more people accumulated in prison. For another thing, the beginnings of the creation of impoverished inner cities in America in the 1960s continued: there came to be a "tide of social disorganization" in hundreds of major U.S. cities with more and more high poverty concentration areas.

Into these festering, increasingly jobless ghetto urban areas, came the underground economy: making do with hustles and informal jobs or small businesses, gravitating into the culture of street crime and its associated vast increase in the selling and use of street drugs: heroin, powder cocaine, crack, meth, as well as marijuana and pills. Because street drugs and drug dealers were made out to be "evil" and even more illegal—a consequence of seeing those involved with street drugs as "the enemy"—a "war on drugs" turned police into an enforcement focal point on retail drug trafficking, which was predictably going to result in a vast increase in African American youth adults going to prison. In fact, the black population of prisoners increased from 30 percent in the mid-1960s to 48 percent of U.S. state prison populations by 1999.

I saw this happening. I was a prison college instructor from 1981 to 2000. From 1983 to 1997, I saw my classroom at Michigan Reformatory (MR), a maximum security prison for seventeen- to twenty-five-year-olds, change from white to black. In 1983 the classes were mostly white. By 1987 the classes were 80 percent black. The impoverished young black males caught up in drug-related crime were swept off the streets of Detroit and Flint in the war on drugs crackdowns.

So why am I angry? I'm angry because none of this needed to happen. The ill-fated war on poverty could have succeeded—ending the trend toward jobless ghettos—if we had not taken on the Vietnam War or at least ended our involvement in that war much sooner; the approach to street drugs could have taken a decriminalization, public health, and harm reduction approach instead of a war on drugs approach that has built the world's largest prison system; we could have anticipated that a shift away from a rehabilitation ideal to a punitive just deserts outlook could be captured by the political right wing. We will return to the historical context of this political shift in chapters 2 and 3.

What about the future? Those who are students today, and other readers of this book, could make changes in the "criminology" of the future. Would you be interested in less "social disorganization" in U.S. cities? Less "magnetism of the streets" for urban youth that leads them to crime and prison? That is, would you like to make changes to solve or greatly lessen the inequality and impoverished conditions that contributes to "the culture of street crime" in American inner cities? Would you be interested in a "public health" rather than a "war" approach to street drugs? That is, would you like to approach addiction as a chronic relapse disease and channel money away from prisons and into health and harm reduction?

How do we explain a lot of crime? Answer: bad neighborhoods and drugs. Do we need to have the "criminology" of too many bad kinds of places? Why do we need "social disorganization" theory—can't there be less of the festering inner-city streets *there* to have the theory about? Do we need to have the "criminology" of Prohibition, of too much "lock them up" policies over drugs? Think historically. People in the 1960s changed pollution into environmental protection, changed sexism into gender equality, changed racism into multiculturalism, chipped away at corporate dominance with consumer rights and occupational and safety rights at work, and changed inaccessibility for the disabled to accessible buildings, with ramps and elevators. The point is that "history" does not have to be frozen into a taken-for-granted present. Look at *why* we need a particular criminological theory.

THE PRISONERS' STORIES

The most thoughtful of the prisoners in my volunteer classes display a similar alienation and anger about the same things. They argue that their being in prison is mostly due to "the way things were" when they were growing up. That is: they grew up in bad, crime-infested neighborhoods and learned those ways of surviving and, in particular, learned how to sell drugs and do drug-related crimes. You want criminology? You got criminology, right there. There's plenty of "behavior" to do criminology about.

Yes, there are individualistic causes of crime, some of which have nothing to do with larger issues and root causes. For instance, family causes of crime, which can be sorted out through therapy and prevention. And this book will review several of these and other explanations of crime. While we will review all of the major theories of crime, the heart of this book is what prisoners think about all this. What do they think when *they* read all these theories?

The author went into and out of prisons teaching prison college and volunteer classes for many years. He learned a great deal and wrote about what he knew in the coauthored book *The Prisoners' World: Portraits of Convicts Caught in the Incarceration Binge* (Tregea and Larmour 2009). From 2008 to 2012, the author worked on the experiential foundation for this book by presenting several "Social Science and Personal Writing" classes in Michigan prisons (see the appendix). This special set of eight, once-a-week classes met at three mid-Michigan prisons during this five-year period. These writing courses presented a different criminological theory each week. The prisoners were asked to read and write a personal story for each class meeting that reflected the "theory of the week." Over these eight-week periods the prisoner-students became a writing group—reading their essays, giving praise and suggestions, and having a discussion.

This book, then, reviews criminology theories and explores these convict encounters with these theories. What did they think about these criminology theories? What issues did the theories raise? What stories related to the theories could they write about?

The Framework

As the reader explores vivid prisoner essays in this book, critical questions guide the reader: "*How* does this prisoner essay provide an example to *this* theory? *How* and *why* does this essay reflect the criminology theory's concept(s)?" In a series of chapters reviewing criminology and associated prisoner essays, the reader is challenged to figure it out: "*Where* are the theory's concepts in that essay? *Where* in the essay does the life story reflect the theory?" In short, each chapter of the book is designed to have the student find criminological theory concepts in each prisoner essay.

This book, *Prisoners on Criminology*, presents a review of major criminology theories and is intended as a supplemental book to help students in a criminology course to learn the major theories. But the book does more. Beyond a novel framework to capture key concepts in the major criminological theories through memorable prisoner essays and excerpts, the book reveals real people in prison and their lives. What were those lives like?

LOOKING BACK: CRIMINOLOGY INSIGHTS

In these five years of volunteer classes, prisoners wrote a total of 230 essays. Their insights, looking back from prison on their life, include:

- as a kid having no money and feeling pressure to have stuff, getting a poor education, and coming up in a neighborhood where crime was "the way things were,"
- growing up in a dysfunctional family with addicted parents who are engaged in criminality,
- acting out impulsively, doing dumb things, having low empathy, being caught up in uncultivated responses of anger and rage,
- selling drugs in middle school and dropping out early from school
- gravitating into gangs, crews, one's "set" or "clique," and experiencing drug-turf violence,
- slipping, in an increasingly "cold" neighborhood, into the guns and violence side of the drug economy, and
- becoming an addict and a thief.

The prisons are full of persons who have had some distinct influences on their lives. Various criminological theories attempt to explain the impact of these influences on crime. In the typical Michigan prison volunteer class I teach, half are white and half are African American and Latino. In the classes there are two types of communities represented: the white experience—suburbs, small rural city, or northern Michigan resort town—and then the black and Latino experience—inner city, jobless ghetto. Part of the prison's role is to serve as crime control; another part of the prison serves as a convenient oppression, channeling those from declining inner ring suburbs and the jobless ghetto into the holding pens of American prisons. Many of these prisoners grew up with chronic exposure to crime and violence (Green 1993). There is a saying: "A child without hope is a dangerous thing."

A large number of nonviolent prisoners (property crimes, DUI, bad checks, drugs) serve short sentences (two to four years) whereas prisoners convicted of violent crimes (murder, assault, criminal sexual conduct) serve long sentences (five to ten years, ten to twenty, twenty to life). This means the prisons fill up with those convicted of violent crime, as the nonviolent prisoners' cycle in and out. About half of the prisoner composition in the volunteer classes I teach are composed of older, long-sentence prisoners most of whom have become transformed (LIFERS 2004).

Jim Austin, former executive director of the National Council on Crime and Delinquency, once said, "I'm not afraid of the older criminal or ex-con; it's the young ones coming up that I'm afraid of." Indeed, the violent crime-prone years (robbery, burglary, assault, homicide) are fifteen- to twenty-five-year-olds. African Americans, 12 percent of the U.S. population, have become 48 percent of state prisoner population (Mauer 1999). Even though crime has been declining since 1991, black male homicide is four times more prevalent than whites (Parker 2008). How are the younger men who come to prison influenced as they are growing up? Part of what Jim Austin is saying is, "Don't be at the wrong place at the wrong time." And that would be finding yourself in a bad neighborhood near, or as a part of, "a drug deal gone bad."

That's what's going on in the streets. What's going on in the prisons? After leaving the streets and coming to prison, what does it feel like for prisoners who come to prison volunteer classes?

ALTERNATIVE COMMUNITY FOR INCARCERATED MINDS

By drawing out a mix of older and younger prisoners to a weekly two-hour evening criminology class very focused discussions on criminological issues were had each night. Prisoners had spent time in their noisy housing unit focusing on writing their paper. For them, the prison yard was "the streets," and coming for these few moments to the program building was a way to hold on to a transforming self. It was a time to tell their story.

Such a format created an opportunity for the prison's older, long-sentence prisoners to come to class and be challenged. Active leaders of the Michigan Chapter of the National Lifers Association (NLA) participated in the author's writing classes at the Gus Harrison, Cooper Street, and Parnall facilities, along with middle-aged and younger prisoners. For older prisoners—the grey heads—a class in the school is a venue to interact, model, and mentor young prisoners just off the streets. The younger prisoners can learn from the yard or they can learn from the grey heads about whatever is going on at the prison school building.

These volunteer classes require self-work—thinking and writing about one's own self and the influences on one's life. Out of the sharing of this self-work the classes open up an "alternative community." In the context of this liberated zone of meaningful discussion reinforcing a different self than the talk on the yard, moments of personal insight and dramatic description occur. As each prisoner reads his graphic story for the week, stark images of their past life are revealed. As each prisoner takes his turn reading his story, common experiences provoke a nod of recognition from the other prisoners. Lessons from growing up into the criminal life connect with criminology insights.

Some in prison came from an economically secure household. Their "coming up" was not strongly influenced by neighborhood or family. But, in looking at their life, there were nevertheless pathways (e.g., addiction) and tipping points (e.g., starting to sell drugs) that—because the United States has a punishment approach rather than a public health approach to street drugs— pushes them into criminality. There are sex offenders, aggravated assault, car boosters, domestic violence, and repeat DUI offenders. But most of the prisoner classroom is composed of convictions for inner-city, drug-related, and often violent street crime.

The largest single offense mode in prison is conviction for drug-related crimes. This reflects the long sentences and law enforcement drug sweeps that came with the "war on drugs." In 1975, there were 6 percent of state prisoners convicted for drug offenses. By 2010, fully 29 percent of state prisoners were convicted for drug offenses.

To simplify: the whites are the drug buyers and the blacks are the drug sellers. The whites seldom carry guns or shoot people, but the blacks, as sellers, are drawn into the ugly side of the drug economy and are often convicted of drug-turf and gang-related gun violence, assault with intent to do great bodily harm, and homicide. Thus, they are arrested and convicted more, and serve longer sentences—and accumulate in prison.

The national crime rate has fallen for more than twenty years (since 1991). However, disaggregating the data on crime decline shows the crime decline is *unequal* (with blacks four times more involved in homicides) than white. Why?

INDUSTRIAL RESTRUCTURING AND DRUG OFFENSES

Karen Parker (2008) argues in *Unequal Crime Decline*, that African Americans in the industrial city central neighborhoods were disproportionately impacted by *industrial restructuring*. City labor market structures were depleted of good quality jobs when the manufacturing, and auto and auto-related parts and service industries, closed down, shifting production to other locations.

The impact of these changes in the labor market—the loss of stable, good quality jobs (good pay, benefits, economic security)—impacted the black family (Parker 2008: 86).

It is not only the loss of good jobs. Also affecting the crime rate are the degree of racial segregation, the concentration of poverty, and the degree of relative deprivation in a context of ascribed status (Blau and Blau 1982).

This employment instability and dislocation, racial segregation, and poverty, as it impacted on the families, led to urban violence.

Parker notes that urban areas with extreme racial segregation showed a white homicide rate in 1980 of 6.89 homicides per 100,000 in the population and a drop to 4.67 homicides per 100,000 in the year 2000. But black areas of extreme racial segregation showed 30.4 deaths per 100,000 in 1980 and a fall to only 18.7 deaths per 100,000 in the year 2000.

The 1980 comparison of nearly 7 homicides per 100,00 per year for whites and 30 homicides for blacks shows that blacks suffer four times as much homicide as whites, and Parker's data show that an unequal crime decline falls with the same ratio (4 black to 1 white) over the twenty-year period (1980 to 2000).

As we see, Karen Parker sets out to explain the "racial gap in homicide rates" (2008: 86–94). Major theories of crime and criminality differ—for instance, whether they are *macro* or *micro* types of theory. Parker's explanation of how industrial restructuring in urban labor markets relates to "unequal crime decline" and black and white rates of homicide is an example of a macro theory. Macro theories "attempt to make sense of the everyday behavior of people in relation to conditions and trends that transcend the individual, and even the individual's neighborhood and community" (Barlow and Kauzlarich 2010: 5–7).

The prison classes I taught, as mentioned, brought out lifers and other long-sentence prisoners who have a several-decade perspective in their writing. They witness in their stories "how it is" to grow up in changing neighborhoods and during drug epidemics—and how it is to grow up within a *context* of neighborhood and family criminality. Macro-historical structures, such as federal and local housing policies that increased residential segregation, the loss of jobs, and corporate business decisions that led to consequent worsening of neighborhoods due to increasing joblessness, were integrated into prisoners' lives through stresses that cause dysfunctional families and disorganized communities. But most criminal justice students have "the social world upside down"—they start out with individuals making poor choices. This is a micro-level approach. But children as individuals do not choose their parents, neighborhoods, or historical times. Micro-level theories, on the other hand, focus on how social interaction creates and transmits meaning.

> Laub and Sampson (1988), for example, predict that structural factors such as household crowding, economic dependence, residential mobility, and parental crime influence the delinquent behavior of children through their effects on the way parents related to their children day by day. (Barlow and Kauzlarich 2010: 7)

Most people start out thinking about crime in a very individualistic way. Prisoners in my volunteer class were given excerpts from Farrington and Welsh's *Saving Children from a Life of Crime* (2007). Farrington and Welsh assess the best large-data-set studies for predictive and protective factors in crime and crime prevention. I created table 1.1 to summarize their findings on individual, family, and community predictive and protective factors related

Table 1.1.   A Public Health Model of Early Childhood Prevention: Early Risk Factors for Offending and Effective Interventions

INDIVIDUAL		FAMILY		COMMUNITY (Environmental)	
Predictive	*Protective*	*Predictive*	*Protective*	*Predictive*	*Protective*
• Low intelligence and attainment	• Preschool intellectual enrichment and child skills training programs	• Criminal or antisocial parents	• Parent education plus day care services and parent management	• Growing up in a low socioeconomic status household	• School-based interventions (middle school and high school)
• Personality and temperament		• Large family size		• Associating with delinquent	• After-school and community-based mentoring programs
		• Poor parental supervision (lack of initiating structure)		• Attending high delinquency-rate school	
• Low empathy		• Parental conflict		• Living in deprived areas	
• High impulsiveness		• Disrupting families			

Source: Table constructed by the author, based on information presented in Farrington and Welsh, *Saving Children from a Life of Crime* (Oxford: Oxford University Press, 2007).

to crime. Some prisoners did write essays on "individual factors," mostly on impulsiveness, low empathy, and low school and work attainment. Most "corrections" workers—probation officers, prison staff, parole officers—need to work on the individual, that is, they stay at the individual level of reality. Family therapy and sociological criminology is not their job.

While some prisoners feel they need to change themselves as individuals, the majority of prisoners felt that their criminality was due, in the first place, to growing up learning the ways of the community. Most of the 230 prisoner essays were not about the individual but rather about the dysfunctional or criminal family and the criminogenic community—and several prisoner essays reflect larger, macro-social changes influencing community and family. A few also saw larger, more encompassing political and economic factors that caused their community to be the way it was.

FAMILY, COMMUNITY, AND SOCIAL CHANGE—PRISONER ESSAYS ON INFLUENCES GROWING UP

As you read the following four essays ask: *How* does this prisoner essay reflect the empirical findings (predictive factors) shown in table 1.1 at the individual (micro-theory) level? How about the family (meso) level? How about the community (meso-macro) level?

How and why does each of these four essays reflect the *predictive factors* in table 1.1 that, according to Farrington and Welsh, are supported in criminology research? *Where* are the predictive factors in each essay? For each essay do we need all three levels of crime causation? Where in each essay does the life story suggest that one or more predictive factors might apply? If we were "saving children from a life of crime" what *preventive* factors (or *protective* factors) might have worked for each prisoner essay? What would a community crime prevention plan look like for these four people?

#####

Prisoner Essay 1.1

"Children are living an illusion, tricked into thinking they're full grown." (10/27/08)
Early on in Al's life it was apparent that he had to develop aggressive behavior to get money or else just try to live without the basics. There were 4 boys and 3 girls and a mother that was a diabetic, over weight, and on welfare. Al was the middle child, so he was usually the recipient of hand me downs and little or no attention. The living conditions were deplorable (roaches

and mice). Al learned early that he could get away with little don'ts because
the family could use a little more. The oldest brothers had friends that came
around and they were into all kinds of illegal activities, from stealing clothes
from the mall to robbing people on the street. Al's house was the rendezvous
point (the spoils came there).

Over time Al learned that he had to lie for his brothers and their friends, he
thus became more aggressive because they would reward him for his tough-
ness. Eventually, his roles grew, he began to answer the door at the home,
give directions to older people. Before you knew it he participated in the selling of items and distribution of narcotics, weapons, nothing was off limits. He
learned that when people want something they do not care who has it, they
will do whatever the person who has it wants.

By the time Al was 12 years old, he sold drugs, hosted gambling parties.
He was responsible for keeping the peace among 30-year-old adults. His
aggressiveness grew knowing that his family had his back. You might wonder why his mother allowed this behavior, well as I stated earlier she needed
the extra money. She had three younger children that were being subjected
to this same exposure.

. . . What he did was what was expected and accepted, not only in his
home but in his areas of the city. If you understand, then you can see how
aggression grows, in order to keep from going to jail and not getting played
out of your product you learn early on that you have to display aggression
and confidence. . . .

The one thing that I feel is not fair is how children can effectively be
robbed of childhood in the typical sense with the school band and the camping and the football. When you look back at a life like Al's you don't see
growth for the better, rather you see children that are living an illusion,
tricked into thinking that they are full grown adults. With responsibilities
equal to "real adults" and that is sad to subject a child to that experience
that early. In the end, the young adult will not have the necessary tools to be
productive citizens, so prison is very real in their future.

#####

Prisoner Essay 1.2

"The Kitchen Smelled of Urine and Wet Dog. . . ." (2/24/10)
The kitchen smelled of urine and wet dog. The walls were a peeling pallet of
avocado green and nicotine yellow. Three days worth of dishes spilled in the
sink. Bread crumbs, beer cans, and backyard dirt filled the floor. The refrigerator fan clicked like baseball cards in bike spokes, when Chris and Randy
trotted in for breakfast, the roaches took their time in scurrying away.

The brothers were used to this. In fact, they didn't know any different. The hallways, the bedroom, the bathroom, it all festered with neglect. The things they wore or played with were found among the piles of dirty laundry, the stacks of old newspapers and the boxes filled with junk. Meals came ala-carte and, since Jackie their older sister didn't usually emerge from her room and the back of the house until after noon, the boys could have their fill.

Together, they explored. Among the corn starch and baking soda, fuzz-filled leftover containers, and the eight cans of beer left over from last night's case, they found half a row of crackers and a chunk of dried-out cheese.

When the microwave sounded that breakfast was ready, their mother snuffled twice, then rolled over on the couch.

Chris began stealing cars at fourteen; Randy was the first to get caught. At sixteen, Jackie got pregnant by a man in his twenties. Throughout this, they had no father; their mother was never far away, but her chief concern remained alcohol.

#####

Prisoner Essay 1.3

"Child Neglect—Left to Raise Self" (2/18/09)
Growing up in my family was easy, and in my life now, I can see how that had something to do with my life of crime.

I had a father and a sister for parents. My father worked at GM so that means he was always gone, but I grew up with a lot of money. Everything I ever wanted, I was given, to make up for family time spent together that never happened.

With school, if I did not do good, so what? If I did not pass a grade, who cares? My sister acted as a mother to me but as far as school, she had her own life to worry about.

By the time I was 13, we moved to a bigger town and I was given everything needed to pass time, and have a blast, and raise myself. Kids with nothing to do and a lot to work with always found something to do.

As I got older, I spent my time going bigger and pushing limits of the laws. At first, I did small crimes. With the family it was always a "oh well don't do it again." So I would be smarter every time I went out. A kid left to control himself.

No matter what I did in home at school or on the streets, the money, time, and nothing to do, and no one to tell me not to do it, was an everyday reality for me. If someone did say "No," it was not anything I have to deal with, so I said: "Who are you to tell me I cannot, or should not?"

That there became part of my grown up thinking. Who can tell me not to do this or that? Wrong or right? I grew up making choices on my own. By this time I am grown—that was who I became—my family factors are the lack of.

#####

Prisoner Essay 1.4

"What a Child Is Learning: Parents Taught Criminality." (2/18/09)
As I look back at growing up the way I did it is obvious that I was raised wrong. But to me it was life. In other words I never had any other life. I grew up in the projects. My father was addicted to alcohol. My older brother was murdered during a robbery that went wrong. My father was very abusive, both physically and mentally. And my mother and I was his favorite victims. I grew up in the era of time where crack was destroying the black community. Not only did I see the change, I personally felt the effects.

My parents had no idea of how to raise children. And their personal habits interfered with any desire they may have had to learn. I watched them, and learned from them. I learned how to be compulsive. I learned how to be irresponsible and the abuse only feed my insecurities. I had no self-love and no confidence. And to make matters worse the school was telling my mother that I had a learning disability. My parents seen that as an opportunity to scam the state as a means of getting checks and it worked. Everything I was told about me I believed it was not until maybe 5 years ago that I realized that I actually don't have a learning disability. I just was not being taught. I can still recall being in the fourth grade and not knowing how to tell time. Nor did I know left from right—because no one had taught me.

But I knew how to steal. Because someone had took the time to teach me and I picked up on it fast. I knew what drugs looked like. Everything I was learning in my home was only preparing me for a life of crime. There was no interest took in my education, instead my father sat me down and showed me how to steal crack. My mother taught me how to deal with the cops if I was ever questioned about a crime. I do not know anything, I have not seen anything and I have not heard anything.

There was a lot of time and interest spends in assuring I know how to be a criminal. And no time spent in teaching me how to do it right. I do not blame anyone for the decision I made. I just understand how important it is to pay attention to what a child is learning, and the benefit of having good role models. And I am the outcome of not having good role models. And when no attention is paid to what the child is learning.

#####

One value of the Farrington and Welsh research (table 1.1) is that they locate individual and family factors that are predictive factors. It would, however, be easy to stay at the individual level of predictive factors.

As mentioned, America has a very individualistic culture. The individual is investigated, arrested, convicted. Individual prisoners will say: "I don't need to change the system, I need to change myself." And at that point in their life they're mostly right.

Prisoners understand they need to put aside the whining and excuses—or techniques of neutralization, such as: "I didn't really hurt anyone," "The authorities are corrupt anyway," "It is a big corporation, they won't miss what I steal," "I had to follow my gang," "I shouldn't do these crimes but I had a bad upbringing" (Sykes and Matza 2005). As Frank Hagan (1994) notes:

> As an illustration of the techniques of neutralization, the song "Gee, Officer Krupke," from the 1950s musical *West Side Story*, has members of the Jets arguing that they are victims of a social disease:
>
> > Dear Kindly Sergeant Krupke,
> > You gotta' understand,
> > It's just our bringin' upke
> > That gets us out of hand.
> > Our mothers all are junkies,
> > Our fathers all are drunks.
> > Golly, Moses
> > Natcherly we're punks.
> >   Stephen Sondheim

But what *are* children supposed to do when they grow up with dysfunctional parents? Other than television advertising materialistic goals, do children know or learn the mainstream cultural values when they grow up in "street families" and are chronically exposed to family and neighborhood criminality and violence? For example, refer back to prisoner essays 1.1 and 1.4 above.

Sykes and Matza theorized in 1957 that "delinquent" youth really did understand and believe in mainstream cultural values—instead of a thoroughgoing "subculture of criminality," there was most often a "drift" in and out of delinquency and conventional norms, and that the statements listed above, such as "I didn't really hurt anyone," were "techniques of neutralization" (excuses). Sykes and Matza criticized the "subcultural theories of delinquency, which rested on the premise that delinquent values were at variance with conventional values." Their theory was that "delinquents" really did believe in the mainstream values and were just making excuses to cover for their behavior. And that was probably true, at that time. But in prisoner essay 1.1 above, the child is not only "tricked into thinking they're full grown," but they are acculturated to what "full grown" *means* to "street families" in their neighborhood—criminality as a way of life. This thorough-going opposition to the dominate culture is also evident in prisoner essay 1.4.

WITH JOBLESS GHETTO COMES NEW SOCIAL TYPE

Sykes and Matza were writing in the 1950s, *before* the economic devastation of the inner cities, before the emergence of jobless ghettos in the 1960s, before the impact of the war on drugs in the 1980s and 1990s into the present, and before the quadrupling of the U.S. prison system, which started in 1986. Sykes and Matza's dismissal of the "subculture of violence" came from a perspective of more than fifty years ago—before the impact of mass incarceration on the creation of "high impact" neighborhoods.

Many changes in the last thirty years in particular have created an "incarceration binge prison culture" that reflects deep cementing of a subculture in the community—a culture of street crime. This subculture includes a back and forth cycle from prison to community and community to prison, that creates a "high impact" neighborhood where people under supervision of the criminal justice system "churn" before returning to prison. This is described more fully in chapter 2, "The Making and Unmaking of the Prison State." In many urban areas "street" values and "code of the street" values *are* at variance with conventional values (Anderson 1999; LIFERS 2004). Elijah Anderson observes:

> In his alienation and use of violence, the contemporary poor young black male is a new social type peculiar to postindustrial urban America (Anderson 1999). This young man is in profound crisis. His social trajectory leads from the community to prison or cemetery. (2008: 6)

While prisoner essays 1.2 and 1.3 paint a picture of families that could be black or white and live in a working-poor or a working-class neighborhood, prisoner essays 1.1 and 1.4 are families that seem to fit into the social context of the high crime, jobless ghetto. Essays 1.1 and 1.4 help to examine what the picture of social disorganization means at the family level—how do there come to be such families? A picture of the descent of organized and stable urban working-class or working-poor neighborhood families *into* socially disorganized, concentrated urban ghetto poverty, crime, and "street families" is described by Elijah Anderson:

> Living in areas of concentrated ghetto poverty, still shadowed by the legacy of slavery and second-class citizenship, too many young black men are trapped

in a horrific cycle that includes active discrimination, unemployment, poverty, crime, prison, and early death.

. . . To understand the origin and nature of the problems and prospects of the black inner-city male, we must situate him in postindustrial urban America. . . . (While) in those last days of the industrial era, black men continued to work hard in factories and on construction while their wives worked as domestics, dishwashers, nurse's aides, and janitors . . . these jobs gave a certain stability to the poor inner-city community. . . .

In time, this situation gave way to the postindustrial era with its recurrent recessions, major economic shifts from manufacturing to service and high technology, and the departure from the inner city of relatively high paying and low-skilled jobs through deindustrialization and globalization. (Bluestone and Harrison 1982; Perrucci et al. 1988; Wilson 1987, 2012; Wacquant and Wilson 1989; Anderson 1990; Anderson 2008: 3–4)

As an achievement of the American civil rights movement of the 1950s and 1960s, African Americans, Latinos, and women won the right to better employment opportunities. As a consequence, a newly expanding black middle class moved to the suburbs. "Inner-city neighborhoods gradually underwent a process of transformation from all-white middle- and working-class to racially mixed but still economically stable to all-black working-class, poor, and destitute" (Wilson 1987; Anderson 1990; Massey and Denton 1993).

This move to the suburbs by educated and skilled African Americans along with urban deindustrialization and globalization led to those left in the now "jobless ghetto" experiencing

poor schooling, employment discrimination, and powerful negative stereotypes. . . . In order to survive, residents created a thriving irregular, underground, and often illegal economy. The crack cocaine trade offered a way to make money, but entailed grave risks to individual and social health (Williams 1992). The violent crimes perpetrated by desperate addicts and greedy dealers reinforced deeply negative public images of the black urban ghetto." (Anderson 2008: 5–6)

An argument can be made, then, that in the contemporary jobless ghetto there is a subculture with different values from conventional culture. As Anderson stated, the contemporary alienated, violence-prone, young, poor, black male "is a new social type peculiar to postindustrial urban America," with a life in crisis that leads from community to prison (or death). How did this "new social type" come to be? Here Anderson theorizes through observations at the *macro* level of criminology theory, and he notes:

(There are) fundamental structural factors that shape the increasingly isolated and impoverished urban black ghetto. The inner city economy at "ground zero" rests on three prongs: 1) low-wage casualized jobs that offer little continuity of employment and few if any benefits; (2) welfare payments, including Aid to Families with Dependent Children and its successors, food stamps, and other government transfer programs; and (3) the informal economy, which encompasses (a) legal activities carried on outside the marketplace such as bartering labor and goods among friends and relatives, (b) semi-legal activities such as small businesses operated out of the home under the radar of regulation, and (c) illegal activities such as drug dealing, prostitution, and street crime.

. . . With the recent drastic reductions in welfare payments and the latest contractions in job opportunities for less educated workers, many inner-city residents have increasingly relied on the informal economy. The more desperate people become, the more the underground economy becomes characterized by criminality and violence. (Anderson 2008: 7–8)

I have been arguing through an historical perspective that the "kind of criminology" that explains these jobless ghetto "kinds of places" developments of oppositional criminality, though needed to understand what's happening, has developed *instead* of a criminology of prevention that we might have had with the 1960s "war on poverty." That is, I agree with Anderson's analysis, and point to the question of "what has allowed us to get to this point" where we *need* a theory of a virulent "new social type of person" enmeshed in their growing up in a "culture of street crime?"

The four prisoner essays above (1.1–1.4) seem to imply family factors, such as criminal or antisocial parents, large family size, poor parental supervision, parental conflict, and disrupted families (see table 1.1). But all families are located in a time and place—a certain historical and socio-logical setting. Looked at as an isolated social unit, poor parenting emerges from criminological research as "the most important factor" in explaining the crime of children in such families. The degree of parent education, parenting skills, and good day care is found to be an important path toward preventing crime (table 1.1; Farrington and Welsh 2007).

Any family can suffer from alcoholism or other addiction (prisoner essay 1.2). Middle-class or working-class family dysfunction characterized by poor parental supervision and neglect is more typical of white prisoners. The parent(s) work and provide a home and material "stuff," but are not involved in their child's life, such as the essay "Child Neglect—Left to Raise Self" (1.3). In contrast, the black inner-city family is more often dysfunctional through the parent's poverty; parental, sibling, and extended family criminality; and living in marginal, high-concentrated poverty, gang-infested neighborhoods (essays 1.1 and 1.4). But in reading through essays 1.1–1.4 it doesn't seem that any of these parents—comfortable or poverty-stricken, black or white—will involve themselves in the proven protective factors: parent education and parent management skills training, plus good day care.

The family is not an isolated social unit. "Family autonomy" is a myth. For example, children leave the home and encounter whatever is going on in the streets every day. The neighborhood the family lives in itself is part of a particular real estate area—a good neighborhood or a bad neighborhood. Parents, affected by dynamic and changing city labor markets often have to take low-income jobs and live in a low-rent marginal neighborhood.

Farrington and Welsh observe that an effective crime prevention program must recognize the *interaction* of individual, family, and community.

> Clearly, there is an interaction between individuals and the community in which they live. Some aspects of an inner-city neighborhood may be conducive to offending, perhaps because the inner city leads to a breakdown of community ties or neighborhood patterns of mutual support; or perhaps because the high population density produces tension, frustration, or anonymity. These may be interrelated factors. As Albert Reiss (1986) argued, high-crime-rate areas often have a high concentration of single-parent, female-headed households with low incomes living in low-cost, poor housing. The weakened parental control in these families—partly caused by the fact that the mother has to work and leave her children largely unsupervised—means that the children tend to congregate on the streets. In consequence, they are influenced by a peer subculture that often encourages and reinforces offending. This interaction of individual, family, peer, and neighborhood factors may be the rule rather than the exception. (2007: 88)

In chapter 6, "The Family and Crime," the feminization of poverty is highlighted as an important topic for criminology. If we want to reduce crime we need to give support to one parent (mothers or fathers) to be home with their children; poor single women with children need better support.

Street Life More Ordinary Than a 9-to-5 Job

Some African American prisoners talk about how their "mothers all are junkies, their fathers all are drunks"; however, unlike the 1950s gangs parodied in Sondheim's lyrics for *West Side Story*, the young black experience in recent decades is closer to *Boyz in the Hood*, a 1990s film about how criminality "was just the way it was" in their neighborhoods. This clear conviction on the part of black prisoners—"crime is just the way it is in the community growing up"—is elaborated best not in the micro-, psychological, or social-psychological study in criminology such as of the "autonomous" family, but rather at the macro or community level. Why are the crime rates higher in certain places? Marxist perspectives on uneven development and surplus population, or the Chicago school in criminology's "social disorganization theory" shed light on this question. That is, we could assume that most people are capable of growing up normal, and that it is the environment (community, economy, politics) that influences their "coming up" the most—especially a "kind of place" as virulent as the American jobless ghetto. But Loic Wacquant (2008) argues this kind of "advanced marginality" is beginning to occur in France and other European nations as well.

Uneven development is a consequence of commercial decisions to disinvest in the central city and reinvest in the suburb, or in Mexico or China. Business decisions result in a surplus population or unemployed urban underclass. Political (in)decisions result in abandonment of this (sub-)proletariat hyperghetto. The ghetto poor lose conventional organization in such things as a livable wage, stable family, and decent neighborhood.

Social disorganization is defined as the inability of the community to enforce its norms and values (through informal social control). The abandoned hyperghetto has a social organization that is a response to the encroachment of street crime culture. Basically, the prisoners are saying that as they grew up, the stronger pull in their lives was "street" (criminality) rather than "decent" (family, school, work) (Anderson 1999; Sullivan 1989).

The March into Illegal Activities

The culture of street crime is stronger as a subculture of violence today, where guns are commonly used—whereas fists and chains were used *West Side Story*. Part of the difference is the shift from industrial city to the postindustrial urban jobless ghetto and the enlarged role of the drug economy and a more widespread political neglect of the central city residential areas.

In the 1950s, gangs were *part* of the community—delinquency was aberrant, kids needed to excuse their behavior (Sykes and Matza 1957). Since the 1970s, gangs and the culture of street crime have *become* the community values and norms in some blighted urban neighborhoods. A common definition of "street life" includes criminal trades such as drug dealing, robbery, burglary, auto theft, prostitution, and lesser forms of street hustling. Trevor B. Milton writes in his book *Overcoming the Magnetism of the Street Life*:

> The criminal justice system was designed to make the average youth afraid to go to prison. But for young boys growing up surrounded by street hustlers, and consequently involved with the criminal justice system, street life may be more *ordinary* than working a 9-to-5 job.
>
> Encouragement to be involved in criminal activities seems to come from all over, whether it's from the diminished expectations of society or the social pressure of local peer groups. According to Elijah Anderson (1994), "for these young people the standards of the street code are the only game in town. The extent to which some children—particularly those who through upbringing

have become most alienated and those lacking in strong conventional social support—experience, feel, and internalize racist rejection and contempt from mainstream society may strongly encourage them to express contempt for the more conventional society in turn."

. . . street life . . . seems to guarantee immediate social rewards amongst one's peers. (2012: 58–59)

Milton concludes that there develops an oppositional culture, which is "a form of retreatism *away* from mainstream society and *toward* a more accepting criminal subculture as if it has a strong magnetic quality to it."

Many urban state prison systems have up to 80 percent of their prisoners from just a few dozen metropolitan burroughs, neighborhoods, or urban areas from just a handful of cities statewide. These urban areas are "high impact" neighborhoods where family members cycle to and from prison, where the percentage of residents in the neighborhood who have been to prison or are on probation or parole is very high (Lynch and Sabol 2001), and where the impact of mass incarceration has been devastating to family and community structure (Clear 2007; Rose and Clear 1998). Trevor B. Milton notes:

> The negative conditions propounded on New York City's former working class neighborhoods have created an acknowledged cultural expectation of criminal deviance; what Loic Wacquant (1999) has called "the regime of urban marginality." Urban youth, in particular, are lining up to join the ranks of the *hustler class* which consequently and effortlessly provides fodder for the criminal justice system. As is said best by Wacquant:
>
>> Post-industrial modernization translates, on the one hand, into the multiplication of highly skilled positions for university-trained professional and technical staff and, on the other, into the deskilling and outright elimination of millions of jobs for uneducated workers. . . . A significant fraction of the working class has been rendered redundant and composes an *absolute surplus population* that will probably never find regular work again. (1999: 1639–47)
>
> Milton notes that a few of these young lower working class men will "bridge the gap to monetary success with a good education and support from family, and some good contact with the job market, but many will "choose the more widely available march into illegal activities." (2012: 8)

The prisoners in my volunteer classes often write about their youth that they experienced chronic exposure to poverty and violence. They often report feeling stressed as a child or teenager because they did not have the money to buy the material goods the other kids had. Chris Hedges, in a recent piece of writing about Camden, New Jersey, titled "City in Ruins," wrote:

"Today's a very hard time to be poor," says Father Doyle, seated in the church rectory. "Because you know you're poor. You hear people my age get up and say, 'We were poor. We put cardboard in our shoes.' We talk like that. But we didn't know we were poor. Today you do. And how do you know you're poor? Your television shows you that you're poor. So it's very easy to build up anger in a, say, a high-voltage kid of 17. He knows he's poor, he looks at the TV and all these people have everything and I have nothing. And so he's very angry. . . . I'm talking about the violence that rises out of the marketing that shows the kid what he could have, creates a huge anger that explodes easily. That I discovered very quickly when I came to Camden. I discovered the anger was so near the surface, you just rub it and it explodes. And there's no respect for you if you have no money." (Hedges 2010: 20)

RISING TIDE OF SOCIAL DISORGANIZATION

Camden, East Baltimore, North Philadelphia, South Central Los Angeles, Detroit, South-side Chicago, East Saint Louis—today there are hundreds of American inner-city urban areas that are jobless ghettos, that are "absolute surplus population," places that are socially disorganized, and in which the *hustler class*, a new social type peculiar to postindustrial urban America, exists. All of this constituting a rising "tide of social disorganization." A recent news article by Associated Press writer Corey Williams comments:

DETROIT—A teenager charged as an adult in a drive-by shooting is the latest of more than a half dozen Detroit youth—including a 12-year-old—arrested in August for crimes ranging from armed robbery to murder.

"Lately, every day when I come to work there are several violent crimes committed by youth offenders. That is a very sad commentary," (Prosecutor) Worthy said in a statement Monday, challenging parents to be more involved in the lives and activities of their children.

The Rev. Horace Sheffield III, a longtime activist in the city, said positive support of any kind doesn't exist for many young people in Detroit.

"We have one of the worst economies that's ever existed, and we don't really have the kind of parental involvement or community-wide intervention that is necessary," said Sheffield, executive director of the Detroit Association of Black Organizations.

"These are kids who don't have anything, who are exposed to people who have a lot of stuff, and have been criminally socialized as a means of getting what they want." (Williams 2009: A3)

Trevor Milton notes that "For young boys in lower economic strata, the pressure to be delinquent is strong." One seventeen-year-old Bronx neighborhood respondent Milton interviewed stated:

"On the block, it's about money. Selling. It's the easiest thing to do. . . . Guys function on envy. Who's doing what? Who's got the flyest girl? Who's got the nicest car?" Going to school and getting a legitimate jobs is a slow path to these social rewards, while the criminal trades offer the quickest and easiest route."

Most of these boys saw money as the means to all other social ends. They believe that, if you possess large amounts of money, society rewards you in kind: you get the girls; you get the respect; you get nice things. If the average drug dealer can make $5,000 a week, and the average car thief can make $10,000 a week, some see these behaviors as worth the use of violent capital, even if it goes against their principles. The magnetism of unforeseen amounts of cash and the insulation provided by street respect is too great to deny. (2012: 59–60)

COMMUNITY-LEVEL CRIME PREVENTION

Milton echoes my own efforts earlier in this chapter and in the book *The Prisoners' World* (2009) to emphasize the need to downscale mass imprisonment and shift from an overly punitive to a more preventative approach.

Criminal justice officials should not only be using fear of imprisonment as a deterrent to crime, they also should be looking at these cultural components as complicit in the causes of crime. Thus far, crime control institutions have gone the way of subtracting the criminal element rather than adding a more stable structure to prevent the crime in the first place. (Milton 2012: 60)

So, we have the uneven development "propounded on New York City former working class," the "post-industrial modernization" creating an absolute surplus population—a picture of a disorganized community (or differently organized community) where the kids "have been criminally socialized." Many criminologists and criminal justice academics share a desire to see more societal focus on prevention. As Robert Sampson, 2012–2013 president of the American Society of Criminology, notes:

Public discourse on crime policy has traditionally been dominated by calls for the ever-greater penetration of official control—especially more police, more prisons, and longer mandatory sentences. Public-health approaches have begun to challenge this emphasis on reactive strategies by the criminal justice system, advocating instead crime prevention (Reiss and Roth 1993; Earls and Carlson 1996). In thinking about the prevention of crime, policymakers have turned to programs that attempt to change individuals (e.g., Head Start; job training) or families (e.g., child-rearing skills; conflict resolution). (2002: 225)

But we have shown, in prisoner essays 1.1 and 1.4, that growing up in a certain kind of "culture of street crime" community and family has had a great influence on prisoners *in their own estimation*. If we are to listen to prisoner voices then we will be guided *to* the community level variables (table 1.1). Sampson continues:

> Although individual- and family-level prevention are welcome partners in crime control, there is another target of intervention that until recently has been widely neglected in public policy circles—the community. This level of social inquiry asks how community structures and cultures produce differential rates of crime. For example, what characteristics of communities are associated with high rates of violence? Are communities safe or unsafe because of the persons who reside in them or because of community properties themselves? Perhaps most important, by changing communities can we bring about changes in crime rates? (2002: 225)

Sampson's main research conclusions on neighborhood social characteristics, crime rates, and policy implications are summarized in the points below:

- There is inequality between neighborhoods. Strong evidence links concentrated poverty, unemployment, and family disruption to the geographical isolation of racial minority groups. This is called *concentrated disadvantage.*
- Crime, violence, arrest, and incarceration are all spatially clustered in the same neighborhoods that are characterized by severe concentrated disadvantage. These are neighborhood "hot spots" of crime *and* criminal justice intervention.
- While individuals move in and out, neighborhoods have a general durability or stability in the relative social positions.
- In turn, mechanisms such as informal social control, trust, moral cynicism, network ties, and organizational capacity are hypothesized to explain violence rates, mediating in part neighborhood structural characteristics and durable concentrated disadvantage.
- A community-level approach to crime implies intervening in neighborhoods, changing places not people. I outline ten strategies, focusing on: neighborhood "hot spot" policing, reducing disorder, building collective efficacy, housing-based stabilization, deconcentration of poverty, municipal services, child development, increasing organizational capacity, community-based prisoner-reentry, and an "eco-metrics" for evaluation (2011: 211).

If we return to table 1.1, Farrington and Welsh locate strong *predictive* factors at the community level—growing up in a low socioeconomic status household, associating with delinquents, attending high delinquency-rate schools, and living in deprived areas. Sampson argues that "not enough attention has been paid to 'noncrime' policies—especially on housing, families, and child development—and how they influence the link between crime and community" (2002: 225).

Farrington and Welsh note two evidence-based *protective* factors at the community level—school-based intervention, and after school and community-based mentoring programs. Studies of children who grow up in concentrated poverty areas and *don't* get in trouble with the law show that, compared to those in prison, the difference was those who escaped the fate of prison had received *mentorship* while growing up. What happens within a community to build family social support and mentorship matters.

I was part of the task force that helped to start the Boys and Girls Club located in Adrian, Michigan. The key to club success is full-time reliable mentors (paid staff with good jobs that include benefits). In the last thirteen years this local club has grown from a membership of 40 to a membership more than 1,000 and with currently more than 120 children coming daily to the club. The small blue-collar city of Adrian (pop. 22,000) during this same thirteen years has had several plant closings and the county it's in (Lenawee) had for several months the highest unemployment rate of any county in Michigan (14 percent as of December 2010). There are a lot of strained individuals and stressed families in Adrian, but the afterschool programs help many kids with mentorship by the paid staff.

The prisoners' voice, "looking backward" from the prison, helps us understand how these family and community level variables work to produce the kind of strain and criminogenic opportunity structure that leads toward criminality (Shaw 1930; Merton 1938; Sutherland 1947; Cloward and Ohlin 1960; Berger 1985; Agnew 1999). Prisoner voices help us connect criminology to people's lives, and to understand prevention and corrections work with early childhood development, families, peers, neighborhoods and schools, and in our communities, and to address the festering hyperghettos spreading over the last thirty-five years.

We are at a turning point. We need the prisoners' voices. We need their voices to help understand how to work at better crime prevention (Agnew 1999; Berger 1985; Farrington and Welsh 2007; Newbold 2003; Rosenbaum, Lurigo and Davis 1998), and to downsize prisons, improve success on parole, and close down the revolving door of home to prison (Jacobson 2005; Petersilia 2003; Richards and Jones 1996).

What *happens to* communities—plant closing, community decline, increasing lack of power to affect policy—are macro criminological explanations *beyond the immediate* community. For example, the decision of corporate boards and managers to move ahead with plant shutdowns in Adrian and shift manufacturing investments to other countries (for instance, Mexico and China) is clearly a different level of criminological explanation than what goes on in the "autonomous" household or in the local family social support network, such as a Boys and Girls Club. The concluding essay of chapter 1 raises our examination to an often neglected, but needed, level of social analysis: What happens to a key thoroughfare in a community area that goes "cold."

#####

Prisoner Essay 1.5

"As Visgar Road Became Cold." (10/21/09)
Visgar Rd, the street that separates the cities of Ecorse from River Rouge, runs through southwest Detroit, approximately one half mile in distance; (it is) where all criminal activity is accepted, and evil is permitted to pollute the minds of the youth and immature teens. It wasn't always like that. And I was fortunate enough to had seen Visgar when it was still attractive. When black owned stores, and businesses overflowed every inch of the street. The people that owned those stores were friends of the family, and lived right in the community.

I witness the change. I seen the business's close down, and what was once a friendly atmosphere, ran by people that knew you, and enjoyed your company, was now been ran by hostile Arabs. Who were not shy in displaying that they only wanted your money. I had seen Visgar become empty and soulless. As crack cocaine established its self in the community, my own parents became addicted to its power. I sold drugs to men that as a child I looked up to, and a woman I previously found attractive who got into crack became unappealing overnight. My friend's mother, a lady we all called auntie, who watched me grow up, tried to stab me because I refused to sell her drugs.

As Visgar became cold, the people became desperate, and acts of atrociousness would follow. I was able to identify the ugliness that existed in the people who so commonly referred to as crack heads. All the while justifying my own actions; oblivious to just how ugly I have become. The streets bred an attitude of selfishness. Those who appear to be the most heartless, is often feared. And fear inspires respect, which is very valuable on the streets. Therefore it was my desire to be feared.

My role models were drug dealers, I watched them climb the criminal ladder of success, starting off as low level drug dealers, and later becoming kingpins; never leaving Visgar Rd. My oldest brother wasn't so lucky. He was born at Sombies Hospital, which use to sit on Visgar between Palmister, and Holford St. As a teenager he sold drugs on Visgar Rd. and as a result of a failed robbery attempt, he was murdered, on Visgar Rd. Directly across the street from where he was born. The funeral home that prepared his burial, also sits on Visgar. Ironically, that's the only black owned business that has not gone out of business.

As the crack epidemic hit urban cities across America, everything started to change. Successful black families started to leave those cities, moving to the suburbs; they didn't want to expose their children to what goes on in the ghetto. I remember in the 80s, people that smoked crack did so in a house or building, it was some privacy involved. I lived in a crack house, so I remember seeing the glass pipe's, the broken hangers with cotton balls dipped in alcohol, making a homemade torch.

Fast forward to the future, and all the privacy is gone, TV antennas replace glass pipes, and those who smoke, do so where ever. I remember seeing a guy walking by with a pipe hanging from his lip like a cigarette. Parents don't shield their children from this activity because it's just too common. And they just don't realize the effects it can have.

With successful people leaving the community, the youth don't have real role models. And the people that give us attention are criminals. So we grow up wanting to be like them, there is no one around to show us a different way.

Even the police are viewed as crooked where I'm from—treating every young black male as a criminal. Feeding the animosity that permanently separates us.

To work for a living is looked at as being foolish where I'm from, especially when crime seems to be more expected, and more profitable. I am my environment, and my actions are its products.

#####

EXERCISES 1.1–1.4: LOCATING IN PRISONER ESSAYS LEVELS OF ANALYSIS AND PREDICTIVE AND PROTECTIVE FACTORS

1. In prisoner essay 1.1, "Children are living an illusion, tricked into thinking they're full grown":
   a. In this essay, what is the illusion the inner-city children are having? Elaborate. Why are they having this illusion?
   b. Can you suggest any *macro* explanation for the neighborhood network of friends that came to Al's house that he is growing up learning from? Locate two quotes from chapter 1 to support your views.
   c. If you agree with the prisoner essay 1.1 author, that childhood *should* have "school band and the camping and the football," and that it's "not fair how children can effectively be robbed of childhood," *why* are children like Al tricked into thinking they're full grown? What *should* "full grown" mean? (Write 2–3 paragraphs.)

    d. Compare the three levels of explanation (individual, family, or community) in this story. Be specific. Which level best describes the robbing of Al's childhood? Why? Explain your answer. Locate two quotes from chapter 1 to support your view.

2. In prisoner essay 1.2, "The Kitchen Smelled of Urine and Wet Dog. . . . ":

    a. Suppose you were in a meeting with five influential county and community leaders designing juvenile justice programs and the goal was to "wrap social support services" around Chris, Randy, and Jackie. The leaders are: the director of County Juvenile Justice (juvenile probation), the probate judge (family court), the local director of community mental health, the local director of the Department of Human Services, and the director of the local county juvenile treatment and detention facility.

       i. What are the levels of explanation you need to be working at? Why? Explain your answer.

      ii. What services would you seek to "wrap around" the three children? Draw on table 1.1 and quote from chapter 1.

     iii. What appear to be their mother's problems? (Consider how many problems she may have.) What approaches would you take with/for the mother?

     iv. How might this case provide examples for *each* of the micro, meso, and macro levels of criminology theory? That is, *connect* individual, family, and possible community level variables. Locate two quotes from chapter 1 to support your views.

3. In prisoner essay 1.3: "Child Neglect—Left to Raise Self"

    a. What specific individual and family level predictive factors may be at play?

    b. Can you see any community level influences? If so, what? Explain. Locate two quotes from chapter 1 to support your view.

4. For prisoner essay 1.4: "What a Child Is Learning: Parents Taught Criminality"

    a. Locate two or three quotes that describe a family level of explanation.

EXERCISE 1.5: LOCATING IN PRISONER ESSAYS MACRO LEVELS OF CRIMINOLOGICAL ANALYSIS

1. In prisoner essay 1.5, "As Visgar Road became Cold"

    a. Identify two or three events in the essay that transformed Visgar Road into an "empty and soul-less place," a half-mile former living neighborhood that had become cold. Locate two quotes from chapter 1 to support your view.

b. What macro sociological explanation discussed earlier in this chapter could explain this negative neighborhood transformation? Locate two quotes from chapter 1 to support your view.

c. As a consequence of this change in the neighborhood, the prisoner describes how people became desperate, ugly, selfish, heartless, and feared. Why was it his desire to be feared? Locate one quote from chapter 1 to support your view.

d. Why were successful people leaving the neighborhood? Why did the youth "grow up wanting to be like the criminals?" Locate two quotes from chapter 1 to support your view.

DISCUSSION AND REVIEW QUESTIONS

1. What is meant by absolute surplus population? How does this relate to mass incarceration?
2. How were the jobless ghettos in U.S. cities created?
3. What is meant by the "magnetism of the streets?"
4. What is meant by a "new social type" as a social role in the jobless ghetto, according to Wacquant?
5. Give examples of micro, meso, and macro levels of criminological analysis.
6. What does Sampson mean by "noncriminal justice" policies for crime prevention?
7. What is meant by "alternative community" for prisoners?

2

The Making and Unmaking of the Prison State

As the United States became a mass incarceration society, with the incarceration rate quadrupling during the 1980s and 1990s, the United States came to have the world's largest prison system. This "prison state" occurred, even though crime rates have been falling since 1991 (Zimring 2007). The proximate answer for why the United Sates built such a large prison system lies in the harsh drug laws established in 1986 during a media-driven moral panic over drug-related crime—leading to a "drug crime" era.

But there were also other causes. The tough-on-crime sentencing laws such as "three-strikes and you're out," long-sentence mandatory minimums, serving longer sentences under "truth in sentencing" laws, eliminating good-time credits, and fewer paroles all contributed to the prison build-up movement (Useem and Piehl 2007). These were all also outcomes of a "governing through crime" representational model (Simon 2007), institutional racism (Tonry 2007; Wacquant 1999), and management of absolute surplus labor in the jobless ghetto (Wacquant 2008). We will review each of these issues in chapters 2 and 3. Addressing mass imprisonment will require the United States to "rethink the correctional project" (Clear 2007).

MOVE BEYOND THE DRUG CRIME ERA

In focusing on how and why the United States quadrupled its prison system, I hope to educate people about the role of power and inequality and to highlight the need to see a *competition* between overuse of confinement and other state priorities; a competition between the state correctional budgets and other state budget priorities such as education, environment, and health; and justice reinvestment in community-level crime prevention. There was a strong public response to increasing crime—a call "to do something"—during the 1986–1991 increase in crime due to the crack epidemic. There has been an increasing debate, however, about whether the response—mass incarceration—is fundamentally inappropriate.

The alternative would represent a new rational public model: more rational sentencing and parole policies, a harm-reduction approach to drugs, greater emphasis on crime prevention, and a pragmatic set of policies to safely downsize the prisons, and shift some of the saved public resources to justice reinvestment in high incarceration communities. Through such an emerging model the American people could move beyond the "drug crime" era, explore and resolve the racism inherent in the incarceration binge culture, and its "new Jim Crow" stigma for ex-felons, end the hyperghetto-hyperincarceration era, and move beyond governing through crime. Before we move beyond the prison build-up era we must understand it.

PRISON BUILD-UP AND MASS INCARCERATION: AN OVERVIEW

How did the United States become the world's largest prison state? For many decades, prior to the incarceration binge, American prisons were hidden bureaucratic posts in rural towns and valleys, far removed from everyday U.S. life. Then, starting in New York, the 1973 Rockefeller mandatory drug sentences politicized prison sentencing in a harsh, punitive, and long-sentence way that was to lead to the growth of U.S. state and federal prisons. In January 1981, when I started teaching in the Pell-grant subsidized Jackson Community College prison college program at Jackson Prison, the state of Michigan only had 8 prisons and 14,000 prisoners. But since the 1986 and 1988 federal antidrug laws crime, sentencing, and prisons became politicized. A public, seemingly fed-up with crime and druggies, led to a politicians vote-getting strategy of the "politics of tough." Behind this was the rise of a new "representational model" where governors and presidents learned to act more like prosecutors and "govern through crime legislation" (Simon 2007). Michigan grew to 42 prisons and 51,000 prisoners by 2008.

For politicians—cynical and sincere, alike—a handy politicized "war" metaphor emerged (Tonry 1999). Cullen and Jonson (2012) note that, in the matter of crime, law, and corrections, American society goes through "swings in the pendulum" from punitive to rehabilitative emphasis, and back to punitive. The United States in the 1950s and 1960s emphasized the rehabilitative and corrective approach to street drugs and crime. By the mid-1960s, the United States was attempting to solve root problems underlying poverty, drug abuse, and crime. Then a shift occurred. An underfunded "war on poverty" and rehabilitative ideal gave way by 1967 to a new punitive symbolic use of crime politics. By the mid-1970s and into the 1980s, the United States moved to a "war on crime" and a "war on drugs" approach, with a punitive emphasis on incarceration (Berger 1985).

"Crime" had developed a particular salience for the American public (Zimring 2006). In our political system, being "tough" and not "soft" on crime became a wedge issue that got votes and re-election (Tonry 1999). In this shift of perspective, prisoners were no longer expected to be rehabilitated, but became "dangerous categories" of people (Feeley and Simon 1992) to be treated as a "waste management" problem (Simon 2007). As demonized "person categories," the solution for the convicted felon shifted from short sentences and rehabilitative treatment, to a rush to "lock them up and throw away the key" in a longer sentence "warehouse prison" (Irwin 2005).

Just as other marginalized segments had their social movements, prisoners needed a movement (Ross and Richards 2003; Richards and Lenza 2012). But prisoners live in prison and have little voice on public matters (Tregea and Larmour 2009). This book, *Prisoners on Criminology*, shows us that ordinary convicts, even those without any college education, can contribute to our understanding of criminology. A few of the older, grey-haired, long-sentence prisoners contributing essays to this book have lived through all the changes described above and this shift toward mass incarceration; most have recently come into prison. More than 80 percent of state prisoners have a history of being victims of child abuse and neglect. Criminogenic "variables" such as family; and community characteristics, such as social disorganization, poverty, street-culture peers, and lack of home ownership, all show up in these prisoners' stories.

In becoming aware of the issue of mass incarceration people often come to the realization that things are the way they are because of certain power arrangements in society. How did the "power world" in our society contribute to making the massive "prison world" at which we have arrived?

One of the easiest things to do is *taking the context of your life for granted*: your current and most recent past—the "facts" you see—this existing historical context can be unquestioned as "the way it is." Reflecting on the historical era of "getting tough on crime" and the rise of mass incarceration, and taking Michigan as an example, the highly respected Citizens Research Council of Michigan noted on June 12, 2008:

> With an incarceration rate of 489 persons per 100,000 residents, Michigan far exceeds the average incarceration rates for the surrounding Great Lakes states (338 per 100,000) and the U.S. as a whole (401 per 100,000).

The single most important contributing factor to the growth of Michigan's incarceration rate has been average prisoner length of stay, which lengthened from 28.4 months in prison in 1981 to 43.5 months by 2005.

Average length of stay, in turn, grew *as a result of various public policy changes* aimed at getting tough on crime including mandatory sentences, lower rates of parole and probation, and harsher sentences. These policy changes were made at many different times, by many different people and generally *with little or no reference to their likely fiscal consequences.*

Because of the state's high incarceration rate, Michigan's spending on corrections has grown to the point that corrections is now:

- the largest program operated directly by the Michigan state government;
- the employer of one-third of the state government's classified work force;
- responsible for $2 billion in annual expenditures or roughly 20 percent of the General Fund budget;
- accounts for 5.2 percent of total Michigan state expenditures compared to a national average spending on corrections of 3.4 percent of total stated expenditures; and
- likely to grow to $2.6 billion/year or more by 2012.

This seemingly uncontrollable growth in Michigan's corrections spending has been a major contributor to Michigan's structural deficit, which is discussed at length in CRC's recent publication, "Michigan's Fiscal Future," (CRC Report No. 349, June 2008) (CRC 2008).

In the second decade of the twenty-first century, several state governments are finally attempting to cap prison growth. But corrections budgets remain high and only a handful of states have really begun to downsize their prisons (Austin et al. 2013).

Before exploring criminology theory we need to explore the public policy changes that led to the prison build-up in the first place. For example, mandatory sentences mean that judges cannot adjust the sentence downward. This means the prisoner serves the whole legislated sentence and prisoners accumulate in prison. Without parole guidelines, state parole boards tend to parole fewer people. Releasing fewer on parole also means prisoners not released accumulate in prison. Eliminating good time means longer sentences. States should revisit sentencing guidelines enacted in the harsh 1990s. Sentencing grids legislating harsh long sentences means prisoners accumulating in prison.

However, some states are beginning to look at their sentencing grids. Representative Joe Haveman, Republican Chair of Michigan's Corrections Appropriation committee currently advocates that legislators revisit Michigan's sentencing policies to reduce the length of sentences.

Michigan has started a much-needed review of its criminal sentencing guidelines—one that will hopefully chart a path for more efficient use of the state's limited resources.

The state has struggled to balance public safety with punishment and rehabilitation efforts that produce good results. Indeed, Rep. Joe Haveman, R-Holland, who heads the House Appropriations Committee, recently told the *Detroit News*: "Being 'tough on crime' above all other concerns simply hasn't created a safer society."

And Michigan's corrections budget, exceeding $2 billion a year, is too large to sustain without damaging other essential services. Indeed, the Lansing State Journal Editorial Board is among many voices suggesting the size of the corrections budget has already harmed the state. Consider, for example, the drastic reduction in state support for higher education, which has resulted in accelerated tuition increases. (*Daily Telegram* 2013: A6)

Establishing Law: Consensus and Conflict

How were these prison build-up policies established? Some laws everyone agrees with, for others there are differences of opinion. However, not everybody has an equal say on what becomes law. As Shelden says:

> *The making of laws and the interpretation and application of these laws throughout the criminal justice system has, historically, been class, gender, and racially biased.* More to the point, as Cole has noted, there are really two systems of justice: "one for the privileged and another for the less privileged" (Cole 1999: 9). Moreover, one of the major functions of the criminal justice system has been largely to control and/or manage those from the most disadvantaged sectors of the population, that is, the dangerous classes. (Shelden 2008: 17–18)

We could argue with Shelden. Laws do not just "manage those from the most disadvantaged sectors of the population." Clearly there is, and always has been for many centuries, wide consensus that certain behaviors are crimes. Those laws are laws of consensus (Braithwaite 1989). For instance, most people agree that the crimes reported by the FBI in the annual Uniform Crime Reports (UCR) should be seen as crimes: murder, rape, robbery, burglary, arson, larceny, auto theft, and serious assaults. These laws are not created for the powerful to "manage" the powerless; rather, they protect the working class and middle class (Young 1979). Useem and Piehl (2008) argue that the prison build-up movement started out as a "rational public" responding to the increase in crime in the period 1986–1991, but that such a "tough on crime" social movement had "weak brakes" over the last twenty-three years, only now beginning to examine itself (CSG 2012; Austin et al. 2013).

Understanding the evolution of morality (Katz 2000) in animal behavior studies reveals a type of "species being" for humans and other primates that is cooperative (Flack and DeWaal 2000: 6–7) validating philosophic observations by Kroptkin and Marx. So it is possible to explain a *human nature* in which there could be "universals"—such as norms and laws about murder and rape and stealing and so forth. There *are* some common human norms. For example, the "norm of reciprocity" (Gouldner 1960), which facilitates the buildup of group norms through repressing power and status in order to be accepted by a group (Blau 1964). Thus group norms and "society" can emerge (Durkheim 1893/1964). But the prison build-up movement of the last forty years is not a result of pure consensus.

The Exploitation and Suppression of the Poor and Marginal through Legal Means

There are cultural conflicts (Sellin 1938) around behaviors related to vices or personal behavior, such as alcohol and other street drugs, gambling, and prostitution. For these "moral vices" the cultural capacity of one societal segment, can "power over" against another societal segment, to establish its' own cultural definitions and *laws* of what is "criminal" (Gusfield 1967).

The cultural power groupings can change from century to century or decade to decade. Moreover, it is not just cultural power struggles over "moral vices" at stake here. There are also historical eras in which powerful social strata use the law to enforce their political and economic interests. The powerful who have gained access to resources (surplus) are able to define laws that keep a social order that favors them. Their ideas and laws become the ruling ideas and laws, protecting society the way it is (Marx 1867/1967; Lenski 1966).

Shelden, describing the rise of early forms of stratified societies, empires, and capitalism, draws an important generality for us:

> [A] centralized power base arose that began to compel or coerce a surplus from the work . . . once (the group that rises to power and has control over the means of production) occurs . . . there comes the threat of trouble in the form of "revolutions, peasant and slave uprisings, labor strife, and common crimes as groups or individuals seek to affect either a personal or more general redistribution of wealth and power" (Michalowski 1985: 74–75). Thus there arises the need for a formal system of "law" to respond to such threats to the prevailing order. (Shelden 2008: 30)

This stark description of "the law" as an outcome of a power system may seem uncomfortable. Many textbooks read by young adults looking to go into jobs in the criminal justice area introduce the "criminal justice" field as *constituted* in work roles—cops, courts, corrections—enforcing commonly agreed upon laws: murder, rape, assault . . . and drugs. But all of the drug and alcohol "prohibitions" have been laws passed just at the point where there is *conflict* over usage and the possibility of normalizing alcohol or other drug use is beaten back by the hurried or "bandwagon" pressure to pass a prohibition law (Chiricos 1995/2002; Gusfield 1967). Tough laws are even passed once the "deviant trend" is diminishing (Musto 1991), like stomping seven times on a bug that is already dead.

It might be expected that a criminology book would start with individualistic explanations of deviant or law-breaking behavior. The laws exist: "Why do individuals break them?" But in the quote above, Shelden says, once a group rises to power, "there comes a threat of trouble" that includes not only the *form* of uprisings and labor strife, but also in the *form* of "common crimes as groups or individuals (who) seek to affect either a personal or more general redistribution of wealth and power." Even though much property crime is related to addiction, the rate of drug abuse is higher in impoverished neighborhoods (Abadinsky 2008) of concentrated disadvantage (Sampson 2011). The "disadvantaged neighborhoods" themselves are created and maintained by urban elites and federal and state policies (Wacquant 2008). This *tension* between the powerful who benefit from the existing structure and those who are disadvantaged by that existing social structure, is built into highly unequal societies characterized by major injustices.

The United States has become a *highly unequal society*. The federal and local policies, corporate decisions, and migration and residential segregation patterns have created inner-city jobless ghettos and the world's largest prison system. This is a reciprocal relationship—just as you cannot have a slave without a master (Hegel 1910/1967), so you cannot have U.S. mass incarceration without the jobless ghetto. This "imprisonment of community" is a *criminogenic relationship* (Clear 2007; Tonry 2007; Wacquant 2002, 2006), and has led to the high impact or high incarceration neighborhoods (Austin et al. 2013; Lynch and Sabol 2001).

More broadly, the United States has become more unequal. There has been overall stagnant individual wages for the last thirty years and rising job insecurity. The loss of home value during the 2008–2009 Great Recession, continuing economic insecurity, even as the richest 1 percent of the population has become immensely rich (Wysong, Perrucci and Wright 2014; Reich 2010). This is a *class relationship*. How does such inequality relate to mass incarceration?

Most introductory criminal justice texts do not go deeply into cultural conflict, inequality, injustice, or class conflict. Rather, most academic criminal justice texts detail the major tension in the criminal justice world as that between "due process" and "crime control" values. These two values exist in a conflictual tension *within* a constitutional and essentially "consensual" society (Packer 1968/2004). Criminal justice students familiar with sociology, because they have taken an introductory sociology course, will recall that a consensual view of society sees society as "glued together" through a set of norms held in common (Durkheim 1893/1964).

But a view of our social context as a normatively consensual society does not accurately describe the cultural conflicts of a complex, pluralistic society. Such a "we all agree" view does not capture the basic economic and power *conflict* systems of past historical societies, such as feudal lord over peasant, slaveholders over slaves in the slave society, or a rising business class over poor peasants and the emerging working class (Thompson 1963).

This chapter raises the question of whether, in the last fifty years of uneven development as the growth of the suburbs led to festering inner cities and the incarceration of their residents in the development of the world's largest prison system, these events can be seen as *an outcome of each other*: a recip-rocal relationship or structural conflict wherein a "formal system of 'law' to respond(s) to" the "threat(s) to the prevailing order" in the form of young blacks "acting up" in the jobless ghettos of U.S. cities (Eitzen and Baca Zinn 2000: 139–73; Irwin 2005: 222–23; Tonry 2007: 23; Wacquant 2007). Several times before the United States needed a "formal system of law" to handle the tensions of a social setting with raw inequalities and social injustice. These included the debtor's prisons era laws and the slavery era laws, such as the fugitive slave laws that culminated in the Fugitive Slave Act of 1850.

Readers, perhaps, will agree that the examples we give—debtor prisons, runaway slave laws—are examples of social injustice, unjust situations caused by an unjust social order. Now think about the current U.S. prison system as, by far, the largest in the world. Think about how the development of this huge prison system is linked to the rise of jobless inner-city areas. Most of New York's state prisoners come from a handful of city boroughs in New York City (Jacobsen 2005; Clear 2007). In Michigan, much of the prison population is from Flint (devastated by plant shutdowns since 1975) and Detroit (with job loss since 1965, loss of more than half of its population, fiscal crisis since 1981, an emergency manager since 2012, and bankruptcy in 2013). As Michael Hallett writes in his foreword to Randall Shelden's *Controlling the Dangerous Classes*:

> As part of a growing body of work bespeaking dissatisfaction with mainstream criminology's myopic focus on hot spots and statistical residues, this book gets to the heart of the matter of social justice versus criminal justice . . . a detailed accounting of the fundamental pattern of the history of criminal justice—the exploitation and suppression of the poor and marginal through legal means—is offered the students who are often encouraged to *ignore* questions of social justice entirely. (Shelden 2008: ix)

Because prisons are so costly to build and operate, and because, increasingly, state legislatures are bothered by corrections budgets larger than public higher education or any other state budget, the *pragmatic* concern to safely downsize state prisons has become a political priority. But a deeper analysis is needed.

We see that the average criminal of today—a "drug crime era" inner-city black—would be described differently than would a criminal in previous decades. The organization of who will be deviant, who will have a "person category" of criminal—like debtor in prison, or runaway slave—is socially constructed through the power world of the day (Best and Luckenbill 1994). For instance, if today you make alcohol in your own basement, are you a criminal? No. But the United States did have a "war on alcohol" during a period of thirteen years (1920–1933) that would have put you in prison for "the production, distribution, and/or sale of intoxicating liquors." Since the 1973 Rockefeller drug crime laws and the federal 1986 and 1988 antidrug abuse establishment of a national street drugs "prohibition," drug-related crime as a percent of prison admittance has increased from 6 percent to 30 percent of state prisoners. It was the fear that street drugs were spreading to the middle class and working class, which then required a "suppression of the poor and marginal through legal means." Reflecting on a similar rural, Protestant, sober, middle-class "dry movement" arising to create alcohol prohibition as a response to urban, immigrant, Catholic, working-class drinking cultures in the period 1870–1920, Joseph Gusfield notes:

> Agents of government are the only persons in modern societies who can legitimately claim to represent the total society . . . their acts makes it possible for them not only to influence the allocation of resources but also to define the public norms of morality and to designate which acts violate them. (Gusfield 1967: 228)

Was the passage of the 1920 alcohol prohibition amendment to the Constitution really a law representing the total society? No. Probably the majority of the American people did not support the law. During the 1960s and early 1970s there was tolerance of street drugs—even acceptance by some. Then, in the 1980s and 1990s, there was a new conservative countermovement or "moral crusade" that brought forth new crime legislation. As Gusfield continues:

> In a pluralistic society these defining and designating acts can become matters of political issue because they support or reject one or another of the competing and conflictual cultural groups in the society.
> . . . [W]e have called attention to the fact that deviance designations have histories; the public definition of behavior as deviant is itself changeable. It is open to reversals of political power, twists of public opinion, and the development of social movements and moral crusades.
> . . . The "lifting" of a deviant activity to the level of a political, public issue is thus a sign that its moral status is at stake, that legitimacy is a possibility. . . .

The present debate over drug addiction laws in the United States, for example, is carried out between defenders and opposers of the norm. . . .

. . . The threat to the legitimacy of the norm is a spur to the need for symbolic restatement in legal terms. In these instances of "crimes without victims" the legal norm is *not* the enunciator of a consensus within the community. On the contrary, it is when consensus is least attainable that the pressure to establish legal norms appears to be greatest. (Gusfield 1967: 228–36)

THE DRUG CRIME ERA

Many 1960s and 1970s youth movements that encompassed civil rights, consumer protection, student power, anti-Vietnam war protests, women's rights, and environmental issues, participated in a cultural rejection of the 1950s conformism. This included vibrant music, smoking pot, and a tolerant attitude toward street drugs. "Do What You Like" was an emblematic song by the late 1960s group Blind Faith. While this movement was mostly a cultural movement, there were also political movement accomplishments in new legislation such as the Equal Employment Opportunity Commission and the Environmental Protection Agency. President Jimmy Carter (1976–1980) continued the "rehabilitative ideal" approach to drug abuse and even proposed decriminalizing marijuana.

But, with Ronald Reagan's election in 1980, all this was to change. A new, punitive cultural conservative outlook and a political shift to the right occurred. Using a new politicization of crime legislation that had started with the Safe Streets Act of 1967 and the Rockefeller drug laws of 1973, a governing through crime representational model (Simon 2007) was emerging (see chapter 3). Politicians touted a new "warrior ideal" for drug enforcement, as part of a new war on drugs.

This chapter argues that the inner-city jobless ghetto and mass incarceration were a historically related, reciprocal, institutional, and political development. After World War II, suburbs were being built with shopping malls. People who could afford to live in the growing suburbs—mostly European-American whites—were drawn to the new malls. They parked and shopped there instead of shopping downtown.

Since the industrial revolution (1870–1920) the United States had always had urban slums and African Americans lived in residentially segregated ghettos (Wacquant 2008: 75–88). But these early American dark ghettos were a place where people could live and *work jobs* in the nearby city factories and warehouses, or work service jobs in the "downtown" and local neighborhood homes and businesses. The building of suburbs away from the central city resulted in downtown business districts, large manufacturing firms, and warehouse corporations closing their downtown operations and moving to suburban and small city industrial parks. Giant office buildings grew up in business centers near highway exits in the suburbs, drawing office workers away from downtown. Small retail goods and services firms were lured away from their central city downtown locations to the new suburban malls to serve the new suburban customers. U.S. inner cities suffered from both "white flight" and capital flight. America's former central city ghettos, where blacks and other minorities lived and worked now became lower-working-class (subproletariat) neighborhoods without the "work"—that is, they became "jobless ghettos" where the truly disadvantaged gathered or remained (Agnew 1999; Clear 2007; Irwin 2005; Tonry 2007; Wacquant 2008; Western 2006: 36–38; Wilson 1996). This process of *uneven development* is a built-in feature of capitalism (Darden, Hill, Thomas, and Thomas 1987; Polanyi 1944; Schumpeter 1950).

The U.S. civil rights movement (1954–1968) had lifted the hopes of tens of millions of African Americans—especially the young, but also their parents. Black political administrations were voted into city government by the new urban black majority populations—a sign of hope. But the city itself was an "empty shell" with few jobs and a diminishing tax base. Now increasingly jobless, ghetto residents saw their youth, restless with despair, hopelessness, and rage, beginning to make trouble as their neighborhoods were festering. Writing about the initial emergence of contemporary U.S. jobless ghettos in the mid-1960s, John Irwin notes:

> The ghetto youths of the late 1960s and early 1970s, excluded from conventional paths to fulfill their intense desires and needs, were available for any activity that promised profit, respect, and excitement.
> . . . They formed neighborhood gangs and carried on wars with other gangs. They pimped or pretended to pimp, used and sold drugs; stole from each other, their neighbors. (Irwin 2005: 222–23)

The South-Central Los Angeles area called Watts burned in a riot of disaffected black youth in 1965. Detroit, Michigan, burned along 12th Street in a similar 1967 riot. The Republicans won the 1968 election. They had used a "Southern strategy" approach to win over Southern Democrats to the Republican Party and the war on crime to rally conservative white votes in the North and elected Richard Nixon in 1968. Then, into the jobless economic vacuum of the now increasingly abandoned and powerless jobless ghetto, the illegal street drug economy began to expand and become a major "employer" of inner-city high school drop-out youth.

In subsequent elections throughout the 1970s and 1980s, the Republicans played on a conservative reaction to the liberal 1960s and used a new governing through crime approach to law making. They beat back the left libertarian tolerance toward drugs with a new conservative, moralistic, and punitive zero tolerance toward drugs. The pendulum had swung from rehabilitation to retribution—compulsive drug seeking behavior or recreational drug use were no longer medical problems or free choice, they were "evil deeds." Moreover, the conservative countermovement began to play the "race card." As Tonry notes:

> If crime and drugs are matters of good and evil, and criminals and drug users are evil, there is little reason to expect sympathy or empathy toward them from the holders of those views. . . . And Wacquant's analysis may help make it clear how and why the race card was played, as Hofstadter more than 40 years ago described. Although, he observed, Republicans historically had sympathy with the plight of U.S. Blacks in the South (quoting Hofstadter, Tonry continues):
>
>> By adopting the 'southern strategy,' the Goldwater men abandoned this inheritance. They committed themselves not merely to a drive for a core of Southern states in the electoral college but to a strategic counterpart in the North which required a search for racist votes. They thought they saw a good mass issue in the white backlash which they could indirectly exploit by talking of violence on the streets, crime, juvenile delinquency, and the dangers faced by our mothers and daughters (Hofstadter 1965: 99).
>
> No informed person disagrees that the national Republican party from the late 1960s through our time pursued a "Southern strategy" of focusing on nominally nonracial issues—law and order, welfare reform, opposition to affirmative action on color-blindness grounds—to appeal to the racial fears and antipathies of white Southerners and working-class voters through the country. (Tonry 2007: 26)

Meanwhile, the inner cities festered and drug sales drastically increased there. Related drug-turf competition and gun homicides, particularly by juveniles, skyrocketed.

The stage was set for President Reagan to respond to middle-class and "Reagan Democrat" working-class voter anxieties over drugs and violence in the cities with a new campaign carrying on Nixon's legacy of the war on crime, but now adding a new war on drugs approach. Reagan announced the new war on drugs in 1982 (Alexander 2012). He pressured the U.S. Congress in the summer of 1986 to federalize laws against street drugs. A national, street drugs "prohibition" now emerged. More federal antidrug laws were passed in 1988. The *drug crime era* had begun.

A drug offense was, by the late 1980s, no longer a minor felony with a presumption of rehabilitative treatment, but now more typically a major felony offense punishable with a long sentence, mandatory minimum prison term. These circumstances (more people entering prison, more staying longer, fewer paroles) rapidly built up state prison populations.

Many observers state that what especially sparked the drug crime era was an epidemic (1986–1993) of crack cocaine (Chiricos 1995/2002; Tonry 2007). Federal law enforcement agencies and U.S. attorneys around the country began to play a major role in what had previously been a state and local drug enforcement effort (CFECP 1998; Obermaier 1996; Heyman and Moore 1996). Federal drug control budgets greatly increased (Diulio, Smith, and Saiger 1995: 456). Federal prisons shot up to 40 percent of their population incarcerated for drug-related federal sentences. State legislatures followed the federal mandatory sentence model with punitive mandatory state drug offense laws, and this spread across the nation. *State prison populations shot up from 6 percent drug related to now up to 30 percent of their prisoners solely from drug-related convictions or drug-related parole violations.*

These new war on drugs laws of the 1980s and the 1990s made production, distribution, and sales of street drugs a new "bandwagon" effect of stiff sentences and enforcement, similar to how "intoxicating liquors" had been made over into a punitive emphasis during alcohol prohibition sixty to fifty years earlier. But, while "possession" and use of alcohol was not illegal under Prohibition, possession and use of street drugs *is* illegal under the war on drugs. "Felony drug possession" has been one of the easier arrests a federal, state, or local law enforcement officer, probation, or parole officer can make. Long sentences can happen if the person is arrested with large amounts of drugs sufficient to suggest "possession with intent to deliver."

These initial Antidrug Acts of 1986 and 1988 triggered immediate police sweeps of inner cities, with the arrest and imprisonment of a host of street drug dealers. The cleanup action came down especially hard on young black drug sellers who had been hawking drugs openly along the inner-city streets of New York, Baltimore, Los Angeles, Detroit, and other U.S. cities. In Michigan, these new young black drug sellers and other white, black, and brown "druggies," began to populate Michigan prisons.

Recall the story of the social context creating these "inner-city street criminals." Suburbs drew businesses and investment out of central city business districts (capital flight) and the result for central-city ghetto residents was to create a set of American jobless ghettos (hyperghetto) that were so bad they were set afire by the frustrated residents in the mid-1960s riots. What was the national response? Starting in 1973 in New York and in 1986 across the nation, a set of punitive laws arose. As Hallet says, "[W]hile both crime and imprisonment rates fluctuate over historical periods, the continued pattern of operation in criminal justice over the centuries . . . is a targeted focus on the poor, the politically powerless, and the socially marginal" (Shelden 2008: ix).

The inner-city riots actually made conditions worse for residents as the "pariah city" suffered political isolation and provided ammunition for conservatives (Darden, Hill, Thomas, and Thomas 1987).

What are abandoned inner-city residents to do? Some can move, but it is hard to move out to the suburbs from the low-rent inner city if you have few job skills or educational credentials. And the poor school systems typical of inner cities are unable to deliver quality education. Then again, there has been very little low-cost housing available in the suburbs. Federal housing policies subsidized suburbia and located low-income housing in the inner city. It was the highway system that built up the suburbs (Wacquant 2008: 69–88). Abandoned low-skilled populations in American inner cities—far away from entry level jobs, in a job-location mismatch—become a "problem population" requiring "management." Available to be designated as deviant and dangerous, the inner-city residents, particularly young black males—now invoking middle-class anxieties and fear of crime—become confined in probation, prison, or parole. Shelden continues:

> As Greenberg and West put it: "Sociological analysis of the history of penalty have *taken as their premise* that institutionalized punishment practices are not entirely determined by the functional necessity of preventing crimes" (2001: 638). Many other things are going on in the operation and unfolding of punishment than crime control—such as political posturing by politicians and social entrepreneurs, confinement and demonization of the dangerous classes, artificial management of surplus labor and official unemployment, profit-taking, and not least, the assuaging of middle-class anxieties about crime and vulnerability. (Shelden 2008: ix–x)

The result has been a rapidly expanded massive new prison world. As mentioned, in the drug crime era state prison admittance for drug-related crimes now shot up from 6 percent to 30 percent drug convictions while federal prisons shot up to 40 percent drug convictions.

Even with a small prison build-up spike during the alcohol prohibition of the 1920s, the U.S. prison population dynamics, for more than one hundred twenty years, from 1860 to 1980, held stable, as mentioned, at a low incarceration rate of 75 to 125 per 100,000. But then the nation went, in a brief twenty-five years, from 329,821 prisoners in 1980 to 2.2 million prisoners in 2007 (Austin and Irwin 2001: 1; Useem and Piehl 2008). Shelden states:

> Convictions for drug law violations (mostly possession) accounted for more than *one-half* of the increase in state prison inmates during the 1980s and early 1990s. Between 1985 and 1995 the number of prisoners in state institutions who have been convicted of drug offenses went up by 478% (Shelden 2008: 56)

This meant that existing prisons were going to become overcrowded. The nation's states were thus forced (and, to some degree, encouraged by federal "truth in sentencing" prison building grants) to hurriedly build more than one thousand new prisons. Thirty-four new prisons were built in Michigan alone. In a state that had previously had only eight state prisons and some camps in 1980, Michigan now had forty-two prisons and eight camps in 2008. Many of the prisoners' lives whose writings are presented in this book, span this entire period.

The Past and the Present—A Similarity

In this recent massive "incarceration binge" the "abuse substances of choice" were street drugs. Sixty-five years earlier, in a very much smaller but equally violence-ridden "incarceration explosion," the abuse substances of choice were intoxicating liquors. Certainly, the few dozen war on alcohol prisons constructed during the Prohibition years (such as Jackson, Attica, and Alcatraz) were far fewer in numbers than the one thousand new prisons hastily thrown up nationwide as "temporary facilities" during the 1986–2008 war on drugs incarceration binge.

Can you say that it's not fair to compare alcohol with street drugs because street drugs are much more dangerous? To the contrary, alcohol is responsible for more death and violence—and more health problems—*than all the street drugs combined*. Abadinsky, citing Li, Smith, and Baker 1994, and Wicker 1987, notes:

> According to scientific and pharmacological data used to classify dangerous substances for the protection of society, *alcohol* should be a schedule II narcotic, a Drug Enforcement Administration (DEA) category referring to a substance that is highly addictive and available only with a government narcotic registry number. *The cost of alcohol is twice the social cost of all illegal drug abuse.* Alcohol is reputed to be the direct cause of 80,000 to 100,000 deaths annually and alcohol-related auto accidents are the leading cause of death for teenagers. (Abadinsky 2008: 2–3) (emphasis added)

For many of the black prisoners whose thoughts we present in this book, their ambition, like that of most young inner-city kids in the "drug crime era," was to become a real life gangster. And, one day, to be a real "player." A person who has everything, while only a teenager! Living life in the fast lane, accumulating fast cash, fast cars, and fast women through the game of selling drugs, just like they saw their fathers, their big brothers, uncles, or other teenagers they admired doing around them.

As we have seen, in the twentieth century the United States passed two major federalizing laws—one criminalizing alcohol and the other vastly increasing the penalties for street drugs. Things were not good before passing the laws: there were health consequences, work consequences, or family and community life consequences for both alcohol and street drugs. And, things were (are) not good *after* passing the law: too much violence in the community, kids growing up having to negotiate "the streets," too many people in prison, families broken up, punishment not solving the problem with continued demand for drugs.

The first major law, Prohibition (1920–1933), made production, distribution, and sale of types of intoxicating liquors illegal. The second major law, the Anti-Drug Abuse Law (1986–present), shifted types of street drugs from a medical problem with short incarceration as minor felonies, to the category of major felonies with long sentences. Hallet concludes:

> [C]riminal justice activities have demonstrably not been about reducing crime or demand for drugs or curtailing addiction—but instead about cracking down on socially reviled groups that have not managed to become part of the mainstream, dominant culture. (Hallett, in Shelden 2008: x)

Today we regulate and tax the alcohol industry, which has become a legitimate business in production, distribution, and sales. We have adult criminal laws applying only to sale of alcohol to minors or the juvenile law of "minor in possession."

Criminality and death are definitely associated with alcohol, such as alcohol-related crimes of assault, domestic violence, and negligent homicide driving while drunk (Abadinsky 2008: 116; Wanberg and Milkman 1998). On the other hand, the *criminalization* of alcohol, street drugs, or tobacco adds the legal dimension of being arrested, charged, convicted in a court (or plea), and sentenced to probation, jail, or prison time. There will often be surveillance while on parole. There may be impacts on one's family, children, and community, and restrictions on employment, housing, and ability to vote after release as a convicted felon (Alexander 2012; Mauer and Chesney-Lind 2002; Petersilia 2003). And then, after years in prison, there can be the problem of overcoming *both* addiction and prisonization (Terry 2003). And to complicate matters, the United States has a severe prison racial disparity issue: African Americans, only 12 percent of the U.S. population, are 48 percent of U.S. state prisoners.

Michelle Alexander argues that the United States has developed a new Jim Crow type of racial caste that emerges from the consequences of mass incarceration:

> Knowing as I do the difficulty of seeing what most everyone insists does not exist, I anticipate that this book will be met with skepticism or something worse.

For some, the characterization of mass incarceration as a "racial caste system" may seem like a gross exaggeration, if not hyperbole. Yes, we may have "classes" in the United States—vaguely defined upper, middle, and lower classes—and we may even have an "underclass" (a group so estranged from mainstream society that it is no longer in reach of the mythical ladder of opportunity), but we do not, many will insist, have anything in this country that resembles a "caste."

. . . Jim Crow and slavery were caste systems. So is our current system of mass incarceration.

It may be helpful in attempting to understand the basic nature of the new caste system, to think of the criminal justice system—the entire collection of institutions and practices that comprise it—not as an independent system but rather as a *gateway* into a much larger system of racial stigmatization and permanent marginalization. This larger system, referred to here as mass incarceration, is a system that locks people not only behind actual bars in actual prisons, but also behind virtual bars and virtual walls—walls that are invisible to the naked eye but function nearly as effectively as Jim Crow laws once did at locking people of color into a permanent second-class citizenship. The term *mass incarceration* refers not only to the criminal justice system but also to the larger web of laws, rules, policies, and customs that control those labeled criminals both in and out of prison. Once released, former prisoners enter a hidden underworld of legalized discrimination and permanent social exclusion. They are members of America's new undercaste.

. . . Merely reducing sentence length, by itself, does not disturb the basic architecture of the New Jim Crow. So long as large numbers of African Americans continue to be arrested and labeled drug criminals, they will continue to be relegated to a permanent second-class status upon their release, no matter how much (or how little) time they spend behind bars. The system of mass incarceration is based on the prison label, not prison time. (Alexander 2012: 12–14)

But now we are in the second decade of the twenty-first century—thirty years after the beginnings of the war on drugs—and there is a potential shift in attitudes: there are increasing calls to end the war on drugs and to downsize the prisons.

Could street drugs be reduced in their harmful effects to the individual and the community through a "health and wellness" social movement? This has happened before. The use of tobacco, another major addictive substance that qualifies as a medical problem to self and a social problem to others, has, in the last fifty years, declined dramatically. This decline in smoking occurred solely through social pressure and social movements (and some class action civil suits), without bringing any criminal punitive penalties to bear with the exception of sale to minors, restrictions on advertising, and restricting smoking areas. Tobacco is another "vice" industry, where it is legal to produce, distribute, sell, and possess, and where the industry is regulated and taxed, like today's approach to alcohol.

THE HARM-REDUCTION MODEL

A *drug-defined crime* would be something like a felony drug arrest for possession or possession with intent to deliver. A low-level *drug-related crime* would be something like home invasion or shoplifting. A high level drug-related crime would be defined as conspiracy for major dealing, wholesaling, or distribution operations, with ancillary drug-related violent crime of "contract" enforcement (killings) and self-help "management" (extortion, assault) (Black 1983/2010). In the United States over the past twenty-five years, the sentencing for these drug-defined and lower-level drug-related crimes has typically involved several years of prison time. Some European nations have moved to a response to first- or second-offense, drug-defined and drug-related crime with an approach called *harm reduction*. This alternative puts aggressive law enforcement and pressure on producer nations (supply reduction). From this view, abstinence is desirable but is not usually a realistic goal. "Instead, this approach examines harm from two points of view: harm to the community and harm to the drug user. The focus, then, is on lowering the amount of harm to each" (Abadinsky 2008: 408).

In the harm-reduction approach, the use of drugs is accepted as a fact. Instead of a "warrior" approach of aggressive law enforcement on *all* drug behavior, as typified by our current zero-tolerance with mandatory sentences, the focus in harm reduction—for low-level offenders without prior criminal records—is placed on reducing harm while use continues. The characteristic principles of the harm reduction approach include: (1) pragmatism; (2) humanistic values; (3) focus on harms; (4) balancing costs and benefits; and (5) priority of immediate goals (Abadinsky 2008: 409–10). In this approach the focus is on reducing the *risky consequences* of drug use rather than on reducing drug use per se. "In place of the 'war' analogy and 'total victory' rhetoric," researchers and practitioners of the harm reduction approach "support even small steps that reduce harm," such as needle-exchange programs. Safer methods of ingestion could be fostered. "Risk would be further reduced by substituting methadone for heroin or other legal substances for cocaine and then by moderating the use of drugs—including nicotine and alcohol—en route to abstinence when this is possible" (Abadinsky 2008: 410).

The British, in the region of Merseyside, do not tackle the problems of economic decline and inner-city, drug-related crime with a massive incarceration binge, as in the United States. Instead, they offer a comprehensive harm reduction program. For instance, in this severely disadvantaged region that includes the city of Liverpool, thousands of unemployed dockworkers are without work because their jobs were replaced by containerization. They have turned to drugs, and a nascent drug economy has arisen. The British criminal justice system (Home Office) supports a program that

> involves needle exchange, counseling, prescription of drugs including heroin, and employment and housing services . . . services are integrated to provide drug users with help when they need it. Pharmacists . . . fill prescriptions for smokeable drugs . . . and other drugs.
>   . . . [T]he police sit on health authority drug advisory committees . . . to refer arrested drug offenders to services. (Abadinsky 2008: 412)

Recall Hallett's view that in the U.S. war on drugs that "criminal justice activities have demonstrably not been about reducing crime or demand for drugs or curtailing addiction—but instead about cracking down on socially reviled groups that have not managed to become part of the mainstream, dominant culture" (Hallett, in Shelden 2008: x). This example of how the British handled the white male, jobless ghetto dockworkers in Liverpool certainly differs from the U.S. approach to its unemployed inner-city black males.

Drugs and Growing Inequality

Everyone knows that drug abuse can happen anywhere in the social class structure. Yet significant drug abuse is not randomly dispersed over the population. Rather, research shows drug abuse tends to be concentrated in areas of poverty. Street drug addiction and related criminality is also often "part of a syndrome that includes family disintegration, child abuse and neglect, delinquency, and alcohol abuse" (Abadinsky 2008: 419–20). The harm reduction model and decriminalization itself does not address the growing inequality within nations.

When we think of the harm-reduction model efforts to reduce "harm to the community" and to reintegrate the drug abuse "offender," we have to ask: into what kind of "community" are we reintegrating the offender? Currie states we need to "simultaneously address the powerful social forces that are destroying the communities to which they must return" (Currie 1993: 279, in Abadinsky 2008: 420), and he alerts us to a need for concern about justice, reparation, and human well-being (Sullivan and Tifft 2001: 143).

Reflect again on the difference between the British response of *harm reduction* with minimal incarceration, for the devastated communities of unemployed, white, dockworkers who get into drugs and street crime in Liverpool, with the *massive imprisonment* of jobless ghetto blacks sucked into drug-related street culture crime in the jobless ghettos of U.S. cities. Too often criminal justice students want to carry a "warrior" outlook of simplification with them into the quest to "become a cop." Abadinsky, citing Gerstein and Harwood 1990, notes:

Our current policy of "shared simplifications" appears to reflect the popular will: allowing the majority of society to be against drug abuse while remaining free to abuse alcohol and tobacco. In other words, laws and law enforcement efforts against substances that are desired by a substantial minority of our citizenry provide symbolic opposition for the majority without actually impairing their own freedom to enjoy dangerous substances and activities—a policy that most Americans would be pleased to "drink to." (Abadinsky 2008: 420–21)

Why does the United States take a war approach to drugs when Britain does not? Chapter 3 tries to answer this question. But the short answer is the unusual U.S. answer to street drugs. Comparing crime and public policy in international perspective, Lynch and Pridemore note:

The United States is unique in its aggressive response to drug offenses, and this too is a major determinant of prison populations (2011: 6).
. . . The aggressive stance that the United States has taken toward drug crime is also a major contributor to the prison population. The United States is more likely to treat drug activity as a crime than most other nations, more likely to sentence convicted persons to prison, and more likely to require offenders to serve more time. Other nations may be similar to the United States in one of these aspects, but none is a punitive in all of these respects. (2011: 44)

The United States, before 1980, along with Great Britain and Europe had long been among nations with few prisons and low prisoner populations. The "prison culture" was not influential in our society. Countries like Russia, China, and South Africa (under Apartheid) were nations that imprisoned massive numbers of citizens. *They* had prison state societies. The U.S. rate of incarceration had remained stable around 100 per 100,000 (rates of 76–124) from 1860 to 1980. The national total prison population stayed in a range of from 200,000 to 400,000. Sentencing was fairly predictable, prisoners moved in and out of prison roughly on schedule, most leaving prison on or before their "minimum" release date (due to a good institutional record), before their minimum sentence because of earning "good time" (disciplinary credits), and nonviolent prisoners often shortened their sentence by going to a halfway house up to two years or more before their earliest release date. Parole served as a "safety valve"—if prisons get a little crowded, more were released on parole (Abadinsky 2006: 1–2), new prisons were not needed.

Since 1986, not only were more prisons needed in the United States—*a thousand* new prisons were needed. And they were always overcrowded with double-bunking cells meant for one. The war on drugs has meant a change in prison culture.

THE WAR ON DRUGS CHANGES PRISON CULTURE

The academic study of the prisoners' world centered on two models, both explaining the origins of prison culture: (1) the endogenous model and (2) the importation model.

In the endogenous model the prison is seen as "a society of captives." The prison, as a *small society*, develops its own subculture. Gresham Sykes noted in his 1958 study that, if men were merely locked in their cell, the prison would be an "aggregate" of prisoners. But Sykes's research for the book *Society of Captives* found that "the prisoners' world" emerges as a subculture through *interactions* at the mess hall, chores, exercise, work, recreation, and school and religious activities (Sykes 1958: 5).

Guards, because of their working conditions, tend to establish relationships with prisoners and cut them some slack. The slightly loose social order the prisoners establish through their interactions with each other and the guards must, however, be held in check by the prison administration that typically, for public relations reasons, holds the values of strict custody and order. And "the prior deviance of the prisoner is a rationalization for using . . . extreme measures (of deprivation) to avoid any events which would excite public indignation" (Sykes 1958: 33).

The Sykes view that the prison culture came pretty much entirely out of the internal tension between prisoner interaction and the deprivations required by administration concern with custody and control (Sykes 1958: 63–83) was challenged in the late 1960s by a view of the prison where prisoners *bring in* their values, norms, and customs. That is, prison culture and life is best explained by the influence of imported subcultures, such as the growing American black Muslim religion entering the prison by 1957 (Haley and Malcolm X 1964), and gangs entering the prison in the 1960s (Jacobs 1977), and particular inner-city neighborhood street cultures becoming imprisoned (Clear 2007). Clearly, both the endogenous deprivation model and the importation model can help in understanding the subculture of the prison.

However, there is a need to update the endogenous and importation models of prison culture. There had been a quadrupling of the U.S. prisoner population, due to the impact of the war on drugs and the development of extreme joblessness in the hyperghetto, since these theories were put forward. With help from older prisoners in my five years of volunteer classes (2008–2012) upon which this book is based, we theorized the rise of a *prison incarceration binge culture*, elaborating several changes over the last thirty years that have altered prison culture:

1. more snitches characteristic of drug prosecutions, means less prisoner unity;

2. an increase in younger prisoners who do not respect older adults on the street and do not respect older convicts in the prison;
3. more people doing long prison time due to tough on crime and war on drugs lengthy sentences;
4. the impact of prisoner reentry initiatives is increasing paroles but mixing lifers with short-timers in Level II prisons;
5. long-term prisoner programs have been cut, now prison programs are more geared toward guys coming in and out;
6. the impact of double-bunking and overcrowded conditions are confounded by more mentally ill persons in U.S. prisons;
7. the fact that, in the war on drugs, so many people come from the same urban areas creates a new neighborhood feel to the prisons;
8. more distinct hoods in prison related to drug-turf gangs;
9. the prison as a school for crime now enhanced as more druggies (addicts) now mix with opportunist criminals in the yard;
10. a new convenient oppression using prisons to solve the problem of jobless ghettos;
11. because of state budget crises there is significantly less in-prison programming, education, and vocational training;
12. there is a new, evidence-based imported "policy culture" around planning for reentry—from control after prison to support after prison creating an expectation in prison to work on reentry plans;
13. the emphasis on prisoner reentry initiatives is changing field services and prison organizational culture—"don't want them back"; and
14. yet high unemployment and lack of good quality jobs means a continuing issue of "what to do with the inner-city black males" who continue to have a violence rate four times more than whites.

Moreover, there is no sign that states are seriously addressing the "functional" premise of the incarceration binge: that prison growth plays a surrogate welfare system role for the inner-city black males. That is, that hyperincarceration is another in a "series of American cultural practices and legal institutions (that) has operated to maintain American patterns of racial dominance and hierarchy for two centuries" (Tonry 2007: 23). It is this strong dose of racism that has helped to orchestrate the growth of the prison system (Tonry 2007; Wacquant 2008; Zimring 2006). Where is the drive—so far—to reduce this dose of racism in our prison system?

Barlow and Kauzlarich (2010: 57–58) state that we need to consider how the "dramatic increase in U.S. imprisonment rates over the last few decades could be negatively impacting neighborhood and community social organization." They cite Rose and Clear (1998: 441):

High incarceration rates may contribute to rates of criminal violence by the way they contribute to such social problems as inequality, family life deterioration, economic and political alienation, and social disorganization . . . (and) undermine social, political, and economic system already weakened by the low levels of human and social capital produced under conditions such as high rates of poverty, unemployment, and crime. . . . The result is a reduction in social cohesion and a lessening of those communities' capacity for self-regulation. (2010: 58)

Exploring prisoner complaints about overly long sentences, lack of correctional programming, getting "flopped" too often for "no reason," and existing in a system that is interested in "keeping us in here and making sure we come back," reveals, in fact, the set of social dynamics and related social policy discussed above.

RACIAL DISPARITY IN U.S. PRISONS

Michael Tonry, giving his presidential address to the American Society of Criminology in the fall of 2007 notes:

[In my 1995 book] *Malign Neglect*, I tried to unravel the reasons why black Americans were so much likelier than whites to be arrested, convicted, imprisoned, and executed. . . .

Here is what I learned. First, although blacks had for a century been more likely to be held in prison than whites, racial disparities began to increase in the 1960s and then shot up to all-time highs in the 1980s: by then blacks were half of American prisoners, although only 12 percent of the U.S. population, and they had an imprisonment rate seven times higher than whites. Second, blacks were much more likely than whites to be arrested for the "imprisonable" offenses of robbery, rape, aggravated assault, and homicide. . . . Third, however, critically, no significant shifts had occurred in racial patterns in arrests for a quarter century, and involvement in serious violent crime could not explain why black imprisonment rates had increased so rapidly. Fourth, the principal driver of the increase was imprisonment for drug crimes, and policy makers knew or should have known that the enemy foot soldiers in the war on drugs would be young, disadvantaged, inner-city members of American minority groups. That seemed to me then and seems to me now a profoundly unwise and immoral exercise of governmental power. (Tonry 2007: 21–22)

At the same time as these two changes were taking place—the fourfold increase in rate of incarceration and the "blackening" of our prisons—the prisoner profile was changing from the long familiar, violent, white "bad guy" image to that of the drug-related crimes of black and white "druggie" prisoner. Unlike the traditional, violent criminal of the past—the robber, rapist, or murderer—or the nonviolent property criminal of the past—the burglar, thief, shoplifter, bad check writer—today up to 30 percent of state prisoners and more than 40 percent of federal prisoners that enter prison are convicted of drug and drug-related crimes. According to the Michigan Department of Corrections (MDOC), 43 percent of prisoners entering prison during the incarceration binge period were classified as nonassaultive (MDOC 1996/2007).

In terms of the rate of incarceration, Blumstein notes:

> The most striking observation (is that) . . . [i]n the 17 years from 1980 to 1996, drugs climbed from the single offense with *almost the fewest* prisoners *to* the one with by far *the largest number*. There were an estimated 23,900 state and federal prisoners for drug offenses in 1980, which represented an incarceration rate of less than 15 per 100,000 adults. By 1996, that incarceration rate had grown to 148 per 100,000, more than a nine-fold increase. (Blumstein 2002: 453) (italics added)

Moreover, the amount of time served for drug offenses rose dramatically. There were now the long-sentence mandatory minimum drug laws (meaning no release for "good time"). There were now fewer paroles once the minimum sentence had been completed. And there were now more parole violations sending people back to prison—often for failure to pass drug tests while on parole (Blumstein 2002: 461).

How did all of this come about? (See figures 2.1 and 2.2.) How did the United States, in a short twenty years, change from having a traditionally low prisoner population into becoming the world's prison and jail leader, with over 2.2 million prisoners?

Was this type of prison growth happening elsewhere in the Western industrialized world? In fact, the incarceration rate remained constant in the other Western nations. Between 1970 and 2000 Europe's custody rate per 1,000 stayed at less than 1, around 0.8 to 0.9, while the U.S. custody rate between 1970 and 2000 shot up from 1.8 to 8.4 individuals incarcerated per 1,000. Clearly huge prison growth has been a peculiarly American phenomenon.

Michael Tonry, in his 2007 presidential address to the American Society of Criminology, in reviewing the work of Loic Wacquant (1999; 2002; 2008; 2008), notes that his historical view can help explain *why* we had a war on drugs. Tonry notes that Wacquant's "basic, functionalist argument is that a series of American cultural practices and legal institutions has operated to maintain American patterns of racial dominance and hierarchy for two centuries" (Tonry 2007: 23).

Highlights

Violent crime rates, 1973-95 (with adjustments based on the redesign of the National Crime Victimization Survey)

Victimization rate per 1,000 persons age 12 or older

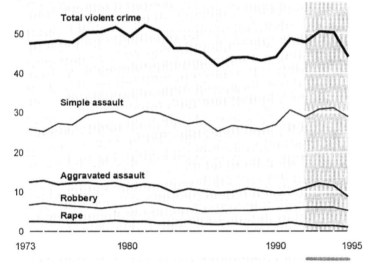

Collected under the National Crime Survey (NCS) and made comparable to data collected under the redesigned methods of the National Crime Victimization Survey (NCVS)

Collected under the redesigned NCVS

Violent crime includes murder, rape, robbery, and aggravated and simple assault. Murder is not shown separately. Sexual assault is excluded, as explained on page 3.

• A decline in the violent crime rate beginning in 1994 interrupted a rising trend that existed after the mid-1980's.

• In 1995 rape, robbery, and aggravated assault, measured by the National Crime Victimization Survey (NCVS), and murder, measured by the FBI's Uniform Crime Reports (UCR), were at or near a 23-year low.

• The rates of theft and household burglary have steadily declined since the late 1970's. In 1995 burglary was at about half the rate in 1973.

• The motor vehicle theft rate in 1995 was well below the highest rate of 1991.

• 1973-91 estimates were adjusted to reflect improved survey methodology put in place in 1992. The adjustments preserve the year-to-year changes in relationships for earlier estimates.

Figure 2.1.   Trends in Criminal Victimization in the United States, 1973–1995. *Source:* U.S. Department of Justice.

Percent of new court commitments
to State prisons

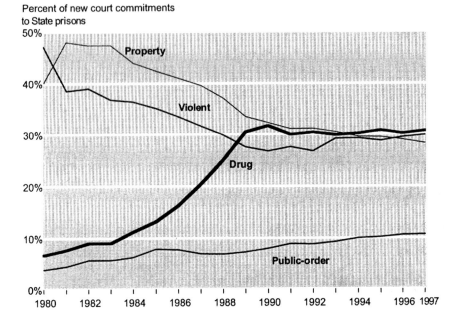

Figure 2.2. Most Serious Offence Convicts Admitted to State Prisons, 1980–1997.
Source: U.S. Department of Justice.

Well, didn't we have a civil rights movement? As mentioned, I've lived through and participated in, the American civil rights movement (1954–1972). That important movement resulted in considerable increased economic and social integration of blacks in American society. However, *when you look at the criminal justice system*, there is a very different story. In U.S. prisons there is a "7-to-1 racial difference in imprisonment rates."

Tonry notes that "32 percent of black males born in 2001 will spend some time confined in a state or federal prison" (2007: 23).

While the civil rights movement opened the job structure to African Americans to produce good working-class, middle-class, and government jobs; and while school integration since 1971 produced a measure of equality between students, the criminal justice system produces devastatingly *reduced* life chances for poor black Americans (Western 2006). The criminal justice system with "nearly of third of black men in their twenties . . . in prison or jail, or on probation or parole" reduces black men's chances for jobs, marriage, being a good father, or being socialized into prosocial values. "There has to be a reason why the criminal justice system treats American blacks so badly, why its foreseeable disparate impacts on blacks and whites are disregarded." (Tonry 2007: 23–24).

To answer this question requires a history of narcotics before the war on drugs and an analysis of the emergence of the war on drugs.

The United States has always had "swings in the pendulum" between tolerance and intolerance regarding "moral vices" such as alcohol and drugs (Musto 1991). For instance, the 1890s were awash with drugs and alcohol, but by 1920 the United States had prohibition and a punitive war on alcohol era. Then drugs flowed again under a period of tolerance during the 1960s and early 1970s, only to run up again against a tide of intolerance driven by tough on crime politics in the 1980s and 1990s. Even with alternating eras of tolerance and intolerance over the decades, a rough stability in the rate of incarceration between 60 and 125 per 100,000 existed, up to 1984.

In the 1980s, events were to change that stability in the rate of incarceration. Guns began flowing into the U.S. cities. The path to gang violence in Detroit resembled that of the gangster period of Prohibition in the 1920s. Bands of armed gangsters competed for control of territories. Similarly, entrance of guns into the 1980s jobless ghetto quickly spelled competition and trouble in Detroit. There was an increase in guns and crack and the crime rate jumped between the years of 1986 and 1991. But it was not an increase in the *crime rate* that was scaring the U.S. public, so much as the alarming increase in the use of firearms in drug and gang turf battles of the city (Zimring and Hawkins 1997). Teenage drug sellers, youthfully headstrong and unschooled in guns, fought with youthful vigor and emotion to protect their particular piece of hard-won turf (Blumstein 2002).

News stories of the wave of homicides and arrests in Detroit created national attention and brought forth, in the summer of 1986, as we have highlighted in chapter 1, a moral panic (Chiricos 1995/2002). The moral panic resulted in the rushed passage of the 1986 and 1988 federal antidrug abuse act and their extraordinarily long mandatory drug sentences. Instead of focusing on the problems of the inner city—urban labor markets and jobs, family support, housing, income, job skills, and education—the United States began a punitive response in the shape of a drastic increase in incarceration.

The United States has, over the past twenty-five years, built up a mass incarceration system with 2.2 million people incarcerated and African Americans, 12 percent of the nation's population, constituting 48 percent of the prisoners. Why? We have described the jobless ghettos in the United States and their relationship to crime, and some of the reasons they have developed. One major consequence has been that one-in-four African American males' ages seventeen to thirty-five go to prison.

Now, thirty years later, we *still* have the jobless ghettos (hyperghetto). How did we arrive at this point? The short answer, beyond swings in the pendulum, crack, and guns, are the metaphors we are governed by. We will address this in chapter 3. What has the strategy of mass incarceration looked like to prisoners? Consider prisoner essay 2.1, below, written by an African American man who went to prison when he was nineteen years old and has been incarcerated for the past twenty years, and prisoner essay 2.2, which give us prisoners' insight to the criminology of mass incarceration.

#####

Prisoner Essay 2.1

"They Lock Older Guys Up—Now We Kids Had to Hustle" (3/17/10)
I can remember when I was young that there were older guys in my neighborhood that people as well as myself look up to. These guys had it all—the girls, clothes, and cars. But most of all they had the money. They would give us money so we could go to the penny candy store or record shop to buy stuff we wanted. This was good cause a lot of times our parents didn't have extra money to give us for these things unless it was the first of the month when everybody expected their welfare checks.

When some of these people got lock up for crimes, it made it hard for us to get extra stuff that we wanted cause they was gone and the money left with them. Now we had to hustle for ourselves to get money and that meant we had to commit crime. Yeah, we could had cut grass, but there was no grass. We could have even collected bottles, but those were all broken. Crime pay is much better cause all we had to do at that time was be a look-about (lookout) or take and package somewhere and keep your mouth shut.

My father for the most part showed me and my brother how the streets can pay. I watch little by little how my parent's neighborhood was getting worse by the day when people started to get lock up on a daily basis. The neighborhood was largely a breeding ground for crime but when people started to get lock up it got worse. People who was alright in the neighborhood who had a little money all of a sudden didn't cause their father or brother was lock up who provided for the household in major way. People on the block would help each other out as much as they could but things was just tight, there wasn't a lot of jobs to be had let alone even be offered. So there was no networking about getting jobs, just hustling.

People who had jobs, had to catch the bus or walk to work. People who had cars got lock up, so going to work every day was hard and in the winter was not even an option. I see how social disorganization in my neighborhood made it worse than it already was when people got lock up. When my father was killed I see how our household went down and the things I was used to having was now gone, so I did the only thing I knew to do at that time which was to commit crime to help out around the house and take care of myself.

When I got lock up this hurt my family as well as the community. I was someone that people knew and could trust for things. I wouldn't let people houses get broke in or their cars stole in my neighborhood. Prison changes that.

So when I got here and seen almost everybody from my neighborhood, I was like damn! This is almost like a neighborhood reunion, minus the fact that we all were lock up in prison.

How does mass incarceration makes disadvantaged neighborhood worse, because the people that keep it safe like myself are gone from the neighborhood. Trust me I have first hand knowledge; I sit here talking to you. I was once part of the problem. There is hope though. We must first clean up our minds! Crime and violence isn't the way to provide for our community. Yeah a lot of money is made, but at what cost? I can write and read about the cost for a year or two and have a new issue every day, we see it on TV and hear it in our music.

I still believe that good can still be done by having after school programs and community meeting where everybody gets together to talk about making our neighborhood safe, having love for our neighbor so we can walk down the street safe. It's start with us, the adult. We tore the community down and the cleanup is on us. We owe it to the community and they look to us for guidance. Let's show them the right way because they are the futures. Let's stop the mass incarceration and start mass living. Because prison life isn't living life but wasting life.

#####

Prisoner Essay 2.2

"Rampaging Juvenile Elephants" (3/17/10)
The earth trembled violently as though it would split in half—swallowing the entire village. Women and children scampered for cover as the men of the village retrieved bolt-action rifles in defense of their homeland. The crack of gunfire mingled with screams and the thunderous trumpeting of the rampaging elephants, creating a sonic kaleidoscope of terror. Under the cover of darkness the dust covered pachyderms moved like formidable tanks destroying everything in their paths. With vise-like grips they used their enormous trunks to wrench trees from the fertile ground. Splintered wood, foliage and rich soil flew though the air as they hurled their timberland projectiles into the small circle of huts. These are the images that played though the movie screen of my mind as I read the newspaper account of what occurred when a herd of juvenile elephants were on a rampage.

I can't recall exactly what village the story took place in, however I will never forget the impression the story left on me. What occurred in a small village of the other side of the world was playing out on city blocks and in trailer parks across the nation, the juveniles were rampaging. A biologist gave her account of what happened when the older bull elephants were taken away and placed in zoos far away from home, leaving behind a herd of female and baby elephants. As the male juvenile elephants grew older they started exhibiting high levels of aggression and violence. When they were young the mother elephants corrected their behavior and guided them back in line. But as they matured, growing in size and stature they rebelled against the matriarchal authority. They terrorized the other female elephants and rampaged though several villages, leaving in their wake of death and destruction.

World renowned biologists and animal behaviorists were called in to find what was making this herd of elephants so aggressive. They analyzed the soil and water where the elephants congregated to see if it was contaminated. They observed the surrounding jungle to see if they were being threatened by other animals or human poachers who often killed them for their tusks. The biologist sedated a couple of the rabble rousers taking blood samples to ensure they weren't infected with any parasites that affected their behavior. Finally one noted specialist recognized there were no adult male elephants present. The scientists got together and discussed the possibility of bringing a couple of the older bull elephants back to restore order. They agreed it was a better alternative than euthanizing the young elephants.

Over the next couple of weeks they returned two bull elephants to the herd. Initially the juvenile elephants were skittish and a bit unsure of themselves. They kept their distance from the older bull elephants for a day or so. After a few days the juvenile elephants were back up to their old tricks. They increased their aggression toward the female elephants, threatening them with their large tusks while spraying them with dirt and water. They pulled trees from the ground and tossed them around like nerf footballs. The older bull elephants observed their behavior before they trumpeted loud enough to shake tectonic plates. Their power and authority burst through the air with a clarity that caused the juvenile elephants to freeze in their tracks. The older bull elephants then went on to corral the younger males along with the rest of the herd and guided them down to the river where they bathed and drank. They taught them how to forage for food and how to defend the baby elephants from the ever present threat of lions. The older elephants successfully redirected the juvenile elephant's energy toward something more productive and meaningful. Within two weeks order had been restored to the herd and the village was once again safe.

When I finished reading the story my heart wept for the juvenile elephants and the young males in my community who are waiting for their version of the older bull elephants to be returned to the village.

It was clear from the story of the elephants what was happening in my own family and by extension my community. Due to the overwhelming loss of strong male leadership the male juveniles were running amuck. The women could no longer walk to the corner store without being molested and the children were no longer able to play safely outside. The quality of life in our contemporary village was in steady decline. The law and order that once characterized our community had given way to chaos. With so many males from our community being hauled off to prison there was no one there to guide the youth and focus their energy on educational, spiritual and financial prosperity. The reality of this grim picture became clearly visible to me as I thought about my son, nephews and lil homies. Like juvenile elephants they were terrorizing the village and threatening to destroy everything in their path, including their future.

Unfortunately the young men in my family and neighborhood were inheriting a destructive legacy that began before they were born. I was the third male member of my family to come to prison. When I arrived in 1991 I had a 3 month old daughter and a son on the way. My oldest brother had just been released from prison and my other older brother was upstate serving a short sentence leaving behind his son. In 1993 my oldest sister's husband came to prison leaving behind a total of six sons. Currently one of his sons is now in prison and two were recently released. In 2005 my older brother came back to prison leaving behind his son again and a daughter who was born when he was released. In 2004 and 2005 two of my cousins followed in our footsteps and landed in prison. One is home now and the other one is waiting to be released, he has two sons. And finally my other brother-in-law came to prison and left my sister to care for their five children. And the impact is being felt throughout our family and community.

Two of my nephews have been to prison and one has had a few minor scrapes with the law. My own son has had several challenges including smoking marijuana and getting kicked out of school. My nephews act out and my sisters are having major trouble trying to keep them out of prison and in school. Over the years I have written my children, my nephews, nieces and younger cousin's in an effort to break the cycle. I warn them about the consequences of gun violence, sexually transmitted diseases, drug abuse and teenage pregnancy. When they write me back or I speak to them on the phone I can hear the desperation in their voices. They crave guidance and structures. They yearn for the discipline and focus that only a man can instill in a young man. They want guidance and help. And like the older elephants the males in my family have been sent off to human zoos where we aren't so readily accessible to them. But I refuse to allow this to stop or deter me from doing my part to guide them, it's my duty, no—it's our duty.

Without realizing it most of us who come to prison are like modern day pied pipers, we lead the youth in our families and community straight into the blood stained jaws of the prison industrial complex, or worse to an early gravesite. It doesn't matter if we are from the hood or the suburbs. When we leave our families and communities we leave a void behind. It doesn't matter whether we are biological fathers or not when we are removed from society the children, and by extension the community suffers.

We know the many ways mass incarceration impacts the community. Tax dollars that would normally go toward education and other important social services are spent on prisons. The guardians that are left to care for the children have to alter the quality of their lives. The wives and mothers left behind have to rely on state sponsored rations to ensure the children are fed and their basic health care needs are met. Property taxes go up. While property values plummet. And the chance of our children coming to prison increases sevenfold. We know (these criminological theories) and we live them. The scientifically articulated data infused analysis paints a sobering and disheartening portrait. However there is nothing as sobering as getting a letter from your nephew announcing his arrival to prison or his proclivity to self destruct. It is these letters and this brutal reality that makes me ask the larger question. What must we do to stop the children from running amuck like the elephant in the village?

#####

Barbara Levine, associate director of Citizens Alliance on Prisons and Public Spending (CAPPS) in her wonderfully comprehensive and precise recidivism study (August 2009) studied 76,000 Michigan prisoners released on parole over the years 1986 to 1999. Her analysis revealed the unnecessary years past earliest release date that many offense category prisoners spend in Michigan prisons (request copy from www.capps-mi.org). In this chapter, we have suggested a "new rational model" of harm reduction and sensible sentencing and prison policies. Such policies will save money for the "new justice reinvestment" movement and for other state priorities. But why did the United States become "stuck" in the politicized punitive model? To answer this we need to review, in chapter 3, the politics that have driven mass incarceration.

EXERCISE 2.1: REFLECTING ON MASS INCARCERATION

Design an alternative to overuse of confinement. What policies can be used that do not require an expensive prison bedspace? What is wrong with a "waste management" approach to prisoners? Explain.

DISCUSSION AND REVIEW QUESTIONS

1. What has been the single most influential type of law that has resulted in the prison build-up?
2. How has prison culture changed as a consequence of the prison build-up movement?
3. What explains the racial disparity in U.S. prisons?
4. What have been the trends in U.S. crime rates since the 1950s?
5. Compare prisoner essay 2.2 to the argument made in chapter 2.
6. Interpret figure 2.1. What have been the trends in crime?
7. Interpret figure 2.2. What has been the "most serious offense" on convicts admitted to prison?

3

The Politics of Mass Incarceration

We have traced the rise of mass incarceration. Social change on the dimensions of a quadrupling of the U.S. prison population in the nearly thirty years from 1984 to 2012 can be explained in terms of the conservative cultural shift from due process and rehabilitation ideals to crime control and retribution values. Yet surveys show U.S. citizens want both punishment and rehabilitation. The biggest shift in the prison build-up movement has been the *politicization* of crime, cops, courts, and corrections. The American traditional correctional project of punishment linked to rehabilitation became buried under layers of politicized crime legislation.

According to Jonathan Simon, much of this can be traced back to the 1968 "Safe Streets Act" and the subsequent development of a political approach he calls "governing through crime legislation." The baby boom—children of World War II veterans after the war—swelled up the ranks of fifteen- to twenty-five-year-olds in the 1960s and early 1970s. This demographic bulge meant that crime would increase in the late 1960s and early 1970s, and the crime rates did go up. The Democratic Party needed the votes from the big cities and President Johnson signed the Safe Streets Act. This crime legislation approach reflected a

"[s]trategic vision for retooling liberalism . . . because it responds to one of the most urgent problems in America today—the problem of fighting crime in the local neighborhoods and on the city street" (Johnson 1968: 725).

In the concluding paragraph of the statement, President Johnson brings the whole constellation into view: the war on crime, its territorialization into streets, and the centrality of law enforcement (Johnson 1968: 728). (Simon 2007: 95–99)

During the 1940s, 1950s, and 1960s there had been, for the Democratic Party that controlled Congress and for the Roosevelt, Truman, Kennedy, and Johnson presidential years a continuation of the 1930s New Deal emphasis on programs for the people and civil rights. This evolved into President Johnson's

"Great Society." But Simon argues that the 1968 Safe Streets Act "was the signal event marking the end of the Great Society era and of the liberal pro–Civil Rights dominance of federal policy." Political theorists Scammons and Wittenberg, in *The Real Majority* (1969), argued only a year after the Act and the 1968 Republican takeover of the White House, that crime was "the central example of how the Democratic Party was in real danger of losing its two-generation-old majority status by ignoring a profound shift of its traditional supporters on a host of 'social' issues, including the race problem, abortion, family values." Democrats traditionally talked about root causes of crime but now were counseled to support tougher law enforcement measures to repress existing criminals (Simon 2007: 99). Politicians began a "game of who could be tougher" on crime. The "logic of representation" shifted: "legislators must be for victims and law enforcement, and thus they must never be for (or capable of being portrayed as being for) criminals or prisoners as individuals or as a class" (Simon 2007: 100).

DRUGS, GUNS, AND THE INNER CITY—A WAR ON DRUGS

As the "war on crime" continued into the 1970s and 1980 (and into the present), this new "representational system" (governing through crime legislation) produced many more examples of the "politics of tough on crime." Many politicians seized on inner-city drug crimes in the mid-1980s as a "wedge issue" to distinguish their political party from the "softer" (other) political party. The Republican Party was particularly good at this maneuver, but the Democrats found they needed to play catch up and be "tough on crime" too. Crime, Simon argues, citing Scheingold 1991, was a political narrative "emphasizing personal responsibility and will over social context and structural constraints on freedom and that could be enacted without fundamental changes in the status quo of wealth and power; (was) a pathway for government innovation" (Simon 2007: 25–26).

Dismayed by urban violence, especially drug-related killings in Detroit's ghetto and other urban ghettos, and aware of the rise in drug use nationwide (by both whites and blacks), President Reagan seized the moment to continue governing through crime by announcing a war on drugs in 1982 and by 1986 pushing through a new package of crime legislation.

The states, having broad powers to police crime, "moved forward as innovators in using criminal law to govern, especially in the 1970s and 1980s" (2007: 29). But the war on drugs also belonged to federal jurisdiction because it involves interstate or international commerce. In the 1980s the federal government promoted the "belief that illegal drug commerce was the underlying cause of violent street crime," as many suburbs and small local communities were sheltered." Additionally, legislation provided federal money to states to adopt truth-in-sentencing legislation that required prison inmates to serve 85 percent or more of their sentence as a condition of receiving federal money to build more prisons. Moreover,

> virtually no constitutional limitations have been found on the amount of prison time as punishment. In short, alone among major social problems haunting America in the 1970s and 1980s, crime offered the least political or legal resistance to government action. (Simon 2007: 29–31)

A new "federalization" of drug law, similar to the 1920s Prohibition Era, emerged (Heymann and Moore 1996). The new federal drug laws imposed stricter penalties and longer sentences for possession, use and sale of drugs. States followed with their own punitive, long sentence penalties for "possession with intent to deliver," or "conspiracy with intent to deliver."

There were several other potential "pathways to reconstructing governance" after the end of the New Deal Politics in the 1960s. The alternative pathways that could have been followed were such as restoring the power of organized labor movement, expanding social insurance programs for working and middle class, environmentalism, expanded mental health programs, and continuing the civil rights movement. But the alternative pathways "were stymied easily when the crime agenda decisively sprinted ahead in the mid-1970s" (Simon 2007: 25–58).

The first pathway of this politicization of crime, cops, courts, and corrections pathways was government action taken at the state level with the 1973 Rockefeller mandatory sentence drug laws, which were followed by passage of the first federal Mandatory Minimum Drug Laws of 1986, in an atmosphere of moral panic (Chiricos 1995/2002). In late 1986, and continuing on into the 1990s, many young drug sellers who had been living "life in the fast lane" in the streets of Detroit's ghetto, and other inner cities across the United States, now found themselves abruptly detained on the streets, arrested, charged, convicted, and sentenced, and condemned to prisons such as Michigan Reformatory and Jackson Prison in Michigan for harsh ten- to twenty-year, and twenty-to-life mandatory drug sentences. The author was teaching prison college in these facilities at this time and saw his prison classrooms of mostly white traditional young criminals in 1983 turn into mostly black drug-related young criminals by 1987. As Schmalleger notes:

> By passing mandatory sentencing laws, legislators convey the message that certain crimes are deemed especially grave and that people who commit them deserve, and may expect, harsh sanctions. These laws are sometimes passed in response to public outcries following heinous or well-publicized crimes. (Schmalleger 2001: 374–75).

Did harsh state and federal mandatory drug laws really deter jobless youth in American inner cities from selling drugs? Schmalleger notes:

An (evaluation of) New York's (1973) Rockefeller drug laws were unable to support claims for their efficacy as a deterrent to drug crime.

. . . Tonry found that . . . sentences become longer and more severe. Mandatory sentencing laws may also occasionally result in unduly harsh punishments for marginal offenders who nonetheless meet the minimum requirements for sentencing under such laws.

In an analysis of federal sentencing guidelines, other researchers found that blacks receive longer sentences than whites, not because of differential treatment by judges, but because they constitute the large majority of those convicted of trafficking in crack cocaine—a crime Congress has singled out for especially harsh mandatory penalties (Schmalleger 2001: 375–76). (FAMM 2008)

Thus, the next twenty years (1986–2006) would see the tremendous prison explosion of one thousand new prisons that Austin and Irwin (1997/2001) labeled as "The Incarceration Binge." The author became a founding member of the Michigan Citizen Alliance on Prisons and Public Spending (www.capps-mi.org) in May of 1998, with an organizational goal to "cap prison growth, cap prison spending, and shift resources to prevention." Sentencing for drug crimes would get ever tougher and prisons nationwide would become ever fuller, reaching the capacity point, leading to double-bunking cells designed for one—and then with ever more prisoners, putting beds in the prison gyms and hallways. The author and his coauthor for the 2009 book *The Prisoners' World* made tours with the warden of San Quentin Prison in California at the start of the drug laws impact in 1990 and again in 2000, describing the increasing problem of allocating scarce bedspace (Tregea and Larmour 2009: 153–58).

Why did the people of the United States "let" a moral panic in 1986 over crack cocaine *lead* to such a twenty-year-long incarceration binge?

We've identified Simon's insights about the politicians "strategy shift" away from New Deal or New Social Movement politics of helping people with social programs to the new tough on crime or governing through crime, where politicized crime legislation becomes an unassailable approach to win votes. But, in this "strategy shift," whose votes were cultivated? Would white suburban parents allow their children, e.g., white working-class or middle-class males seventeen to twenty-five years old, go to prison on a scale such as what has happened to urban African Americans youth? There *was* an increase in crime in the cities, mostly drug-related due to the crack epidemic, leading up to the 1986 federal laws (Useem and Piehl 2008). However, the federal legislation was passed in a hurry in an atmosphere of high anxiety and fear that the 1986 crack epidemic inner-city gun violence would spread to the suburbs. Zimring and Hawkins wrote an insightful 1997 book arguing that what the public was most afraid of was gun violence, and not so much drug addiction. Chiricos notes:

> Hysteria over violent crime is a classic example of "moral panic." This concept was developed by Cohen, who noted that at certain times a "condition, episode, person or group of persons emerges to become defined as a threat to societal values and interests" (Cohen 1972: 9). He notes that typically the threat is presented in the media in a simplistic fashion; spokespersons such as editors, the clergy, and politicians man the moral barricades; and experts pronounce their diagnoses of the problem and present solutions. As he emphasizes, the point of a moral panic is "not that there's nothing there," but that societal responses are fundamentally inappropriate (Cohen 1972: 204). (Chiricos 1995/2002: 59)

So, the war on drugs with the police crackdowns and the long-sentence mandatory minimums, led to massive incarceration getting the now reviled crack dealers off the streets and into prison. Then, another young inner-city black youth would step forward to sell the drugs. But for every violence-prone, street-corner, gang-affiliated drug dealer making money off of selling crack there were many more "druggies" (white, black, and brown) who bought the drugs and became addicted. These people often then, through drug abuse, started to do home invasions, petty larcenies (like shoplifting), writing bad checks (uttering and publishing), robberies, or selling drugs themselves to support their expensive drug habit.

Who Is in Prison?

Prison is a "mixed bag" of several types of criminality, but since 1986 "persistent property offenders with a drug problem" became the largest single category of prisoner. For instance, the Michigan Department of Corrections (CAPPS 2008) admittance statistics reported state prisoners charged with *drug-defined* crimes (possession, intent to deliver) entering the prisons were at an historical high of 21 percent in 2007, up from around 5 percent in 1980. And, under sentencing guidelines, second- and third-felony offense prisoners were getting long sentences.

Definitions and Issues

A lot of prisoners are nonviolent. Michigan MDOC reported that 43 percent of state prisoners *admitted* were "nonassaultive," while 38 percent were "assaultive." Some of those charged as assaultive are burglaries or home invasions, which are often *drug-related property crimes.* "Home invasions" involve breaking and entering a home, while "burglaries" involve breaking and entering places that are not homes, such as warehouses or commercial buildings.

Some of those who do burglaries and home invasions are violent, some are not. The prison-admittance who are in the assaultive category can be broken down into a rough approximation of perhaps half who have violent tendencies (carry guns or engage in other opportunistic assaultive crime) and half who are nonviolent (no guns or assaults, no other violence in their court records).

Adding together drug-defined crime, the nonviolent category of home invasion, burglary, and other nonassaultive convictions, a good estimate is that 50 percent *of those entering prison* are nonviolent prisoners. That is, nationally, we have "one million nonviolent prisoners" currently *entering* our prisons each year.

The cost to Michigan taxpayers as of 2008 was $32,000 per prisoner bed-space, per year. There is, then, a tremendous cost in potentially misplaced priorities in state sentences when we incarcerate nonviolent people for long sentences who we are *irritated at*. On the other hand, we want to reserve a prison bedspace for violent people who we are *afraid of.*

So, in this regard, it is important to distinguish who *goes* to prison each year (prison admittance) and what types of people *are in* prison at any particular time (prison population).

Violent prisoners, as we've indicated, may represent only about one-half of all prison admittance. However, conviction for violent offenses typically involves longer sentences with fewer paroles at earliest release date. Convictions for many nonviolent crimes (other than mandatory drug crime sentences) can be short sentences. We want to keep violent predators off our streets *during that period of their life* when they are violent. On the other hand, those with nonassaultive convictions have short sentences and are released more often at their earliest release date—they come and go from the prison. The exceptions are long war on drugs sentences, and, in general, the tough mandatory minimums and three strikes laws. So, those with a violent conviction in their record, or criminal sexual conduct offense, have longer sentences and are paroled less. Those with a violent conviction "pile up" in the prison and constitute roughly 75 percent (75 percent) of the *total prison population* at any given time.

So, yes, it can be said that our prisons are "full of violent predators." But only because many others come and go from the prison, leaving the more violent category of original offense, with very long sentences, to accumulate as a larger and larger part of the prison population. Thus, we need to distinguish between three types of prisoner population: overly long nonviolent drug-related sentences, other short nonviolent sentences, and longer violent record, or criminal sexual conduct sentences.

It's important, also, to note that not all "violent predators" are *still* violent predators after many years in prison. Prison authorities recognize this when they move violent conviction prisoners down from level five (high security) to level two (low security), due to a lowering of the risk of violence assessment to staff or other prisoners, during the course of serving their sentence. Recent recidivism research also notes that murderers (as well as sexual offenders) are some of the *least* likely prisoner categories to reoffend when, (or if), they are released (CAPPS 2009). Many youth that, at seventeen, eighteen, or nineteen got caught up in drug-related violence (turf war homicides and deadly assaults) and are serving very long sentences, mature-out in prison. They become nonviolent people after staying so long in prison. After ten or twelve years they've wised up—but still have many years to go on a twenty-to-life, or parolable life, or life sentence. Because prisons also accumulate rough customers committed to criminality, the "aging out" and self-transformation effect for some (becoming nonviolent) is offset by a "jail learning" effect (deepening criminality) for others. There is not only a positive incarceration effect that reduces crime through incapacitation; there is also a negative incarceration effect that increases crime through social learning of criminal techniques and attitudes inside the prison.

Thirty Percent State Prison Admittance Nonviolent Drug-Related

How many state prisoners are war on drugs prisoners? Adding together the historical high of 21 percent drug-defined (MDOC 2007) and an additional estimate of 9 percent conviction for home invasion *where* the case file would show a nonassaultive individual with nonviolent drug-related behavior, we have a reasonable estimate of a total of 30 percent of Michigan's state prisoners who come into Michigan's prison as nonviolent offenders caught in the incarceration binge as a consequence of the war on drugs. For federal prisons the war on drugs prisoners are 40 percent of those admitted. Why are we putting *these* people in prison, and for such long sentences? Blumstein notes:

> Unfortunately, our political system has learned an overly simplistic trick: it responds to such pressures (demand to do something about drug problem) by sternly demanding punishment. This approach has been found to be strikingly effective—not in solving the problem, but in alleviating the political pressure to "do something" . . .
>
> As a result, there has been a succession of punitive efforts to attack the drug trade. Many states have adopted mandatory-minimum sentences for drug dealing that are comparable to the sentences for homicide. The consequence of these efforts has been a dramatic growth in the number of arrests for drug offenses and the filling of prisons with drug offenders. (Blumstein 2002: 466–67).

Racial Disparity and Drugs

Writing in 1999, Marc Mauer notes that African Americans, who constitute 12 percent of the U.S. population, accounted for only 21 percent of the drug possession arrests nationally in 1980, and that, as the 1986 federal drug laws emerged, followed by state drug laws, the number of black drug arrests "rose to a high of 36 percent in 1992. . . . Importantly, for juveniles, this rate . . . climbed to 40 percent by 1991, before declining to 30 percent in 1995" (Mauer 1999: 145).

> Do African Americans use drugs a great deal more than whites? Mauer notes:
>   Looking at the data for 1995, we find that while African Americans were slightly more likely to be monthly drug users than whites and Hispanics (7.9 percent versus 6.0 percent and 5.1 percent, respectively), the much greater number of whites in the overall population resulted in their constituting the vast majority of drug users. Thus, the SAMHSA (Substance Abuse and Mental Health Services Administration) data indicate that whites represented 77 percent of current drug users, with African Americans constituting 15 percent of users and Hispanics, 8 percent . . . it is difficult to imagine that African American drug use is of a magnitude that could explain blacks representing 15 percent of current drug users yet 33 percent of arrests for drug possession. (Mauer 1999: 147)

Ignoring Root Problems of Urban America

Chiricos had identified the 1986 Anti-Drug Abuse Act mandatory minimum and massive prison build-up as a fundamentally inappropriate response. He says:

> But instead of waging war on the inhuman conditions fostered by policies of disinvestment and de-skilling, that have hollowed our inner-city neighborhoods, we wage war on those individuals dehumanized by the lack of reasonable choices. Instead of waging war on unemployment, inadequate schools, and the loss of hope we wage war on individuals destroyed by those very conditions. Instead of waging war on the factors contributing to an increasingly isolated underclass— for whom life has less and less meaning—we wage war against individuals who seek meaning in drugs and violence.
>   Instead of seeing the world as it is—one in which investment decisions by the owners of capital have caused the devastation of inner-city neighborhoods, communities, and families and the economic stagnation of almost all others—these moral panics force us to see as "in all ideology, men and their circumstances . . . upside-down as in a *camera obscura*" (Marx and Engels 1846/1970: 47). The greatest victims of private and public policies that have literally determined that people will count less than profits are demonized by moral panics and herded behind ever-widening walls of exclusion.
>   As noted above, the real danger of the recent moral panics is that they treat problems that have been *substantial* and *enduring* for several decades in many

inner-city neighborhoods as if they are a *sudden* firestorm. An atmosphere of panic mobilizes demands for immediate repression and causes us to ignore the root problems of urban America, which have grown and festered for decades. The same media frenzy that raises *decisiveness* to the cardinal virtue of public policy, lowers the chance that meaningful response to enduring problems will be undertaken. (Chiricos 1995/2002: 72–73)

WHAT EXPLAINS PRISON BINGE GROWTH?

The U.S. prison and jail system has "been on a binge," becoming the world's largest. Is this because the crime rate has been increasing? Hardly. While there was an increase in crime rates from 1960 to 1975 and again from 1986 to 1991, in fact, the U.S. crime rate has been falling every year since 1991 (Zimring 2007). Researchers note a steady decline of adult violence, particularly homicide and robbery, for over thirty years.

How are we to explain this massive 400 percent growth in the prison system (1986–2008) when the U.S. population in the same period grew only 25 percent from 240 million to 300 million? And how are we to explain rapid prison growth even as there has been a decrease in crime, and even a decrease in violent crime? True, you cannot imprison so many without lowering crime. So, in this view, increasing incarceration lowers crime. However, the best research indicates that the use of mass incarceration lowered crime at most, perhaps 20–25 percent in the 1990s (Conklin 2003: 79–98). Cullen and Jonson summarize their careful review of "incapacitation effects" this way:

- There is an incapacitation effect, and it is meaningfully large. Prisons prevent crime. Letting people out of prison will increase criminal victimization.
- It is deceptive to compare the amount of crime saved by placing an offender in prison compared with *doing nothing* and allowing the offender to *roam free on the street*. The proper comparison, which is never done in incapacitation research, is how much crime would be saved if we used a similar amount of money and *invested it in alternative correctional interventions*.
- Prisons should be used judiciously and only as part of a comprehensive plan to intervene effectively with offenders. (2012: 100)

What would these alternative correctional interventions be? Resources saved from prison downsizing could be invested in more probation, and other community corrections such as electronic tethering; more early childhood enrichment and parent management skills; more job skills training and education; and more community policing. Some of the money saved could be shifted to the justice reinvestment movement—i.e., be reinvested in the high incarceration communities where a large percentage of prisoners come from (Austin et al. 2013; CAPPS 2013).

Reducing Concentrated Disadvantage, Reducing Chronic Unemployment, and Increasing Social Supports Lowers Crime Rate More Than Prison

Returning to the Conklin (2003) estimate that 20 to 25 percent of the crime reduction is due to an incapacitation effect—this still leaves 75 to 80 percent of the fall in crime rate due to many other factors. That is to say, there are *multiple factors* or variables that explain the rise or fall of crime rates and that, if resources were put into crime-prevention programs related to these other variables, the crime rate could drop further. Pratt (2009) says

> compare the extent to which expansion in incarceration predicts crime rates relative to other social and economic factors. For example, Pratt and Cullen's (2005) meta-analysis of over 200 studies on the predictors of crime rates found that the overall "effect size" (interpreted as the strength of the relationship) of incarceration variables that have been adjusted for endogeneity and crime rates was among the weakest of the 31 different predictors assessed. The strongest predictors of crime rates were found to be variables that tapped into "concentrated disadvantage," which is the intersection of *economic deprivation and family disruption concentrated with particular racial groups* in society (see also Sampson, Raudenbush, and Earls 1997; Sampson and Wilson 1995; W. J. Wilson 1987); *long term chronic unemployment* (see also Land, Cantor, and Russell 1995); and *stingy social policies that undermine levels of social support for citizens* (see also Cullen 1994; DeFronzo 1996, 1997; Pratt and Godsey 2002, 2003).
>
> The unmistakable conclusion from this collection of studies is that policy makers' claims of massive reductions in crime that can be attributed to the expansion of the prison population are patently false. Even the meager percentage of reduction in crime that prisons give us is not a small matter in a country that experiences far more violent crime than any other Western nation. The impact of prisons on crime, however, which perhaps more than any other single factor has enabled our dependence on incarceration, is quite weak when considered in light of the dollars that state and federal corrections budgets absorb that could be spent addressing the underlying social factors more strongly related to crime rates. (2009: 67–68) (emphasis added)

Crime's been falling since 1991. Since the continuing prison expansion after 1991 did not occur in the context of an increasing crime rate, why has there been such political support for a massive prison system after 1991?

We have explained that a shift (in general) to *crime legislation as a way of governing* (Simon 2007) set up a metaphor of war on crime. We've also explained that the tougher drug laws were the primary reason for more arrests and convictions. It was the sharp punitive set of drug laws initiated by President Reagan and passed by Congress in the late summer of 1986 that launched the prison build-up (figure 2.2).

Writing about his twenty-year prison college teaching experience, the author reflected:

> In 1986, I attended my first prison college graduation at Soledad Prison in California. Driving down from El Cerrito, near Berkeley, for two years, I had taught business classes at the prison for Hartnell College. On the occasion of the graduation, about 150 prisoners and 50 teachers, administrators, and guests attended.
>
> In most college graduation ceremonies the discussion is about the bright prospects ahead, the promise of the future. (Tregea 2003: 320).

But, while many prisoners were familiar with many drugs, these graduates of the Hartnell College Associates of Arts degree program at Soledad Correctional Facility who were also near their release date from the prison now faced a new crack drug epidemic that, at that time, was starting two-hundred miles south in Los Angeles. Simultaneously, politicians in Congress were calling for tough, new penalties. In describing the Hartnell graduation, Tregea continues:

> This prison college graduation was a ceremony of dark warning. The talk was about how the pull of the street, the lack of employment, inadequate transition services, combined with the virulent addiction potential of drugs and alcohol and money from the drug trade could spell disaster for many graduating prisoner-students. (Tregea 2003: 320)

What were all the situational factors that could let this summer of 1986 drug scare, and the rush to pass the 1986 drug laws, escalate into a quadrupling of the U.S. prison system? There had been drug epidemics, drug scares, and drug laws before—but we had never quadrupled our prison system before. What mainstream, "Big Politics," institutional "players" could facilitate such a growth of the criminal justice apparatus, (cops, courts, corrections), into a gargantuan organizational field (Kraska and Brent 2011; Scott 1992; Stenson 1991)? Why is crime—at certain times—so important to Americans? That is, what explains the *salience* of crime as peculiar to America, and how does that salience of crime underlie the tendency to authorize the massive prison growth (Zimring 2006, 2007)?

We have reviewed Simon's account of how *governing* through crime legislation had, by the mid-1970s, become a major "political formula." On a more pragmatic level, it is true that between 1986 and 1991 the crime rate *was* increasing. This is an important point because the prison build-up movement could be seen as a design by a rational public to dampen down crime.

And it is true that the growth of the prison system dampened down that late 1980s, early 1990s crime rate growth by getting people off the streets and into prison.

How much did incarceration of so many reduce crime? Establishing any "general formula" for how much effect increasing incarceration reduces the crime rate is probably inadvisable. Some researchers suggest that increasing incarceration rate between 1986 and 1991 decreased the crime rate by about 20 to 25 percent. Other estimates go as low as 13 percent and as high as 50 percent. In typical cost-effective analyses, the cost of financing the increase in incarceration is weighed against the cost of the crime deterred. John Irwin and James Austin note:

> Annual spending (in the 1990s) on corrections has risen from $9.1 billion to nearly $32 billion, far outstripping any other segment of the criminal justice system. . . .
> . . . Significantly, the costs of crimes to victims is far below the costs of criminal justice. In 1992, the total costs of crimes to victims, as reported in the U.S. Department of Justice's National Crime Victim Survey (NCVS), was $17.6 billion, or about $500 per crime; the majority of crimes had value losses below $100. These costs include economic losses from property theft or damage, cash losses, medical expenses, loss of pay caused by victimization, and other related costs.
> . . . Given the enormous costs of aggressive imprisonment and its doubtful effectiveness on crime, one must question the wisdom of our current sentencing policies. (Irwin and Austin 1997)

But it matters which decade you are talking about. The research is clear that *some* important reductions in crime occurred during the 1990s as the prison system grew (Conklin 2003: 79–98). But, as we've entered the twenty-first century, a pair of the most careful policy researchers on the growth of "the prison state" have concluded, regarding the prison build-up, that "for many jurisdictions the point of accelerating declining marginal returns may have set in" (Useem and Piehl 2008: 51–80).

The conclusion that all of our massive prison growth is "not paying off" anymore in terms of "cost-effectiveness" suggests that the problem of explaining the growth in the prison apparatus has become more than an academic exercise. People are really becoming concerned about overuse of confinement, especially governors and state legislatures (Cullen and Jonson 2012: 205–15).

In order to fully address the *reasons* for the dynamics underlying the incarceration binge—which it is our premise *began* as a moral panic over a drug epidemic combined with a good dose of racism—and look at what explains the *continued* push for ever greater prison growth all through the latter 1990s and through the period of 2000–2008 we need to ask: Why did we *let* drug laws and the prison build-up continue for fifteen years after the 1991 start of the decline in crime rates? This question is still relevant as each state confronts budget crises but also continued political pressure to be tough on crime. For instance, Michigan's Republican governor, Rick Snyder

has chosen as his new corrections director a sheriff who vocally opposed former (Democratic) Gov. Jennifer Granholm's actions to release more nonviolent prisoners eligible for parole . . . he's studying how the department can rein in spending while keeping the public safe, and plans to visit neighboring states to look at what they're doing to hold down costs and crime. (*Daily Telegram* 2011: A3)

Simon argued in his 2007 book that we cannot break the cycle of prison growth unless we change the underlying "representational style" of *governing* through crime legislation. He argues that

[t]he three-strikes law, with its expressly populist tone and scarcely disguised contempt for the judicial process, embodies the categorical logic of mass imprisonment, which promises to substitute rigorous rules for the soft and untrustworthy judgment of judges and other government officials insulated by bureaucracy and expertise from direct engagement with the public. (Simon 2007: 156–58)

Simon agrees with Tonry and Wacquant that the mass incarceration strategy has an effect in terms of racism and a "convenient oppression" or malign neglect effect of repressing an absolute surplus of labor in the jobless ghettos, but he argues that the *origins* of mass incarceration lies in its "fit" as a policy solution "to the political dilemmas of governing through crime." He notes that

[m]ass imprisonment is a stable solution to the highly competitive political logic established by governing through crime. As the following examples will suggest, executives (especially governors and presidents), lawmakers, and courts attempting to play to their strengths in the era of governing through crime must embrace mass imprisonment. (2007: 159)

While Jonathan Simon's analysis of "crime legislation as governing through crime" leading to mass imprisonment is a powerful critique, it raises two issues: would white Americans allow a governing through crime with the effect of sending a high proportion of *their* children (young white males) to prison? And, second, with state budgets tight, legislators began looking to reduce corrections budgets. In 2008, a year after Simon's book came out, the Council of State Governments (CSG), reflecting the pressures on state budgets posed by overuse of confinement, began working on a Justice

Reinvestment Initiative (JRI) to shift money saved by legislation to *downsize or cap prison growth rate* and reinvest in community corrections (probation, parole) and policing. Yet there has not been significant *reinvestment* in high impact communities (Austin et al. 2013). Moreover, the corrections budgets and prison populations still remain high.

Explaining Prison Growth

The prisoner voices in the essays in this book reveal their thinking and feeling as they witness their lives before entering the prison system. However, it is necessary to ask questions they, themselves, may not have asked: what "behind the scenes" social dynamics are shaping this "experiential world" of individuals, families, and communities as the United States transformed into the worlds' largest "prison state"? Chapter 2 described how the prison culture has changed over the last twenty-five years to include the subcultural consequences of more snitches, less respect for older prisoners, overcrowding, double-bunking, more druggies, fewer correctional programming services, longer sentences, fewer paroles, and more "revolving door" offenders coming back into prison from mostly drug-related parole violation—developing an in-prison "incarceration binge culture." I suggested in chapter 1 that there is a connection between the inner-city jobless ghetto becoming a "hyperghetto" and the quadrupling prison system becoming a "hyperincarceration." The connection is not only that they feed off each other and are a "symbiotic system" (Wacquant 2002), but that this connection is a "convenient oppression" (Tregea and Larmour 2009).

Chiricos (1995/2002) had noted that a moral panic in the summer of 1986 over the crack epidemic led to an escalation of the prison build-up movement (see figure 2.2). But why, over the subsequent twenty-five years, did those with the power to decide *ignore* the root causes of persistent and enduring concentrated poverty, violence, and drug crime in the festering inner city? Why were there not policies to reduce concentrated disadvantage, chronic unemployment, and increase family social supports?

Tonry suggests this was a *malign neglect.* Tonry asserts, following Loic Wacquant and Richard Hofstader, that the U.S. Republican Party's "Southern strategy" used the simplistic trick of "getting tough on crime" as a wedge issue to get votes; and, more deeply, that the massive prison build-up represented another "in the series of American cultural practices and legal institutions (operating) to maintain American patterns of racial dominance and hierarchy for (the last) two centuries" (Tonry 2007: 23). Simon (2007) argues that while all of this may be true, the *impetus* for mass incarceration lies in a trend since 1968 toward governing through crime with building prisons as a winning political program of public goods.

In this section, drawing on chapter 3 of *The Prisoners' World* (Tregea and Larmour 2009), we want to review several more basic theoretical orientations that can help explain the causes of prison build-up, *in addition to governing through crime, drug laws, and racism.*

Binge Growth Theory

Peter Kraska and John Brent's *Theorizing Criminal Justice* (2004/2011), introduces eight theoretical orientations, each of which can be used as a *different* "theoretical lens," to answer the question: "What accounts for the growth of the criminal justice apparatus (cops, courts and corrections)?" These eight theoretical orientations are: (1) rational/legal; (2) systems view; (3) crime control versus due process; (4) politics; (5) social constructionist stance; (6) growth complex; (7) oppression; and (8) late modernity. While the Kraska reader is meant to introduce criminal justice students to the issue of growth in the *entire* range of the "criminal justice apparatus," we want to focus on how his collection of perspectives can contribute to corrections and prison "binge growth theory."

We begin by integrating these eight theoretical orientations into three sets of interlocking explanations of prison growth. In summary, we argue that what may have started out as a rational public prison build-up movement responding to crime turned into a binge growth through the *orchestration* of continual massive prison growth over the past twenty-five years (1986–2011) through three sets of interacting social forces.

First, there has been a *rational and legal* response by an American public that, during the period 1980–2008, wanted to shift values from due process to a crime control model (Useem and Piehl 2008). The American public has been expressing an increase in security consciousness (evident in all Western nations), *and* a peculiar salience of crime characteristic of America (Garland 2001/2004; Zimring 2007). While there was an increase in the crime rate from 1986 to 1991 that the original crack epidemic prison build-up movement tried to dampen down, there was also throughout the period 1986–2008, a shift to crime control values, even as after 1991 there was a decrease in the crime rate. Using prison cells or an incarceration strategy is what Jonathan Simon views as a "waste management" policy—a use of public goods that has a political upside, but (seemingly) no political downside.

At the same time during these twenty-five years (1986–2011), there has been a simultaneous interest in community-level *crime prevention.* Americans may be beginning to connect with issues of community crime prevention (front end) and success in prisoner reentry (back end), but have not yet shown signs of analyzing the policies driving prison binge growth. *Wanting* a rational and legal response to crime that shifts values from due process to crime control is not the same as *getting* a rational and effective crime control system. Is it rational to have the world's largest prison system?—To quintuple the rate of incarceration over the course of just twenty-five years? Overuse of confinement has begun to eat up state budget resources, at the same time that there are not enough resources for crime prevention. The prison build-up movement is now acknowledged to have "weak brakes" and to have "decreasing returns." Would not a shift of some resources from capping and reversing the prison build-up movement to an evidence-based crime prevention movement (Cullen and Jonson 2012) that included a harm reduction approach to drugs and a justice reinvestment strategy be an alternative rational crime control model?

Second, there is a history of *politics, media, and fear* that combined with how the criminal justice network seeks coherence as a system acting to maintain its own interests as a growth complex. Similar to the rise of "tough on alcohol" during the campaign to build-up alcohol Prohibition, in the politics, media, and fear view, the question has to be asked: what politician can oppose the "bandwagon" prison build-up movement? The public *wants their tax money to do something.* They may no longer want overuse of incarceration, but up to very recent times, the politicians can't stop supporting it, or run the risk of appearing "soft on crime." On this issue, and for the period he described (1968–2008), Simon was correct. For many years support for a "bloated prison bureaucracy" was amplified by fear through a governing through crime political formula (Simon 2007) involving politicians as "tough." Prosecutors became a model for political authority. Through the war on crime governors can act in the "prosecutor role," spending federal crime control money steered to the states; supporting the state legislature in stiffer punishments; and not emphasizing community corrections sentences. Governors, however, in governing through crime, also became politically responsible for heinous parolee crime happening on their shift (Simon 2007: 71).

The media driven "drug scares" and moral panics interact with the politicians call to be tough on crime. Thus, more laws increasing the sentence length occurred, more prisoners stayed longer in prison, and the prisons grew. In this situation, the prison systems have "had the upper hand" in state budgets for decades.

However, this political quagmire has reached a tipping point. Partly because they cannot afford it anymore, state governors and legislators have started to cap prison growth through revisiting sentencing and parole policy. Money saved has tended to go to community corrections (probation, parole) and law enforcement. Now that many effective evidence-based programs are known, a shift of states' tax resources to evidence-based crime prevention is possible.

The racial disparity is still embedded in the U.S. prison system. The *convenient oppression* that the growth of the U.S. criminal justice apparatus provides for "managing" the surplus labor in the jobless ghettos is a difficult reality to face up to. Simon notes:

> At the center of this new lawmaking rationality is the crime victim. Crime victims are in a real sense the representative subjects of our time (Garland 2001a: 11–12).
> The nature of this victim identity is deeply racialized. It is not all victims, but primarily white, suburban, middle-class victims, whose exposure has driven waves of crime legislation (2007: 75–76)

I asked earlier in this chapter: "Would white Americans have allowed the 'governing through crime' political formula outlined by Simon if it had had the effect of sending a high proportion of their children (young white males) to prison?" The public may not believe they are supporting the oppression of urban "high impact areas." Aren't people who have broken the law supposed to go to prison? Yet, prison binge growth has created a massive overuse of confinement and prison spending is now coming up against the pragmatic concern of state budgets in crisis. The corrections budget has become the largest state general fund expense (CRC 2008; CSG 2012). Michelle Alexander argues that even though state legislators are beginning to look at state prison budgets, there is still a strong discrimination against black males who are yoked with the *prison convict label*—legally denying the black ex-con rights and privileges *after* their release—a situation that amounts to a new Jim Crow system (2012).

The 1986 federalization of drug laws started the drug-crime era prison build-up movement that, through federal grants to build new prisons, spread the mass incarceration trend to the states. But the "representational model" of *governing through crime* from Simon's view, starts with the 1968 Safe Streets Act.

The *crime legislation model* Simon describes required a president to push the policy. It will take a new focus from Washington to address the urban problems that have led to the existing incarceration strategy that is based upon "imprisoning communities." Can the taxpayers afford not to? To truly address crime we need to pay either way—prisons or prevention—and it's coming down to a choice: respond to the hyperghetto either through continuing the world's largest prison system or through an increase in prevention. It is an inconvenient choice because there is not enough money to do both. Is it time for Americans to face up to its "inconvenient oppression?"

Jeffrey Reiman reports in his book *The Rich Get Richer and the Poor Get Prison* that he asked his students to imagine that, instead of designing a correctional system to reduce and prevent crime, we had to design one that would maintain a stable and visible "class" of criminals. What would it look like? The response . . .

First. It would be helpful to have laws on the books against drug use or prostitution or gambling—laws that prohibit acts that have no unwilling victim. This would make many people "criminals" for what they regard as normal behavior and would increase their need to engage in *secondary* crime (the drug addicts need to steal to pay for drugs, the prostitute's need for a pimp because police protection is unavailable, and so on). (Reiman 2004: 2–3)

It appears that several states have managed to cap prison growth but still maintain an overly large prison system (Austin et al. 2013). Is the time coming when the American people are past the *incarceration binge* culture? Could the American people push for and support a harm reduction and "health and wellness" approach to reducing street drugs? This would be a path similar to the U.S. history repealing Prohibition and adopting a wellness approach to alcohol—and in reducing tobacco use.

ALTERNATIVE RATIONAL CRIME CONTROL MODEL

Polls suggest that the public is of two minds—they want tough punishment but they also want their tax money to rehabilitate—to change criminal thinking through treatment and to "do" something, to "fix" or reduce the drug abuse and addiction problem. For drug abuse a harm reduction approach, combined with more decriminalization of drugs, would include education and treatment, and might result in a gradual cultural shift away from street drug use and abuse. A lot of money—tens of billions of dollars each year—could be shifted away from the punishment priority (prison system) and reinvested in rehabilitation and a justice reinvestment priority through utilizing evidence-based crime prevention programs and investing in the inner-city high crime neighborhoods.

More generally, the American people have been interested in effective community-based crime prevention for several years. David Farrington and his coauthors have researched several evidence-based programs of "what works in preventing crime," including such institutional areas as families, schools, communities, labor markets, places, police, and courts and corrections. For families they have identified home visitation, parent education plus day care/preschool, school-based child training plus parent training, and multisystemic therapy. For schools they have identified school and discipline management (crime, alcohol and other drugs, assaultive behavior) and establishing norms for behavior, along with mentoring, tutoring, and work study. For labor markets they have identified ex-offender job training for older males no longer under criminal justice supervision; intensive, residential training programs for at-risk youth, such as Job Corps (Welsh and Farrington 2002/2006: 408).

Beyond the warehouse prison, Welsh and Farrington find specific criminal justice prevention programs that are effective, such as

> *Courts and corrections:* Rehabilitation with particular characteristics (e.g., target specific problems of offenders, intensive treatment); prison-based therapeutic community treatment of drug-involved offenders; in-prison therapeutic communities with follow-up community treatment; cognitive behavioral therapy; moral reconation therapy and reasoning and rehabilitation; Non-prison based sex offender treatment; vocational education for adult offenders and juvenile delinquents; multi-component correctional industry programs; community employment; and incapacitating offenders who continue to commit crimes at high rates (Welsh and Farrington 2002/2006: 408)

Once you see these noncriminal justice options (family, school, labor markets) as *competing alternatives*—more money for mass incarceration or more money for crime prevention—it becomes possible to vote against overuse of confinement (CAPPS 2008).

What causes drug use and drug-related offenses? Beyond experimental and recreational use of alcohol and other drugs, heavy drinking and drugging can be traced back to personal trauma, the family (child abuse and neglect), and the community (neighborhood poverty and gangs). Once you are addicted you've got a brain disease and so relapse is characteristic, making getting off drugs—and staying off—difficult. There is a need for access to drug treatment therapy. And, of course, there is the drug economy that has long ago entered the jobless ghetto. So we cannot solve the underlying problems of such communities and families without a massive shift of scarce resources away from the overuse of confinement and into effective crime prevention and community development.

Could the American public shift from one rational paradigm (more laws, more prisons) to another rational paradigm (more family and community support and other evidence-based crime prevention)? This second rational paradigm would include a reduction in poverty, inequality and more jobs, job skills and education, a harm reduction approach to drug problems, short "treatment-based sentencing," simultaneous early child development, parenting support, and community development to address the "moral vice" problem of street drugs and reduce the culture of street crime in the United States.

Herbert Packer, in his 1968 article "Two Models of the Criminal Justice Process," articulated two value clusters that characterize attitudes toward, and within, the American criminal justice system.

One value cluster is *crime control*. From this view the main value of the criminal justice apparatus is to repress or control crime. To do this, "efficiency" is necessary. The fact-finding administrative agency (police, sheriff's departments, FBI, other federal crime control investigating agencies) knows what it is doing, and should be trusted. The premise is that such criminal justice agencies gather facts and know who is guilty. There is a presumption of guilt.

The other value cluster is *due process*. From this view the main value of the American criminal justice process is its value on protecting the rights of the individual; ensuring their right to due process—no search without a warrant, the right to an evidentiary hearing, trial, and appeal. To hold fast to this value, "obstacles" to the states crime control process are necessary: the state must "prove its case" in a series of required hearings with rules surrounding admissible evidence. The premise is that the state and criminal justice apparatus can make mistakes, or become oppressive, and should not be trusted. There is a value on the fate of the individual, and a distrust of state agencies, and a presumption of innocence.

Overall, writing in 1968, Packer believed that the American justice system is ambiguous on these values and at that time there existed a tension-filled "balance" between crime control and due process. Packer was worried that crime control might take over. Since Packer wrote, the American people have "leaned" markedly during the twenty-five-year societal incarceration binge culture (1984–2008) toward the value of "crime control." The growth of the prison system and its' internal incarceration binge culture, can, thus, be explained by a growth in the emphasis on the *value* of crime control and punitiveness.

Bert Useem and Anne Morrison Piehl, in their 2008 book *The Prison State*, argue that, to an extent, this growing emphasis on the value of crime control and the prison build-up movement was not an outcome of irrational racism but a pragmatic and a rational social movement responding to the initial increase in crime rates during the period 1986 to 1991. However, they note certain limits to the "rational public" model:

> The prison buildup movement, we have argued, was a pragmatic effort to deal with an escalating crime rate rather than, as the critics claimed, an irrational expression of a disturbed population or an effort to achieve an otherwise extraneous political agenda. The critics include David Garland and Loic Wacquant, in a tradition that springs from the work of Michel Foucault. These attributions of irrationality, we found, do not fit the available facts. Yet, more generally, although social movements are pragmatic efforts to create new social forms, they are not deliberative bodies or research seminars. They do not collect evidence on the structures that they are seeking to bring, or have brought, into being. Data analysis (with all its complications) is not part of their "repertoire" for contention. Social movements are rational, but they are not hyperrational. If successful

in achieving their immediate goals, they may not know how, or even when, to stop. More prisons, even if effective up to a point, may have exceeded that point during the buildup, as well as damaged society in other ways. The prison buildup movement may have unknowingly gone too far. Although social movements are strong in their mechanisms of mobilization, they have weak brakes. (Useem and Piehl 2008: 169)

There is also a third set of social values, beyond the "just deserts" punishment crime control model and the "rights-based" type of justice rooted in the due process and evidentiary hearing aspects of the U.S. Bill of Rights. This third set of values emphasizes "human needs" that transcend "crime control" and "due process." What does the community need? What does the victim need? What does the offender need? This can be more of a *harm reduction model* and *restorative justice approach* that de-emphasizes both crime-control "efficiency" and rights-based due process in favor of a community justice, victim-offender mediation, and needs-based justice (Braithwaite 1989; Clear and Cadora 2003; Miller 1976/1989; Sullivan and Tifft 2001, 2005).

After twenty-five years of tough on crime politics, is the United States ready to reassess its values, emphasizing human needs? Such a change in emphasis would require both a cultural and a political shift away from the incarceration binge culture in the United States.

A pattern of "jobless ghettos" developed as a result of the business disinvestment in the major American cities, by the early 1960s. These developments resulted in economically devastated "inner cities" emerging in the United States (Darden et al. 1987; Wacquant 2002; W. J. Wilson 1996).

Watts, such an inner-city context in Los Angeles, had an "inner-city riot" in 1965 and Detroit, also affected by this trend, had an inner-city riot in 1967. Police were held in increasing disdain by inner-city residents. As Louis Radelet and David Carter note in *Policing and the Community*,

The riots and violent upheavals that occurred in various cities during the summer of 1967, and thereafter, marked a turning point in police-community relations programs. Suddenly, the nation was jolted into a realization of intense and profound divisions among its people, both racial and social. . . . There was widespread bewilderment (among police officers). Some simply withdrew from further efforts; many adopted a "get tough" philosophy. Another presidential commission, the National Advisory Commission on Civil Disorders (popularly known as the Kerner Commission, after its chairman), proclaimed in its report that "our Nation is moving toward two societies, one black, one white—separate and unequal." (All this was affecting) police-community relations:

The police are not merely a "spark" factor. To some Negroes police have come to symbolize white power, white racism, and white repression. And the fact is that many police do reflect and express these white attitudes. The atmosphere of hostility and cynicism is reinforced by a widespread belief among Negroes in the existence of police brutality and in a "double standard" of justice and protection—one for Negroes and one for whites.

. . . It is worth reflecting that a generation has passed since 1955. The police and civilian participants in the (community policing) institutes of the 1950s and even of the 1960s are today's "golden agers." The programmers have changed, as have the programs, but the apparent problems in the localities that are in the headlines as a result of flare-ups and tensions in police and community relations seem to be very similar to what they were in the publicized places of fifteen to twenty-five years ago. Racism, urban decay, rampant violent crime, citizen anxiety and fear, and the sharp increase in apparently permanent unemployment are all evidences of community deterioration. The link between these problems and police-community relations has long since been established and were clearly demonstrated in Los Angeles and other cities in 1992. (Radelet and Carter 1994: 27–31)

The Democratic administration of Lyndon Johnson (1963–1968)—under pressure from the decade-old civil rights movement—had just completed signing the historic 1964 Civil Rights Act to enfranchise African Americans and make discrimination illegal. This was a political voting rights reform— African American and other "minorities" now had a voting rights law with teeth in it—but the *economic* problems of the inner cities described above (disinvestment, high unemployment, poverty, loss of a tax base for social services) was causing the inner cities to "fester," like a wound without healing treatment. The inner cities became "occupied" by white police departments protecting the nearby suburbs and enforcing order on an increasingly restive urban black and poor population.

Yet, this was a period in U.S. history when most people had been experiencing a tremendous economic boom for twenty years after the end of World War II (1945–1965). Journalists and politicians talked of "pockets of poverty." There were book exposes on the "remaining" poverty as "the other America." And there was a belief that all the American people could be brought along in the economic boom—that "all boats rise with a rising sea"—and that poverty in the United States could and should be eliminated.

President Johnson had, in fact, launched, in 1964, not a war on crime but a "war on poverty." He wanted to work toward reducing the national inequalities. He also appointed a Crime Commission—the 1967 Kerner Violence Commission—in response to the urban conflagrations. America, in the 1960s, was looking at its social problems.

As the American capitalist environment changed, bringing forth festering inner cities, the *focus* in criminal justice education turned toward problems of the *administration* of justice instead of efforts through applied criminology and social policy to *solve* the underlying urban problems. From the beginning, the emphasis of university criminal justice education programs, which were *born* out of the conflagration of the 1960s inner-city violence, was a selfish "agency and system" orientation.

So then, what explains the growth of prisons from this "systems" view? It is still the *increase in crime rate*, or in *laws making drug-defined and drug-related behavior more of a crime (and of flows of funding)*. In these circumstances the system must grow. More crime, and/or more laws, creates a "forced reaction" of prison growth. Also, note that the very academic discipline of criminal justice in colleges and universities grew out of a changing societal environment—the emergence of "festering" inner cities—that "required" a system view to examine the *efficiency*, changing administrative needs, and professionalism of the crime control process within criminal justice agencies.

Could we have, instead, eliminated, or greatly reduced, the inner cities themselves as a "social problem?" This could have been accomplished through massive governmental economic development programs instead of what we did, in fact, get—a massive "more efficient" growth of the criminal justice administration and a quadrupling of the prison system (Wilson 1996). What were our values in all of this?

The criminal justice apparatus, and especially the penal system, is pushed to become more oriented toward "risk management" through (excessive) use of confinement. This "waste management" takes on a statistical form—actuarial techniques of counting what categories of people are more dangerous than others—and this approach *replaces* a former emphasis on individualized justice, treatment, access to programs, rehabilitation, and restoration. Recently, however, there has been a slow shift toward a focus on prisoner reentry.

While Useem and Piehl argue the prison build-up movement was a pragmatic effort to deal with the escalating crime rate of 1986 to 1991, it is hard not to conclude—with a late modern fetish for safety and its tendency toward an exclusionary society—that there was an element of *fear* and racism cemented into the incarceration binge culture: "an irrational expression of a disturbed population" (Useem and Piehl 2008: 169). The recent emphasis on prisoner reentry could represent, when combined with capping prison growth, a trend toward scaling back the prison build-up.

POLITICS, MEDIA, AND FEAR: THE BINGE GROWTH COMPLEX

Pretty much all organizations want to get bigger: executives and managers have more status the bigger the organizational budget and personnel roster, regular employees know their job will be more secure if the organization is growing larger, communities are happy to have permanent organizations.

State prison systems, and their host towns, are not much different—opening up one thousand new prisons between 1984 and 2001 created many new prison and community employment opportunities.

It is pretty clear to see that the criminal justice network seeks coherence as a system acting in its own interests—and as a growth complex. However, if you are going to have a growth complex, it helps to have normal organizational ambitions grow even more with growth amplified by fear. There is an aspect of the incarceration binge culture that is a governing through crime formula (Simon 2007), with politicians being tough on crime, the media driving drug scares and moral panics, and the criminal justice network itself that is in a mode of rapid organizational growth, all is amplified, in fact, by fear. Unlike decades before, when cops, court, and corrections were a slow moving, low-profile area of public bureaucracy, mere "street level bureaucrats" (Lipsky 1980), in recent years politicians have learned to exploit complex crime problems in simplistic ways for political votes. This has had the consequence of politicians "fanning the embers of fear" in the public and then offering them tough on crime incarceration growth solutions (Tonry 1999).

In the "politics-causes-prison-growth" theoretical orientation the explanation of massive *growth* in the prison system is sought by looking at political orientations, ideology, legislators, policy making and its implementation, and the role of media. The uses to which the criminal justice apparatus are put come largely from "the political climate" and power world, as discussed in chapter 1.

So, the 1950s and 1960s emphasis on short sentences, rehabilitation, and drug treatment for drug addicts has, in the last three decades, become buried under a politicized drug war. Prisons and crime became highly politicized by the 1986 federalization of drug law (and earlier in the 1973 the New York state Rockefeller mandatory drug laws). This occurred under President Reagan, and politicians felt they could not afford to vote against this trend—just like, as we've mentioned, the politicians of the period 1890–1920 felt they could not vote against "dry" proponents' legislation in the "war on alcohol." Criminal justice policy became a "wedge issue" or tool for politicians. Politicians would say: "I am for getting those violent predators off our streets. And I am proposing a tougher law than my opponent, who is soft on crime" (Tonry 1999).

Seen in terms of political values, the United States underwent, from the 1980 onward, a more "conservative" tilt emphasizing "right-wing values." Walter Miller, in 1973, noted the differences in political ideology of the "right" versus the "left."

> The *Right* constellation of values: There is excessive leniency toward law-breakers, erosion of discipline and respect for constituted authority, excessive permissiveness; with assumptions that the individual is directly responsible, a need for a strong moral order, with a paramount importance of security.

The *Left* constellation of issues include: We have a tendency toward over-criminalization (e.g., drug laws), too much labeling and stigmatization, overuse of confinement, discrimination; and assumptions that the primary sources of criminal behavior lie in conditions of the social order, that there is a need to alter the social conditions that breed crime, that the social and political order does not meet the fundamental needs of the majority of its citizens (health, education, jobs, environment); and that the criminal justice system is inequitable and unjust (Miller 1973, in Kraska and Brent 2011: 124–34)

It is possible to argue that we need *both* of these sets of views. A thoughtful writer, such as Wright, asserts that it may be desirable to have "goal conflict" within the criminal justice system—that is, to have both left and right values at work (crime control and tough punishments but also due process and treatment and restoration) (Wright 1981, in Kraska and Brent 2011: 135–39).

On the other hand, this begs the question of which ideology, since 1980, has "won the day." Which way was the tilt? And, over the past thirty years, it is clear that the more right-wing, conservative, punitive set of values had prevailed and that the criminal justice apparatus has needed to adjust to the political context or "swings in the pendulum"—building ever more prisons, with longer sentences due, primarily, to the punitive drug laws. Efficiency of the criminal justice apparatus became more important. In turn, the punitive drug laws were the outcome of a divisive political conflict that has involved the temptation to politicize crime. Writing in the early 1980s, Scheingold noted that crime was an issue that can provide "a simple and credible answer that the public is only too happy to embrace" (Scheingold 1982, in Kraska and Brent 2011: 140–49).

So, from the *politics* theoretical orientation, what explains the *growth* of the prison system? Is it increasing crime rates? No, the crime rates have declined steadily since 1991. Other external factors, the economy and demographics, have had ups and downs, but the prison system had continued to expand until about 2008. This "politics" explanation of the expansion of the prison system is not a "forced reaction" to a larger population or increase in crime rate type of explanation, but rather an explanation emphasizing a political atmosphere of more crime control values undergirding the creation of more crime *law*. The value cluster of "crime control" came to the fore with a more right-wing or conservative political *ideology shift*, and this explained the increased use of incarceration. And, this process of prison growth has *been caused, from the politics point of view, by politics itself*—and this includes the politics of self-serving aspects of news and entertainment media, politicians, and the crime control establishment.

What are we to conclude today, in the second decade of the twenty-first century, with thirty years of prison growth behind us? Is crime control such a big issue these days? Are we tired of the "politics of tough?" Both state budget crisis and recent changes in the political climate and economy have polls showing that "education and health care were more important than crime." There is a "growing awareness among the general public that increases in corrections spending come at the cost of other governmental spending and services" (Vera Institute of Justice 2006).

In May 2008 Michigan's then-governor Jennifer Granholm—in the context of a budget-strapped state—called for prison reform, including release of nonviolent offenders (Granholm 2007). As of the summer of 2008, the United States was moving into a recession. People became worried. They worried about the cost of gas. They worried about whether the United States could achieve energy independence. Many people were interested in promoting more sustainability and slowing global warming through alternative energy and lifestyle changes. The "Great Recession" (2008–2009 and continuing) has increased economic insecurity as firms are slow to hire, continue to downsize and outsource. While the U.S. economy is slowly adding jobs as of 2013, the United States may move back into recession as Europe falls deeper into recession and China slows its growth. All of this seems a greater issue than crime rates. And, by the way, crime rates continue to fall (as of late 2013).

Has the degree of danger that some convicts sent to prison for nonviolent crimes been exaggerated? Does our massive prison system—more than twenty years after the last crime rate rise (1986–1991)—seem to be somewhat an outcome of a fear and punishment response? A response that does not solve underlying root problems? Is it time to recognize that our "prison state" is a fundamentally inappropriate response, and that now is the time to "put the brakes on?"

Kraska and Brent (2011) note that a lot of criminal justice legislation and policy, media focus, and public reactions are related to "moral panics," drug scares, and other mythic and ritual-like social processes, rather than a rational "forced reaction" to a growth in the actual crime rate. The "crime problem," thus, is often not constructed on a basis of actual data—for instance an actual increase in crime—but in a *media-driven "story" that exaggerates* the situation into a "scare" or "panic." The public responds with moral concern, and the politicians dutifully step forward with simple, punitive legislation to take care of the problem.

In Michigan, in 2006, a prisoner named Selepak, mistakenly released on parole, killed some people. The media-driven moral panic pushed Governor Granholm to pull back from a planned release onto parole of thousands of nonviolent prisoners. From the prisoners awaiting release point of view "One person spoiled it all for the rest of us." From the taxpayers' point of view, this panic postponement of prison release can be seen as unnecessary use of confinement. This overuse of confinement (at $32,000 a year per prisoner) cost the state hundreds of millions of dollars during a severe budget crisis—at a time when public school teachers and other local and state services were being cut back.

Victor E. Kappeler notes that "Images of justice are not happenstance. While it is comforting to think of criminal justice as a fixed reality void of political and ideological influences, nothing could be further from the truth." (Kraska and Brent 2011: 186).

Where do myths about criminal justice come from and how are they learned? Well, think about the fact that major media (TV news, cable crime shows, newspapers, tabloids, movies, games) are *businesses* and have vested interests in the promotion of criminal justice myths that can create top drama to keep us entertained. Kappeler notes:

> First, the public is fascinated by sensational crime. Crime has become a media product that sells perhaps better than any other media commodity. Attracting a larger audience translates into more advertising dollars. . . . Second, alternative explanations of criminal justice (than the myths) rarely resonate with the viewers. . . . Third, expression of views that contradict official government positions can lead to enhanced regulation of the industry and a loss of news sources. Media depictions of criminal justice are intertwined with government, money, and ideology. The media are therefore compelled to present a very simplistic, standardized view of justice that does not alienate those who either control or consume it. (Kappeler, in Kraska and Brent 2011: 186–87)

Meanwhile, what had once been a few sleepy, rural, and small scale prison system facilities out of the limelight—a slow bureaucratic career organizational territory of guards, housing supervisors and wardens—has, since 1986, become not only a highly politicized and media-driven prison industry, but in some theorist's view, a type of "growth machine" expanding in its own interest.

It is possible to look at the *growth* of the massive U.S. prison system as partly an outcome of "bureaucracy building." From this view some aspects of prison growth are self-serving, creating jobs for correctional officers, those who supply prisons with goods and services, and the construction industry that builds prisons. Also, with the advent of "privatization" of prisons this "growth complex" view takes on a new alarm since, in the private prison, the profit motives may push to keep the number of prisons stable or growing (Mobley 2003; Perrone and Pratt 2006; Robbins 1997). Rural communities also may think they want the state to build more prisons in their area as a source of tax revenue and jobs (Beal 1998; Hernandez 1994; Thomas 1994; Walsh 1994).

Consider the California Correctional Peace Officers Association (CCPOA). This very large union has tens of thousands of both prison guards *and* parole officers in its ranks. There may be seen an *interest* on the part of parole officers to send parolees back to prison—thus continuing to grow the prison from both new crime admittance and parole violation admittance. This latent self-interest aspect has plenty of Californians worried that their tax dollars are unnecessarily tied-up in excessive confinement partly because of such "bloated bureaucracy" interests of the CCPOA guards and parole officers (Petersilia 2003: 240).

In this view, prisoners and parole violators become the "raw material" for an industry, or "prison-industrial complex." Because such a growth complex can become politically powerful, it can be perpetuated by policy favorable to it, such as legislative parole and sentencing laws that result in more prisoners and keeping them longer. In California the CCPOA was the largest campaign contributor to two governors that ran for, and were elected to office in the late 1990s and early 2000s. The CCPOA is a powerful lobby interest group in California (Page 2011).

Kraska reminds us that the United States incarcerates five times more people per capita today than it did just thirty years ago. He notes:

> A number of scholars do not see this growth as merely a forced or rational reac-
> tion to a worsening crime problem (rational/legal and systems), or a pendulum
> swing toward retributive values (crime control/due process), or even the result
> of shifts in politics. Their position, while acknowledging a partial role for these
> forces in the initial stages of development, stresses that today's criminal justice
> apparatus constitutes a *growth complex,* an entity that has taken on a life and
> logic of its own for its own sake. (Kraska 2004: 178–79)

Shelden and Brown ask "Why has a 'crime control industry' emerged at this point in American history?" They answer: such a growth complex reflects the workings of capitalism: "That is to say, it is driven by a need to make a profit anywhere possible and the need to control an inevitable and growing 'surplus population'" (Kraska and Brent 2011: 218). Is it possible in our "the rich get richer" society where "the poor get prison," that there is some *convenience* for the powerful not to fix the inner cities, not to reduce poverty, not to increase jobs and, in general, not to support programs to reduce the syndrome of family disintegration, child abuse and neglect, delinquency, and alcohol and other drug abuse, that are the roots of crime?

CONVENIENT OPPRESSION: BINGE GROWTH AND HIGH IMPACT COMMUNITIES

The convenient oppression existing in the growth of the U.S. criminal justice apparatus is this: hyperincarceration provides a way for "managing" the surplus labor in the jobless ghettos through an incarceration strategy. This "symbiotic relationship" between (several hundred) impoverished inner city neighborhoods and the state prison system (Wacquant 2007) can result in a strategy of "imprisoning communities" (Clear 2007).

Inequality has increased in the United States. Along with festering inner cities, the U.S. economic landscape reveals towns devastated by plant closings, cities reeling from cutbacks in education, and lowering of manufacturing wages and benefits, a growth in low-wage service jobs and temporary and part-time jobs, cut-backs in the social welfare safety net, even poverty in the suburbs. In 2008–2009 the United States moved deep into the Great Recession the effects of which, as of 2013, are still persisting.

Conservative Americans with right wing values typically do not focus on the reality of inner cities, plant shutdowns, low wages, economic insecurity, but see, instead, a prosperous America led by "freedom to choose" free market business values. However, economic insecurity conditions "marginalize" people, requiring them to live in low-rent districts. With less power, under these conditions of inequality, people have less "enfranchisement" or status in the society.

Kraska notes that the criminal justice system can be seen as a means to oppress those who are marginalized in U.S. society. The criminal justice system is riddled with class inequalities and racial disparity. By focusing on lower working-class crime, the "under" class, the criminal justice system diverts attention from the rich and powerful, the "over" class. Tonry states:

> It was foreseeable that wars on crime and drugs would worsen racial disparities in jails, courts, and prisons. Any experienced police officer, for example, would have known that the War on Drugs' emphasis on arrests of low-level drug dealers would have little lasting effect on the drug trade but would result in many more arrests of young males from deteriorated inner-city neighborhoods. And that is what happened. (Tonry 1995: v)

No war against crime will ever be won. Crime rates are the product of demography (number of fifteen- to twenty-five-year-old males in the population) and underlying criminogenic factors. Recall that 80 percent of state prisoners have a history of child abuse and neglect, have not finished high school (see chapter 4), and have few job skills. Yet both the Reagan and senior Bush administrations slashed the federal safety-net funding for education, housing, and social programs for the cities. "Presidents Reagan and Bush *promoted a strategy of federal disinvestment in the inner cities,* (accelerating their deterioration) and diminished the scope and quality of urban public services. The Reagan and Bush administrations thereby increased criminogenic pressures in the cities" (Tonry 1995: 40) (emphasis added) (see Wacquant 2008: Ch. 2).

At a time when drug use in small university cities was mildly tolerated, and drug treatment still remained the mainstream solution to addiction problems in suburban communities, the 1970s saw big city policy over "drug crime" enter the "big politics" realm, politicizing drug crimes with stiff mandatory penalties.

What was clear both then and now is that a program built around education, drug abuse treatment, and social problems designed to address the structural social and economic conditions that lead to crime and drug abuse would have much less destructive impact on disadvantaged young blacks. (Tonry 1995: 123)

Why was street-level enforcement and prison binge growth the chosen tactic? Tonry argues that the choice of arrest and lengthy incarceration of street level dealers was a *political* decision that had "foreseeable disparate (racial) impacts," and that the disadvantaged black Americans were *used* "as a means to the achievement of politicians electoral ends" (Tonry 1995: 123). Christian Parenti (1999) writes:

To reiterate how this buildup occurred, recall that politicians in the age of restructuring (lowering wages, reducing security, breaking unions, and increasing profits) face a populace racked by economic and social anxiety. The political classes must speak to and harness this anxiety, but they cannot blame the U.S. class structure. So they invent scapegoats: the Black/Latino criminal, the immigrant, the welfare cheat, crackheads, superpredators, and so on. These political myths are deployed, first and foremost, to win elections. But the eventual *policy byproducts* of this racialized anti-crime discourse are laws like three strikes and mandatory minimums. Most important, of course, are the drug laws. Drug offenders constituted more than a third (36 percent) of the increase in state prison populations between 1985 and 1994; in the federal system drug offenders make up more than two-thirds (71 percent) of the prison population. (Parenti 1999, in Kraska 2004: 272)

RECONCEPTUALIZING THE CORRECTIONAL PROJECT— A COMMUNITY JUSTICE CONTEXT FOR DECARCERATION

Todd Clear, former president of the American Society of Criminology, has studied the impact of high levels of incarceration in the disadvantaged neighborhoods of America's largest cities where as many as 20 percent of adult men are locked up on any given day, and almost every family has a father, son, brother, or uncle who has been behind bars. In his 2007 book, *Imprisoning Communities: How Mass Incarceration Makes Disadvantaged Neighborhoods Worse,* Clear makes several points:

The extraordinary growth in the U.S. prison system, sustained for over 30 years, has had, at best, a small impact on crime.

The growth in imprisonment has been concentrated among poor, minority males who live in impoverished neighborhoods.

Concentrated incarceration in those impoverished communities has broken families, weakened the social-control capacity of parents, eroded economic strength, soured attitudes toward society, and distorted politics; even, after reaching a certain level, it has increased rather than decreased crime.

Any attempt to overcome the problems of crime will have to encompass a combination of sentencing reforms and philosophical realignment. (Clear 2007: 5–6)

Clear, in emphasizing the need to really address community well-being in the inner cities, argues we need to "reconceptualize the correctional project":

In the end, we cannot reform sentencing procedures without reconceptualizing the correctional project itself. It goes without saying that the narrow range of concepts about corrections that we hold currently cannot help. Phrases such as "getting smarter rather than tougher," "providing more programs," and "investing in reentry" are not bad ideas, they are just irrelevant to the problem of mass incarceration of people from poor communities. To deal with that problem, we will have to make community well-being a central objective of our penal system. We will have to embrace an idea of community justice. (Clear 2007: 13)

As many state budgets have been in crisis since 2003 there has developed a tightening noose around state prison systems pressuring them not to expand (Jacobson 2005). Parole guidelines to increase the percent released after their earliest release date (ERD) (CAPPS 2008), and reentry initiatives to slow down the recidivism rate (CEA 2003; MPRI 2008), have become a recent focus in several states (Austin et al. 2013).

There have been some changes in thinking about the "imprisonment binge" now that many states have gone into budget crises. Certain states have repealed mandatory minimums, or scaled back the length of some sentences (Michigan in 2002, New York in 2005), and a handful of states have begun to emphasize a sentence to mandatory treatment instead of prison for drug cases (Arizona 1996, California 2000). Drug courts to accomplish oversight of this approach have increased. Michigan cut its prison population from 52,000 to 44,000 between 2008 and 2012. Yet the corrections budget in Michigan remains high, at over or near $2 billion, still larger than all of public higher education in the state. And the prison population has crept back up to 45,000 (see CAPPS website at www.capps-mi.org).

The tough on crime rhetoric, so characteristic of the past thirty years (1980–2010), *continues* into the second decade of the twenty-first century among state and federal legislators. Yet state legislators are looking for ways to cut the state corrections budgets; in the summer of 2013 there are several bills in the Michigan legislature proposing parole guidelines and other prison-reduction measures. CAPPS is exploring justice reinvestment. Are we on the cusp of social change toward community well-being, or are we at an impasse because we are unable to solve the root-cause problems of the hyperghetto?

WHO IS RESPONSIBLE FOR CRIME PREVENTION?

It is true that people in prison need to take responsibility for their lives and, if they are ever released, not to behave in ways that bring them back to prison. Because they've been put in prison after convictions in the community, few are sympathetic with the convicted felon. As a criminal justice major, the student can understand this lack of sympathy for the convicted felon. Neighbors and family of the victim often "make the call" to the police, become witnesses, and want conviction and to send those individuals with criminal behavior away. For the presumed guilty, police make efforts to "catch them." Prosecutors make political reputations by making sure the guilty individuals are convicted. Over 90 percent of cases result in a plea bargain: the system is tilted toward conviction (McBarnet 2004: 17–134). Judges preside and sentence—and are elected on their record. Probation officers guide the convicted when they remain in the community rather than prison. Correctional officers, Wardens, and various Housing Unit Managers and Assistant Deputy Wardens, "keep" the convicted individuals. Parole officers keep tabs on the released and now-under-parole individuals. In recent years, state prisoner reentry initiatives attempt to wrap services (housing, transportation, clothing, training and education, and jobs) around the formerly incarcerated individual as they enter the community to help in transition.

All of this criminal justice system activity can happen, through laws, politics, agencies carrying out the laws, sentencing, and correctional and reentry policy. But, as a criminology student, you may begin to realize that the whole criminal justice apparatus—from arrest to parole—can happen without regard for causes in the criminological sense. That is, the criminal justice system may be designed to correct *individual* behavior, but is *not designed to understand or work concertedly* on the causes of criminality beyond individual rational choice, deterrence, routine activities theory, and some minimal mandatory cognitive-behavioral treatment. Criminal intent is required under law to convict—it is not necessary in the criminal justice occupational roles to "fight crime" by understanding its family, community, social, or economic origins of crime, or to join in action with others to reduce the root causes. There is some exception to this generalization with the example of a thorough-going problem-oriented community policing (Goldstein 1990). But research on policing suggests that solving root problems is not a big part of contemporary policing (Greene and Pelfry 1997: 432–68). For instance, victims and the criminal justice system occupations (police, courts, corrections) are not, usually, in the business—are not paid—to develop noncriminal justice solutions to crime: jobs, housing, family social support systems, good neighborhoods, reduction in the extremes of inequality and discrimination, and some power over decisions that affect the "criminogenic conditions" of our lives (Sampson 2011).

When main-campus students, often coming from stable working-class and middle-class families, are first brought into the prison with the author, to the volunteer "Social Science and Personal Writing" class he teaches, they are very judgmental, thinking prisoners' free will choices and bad decisions got them into prison. And, of course, this is true. After sitting and listening to the vivid weekly *prisoner stories*, and coming to grips with the conditions that the often lower-working-class (underclass or subproletariat) prisoner experiences growing up—criminality in family and neighborhood—the main-campus students turn to "soft structural determinism" to explain crime, saying, for these prisoners: "It's due to their environment."

For their part, however, many prisoners are struggling to take responsibility for their life "going forward." They are building up their will-training, their self-narratives of transformation (Maruna 2001). Of course, the parole board needs to be convinced of personal change. These convicts argue strongly that arriving in prison—their life in the past—was due to their free will choice. On the other hand, some prisoners stick with the theory of family and neighborhood determinism, perhaps reminding the habilitating, newfound "making good" prisoners of their origins and the effect family, peers, and the jobless ghetto had on their lives. It is a delicate scene of receding determinism and fate versus emerging free will and responsibility.

So, while this book explores this tension of social psychological (and existential) "personal responsibility and determinist upbringing" and the transformation from the latter to the former, it is the structural sociological message that "America's Got a Problem: Criminality in Family and Neighborhoods due to Socially Disorganizing Processes" that most impresses the author as to what is the main African American prisoner story. That is, the overwhelming story from the black male prisoners regarding their criminality coming up is that "It was just the way it was coming up." The overall national crime rate has gone down, yet that fall in crime has been uneven: certain places have a high rate of both economic crime and violence against person, and African Americans have a much higher rate of violent crime (Parker 2008).

This book assesses criminology theories that acknowledge a "social problem" perspective on how the United States has gotten to the place where bad neighborhoods or "the other side of the tracks"—even stress within sub-urban family and neighborhoods—have persisted and grown larger, produc-ing more crime-prone neighborhoods.

We began our discussion of the causes and consequences of "social dis-organization" earlier in this chapter. How is this phenomenon (social disor-ganization) translated into individual criminality? What are the mechanisms or processes through which the large context (society, city, community, and the city labor market) becomes a dysfunctional family or "strained" kids who want "stuff" living in bad neighborhoods, in poverty, with poor schools and few job opportunities. How do the "life chances" of these individuals—"trapped in a horrific cycle that includes active discrimination, unemploy-ment, poverty, crime, prison, and early death"—connect back to the larger context, or root causes? We need to bridge micro-level (individual, family) factors with macro-level factors (neighborhood, community, city labor mar-ket, globalization, technology, and political abandonment of the hyperghetto).

Prisoner essays 1.1 through 1.5 in chapter 1 examine the prisoner critique that crime is not only a matter of individual factors, but also neighborhood and family. Each chapter of this book pursues themes raised here about "America's Problem"—the larger social context of both the long-festering inner cities, and more generally, increasing stress on families in various neighborhoods as that relates to "strain" influences on crime rates and cultural choice of crime; and the reciprocal effects of social disorganization and crime in troubled neighborhoods that perpetuate a "culture of street crime."

At a higher power level than the individual, the family, the neighborhood, or even the city labor market, is the decision-making power structure where urban elites, state government, the U.S. government, and top corporate offi-cers of huge enterprises have the last word (Wacquant 2008). Large business in the United States *could* be structured like German large business. Under German law, 50 percent of the corporate board of directors is made up of capital (that is, large banks and other large stockholders) and 50 percent of the board of directors is made up of labor (unions and employees). This is stakeholder capitalism. If there is a need to cut costs there can be open books and a discussion between labor, state officials, capital, and academic policy researchers about how to go about downsizing or plant shutdowns with the minimum disruption to the community.

This is not how it works in the United States. Big business makes the deci-sions, with a lot of pressure from shareholders for short-term profits. This is shareholder capitalism. In the United States, if business won't agree to take care of the communities, families, and individuals affected by business decisions, then that leaves government (city, county, state, and federal) to "pick up the pieces" through social supports and needed programs. But if the economy goes into a Great Recession (2008–2009 and continuing), the states' revenue from taxes falls, resulting in less state revenue and cuts in revenue sharing to counties and cities.

What caused the recent Great Recession? The short story is that the average individual wage has stayed flat or declined for thirty years. People in the 1990s and up to 2008 borrowed against the equity in, and growing market value of, their houses (a "wealth effect") and also used credit card debt to continue a higher level of consumption than their falling salaries and wages would support. Then, the housing bubble (unusual increases in housing value) of the 1990s up to 2007 collapsed, evaporating household wealth. People could no longer get a second mortgage, or borrow against the value of their house. They were "underwater" (market value of home less than the amount of their mortgage). This led to a rapid reduction in consumption, which, combined with risky, speculative, and unregulated bank deals, perpetuated by the largest U.S. banks, plunged the United States and global economy into a recession (Reich 2010).

The big banks had maneuvered President Clinton's administration and Congress in the mid-1990s into deregulating the banks. The consequence of this lack of bank regulation? The big banks, financial and insurance companies developed, in the late 1990s and up to 2008, risky financial games (credit default swaps, derivatives, inappropriate mortgage arrangements). When the housing bubble burst, these risky financial games caused the stock market to plunge, and sent the economy deeper into a Great Recession.

The American people witnessed the Obama administration and Democrats in Congress vote to tighten regulation on big banks and financial firms in 2010. The Republicans voted no. After three rounds of extending unemployment benefits (at this writing up to ninety-nine weeks) unemployment in 2013 is still at 7.3 percent and millions cannot find jobs. The number of months the unemployed have been out-of-work is longer than ever before. The private sector is not creating enough jobs, and the public sector is now facing drastic cuts. Nearly a trillion dollars in stimulus spending was injected into the economy, mainly bailing out the big banks (so the already drastic economic collapse would not get worse).

As of this writing business is creating only slightly more than the 150,000 jobs a month needed just to keep up with the growth of the U.S. labor market, and if Conservative Republicans can force major cutbacks in federal government spending, or Europe's recession gets deeper, or China's domestic demand weakens, these and other issues may cause the already slow U.S. economic recovery to slip back into a recession again. One solution is to create a large number of public jobs: fixing infrastructure, helping people, improving community services. When corporations cannot get the economy going again public spending can—this is known as Keynesian fiscal and monetary policy. This is what happened in the 1930s Great Depression. Even such modest proposals, however, will meet opposition from the current Republican Party, which is dominated by ultra-conservatives who want to greatly reduce the role of the federal government. The Republicans, along with some Democrats, worry about the growth in the federal budget deficit, which would threaten economic growth five or ten years from now.

Yet, a return to bank regulation, stimulus spending, proposals for public jobs, and debates over the federal budget deficit do not signal a fundamental political reorganization of large company's responsibilities. Big firms can still shut plants and devastate communities without regard for the local consequences. And, as we move further into a global economy, this unequal power arrangement between the transnational corporations and communities will continue to grow (Dicken 2007; Williamson, Imbroscio, Alperovitz 2002).

Thus it remains an unchanged power relationship that can create "loss of jobs" in urban economies—causing socially disorganizing processes in urban communities (sets of neighborhoods and city blocks), that, because of weakened informal social control networks, leads to crime.

How far can the government go in becoming a countervailing power, or facilitating through unions and community-development policies, a countervailing power to big business? This was the question in the 1930s Great Depression. As of 2013, federal government economic policies are again being discussed. Some progressive federal economic policies can increase the localization of investment to provide community economic stability.

Can an alternative economy be built on local food, a network of community markets (farmers markets, production cooperatives), local small business, regional and local energy, public ownership of utilities and more public retail city services (Apollo Alliance 2007; McKibben 2007; Williamson, Imbroscio, and Alperovitz 2002)? This faint but emerging vision could be combined with further development of community justice: drug courts, community courts, justice reinvestment—that is, beyond capping prison growth, actually downsizing prison populations and shifting resources to investments in the hard-hit communities where crime rates are high.

Chapters 2 and 3 of this book have presented the context and several causes of the rise of mass incarceration in the United States. This context has brought forth the person category of prisoner.

Who are these "person categories" in our "late modern" society? And what were the causes of their crime(s)? The rest of this book presents many prisoner voices on criminology. We start the next chapter with prisoner voices on their education before (and during) prison, and how this relates to their pathways to prison.

#####

Prisoner Essay 3.1

"The Sons of the Incarcerated: Living for the Moment Because There Is No Hope for the Future" (3/17/10)

It may seem that the most reasonable solution to crime is to simply remove the offender from society, but from my experience, it's surely not most effective way to prevent crime.

I didn't grow up in an area known for crime. In fact, I was in the 6th grade before I knew someone who was sentenced to prison. It was a huge scandal. I remember seeing parents talking to each other about it in hushed tones, and many of them wouldn't allow their children to play with that man's kids, as if criminality were a communicable disease. It didn't bother me, however, because it didn't affect my life in any way. I still had my father. The only thing that intrigued me about the whole situation was that it was another house which had no parental supervision during the day and a lack of repercussions from an overworked single-mom. But it wasn't until years later, after I got myself thrown in prison, that I realized who the victims of incarceration truly are.

I was sentenced to prison at twenty-one, leaving behind a four-year old son and a wife who just entered army basic training. She couldn't care for him then, and as circumstances unfolded, it would be several years before he was able to live with her. My parents took him without question, but they had thirteen other children to deal with. My son didn't receive the attention a hyperactive child struggling with the loss of both parents requires. He would grow up in an overcrowded house with a mother serving her country half the world away and a father serving a sentence that would last into his adulthood.

No matter the minutes spent on the phone or the hours in the visiting room, there was no way I could be there for all the things that a father should for his son. No playing catch in the back yard, no shouting encouragement from the soccer field sidelines, no fishing at that lake up north, no kitchen-table talks about slipping grades, no teaching him how to drive, or to shave; no setting an example of how a man is supposed to care for his family or how to handle life's mounting responsibilities. By the very act of conceiving him, being his father was my responsibility, my place in this world, but since I was not there, someone else would have to step in—or no one at all.

My son entered his teen years while living on an Army base, where most fathers took active roles in their lives, so, in an attempt to fit in, he told potential friends that his own father was still in the Navy. It is impossible to know how he escalated from telling such stories to attempting to cash checks he'd stolen from his mother's purse at the PX. Getting caught didn't dissuade him from continuing to act out. Not long after, he took off in his mother's car and got it stuck in the mud, only to ruin the engine trying to get out. Thinking a change in environment might help with his attitude, his mother moved off base; a month later he stole a golf cart from a nearby course and drove it to school. It resulted in felony charge, two years probation, and ultimately, after getting caught with a tiny amount of marijuana on his school bus, a three-month stint in a Florida correctional camp for boys.

To say that my son would never have gotten in trouble if I was there to guide him is hubristic at best, but I have no doubt he would have stood a better chance. He wouldn't be so far behind maturity-wise, he most likely would have graduated from high school, and he probably would have more ambition in life then to sit around playing guitar hero while getting high.

I'm thankful he's not in prison, especially considering that he was heading down that dark and treacherous road like so many of those with whom I'm forced to share my every waking moment. Their fathers, uncles, brothers, cousins, and neighbors have, or are currently doing time. I can only imagine what it's like to grow up in a community with so little positive male influence. Without real men to show a boy how real men are supposed to behave. The more who are locked up, the less there are to instill values and realistic, attainable goals. Not to live for the moment, because there is no hope for the future.

Removing the offender from society may be a reasonable solution, but sentencing guidelines only account for the victims of the crime committed, never the victims such a removal creates.

#####

EXERCISES 3.1–3.4

Exercise 3.1

In prisoner essay 3.1 the writer says "there was no way I could be there for all the things that a father should for his son." How does this relate to the degree of free will and determinism affecting his son? Discuss. What prison policies might help? What sentencing policies might help?

Free Will and Determinism. Criminology students often argue strongly for a "free will" perspective on crime—that criminality is a choice. Often this is a way to affirm moral values: "I would not choose to do this crime!" After visiting the volunteer prison class I teach and hearing prisoner life stories, many main campus college students switch sides and talk earnestly of "determinism" in people's lives. Now a more sociologically informed moral value takes hold.

Exercise 3.2

Describe the governing through crime society depicted by Jonathan Simon.

Society and Subcultures. Some students come to a relativism perspective and appreciate a kind of "When in Rome, do as the Romans Do" view of the subcultural of crime. That is, the student perceives that those "in the criminality life" have a subculture of their own (as do "straight Johns"). How are society, its class structures, institutions, and subcultures formed in ways that increase criminogenic conditions? What are the assumptions about society that are made in each criminological theory? A goal of each chapter is to present the "view of society" that that particular theory has. What are the assumptions of how society is arranged in this criminological perspective?

Power Arrangements. Neighborhoods do not stand alone. They are connected to the labor markets in the larger communities (e.g., cities). For instance, what power arrangements in the cities, and the city's links to regional and national corporations, the federal government and the global economy, can cause or facilitate socially disorganized neighborhoods? Parker has documented how the loss of manufacturing jobs in U.S. inner cities had a disproportionately large impact on African American males—devastating family and household stability, and disrupting neighborhood informal controls through weakening parent networks (2008). Anderson has traced the changing history for young black males: from industrial city to urban postindustrial ghetto poverty (2008). The result: more violent crime.

Exercise 3.3

What power arrangements could bring a *significant reduction* in your state's prison population? Who would be the members of a coalition to *shift money saved* from prison downsizing to *justice reinvestment* in high impact communities?

Who decides that a community (e.g., labor markets in the city that supplies jobs to families in neighborhoods) will undergo "loss of manufacturing jobs?" In his first film (1989) Michael Moore chased GM chief executive officer (CEO) Roger Smith to try to interview him after Smith made decisions to shut down Flint GM auto plants in the late 1970s. This book includes older prisoner essays that graphically describe how their neighborhoods changed (from good to bad, and how crime increased) after the auto plant shutdowns.

Levels of Causation, Levels of Explanation. At what level of your explanation do you stop your analysis? Is crime due to disrupted family? Yes, but disrupted family can often be a direct or indirect consequence of plant shutdowns, neighborhoods economic decline, increase in household poverty, and the development of concentrated poverty (40 percent or more households in neighborhoods at or below poverty line). So: does concentrated poverty relate to higher crime? Yes, due to loss of family stability and parent networks and influence of crime in the streets. But the *development* of jobless ghettos (concentrated disadvantage) can be traced back to business decisions to disinvest in that community. And, because of power arrangements, an inability to moderate the consequences of business decisions the jobless inner city develops, and inadequate government responses to the problems of the city in the face of business power. Our basic institutions are in conflict: the market institutions overwhelms other societal institutions such as the family (Rosenfeld, Quinet, and Garcia 2010).

Exercise 3.4

Describe what levels of causation are needed to understand jobless ghetto crime?

DISCUSSION AND REVIEW QUESTIONS

1. What was the 1968 Safe Streets Act? How did it influence the subsequent prison build-up movement?
2. What is meant by "a new federalization" of drug laws? How does this relate to the 1986 Anti-Drug Abuse Act?
3. What is meant by a "mandatory minimum" sentence? How does it relate to prison growth?
4. How much does it cost to house one average prisoner in Michigan?
5. What is meant by a moral panic and how does it influence prison growth?
6. What does Simon mean by the phrase governing through crime?
7. Why do U.S. inner cities have the use of a lot of handguns?
8. What is meant by "justice reinvestment?"
9. List a few evidence-based crime prevention ideas.

4

Prisoners on Education

Who are the prisoners? Four out of five state prisoners enter prison without a high school diploma and with few job skills. Many read at or below an eighth grade level and have only third grade math skills (DeRose 2007 and 2010; MDOC 1996). Who is going to hire them in an economy with few manual labor jobs; an economy with only 10 percent manufacturing and 90 percent service industry, where there are already many unemployed with good manufacturing skills and good service industry "soft skills," along with millions of recent immigrants, all competing for jobs in a slow job growth "recovery" that is expected to remain slow job growth for several years into the future? Clearly better basic skills and some postsecondary education and skills training would benefit contemporary prisoners.

ALIENATED UNDEREDUCATED UNEMPLOYED KIDS HANGING OUT

I traveled to the Parnall facility, a mid-Michigan "reentry prison" to offer eight Saturday afternoon two-hour education workshops over a three-year period. These workshops were titled "Going to Community College after Release." In total, while conducting these Saturday workshops I collected 54 prisoner essays. Along with introducing them to community college curriculum and how to fill out Pell grant FAFSA forms, I asked them each to write for twenty-five minutes on their educational background. For me, this was instructive. One prisoner wrote the following.

#####

Prisoner Essay 4.1

"Making Everyone Think I Could Read" (10/4/08)

When I was in grade school from day one, I never liked going, until I was kicked out in the 12th grade. The reason why I never liked school is because I never set time aside to learn how to read or to do anything else.

I came up on a farm where my family was a share cropper and most days my day began early in the morning with my feeding my livestock, and making sure fires was in the heaters when my family got out of bed.

At such a young age, I thought my whole life was going to be nothing but farm life. Once I began going to middle school, things got real rough for me because of me not preparing myself, for what was to come. When the older children found out I couldn't read or understand what was in front of me, I began to start trouble for myself and everyone else. I would fight in school most days when the teachers were not around. But as soon as I was caught, I was kicked out and made to stay at home for two weeks. Still not doing anything to help myself, I continued to fall behind more and more. By the time I got to high school, I was really lost. I faked my way around school making everyone think I could read when I could "not." I got kicked out of high school about six times and then began my life of prison.

Upon coming prison I was told I had to go to school and get my GED I put it off as long as I could, because in the back of my mind, I still didn't like school but once I started my studies, little did I know, school became a place where I wanted to be, because I wanted to be like the rest of my family and finish school.

#####

Why does educational attainment matter in studying criminology? If a prisoner reports that their "Parents were having marital issues, got divorced, became a single parent household and that 'I had stress with school,'" does that hold potential for later criminality or trouble with the law?

Farrington and Welsh (2007) found that at the individual level, low educational attainment is a "predictive factor" of crime (see table 1.1). It may seem that prisoners, who know little about reading and writing, and math, should know a lot about cops, courts, and corrections. But most prisoners as youth coming up actually know very little about *law*.

#####

Prisoner Essay 4.2

"With the Streets as Our Father We Learned about Laws Too Late" (11/8/08) Due to the fact that I am a juvenile offender who didn't know his rights until they were taken away I believe that every school in America should

have a mandatory criminal law class. I think this class should educate children on crime and punishment, and mandate that each child understand about crime, what it can do to their life and how it effects someone else's life.

This class will teach them the understanding of automatic wavier to help them understand just what they will face, as a result of committing crimes. This class should both act out actual criminal trials and as well have documentaries to help expose them to prison—especially those who were under the age of 18, when they committed their crime. Also this class will educate them on what a victim, or a victim's family, feel like as a result of the crime. Since a person can forfeit rights before actually having rights we should at least ensure that every child knows what his/her rights are. This class should ensure that every child understand emotional and psychological scars. It is key that whomever teaches this class will see to it that every child in that class understands. I do believe that it will help be an effective crime deterrent.

Farrington and Welsh say that those raised in inner city and influence by peer-pressure has shown a greater rate for criminal behavior. As for myself, I grew up in the projects in River Rouge, Mich., in an area known as the back street. The back street project boys were known for being rebellious. As a child the older guys used to tell me, "Lil dog, you are from the back streets, so you better represent."

Most of the children in this area were from single parent homes and in most cases that parent had some kind of an addiction. So the streets became our fathers and the older cool guys were like my brothers. As children we are very impressionable. We want to learn how to fit into our environment. Our brains soak up all the information around us. Be it good or bad, just so happen, in the back street projects, it was bad for mostly all the people. I looked up to the criminals. Some sold drugs; others were pimps encouraging women to prostitute themselves. I would watch them and imitate their style. I wanted to dress like them, talk like them. I wanted to be like them. There was no doctors in my community, no lawyers. No engineers. Just a lot of criminals. So I never saw a moral wrong in committing crimes. I never knew just how much being a convicted felon could affect someone's life. I just wanted to be like the guys I looked up to. And I had their approval, and encouragement.

#####

Why is it that typical prisoners entering state prison systems have not completed a high school degree, have few job skills, may read at or below an eighth grade level? As these two prisoner essays show, their family may be rural poor—or, they may come from "streets as their father." There are social pressures *away* from school as a social goal. As Trevor Milton notes:

> Malik—a 16-year-old from Harlem—explained that, even if they don't want to, "men in certain neighborhoods are pressured into selling drugs, robberies, staying on the corner (loitering). . . . Doing dumb stuff! . . . Some guys try to put you down for knowing more than them." Both Felix and Malik stated that academic success did not accord much status. (2012: 63)

Many ethnographers have shown the process of dropping out, such as Simon and Burns in *The Corner* (1997) and Jay Macleod in *Ain't No Makin' It* (1987/2008).

Proximate reasons for school failure are parental neglect, living in abandoned neighborhoods, and going to drug- and gang-infested schools. A short story for the pathway to prison is dropping out to sell drugs (Tregea and Larmour 2009: Ch. 5). A more macro-political economy story is that business and large industries "capital starved" the decaying central city and "flowed capital" to the growing suburbs—producing uneven development into which the illegal drug economy moved to dominate the now jobless ghettos. The reason this book starts out with chapter 2, "The Making and Unmaking of the Prison State," and chapter 3, "The Politics of Mass Incarceration," is because it is necessary to set the historical stage of mass incarceration in the drug crime era to set the context for "the way it was" as many prisoners were growing up.

As explained in chapter 1, in each historical era the definition of what is a crime must be established to understand the *social context*. Mass incarceration as a "governing through crime" era established tough on crime laws on street drugs and long mandatory sentences during a period of uneven development producing the "high impact" neighborhood—a neighborhood that has many going to prison (convicts) and many returning from prison (parolees), and many committing more new crimes or violating their parole (recidivism).

Another more functional or normative theoretical story is a social critique that sees "institutional anomie" in the United States—a society that allows an extreme market economy institution to dominate other institutions such as family, neighborhood, and school (Polanyi 1944; Rosenfeld, Quinet and Garcia ASC 2010). In other words, "making conditions good for business" through policies of low taxes and deregulation, but undermining norms of support for home life, neighborhood, and school, thus bypassing social investment in effective crime prevention strategy. This can also be seen as a political decision to abandon the hyperghetto—a conflict view. Whether you take a normative (consensus) view or a conflict (power) view, the schools in the U.S. hyperghetto neighborhoods are bad, and affected many of our prisoners growing up.

SCHOOL FAILURE AS FIRST FLAG FOR DELINQUENCY

How does school failure and school dropout relate to developing criminality? Joy Dryfoos (1990) researched this question from a prevention point of view, identifying school failure as a "first flag" for later delinquency. She made the case that single problem, short-term programs won't succeed. An effective community crime prevention strategy requires long-term comprehensive multiproblem programs. This is the kind of large-scale program that does not occur because of the institutional anomie we mentioned. She argued:

> Low achievement in school has been shown to be an important predictor of substance abuse, delinquency, and early sexual intercourse. . . . Understanding the epidemiology of school failure and dropping out is fundamental to this book's argument: that high-risk behaviors are interrelated and, therefore, interventions must be comprehensive.
>
> School failure is a process rather than a single risk event. A young person initiates hard drug use or has early unprotected sexual intercourse or first commits a delinquent act at a specific time and place. Usually these actions are voluntary and follow a personal decision (although they are heavily influenced by the social environment). Low (school) achievement results from an array of forces, many of which are outside the control of the child. The quality of the school is, of course, a major factor, as are the actual classroom practices and attitudes of the teacher. (79)

The consequences of dropping out are well documented. Dryfoos lists several short-term and long-term consequences of school failure and dropout. For the behavior of low achievement and poor grades the short-term consequences can include being held back a grade, truancy, and absenteeism. The long-term consequences can include dropout, low basic skills, low employability, and lack of a college degree.

Dryfoos notes that for the youth who experiences nonpromotion, or is left back a grade, the short-term consequences include low self-esteem, low involvement in school activities, problem behaviors, and alienation. The long-term consequences can include becoming a dropout. A prisoner essay describes this: "Being held back twice, once in 7th grade I felt like I was grown. Memories of high school were almost non-existent because I never went—skipped a lot. I started to get into a lot of trouble."

> School dropouts have significantly fewer job prospects. They make lower salaries and are more often unemployed (some permanently). Dropouts are also more likely to be welfare dependent and more frequently experience unstable marriages. Dropouts are much more likely to be involved in problem behaviors of all kinds, including delinquency, substance abuse, and early childbearing.

The chances of becoming an adjudicated criminal and serving time in prison are much higher for dropouts than for graduates . . . in the past, dropouts could find legitimate employment opportunities in industrial and service jobs. With increasing technical demands, ill-equipped job-seekers more often turn to illegitimate sources of employment, such as drug dealing and fencing "hot merchandise."

Finally, society suffers the consequences of dropping out in terms of lost revenue from diminished taxes and increased welfare expenditures. In more graphic terms, it is unhealthy for a community to have a bunch of alienated undereducated unemployed kids hanging out on street corners and getting into trouble. (Dryfoos 1990: 81)

#####

Prisoner Essay 4.3

"My Father Encouraged Me to Steal—This Is How I Grew Up" (3/25/09)
Many of the children that get involved in criminal activity be children that have a lot of free time, and a lack of self confidence. If the community, school and churches get involved in a child's life early there is a chance that collectively they can deter him/her from getting involved with the wrong crowd, and or getting involved with crime.

A lot of times citizens don't want to get involved because they feel like it's not their responsibility. They expect the child's parents to play the positive role in the child's life. What if the parents are on drugs or the parents have some other problem, or habit preventing them from paying attention to their child? Who then is responsible? The measures that have been taken in the past are not working. Foster care does not work, a lot of times the child ends up a victim of some kind of neglect. Those so-called scared straight programs do not work, a lot of the kids that participated in those programs still ended up in prison.

What's needed is an honest approach, programs that seek out the talents in each child and people that are able to give the child confidence in his/her self. In order to save a child from a life of crime, someone has to pay attention. Listen to what excites them. Allow them to freely express how they feel, then question them on why they feel that way. So if they child shows signs of greediness, knowing that greed can be a destructive trait in his personality, someone should step in and help him with that problem. But if no one is around or no one is paying attention then that greed is only going to get stronger. As he grows, so will his greed.

When I was a child, my father often encouraged me to steal. I was easily distracted by money and possessions and no one cared. As I got older, I learned more ways of how to steal and what to steal. I went from going in a gas station and stealing a pack of candy to going in a gas station sneaking in the back, opening the back door, and stealing everything I could get my hands on. By the age of thirteen I was a full fledge criminal. Everywhere I went every store/gas station I walked into. All I thought about was stealing. What can I steal? I even tried to learn how to pick pocket people, but I never could learn. So I stuck to what I know. The more I stole the more brazen I became. I went from stealing from store/gas station, to going in restaurant ordering food eating and leaving without paying. I even went into a barbershop and told the barber my mom was going to come pick me up and pay him. After he finished cutting my hair, I went and sat by the door, acting like I was waiting for my mother. A random car pulled up and I just walked out.

This progressed into breaking and entering and even armed robbery. I cannot remember ever having a dream of being something professional. It took me to come to prison before I realized I have talent for writing poetry. As a child, I had no self-confidence, I had a lot of free time and the people only encouraged the negative thoughts that were going in my head, so that what I grew into.

#####

Dryfoos presents an analysis that suggests that risk behavior be measured in terms of two dimensions: risk of failing and risk of dropping out. "Three kinds of measures will be used here to estimate target populations for intervention: the prevalence of being one or two years behind, the prevalence of low test scores, and the prevalence of dropping out" (Dryfoos 1990: 81) As she elaborates: "In this discussion of the antecedents of school failure and dropping out, we return once again to the 'chicken and egg' quandary. Which variables precede failure and dropout, and which ones are the results of alienation from school?" (88).

Dryfoos assembles a list of "Antecedents of School Dropout" in terms of demographic factors (age, sex, race, and ethnicity), and personal factors (expectations for education, school grades, basic skills, school promotion, attitude toward school, conduct, general behavior, peer influences, school involvement, and involvement in other high-risk behaviors). She then reviews several studies that locate *major predictors* associated with dropping out, for these antecedent demographic and personal characteristics.

For example, for demographics such as age and race/ethnicity a major predictor for dropping out is "old for grade," and "Native American, Hispanic, Black." And, for example, for personal antecedents such as expectations, grades, skills, promotion, attitude, conduct, and peer influence, major predictors are "low expectation, no plans for college," "low grades," "low test scores," "left back in early grades," "strong dislike of school, bored," "truancy, 'acting out,' suspension, expulsion," "friends drop out," "low interest, low participation," and "high rates for child bearers."

She also had antecedents for family (household composition, income/power status, parental education, welfare, mobility, parental role/bonding/guidance, culture in home, primary language), and antecedents for community (neighborhood quality, school quality, and employment). For example, for family major predictors are "family in poverty," "low levels of parental education," "lack of parental support, authoritarian, permissive." For example, for community major predictors are "alternative or vocational school," and "segregated school" (89).

Joy Dryfoos mapped out a comprehensive community prevention strategy that links to the *ability* of a community to plan out community norms regarding school failure and dropout rate. The problem is often that higher poverty areas (40 percent or more at or below poverty level) and high impact areas (many people coming and going to prison, on probation, or parole) have difficulty in mobilizing community assets and sustaining community development (Kretzmann and McKnight 1993). How will such communities "plan out community norms regarding school failure and dropout rate?" We return to descriptions of the high crime communities in chapters 7 through 9.

We also want to search the prisoner views about why they encountered school failure and dropped out. We will find many links to individual, family, and community (chapters 5–7) and to the kind of social disorganization, differential social organization, social structure, social process, and power arrangements (chapter 7–9) that make a planning process to achieve comprehensive community strategies difficult.

Jay MacLeod (1987/2008), in his classic book *Ain't No Makin' It*, found in studying a white youth group of "Hallway Hangers" and a black youth group "The Brothers," that parental involvement and expectations for the black youth were that they would do well in school, whereas the long-term welfare-recipient parents of the white group had low expectations regarding school for their sons. The Brothers stayed out of trouble. However, in the end, The Brothers didn't do much better than the Hallway Hangers in term of jobs because the economy (since the 1980s to present) did not create a lot of good jobs for lower-working-class (or underclass) youth, regardless of whether they stayed in school.

For many prisoners, education (and crime prevention) starts in the prison.

How *are* state prisoners going to overcome their educational and job skills deficit if strong GED, vocational training, and accredited postsecondary correctional education (PSCE) programs are not available in the prison?

Can the state prisoner reentry initiatives facilitate such advanced training and education, so that the prisoner has better chances of getting, and keeping, a job? The current Michigan budget for the Michigan prisoner reentry initiative (MPRI) has been cut. A good deal of the money that is allocated for MPRI steering committees goes to housing, contracts for substance abuse treatment, and contracts for sex offender treatment. There is very little, if anything, left over for the local MPRI steering committee to pay for the formerly incarcerated to receive advanced job training and job placement services, other than to encourage they apply for Pell grants and visit the local employment bureau, Michigan Works! Yet prisoners reentering society as the formerly incarcerated need *extra* educational skill sets and credentials to overcome the stigma encountered in the labor market.

Prisoner reentry programs have been spreading across the states since January 2001, when President Bush, through an executive order that authorized a total of $50 million for the states to start prisoner reentry initiatives. This history of recent United States prisoner reentry initiatives was an effort to mobilize the "thousand points of light"—to help local city and county resources come together with *existing* services to facilitate prisoner reentry. In Michigan $25 to $55 million annually has been budgeted from the state budget for the MPRI. This amount when you are distributing to eighty-three counties and are trying to pay for substance abuse counseling and other expensive counseling, and housing, doesn't go very far and is not enough to pay for the kind of focused advanced skills training that is required.

The author was a participant in the National Institute of Justice (NIJ) Data Resources Program Workshop, "Prisoner Reentry and Community Justice," June 18–22, 2001, held in Ann Arbor, Michigan, at the Inter-university Consortium for Political and Social Research (ICPSR) (Institute for Social Research). The week-long workshop was held just six months after the federal government announcement of the money for each state to start prisoner reentry committees to explore how better to transition prisoners to society.

In the past the prisoner reentry process was mostly the job of state or county parole officers (Abadinsky 2006), with some help from faith-based organizations like Criminal Justice Ministry (Ashby 1998). Now, added to this, would be new state prisoner reentry programs. The NIJ–sponsored workshop was to raise prisoner reentry as more of an academic issue—a research and policy issue for university professors, their graduate students, and think tank professional researchers.

Assembled at this workshop were some of the best scholars on prisoner issues. What were the considerations of reentry the prominent academics and policy analysts asked? The author was asked by the workshop coordinator to be a participant. Outlined below is the author's narrative sketch of each day's activities of this historic launch to the prisoner reentry issue as an academic subfield.

#####

Author's Narrative 4.1

"Prisoner Reentry Becomes an Academic Issue"
We arrived on Monday, June 18, 2001, on the University of Michigan campus
to listen to William Sabol of Case Western Reserve University, give his opening talk on "Prisoner Reentry in Perspective," followed by "Prisoner Reentry:
State Variations, Issues, and Developments" presented by James Austin,
George Washington University. These talks were followed by a research
roundtable for the participants where we all discussed the presentations. Several doctoral level graduate students from universities across the nation were
also part of this week-long workshop. They were looking for PhD dissertation
topics and deepening their grasp of this new "cutting edge" field—a field that
also held some promise of foundation research grant money.

The second day featured "National Overview of Prisoner Reentry: Exploring the Trends, Challenges, and Consequences" presented by Michelle R.
Waul, of the Urban Institute, and "Returning Home: Understanding the Challenges of Prisoner Reentry," by Christy Visher, Urban Institute. A related
presentation, "Prisoner Reentry: Conceptual Revision Emerging from
Program Experience," by Faye S. Taxman of the University of Maryland,
rounded out day two. The participants numbered about 35 academics and
we were becoming a lively colleague group by day two. The Urban Institute,
a foundation-supported think tank, was launching a large focus on prisoner
issues and was to become a center for prisoner and reentry studies in the
decade 2001–2010.

Day three featured "Restorative Practices and Lessons about Prisoner
Reentry from a Community Safety Initiative" (Edmund F. McGarrell and
Kathleen Olivares, Indiana University and the Hudson Institute), "Ground-
ing Prisoner Reentry: A Convict Perspective" (Chuck Terry, University of
Michigan-Flint), and "The Manhattan Parole Reentry Court" (Alfred Siefel,
Center for Court Innovation, New York, NY).

All through the period 1989 to 2010 there has been a growing interest in
restorative justice, in part sparked by the book *Crime, Shame and Reintegration* by John Braithwaite (1989). Chuck Terry represented the new Convict
Criminology Movement, pushing for ex-convict academics participation in
giving voice to prisoners' reentry needs (Richards and Jones 1996; Ross and
Richards 2003; Newbold and Ross 2012). This movement has made a significant impact on the American Society of Criminology (ASC) in the years since
1999 with sometimes 7–10 sessions each year at the ASC annual meetings
featuring the several dozen ex-cons who have gone onto graduate school,
getting the PhD, and who were now professors in American universities
producing research articles, books, and policy papers. I invited Chuck Terry
to a Citizens Alliance on Prisons and Public Spending (www.capps-mi.org)

and Michigan Council on Crime and Delinquency joint-sponsored Michigan Conference in the Fall of 2001.

Day Four of the workshop featured "The Massachusetts Reentry Programs," (Rhiana Kohl, Massachusetts Department of Corrections), and "Community Notification" (Mary Ann Farkas, Marquette University). Workshop participants, who were from several states, were looking for model programs.

Day Five, and the last day of the NIJ-sponsored workshop, featured a morning workshop: "Prison Education and Skills Training in the Transition to Community" (William S. Tregea, Adrian College, and John Linton, U.S. Department of Education Office of Correctional Education, OCE). The author had received foundation grants in 1997 and produced a report on PSCE in 1998; and produced three newsletters as co-founder of the Michigan STEPP Coalition (accredited skills training and education for prisoners and prevention). He had also organized an Academy of Criminal Justice Sciences (ACJS) research session on PSCE in 1999, had written a grant for prison college in Michigan and engaged in educating Michigan legislators to support PSCE, working with Steve Steuerer, Director of the International Correctional Education Association (www.cea.org). John Linton was the new Director of OCE, and had a history of helping with correctional education in Maryland.

These daily workshops in this week-long NIJ-sponsored program launched the academic side of the federal push for state reentry initiatives in what were to become a series of research reports, books and other academic writing, and public policy papers. A representative policy book to come out of this new focus was *When Prisoners Come Home* (Joan Petersilia 2003). This author's book *The Prisoners World: Portraits of Convicts Caught in the Incarceration Binge* (Tregea and Larmour 2009) is also a representative academic supplementary book. The 50 states then began, starting in fall of 2001, to assemble reentry committees, attracting 100–150 of the most active and knowledgeable people in each state to form planning committees on reentry—and hammering out a state reentry program design.

In Michigan this two year process of developing a reentry program became known as the Michigan Prisoner Reentry Initiative (MPRI) with a state budget that started with 13 Million in 2003 that grew to 55 Million in 2010. Michigan is the only state that has MPRI Steering Committees for each of its 83 counties (for information contact: www.michpri.com).

#####

The author, who subsequently became a member of the Lenawee County MPRI Steering Committee, helped develop the overall plan for Lenawee

County. His specific part of this plan is to travel to the Parnall Correctional Facility and offer two-hour workshops "Going to Community College after Release." Prisoner essays from these workshops are reported on in this chapter.

Parnall, located in Jackson, Michigan, is the state's mid-south regional center for reentering prisoners, and thus for prisoner reentry in Lenawee County where the author lives. During the period 2007–2011, the author presented eight of these educational workshops to reentering prisoners. To recruit prisoners to the workshop, the prison MPRI director distributes flyers in the housing units (appendix A). In the two-hour workshop the prisoners wrote twenty-five minute essays on *What your educational experiences have been—from grade school to the present—and what vocational skills training you have gotten, on the outside or in prison.*

This writing assignment showed "beyond the statistics," something about the fifty-four prisoner experiences "coming up."

The national high school drop-out rate is 30 percent. However, some inner-city high schools have a 50 percent drop-out rate. Of the fifty-four prisoners participating in these Parnall "Going to College" prison workshops, 74 percent dropped out of or were expelled from high school (N-40).

Of the fifty-four workshop participants there were 14 or 26 percent who actually finished their high school by "staying in school." Of those who grad-uated high school, three went through a year or more of "alternative school" and one got his GED through "Juvy School" to complete his high school diploma, and, among the ten who graduated by staying in a regular high school, two also took an area career center set of vocational-technical courses.

These vocational technical training centers are offered as part of the county intermediate school districts. Students from area high schools can take techni-cal or vocational courses during their high school years and others, who have graduated or who are working on their GED, can also take courses. Staffed by area educators who are knowledgeable in the several vocational areas offered (firefighter, correctional, electrical, building trades, horticulture, graphics, etc.), these "area career centers" help high school graduates and GED holders get advanced skills training relevant to getting a job.

At the national level, some 700,000 formerly incarcerated people reenter society each year. In Michigan, approximately 14,000 prisoners reenter society each year. Julie DeRose, MDOC director of correctional education, advocates for an "area career center" specifically for reentering prisoners. The formerly incarcerated could transition to such a center, be paid a small living wage to help in transition and learn a trade or certificate. I believe this is a good idea.

Also, *accredited* postsecondary programs *inside the prison*, such as prison community college programs with 15 credit skills sets, 30 to 60 credit concentrations and certificates, and Associates of Arts degrees, and university or college-level Bachelor's degrees, have proven to be a contributor to reduced recidivism and success in reentry (CEA 2003; Petersilia 2003; Tregea 1998, 2003). Even one community college course can help in shifting a prisoner to adopt an affiliation as a "student" and "become interested in other things" (CEA 2003; Duguid, Hawley, and Knights 1998; Duguid and Pawson 1998; Tregea 1998; Wenda 1997).

However, the State of Michigan Budget has embedded in it every year the phrase: "No state appropriation shall be used for the purpose of Prison College." Some states, like Indiana, Massachusetts, Texas, and Ohio do have state-sponsored PSCE programs, but most states, like Michigan, do not.

It is important to keep the pressure on state government to provide what they can to support PSCE and to continue to push for the reinstatement of the federal Pell grant eligibility for prisoners. The current federal dollars that are available for PSCE is a small amount funneled through the Youth Offender Program (YOP) which, in Michigan is known as the CERT program. The YOP/CERT program is for prisoners age thirty-five and under who have no violent or sex offense conviction and will be returning to society within two years. Montcalm Community College runs the YOP/CERT Michigan program, providing up to nineteen credits of a "Business Management" certificate in the form of Continuing Education Units (CEU) that can be turned into credits if the prisoner, upon return to society, enrolls at Montcalm Community College. (These CEU credits get around the language "no prison college" in the state budget since the money for the program is federal.) This program serves one hundred to two hundred prisoners a year.

A second new program "Pathways from Prison" started up in the fall of 2013, a pilot program funded through Vera Institute and Kellogg Foundation, with a $1 million budget. This small pilot program might service two hundred or three hundred prisoners. The MDOC has a population of 45,000 as of early 2014, 14,000 of whom return to society each year, but only 3,500 of these prisoners returning to society have received any skills training and education beyond the GED. The Vera Institute pilot program announcement notes: "According to the National Center for Education Statistics. . . . Seventy-eight percent of the prison population lacks postsecondary education, compared to 49 percent of the general population. Moreover, studies suggest that graduating from college programs can decrease recidivism by approximately 72 percent" (Vera Institute 2013).

Reflect, again, on the prisoner situation: coming into the prison with no high school diploma and few job skills, reading at eighth grade level, and math at third grade level. What is his self-concept? What kind of person is he?

What kind of educational experiences has he had? What kind of self-concept and sense of self-worth will he have leaving prison?

Of the fifty-four prisoners who took the author's educational workshops their proportion ($N = 40$, or 76 percent) who did not complete high school match the 1996 MDOC survey data that showed "Eighty percent of MDOC prisoners enter prison without a high school diploma, and with few job skills" (MDOC 1996). For the 26 percent ($N = 14$) who did graduate there is an advantage in this research in the form of the twenty-five minute personal essays, which offer a more detailed, in-depth, understanding of these "outliers"—where the story of the typical prisoner is not staying in school, these few did finish high school. The highlighted bullets below present excerpts from those who did finish high school and yet went to prison. Compared to the "average" college student (who didn't subsequently go to prison) their educational history and life is probably quite different.

List 4.1 Finished High School. Five excerpts from personal stories of twelve workshop participants who finished high school (26 percent of sample) include:

- By 10th grade I was selling drugs mostly to support my own habit but also for the latest things of my era. I graduated high school and went on to college for one year. But then I had my first child, dropped out of school (college) to support my baby and her mother and kept selling drugs and using them as well. By 1990 I was on my way to prison for the first of four times.
- Dad, wherever he was, was not at home. So the discipline was left to a single mom. . . . She was spread too thin between work and my younger sister and brother. I became the "lost boy" and school became the arena for my needs of attention. My grades suffered—I had to attend summer school for 7th grade so I wouldn't fail. I had many more close calls. By the time I reached high school my motto was: "Squeeze through the radar," and I did. Several close calls and "D's" later, I graduated high school. Sometimes the discretion of coaches and close teachers, and sometimes because I worked just enough. At 18 I moved out on my own and started a blue collar career.
- Outgoing, intelligent kid in an alcoholic abusive home. Bounced from school to school. Adopted at 12 where I was brought to Michigan. Middle school started extremely with drugs, alcohol and partying. High school drug use and alcohol got worse but I managed to graduate through the love of football. Went on to obtain a nurses aid certificate, had hopes and dreams of becoming a male nurse
- Great childhood, good education, high school athlete, partial football scholarship to Ferris State, then lost focus—missed friends, didn't want

to be three-and-a-half hours away from home. Grades went down, lost my scholarship, eventually kicked out. Wish I had gone to community college first year (after high school graduation).

- No job growing up, only chop cotton and pick pecan. Well, my mother was a drunk. . . . So I drank. Went to school to eat food and play. I never read a book. . . . My father (who he met and moved in with at 18) had a drug habit. I used drugs. I get two kids—I use to smoke dope and trick the girls. So now I have two trick babies and I left them. In and out of jail, rehabs and homeless shelters was my way of life. . . . I went to Kalamazoo probation enhancement program 18 times that taught me how to live. Oh, I graduated at Kalamazoo Central High School. How, I don't know. One day I was getting my mind right, I thought—wow, why is all these people going to school and so I started going. . . . I came back to prison in 2007–2008 as a Parole Violator and I have started getting an Associate's degree and have 9 credit (Montcalm Community College CERT program, Continuing Education Units).

To repeat, out of the fifty-four participants in the six workshops, only fourteen had graduated high school, as described in excerpts from their personal stories above. Looking deeper at these fourteen, an examination shows only three out of the fourteen went to college immediately after high school graduation. Of those, one dropped out because he had a child to support and kept selling drugs and using drugs, another left college after getting into drugs, and one didn't finish the associates of arts degree. Three out of fifty-four even tried to go to college after high school graduation—and none of these three stories indicate the kind of *focus* required to "go to college and succeed."

The stories of the eleven high school graduates (HSG) who did *not* go on to college reveal individuals who are not typical "college-bound" students. HSG participant #1 has a rural poverty background with a mother who was a drunk and a father with an illegal drug habit; two babies from prostitutes; in and out of jail, rehab and homeless shelters due to his own addictions. It appears he learned enough "about how to live" from the Kalamazoo Probation Enhancement Program to complete high school—but he was prison-bound.

Five participants immediately sought a blue-collar job or a low-wage white collar or service sector job after high school graduation. One of this set sought adventure in travel and art internships. One participant had a child at nineteen and sold drugs. One participant did take graphic arts at Lenawee Vocational Tech in the eleventh and twelfth grades, but as an outcome of his dysfunctional "rebellion" outlook he went to prison soon after graduating high school.

The conclusion we can draw is that the 26 percent of the sample that completed high school were not focused and/or guided in their behavior into college or university undergraduate careers. If this was the case for those minority who did graduate high school, what are the personal stories of those forty in the sample who *did not* graduate high school? List 4.2 presents some of their profiles.

List 4.2 Did Not Finish High School. Profiles or patterns of causes or contexts of school failure and dropping out reported from 76 percent of workshop participants who did not finish high school include:

- Went through juvenile justice education—"Went to school in Juvy" (county facility); Parents having marital issues, divorce, single parent— "I had stress with schooling"; Report of being a child bully—e.g., "I was a 3rd grade bully and things got worse"; Social promotion—"The teachers promoted me to next class just to get rid of me."
- Rural poverty background—"My parents lived on a farm, I did farm chores. School was a big adjustment and I didn't put aside enough time for studying."
- Social class differences—"Fellow students made school hard: 90 percent of students' households were considered upper class . . . my parents managed to scrape together enough to rent a decent house on the edge of town. I hated school. Every year I was treated worse and worse" (by fellow students).
- Lost focus—"I wasn't a stupid kid—I just lost focus and was bored"; high school, started "hanging in the streets"—"High School, it was cool. I got caught up running the streets—fast money, cars and girls. I did go to school but I wasn't focused like I should have been; high school immaturity—"I thought I was the man. You couldn't tell me anything. That's when I started to get into trouble more—drinking, smoking weed, breaking the law, doing dumb stuff."
- Middle school using drugs and alcohol—"I started drugs and alcohol, school work suffered, grades dropped"; middle school selling drugs— "I started selling marijuana and other drugs—locker raided, expelled several times, wound up in alternative school in High School"; became addicted—"Now, coming to the edge of death—overdosing on phentenal—and coming to prison," this now older prisoner, long in and out of prison, continues "and losing a 19 year old daughter. I've conceded. Admitted utter defeat. My addictions whopped my ass."
- Moved to new school and neighborhood—"Moved to whole new school with my mother. Moved again as entered 9th grade. Was a 'freshmore' and behind in school. Started taking drugs, was expelled"; Skipped school a lot (truancy)—"Being held back twice, once in 7th grade I felt like I was grown. Memories of high school are almost non-existent because I never went. Skipped a lot. I started to get into a lot of trouble."

- Inconsistent parental discipline—"My home life wasn't too strict. My parents divorced when I was 15. I remember that's when I didn't even make it to school anymore"; large family—"Three brothers and a sister, I am the youngest. With five kids my parents said: 'By the time for my education, they were wore out, therefore the discipline was absent.' Because of this in middle school I became involved with criminal activity while experimenting with drugs"; Parent incarcerated, physical abuse—"I enjoyed being acknowledged as one of the smartest throughout school. . . . Middle school was the same until after my mom got incarcerated halfway through 6th grade year. I moved in with my aunt and switched schools. I went through a lot of abuse physically which weighed heavily on my mental."

A common pattern among white male prisoners' outlook is that they are uncomfortable with their low level of education. In a world where social and job expectations for speech patterns, advanced literacy, math, soft productivity skills at retail and service interactions are important, the male prisoner who is uneducated knows he is at a severe disadvantage. This pressure starts in school (MacLeod 1987/2008; Willis 1977).

Joy Dryfoos (1990) talked about school failure and dropping out *as a process.* One prisoner who did not finish high school said:

I went to class but hardly did the work. Teachers asked me what was going on. I always replied "nothing," coaches wanted to know why I didn't try out for any sports. I always replied "don't have time." I was beginning to lose interest in school. The street life was beginning to look good to me. And before I knew about school, I thought I was smart enough. I knew everything and nobody could tell me nothing. So the street became my life. There's only two things that will happen when you choose the street life: dead or locked up. In my case I got locked up and spent nearly 12 years of my life in prison "straight"—I guess the saying is true. When you're older you will look back and wish you could do your school years over.

Some high school dropouts want to change. After being in and out of prison, this thirty-year-old wants to take education seriously:

I ended up going to prison at age of 18. I obtained my GED in prison. I've been in and out now 3 times. This time getting out is different. I'm 30 years old and I do not want to end up back in prison. It's hard to get stable employment being a convict. I do want to further my education for myself and for my family. I do realize how serious my education is now and will not take it for granted anymore.

A careful look at the forty who did not graduate high school before prison finds a type of self-select prisoner who comes to an in-prison volunteer program like the two-hour "Going to Community College after Release" provided by the author at their prison. A disproportionate number of prisoners who have sought self-improvement will come to these presentations (a "self-select" in terms of research sample). In prison, then, offering a volunteer class, you will meet some of the prisoners who have really pushed to get an education:

There were a lot of problems at home that existed all along. I just started to take notice of them.

High school was the period where I feel I started to become a man, while I was still attending school, I was spending more time away from home and around older guys who were getting into trouble. The trouble from them was so much so that after the 10th grade I elected not to return to school and join the Navy instead.

It was in the Navy that I got my G.E.D. it's at this point that I need to back up a year or two. I recall a bus from Inkster so Ypsilanti where I shared a seat with an elderly black man who asked if I was returning to college. My reply was "no." He then said: stay in school son and go to college, even if you only take one class that class will stay with you for the rest of your life. I always remembered that. I believe that's where my desires for a college degree began.

Since that time I went to prison and actually, in 1983, I took my first prison college class, now in 2004 I got an associate degree and in 2006 I received my bachelors degree in general studies from Indiana University through a correspondence course, (pushing along while in prison) one, two, or three classes at a time.

John Irwin, writing about the last thirty-year trend toward the "warehouse prison," observes that:

An increasing number of prisoners choose to radically change their lives and follow a sometimes carefully devised plan to "better themselves," "improve their mind," or "find themselves" while in prison. Improving oneself may start on a small scale, perhaps as an attempt to overcome educational or intellectual deficiencies. The initial, perfunctory steps in self-improvement often spring the trap. Self-improvement activities have an intrinsic attraction and often instill motivation that was originally lacking in the prisoner.

In trying to improve themselves, prisoners glean from every prison source available. They read philosophy, history, art, science, and fiction. Besides this informal education, they often pursue formal education. Convicts can complete grammar school and obtain a GED in the prison educational facilities. They can attempt to learn a trade through vocational training programs or prison job assignments, augmented by studying trade books, correspondence courses, or journals. They study painting, writing, music, and other creative arts. There are some options for these self-improvement pursuits sponsored by the prison administration, but these are limited. (Irwin 2005: 108)

Many prisoners have been incarcerated for selling drugs and becoming implicated in the violence that attends the illegal drug trade. As this next prisoner essay reveals, there is some truth to the prison wardens saying: "Burn a few years off them, (in prison sentences), and they will change."

#####

Prisoner Essay 4.4

"I Am through with Selling" (10/9/08)
Here is a story about my life dealing with my educational point of view in grade school, middle school and high school. Grade school I was always into something bad—never wanted to be there. Never took time to study, but I passed all my classes. Education was not for me. Despite me being expelled a lot, I did barely pass to middle school.

Middle school was the same as grade school. I was into selling drugs then. I sold weed, heroin and cocaine. I was expelled for being caught with weed in my locker—went through Juvenile courts and probation. Also I was kicked out of middle school because of it. It wasn't until I went through a Juvy school, which by me doing good I was then allowed to go back to a public school.

Once in high school I was the man, my own car, crib, I was selling a lot of drugs by then. Then one day about 2 months into school they raided my locker, they found more weed. I was supplying half the school. Someone told, I guess I was doing it too much. So I was kicked out of school for good. It was there that I decided I did not need school. It was when I turned 17 I was an adult. I was just turned 18 when I was sent to prison for attempted murder.

I came to prison in '88 was released in '98, came home. It was there that I wanted to do some good so I enrolled in K.V.C.C. (Kalamazoo Valley Community College). Man, I thought I had the streets back. I was in school for one semester and caught another case. Never finished school. Once again, never finished, wanted to but never had the chance. I am about to be released Jan 13, 2009. I am through selling. I want an education. I have a GED.

#####

The kind of bitter belligerence characteristic of some prisoners, and its context, is on display in the next essay, as well as the growing conviction that there is more to life than crime.

#####

Prisoner Essay 4.5

"Who's To Say You—The Police, Judge, Government—Could Raise Me Right?" (11/9/08)

I was a good kid in elementary all the way through mid-school till I reached junior high. In junior high I started using drugs and alcohol, so by the time I reached high school I dropped out. The streets were calling. Not only did I have a drug problem, I had an addiction or an urge to get into criminal activity and behavior. Selling drugs is what I began to do in my spiral toward a path that led to jail and prison. Somehow I convinced myself that what I was doing was right, and everyone who opposed me, or thought wrong of what I did, was wrong. They did not understand me or my ways. I felt the laws I was breaking were put there to get a cut of my work or control me. My father was never there so to me, if he was not there to control me or raise me right, who's to say you—the police, judge, government, etc.—could control or raise me when my father would not. Now after I have almost a decade in prison or jail I realize there is much more to life than what I have led. I obtained my GED and have since then pursued college. I have learned a lot about people, I taught myself how to cut hair and believe I am one of the best at doing that and much more but I learned more about myself than I ever knew. I know now that I want more out of life than what I have gotten so every day I pursue that and pray that I get more out of life than I have, not only for me, but also for my two children. I need to be there for my children.

I have taken a vocational training class in business education and now would like to go to school to get my barbers license. I will teach my children as a father, knowing my father was the streets and the streets made me a better man then I was yesterday, and I will be a better father than my father is today. One thing I can say is my mother has always been there and she played both mother and father position and is stronger than any man I know today.

#####

As John Irwin noted in his 1970 book *The Felon*, some prisoners are very interested in gleaning—getting any information or programs that can help them. Some struggle with large families and little job training.

#####

Prisoner Essay 4.6

"Looking for Skill Training That Can Support a Large Family" (11/9/08)

I started grade school at 4 years of age, I remember lying to my kinder garden teacher telling her I knew how to tell time, I remember that she asked me what time it was at that moment and needless to say I didn't know. I had to stay after school each day and wait on my older sisters to get out so she could take me home because in the 50's there were no such thing as buses especially for black, only plenty of footwork.

I was kind of smart so grade school was a breeze, junior high was pretty easy too. I just had to figure out how to get in trouble so I started running with the wrong crowd and doing crazy things that didn't make any sense whatsoever.

I quit high school and later ended up in the Michigan Training Unit (MTU) where I took a GED test and passed averaging, I think, 51 and also took up a machine shop course which I completed, consisting of blue print reading and learning to read different gauges for measurement, micrometrics, etc. I learned to operate lathes, milling machines, different grinder's, even surface grinders where you measured and machined different projects and materials within 100th of an inch. That went well because I liked machines.

I later went to Brooks Prison in the late 70's and took a course in food machinery where I learned to prepare different foods. Butchering different food portions, how to recognize and present them, also a course in sanitation. I found this was something that I enjoyed doing but, as far as work went, this was the problem area because the job just wasn't worth the chase as far as money went.

Recently I took a barber class in Kalamazoo at the college of barber and beauty but I had to stop because with 12 children I had to work a lot of over-time and I couldn't find time. Now there are only 5 children. I would love the opportunity to get back in school.

#####

People who are in prison typically have been heavy into drugging and drinking. The next prisoner, now an excellent gleaner of programs in prison, wondered if he had been made stupid by bad drug reactions?

#####

Prisoner Essay 4.7

"Stupid as a Result of Drug Use?"

I am currently a tutor in auto school and have been state certified in engine repair, electronics/electricity, heating and air conditioning, engine performance/tune up, and steering and suspension. I always convinced myself that though I was once smart in my childhood, I was now stupid and unable to learn and retain information as a result of a wide variety of drug use, including cocaine, methadone, mushrooms, acid, marijuana and alcohol to name a few. However, since I have taken this course in auto school from which prior to this facility I had absolutely no knowledge of cars whatsoever. I have realized that I am in fact still smart.

This list of accomplishments led me to enroll in two creative writing U of M classes here at Parnall, and also I am currently serving as a devotional member in my church, and co-facilitating a bible study group as well. I am very hungry for knowledge and refuse to stop climbing. Now that I am convinced I have an ability and a gift to learn, and/or help others learn, I am very serious about finding a way to get into some college classes to further my education, not only for the future of my two children and family, but for the sake of others around me, that maybe I may be able to reach or encourage. I am hoping that I will be able to obtain some helpful information to lead me in the right direction. At this point in my life, my days consist of not much more then constant studying and reading, any class that is posted in my unit, I am eager to be a part of. For there is one important thing, if nothing else, that I have learned here in my two-year stay, it's that there is always something new to learn. Even if not to benefit yourself, you may be able to pass on something to another. Someone once said, "Knowledge is key." I would have to agree to the 10th power! (Parnall in 2009).

#####

The same fifty-four prisoners who dropped out of high school show up in this set of eight 2-hour educational workshops as people who have become transformed—more mature, more focused on their need for advanced skills training and education, as displayed in the bullets below.

Excerpts reflecting transformation of fifty-four workshop participants toward a positive attitude about advanced skills training and education include:

- It wasn't until I came to prison that I got my GED and have now decided to further my education; I look back now and wish I would of went to a community college first year (this after losing focus at a four-year university)
- One thing I remember the most is how good it felt to get a test back with an A, or get good remarks on reports. I now know, that may be the only way I'll stay out of trouble—by getting my education on track. I am now currently enrolled in the Youthful Offender Program (YOP) and am taking courses through Montcalm Community College (MCC) for an entrepreneurial certification. I want, need to be educated and a

business owner; I came back to prison in 2007–2008 as a Parole Violator and have started getting an Associate's degree (through YOP/MCC) and have 9 credits.

- I signed up for and finished the (prison) building trades program, and then I was hired as a tutor for the program. I did excel in the program and worked there until the program was closed in 2003. I have taken many classes taught by other inmates and I did very well in all of them. [Note: in 2006 the MDOC required that all "prisoner taught" classes have a guard in the room—this put the damper on prisoner taught classes because the MDOC was often unable to dedicate a guard to a class sit-in duty]
- But now with 3 children I hope to get a new education, to get away from construction, which is a trigger to drink for me. I hope this will be my prison time for more education. And I hope to be a good example for my kids and myself.
- While in prison I did complete a course in horticulture and would like to continue education, possibly into social work or substance abuse counseling; In here I've changed a lot for the better. I got my GED and was involved in the auto school program.
- Now I'm 31 years old with no education or trade. I have received nothing from the prison system far as education goes. It may be too late for me to go back to school. But it's not too late for me to learn a trade. This is my last chance to build a life for myself.

As these quotes show, there are prisoners who, not having graduated high school before prison, get their GED in prison, and find themselves ready for—and interested in—advanced skills training and accredited PSCE (Tregea 1998, 2003).

State and federal legislators need to invest in prisoner skill training and education. Two dollars are saved for every dollar invested (CEA 2003). The prisoner that gets PSCE is better prepared for getting, and keeping, a job—and not returning to prison (Petersilia 2003).

There is, however, very little postsecondary opportunity in state prison correctional programming. After the 1995 elimination of Pell grant eligibility for prisoners, the 770 prison college programs, offered mainly through community college prison programs, collapsed.

Correspondence college programs are possible for only a very few prisoners and are out of reach for the vast majority who are too poor to pay the tuition. Pell grants have not been available to incarcerated prisoners since 1995. Also, many prisoners have never thought of going to college. When they arrive in prison, without a high school diploma and with a background of dropping out of high school to do drugs and crime, they find the other prisoners in the yard and housing units, with a similar past, also downgrade education. For most, their education was in the streets. Now, in the prison yard, their "jail-house education" starts—how to do crimes better the next time.

The prison college programs, where and when available, as well as strong vocational trades programs, become a counterweight to "jail-house learning" through the role models and "alternative community" that formal education provides.

Given the poor educational background of state prisoners, it was an important investment by states to begin requiring work toward completing the GED as a condition of parole. This legislation passed and was instituted in Michigan in 1998. Several other states passed similar legislation. So, upon entering prison, most state prisoners need to start working on their GED (an equivalent to high school diploma).

However, in today's job market, there are very few, if any, good jobs to be had with just a high school diploma or GED. From the 1950s to the 1980s there were manufacturing jobs with good wages and benefits that could be had right out of high school. However, in recent decades, the United States has shifted from 70 percent service economy and 30 percent manufacturing in 1970 to a 90 percent service economy and only 10 percent or less manufacturing by 2013. Moreover, the large corporations in the manufacturing sector have, over the last thirty years, pushed jobs out of the large plants into a network of smaller manufacturing suppliers with a just-in-time inventory system and these smaller parts suppliers jobs pay much less, and also tend to want some manufacturing-specific skills courses from a community college.

As the factories downsized and outsourced, the unions downsized (lost membership) and became less powerful. Wages and benefits have been negotiated steadily downward so that now, with a "two-tier" system, new employees entering manufacturing have a much lower wage (from $27 an hour in the past down to $13–17 an hour currently).

Do the math. A forty-hour work week times 50 weeks a year equal 2,000 hours a year. At $27 an hour full-time manufacturing work times 2,000 hours brought into the household an annual $54,000 plus overtime and benefits, so that an average steel or auto worker could expect to make over $60,000 a year. However, new manufacturing employees coming in at $13 an hour would gross, as an individual, $26,000 to $30,000 a year. That is a "Low Economy Budget" (Schwartz and Volgy 1992)—and it's a tight household budget. Typically a person in this situation needs to find a second, part-time job and/or marry someone with an second income. More than 45 million people—the "working poor"—live at the individual income, or under, $30,000 a year, as of 2010. Try doing a household budget for an urban family of four—the poverty level is currently $24,000. How much for rent? For utilities, food, car, medical/dental, clothing, and other necessary items? Thirty-thousand dollars a year is not enough, so people have needed a two-income budget to run a household and to raise a family over the past thirty years.

In the 90 percent of the labor market that is the service sector, there are basically two kinds of jobs: low wage without benefits and good jobs with high pay and benefits. The good jobs require advanced education beyond the high school diploma. That is, good jobs require a professional certificate or concentration from a community college, a trade apprenticeship, a bachelor's degree, or a master's degree or professional training such as doctor, dentist, veterinarian (medical school and internship), lawyer (JD), or professor (PhD).

The in-between, or "average" salary jobs such as police, firefighter, corrections, electrician, and other trades (around $17.50 an hour) averaging $35,000 a year, as entry-level salary, up to $60,000 a year with overtime and pay grade increases. These are good stable occupations but are limited in number. And, over the period 2001–2013, public sector jobs have been subject to cuts as state budget crises occur.

The stability of manufacturing jobs and of jobs generally, has decreased in the last thirty years, as corporations developed "pulsating forms" that hired in low-wage temporary and contingent employees during a boom, keeping a smaller set of core employees with better wages, benefits, and training. Then, when the economy contracts—as in a recession—the corporation eliminates the temps and contingent employees, and downsizes to weather out the bottom of the business cycles. Jobs used to be added back to the economy rapidly during the economic recovery phase. In the longest recession since the 1930s, the "Great Recession" (2008–2009 and continuing) this has not been happening. The "job machine" is not working to add jobs during a very weak recovery. Temporary jobs and part-time and contingent workers are frequently the kinds of jobs being added on during the recent "jobless recovery." As of the summer of 2013 profits for corporations have been going up since 2009 but jobs have been added to the economy only very slowly.

Technology has advanced, facilitating the corporations' decisions to invest in computers, servers, software, robotics, telecommunications, and so forth to increase productivity. But this has occurred in a way that, generally, reduces wages, eliminates jobs, and may even involve outsourcing once remunerative white collar jobs or information technology jobs overseas to lower wage China or India. Getting a "good job with a big corporation" is much harder in twenty-first-century America than it was forty-five years ago.

As of mid-2013 the unemployment rate is staying above 7 percent. The "normal" unemployment rate of 4 percent is expected to rise. Having 7 percent of the labor force unemployed may continue for several years. Each percent of unemployment over the normal rate is approximately 2 million workers. So, for instance, with 7 percent unemployment rate, the unemployment number is 6 million people. This is a vast number of people who are unemployed and seeking work, with no jobs in the economy for them. The true unemployment rate goes up to 17 percent if "discouraged workers" who have dropped out of the job hunt are counted. People have been required to remain unemployed longer—in this period (2008–2013) there were three to six people for every one job available. It takes a long time to find a job.

How are prisoners who encountered school failure and dropped-out—even if they've gotten the GED in prison—going to compete for jobs in this discouraging labor market? Further difficulties for state prisoners are that many state budgets have gone into crisis in the long recession and its slow job growth aftermath. Due to underlying structural imbalances (declining revenue, growing expenses, and spending), many states for the decade 2003–2013 have run annual deficits of several hundred million to several billion dollars. Cuts must be made each year to balance the state budget. The cuts include cuts to revenue sharing to the cities and counties—cutting city police and local sheriff departments along with school budgets. Michigan had its first state budget surplus in over a decade in 2013. The money mostly went to fix roads.

In the earlier, more munificent years of the 1990s, states ran up huge corrections budgets, through prison building and "tough on crime" laws. Michigan, and many other states, have a General Fund that includes higher education, corrections, Medicaid, and social services. Medicaid cannot be cut by federal law, and state social services have often been already cut 60 percent or more and cannot be squeezed further. Other state expenditures press on the budget, such as public employees' pensions, environment, roads, and health care. Ordinary state citizens and their families can be hurt—for instance, state public university systems have seen their budgets cut by the state legislatures and have had to raise tuition.

In the context of these state budget crises, there is pressure to cut even the minimal, existing, prison vocational and education programs. In Michigan there was a legislator who wanted to cut the prison GED program. In a meeting the author sat in on, the Director of Correctional Education for Michigan, Julie DeRose, argued with the legislator that people entering prison with third grade math and eighth grade English need the GED program just to get minimal job skills in the labor market (DeRose 2007). In 2010, pressured by budget deficits year after year where it's been necessary to cut in different areas, the Michigan Legislature cut the MDOC prison vocational education budget.

The author reported on the current status of correctional education in Michigan at the Lakeland Correctional Facility "Legislative Seminar" on August 21, 2010 (see author's narrative 4.2, below). This seminar, organized by the National Lifers Association (NLA), had five state representatives, and two academics, Lora Lempert of University of Michigan–Dearborn, who is the "Prison Inside-Out Exchange" coordinator for Michigan, and the author. Included among the state representatives was Alma Wheeler-Smith (D-Detroit), who had just withdrawn from the governor's race due to lack of financing. She is knowledgeable about prisoner and related tax-payer issues surrounding prisons. Turning a state Department of Corrections (DOC) and its forty prison wardens around toward more prisoner education programs is like "turning a battleship." This is the speech I gave to the two hundred assembled prisoners and legislative guests that day.

#####

Author's Narrative 4.2

"Getting Michigan Prison Wardens to Support Prisoner Skills Training and Education Is Like Turning a Battleship" (8/21/10)
Eighty percent of Michigan prisoners enter prison with no high school diploma, no job skills, and many reading at 8th grade level and with less than 3rd grade math skills. Michigan Department of Corrections (MDOC), with a prisoner population of 45,000 has 13 vocational programs—such programs as custodial, food service, horticulture, auto mechanics, computer repair, and building trades. Any one prison may have only two or three of these programs. Of the 14,000 prisoners released from MDOC each year only 25 percent, or 3,500, have received any vocational training beyond the GED. Most of these are custodial, food service, and horticulture training. Julie DeRose is the MDOC Director of Correctional Education. In addition to MDOC vocational programs there are also a handful of volunteer post-GED instructors and a small federal Youth Offender Program (YOP). The Youth Offender Program delivered through Montcalm Community Colleges' CERT program uses a small amount of federal funds (under $800,000) to provide a 19 credit postsecondary business education program for 200–250 prisoners a year, or less than ½ percent. In other words, in today's tight labor market less than ½ of 1 percent of Michigan prisoners returning to society have any access to community college training.

I am on the MPRI Steering Committee for Lenawee County. I go into the prisons and teach a workshop about "How to get Pell grants and go to community college upon release." Getting a job upon release is getting harder and getting some vocational training is important. So I interviewed Barbara Levine, Executive Director of Citizens Alliance on Prisons and Public Spending (www.capps-mi.org) on Wednesday, August 18th, 2010. Barb Levine mentioned she had

heard Julie DeRose speak a few months earlier at a re-entry meeting about how they're redoing their vocational education programs to fit better with the kinds of jobs people can actually find when they get out. I don't recall her giving a lot of specifics. But I was wondering if this was a spin as a cover for cutting back. It's one thing to bring programs up to date and eliminate training for jobs that don't exist anymore, But: if they're just eliminating the more expensive programs or aiming at the lowest common denominator, this sounds really regressive and counter-productive. I would encourage you to try and reach her and press hard for details.

Dena Anderson is an associate of Barb Levine at CAPPS. Dena has been a reporter for the *Lansing State Journal* and has long followed prison issues. I also interviewed her the same day. She said:

It seems they are cutting vocational education programs. To get support for prisoner vocational education you have to find a sympathetic legislator. They can put a requirement for vocational education/job training into the boilerplate of legislative bills or the budget.

I asked her, with the recent downsizing of Michigan's prison system from 51,000 to 45,000, why we couldn't get some of the money saved shifted to investments in prevention, such as advanced skills training and education. She replied:

Yes, that is a good question: Why, if the prisoner population is down 6,000, why are we not able to reduce the MDOC budget (and spend more on vocational education?) The MDOC budget is the same now (at 45,000 prisoners) as it was when they had 51,000 prisoners. What are the expenses? CAPPS is going to make this one of our next projects—to get an answer to this. They are not only cutting vocational programs, there is now no ketchup, no coffee for prisoners, and they've raised prices in prisoner's concession. They're trying to squeeze the prisoners.

So, I interviewed Julie DeRose, director of correctional education for the MDOC, on Thursday, August 19, 2010 and she described some of the current directions and issues for prisoner education:

She states that she has been constantly pushing her "Career-Employment Committee" and even her "Academic Committee" to look at trends in jobs out in the economy. For instance, there is some push from prisoners for cosmetology school or health care training, but those are jobs that ex-felons are not allowed to take. (This is due to laws prohibiting ex-felons from entering certain occupations). She has been following closely DLEG (Dept. of Labor and Economic Growth) 2014 projections: some jobs dying out. And there is a need for MDOC to improve and upgrade on trades.

A criticism she has is that some wardens push for just three types of vocational trades: horticulture (because they want plants along the walkways), food technology (to help run the kitchen), and maintenance (to keep the place running). She says persuading wardens and others in the MDOC and the legislators to have better vocational training for prisoners is like "turning a battleship"—hard to change a big system. But jobs oriented to caring for the prison (custodian, cook's helper, gardener) are not necessarily the right focus for most formerly incarcerated persons reentering the labor market.

Julie DeRose also stated that "keeping prisoners busy is not helpful." More important is to have or encourage prisoners to be taking apprenticeship with national certification. She emphasized that "most of our trades have national certification and promise of employment" (e.g., electrician, building trades).

She mentioned that she has been following two regional economic areas: southwest Michigan, which has a need for tool and die, but the MDOC program for tool and die is in facility near Hammond, Michigan and that some of those released from the Ionia area are heading to Southwest Michigan for the tool and die jobs.

There is a growth in hotel and hospitality in South East Michigan.

But, because in any facility we have a hodgepodge of prisoners: some in a facility want tool and die, some want hospitality, and other types of jobs, but in any one prison there are not programs for all the prisoners.

She is looking into a new job-growth area of "Warehouse management"—it's a matter of getting MDOC vocational programming funding. "We're keeping our ears to the ground, for opportunities—we're not teaching any voc tech that's completely right on the labor market, yet we're trying to be more responsive."

"There is direct opposition to prison education from the way prisons are run" (prisoners are not supposed to get helpful things, principal of least opportunity/privilege). "We've stayed the course . . . but. . . . "

I asked Julie DeRose: "So you've got GED, you've got the old YOP/CERT 18 credit business certificate (CEU) through Montcalm C.C. that serves about 200, and then you've got the 13 voc tech programs with two, three, or four in each prison. You've got a hodgepodge of prisoners in each facility, each with different vocational needs, and in each facility there are not vocational technical programs for each category of prisoner interest. If you had a 'wish list' what would be on that list?"

Her answer was:

1. Our MDOC Correctional Education budget is being cut—need more money.
2. Space is an issue. Even if I had the money for a preparatory program I don't have space. So: need to evaluate the space (in the different facilities).

3. Also: regarding using prisoner education as part of MPRI Reentry, I would like to develop a social enterprise that pays prisoners a little to build and learn trades: Something like Peckham Center in Lansing. (For this presentation here at Lakeland Correctional I will try to clarify Julie DeRose's vision: She visualizes a large center for people with educational and vocational deficits or needs to train for the labor market. Such a "prisoners-in-training when they get out" center would be similar to the "area career centers" run by intermediate school districts, except this career center would pay a small wage to prisoners and would be for reentering prisoners. Julie DeRose described this as a kind of social enterprise—paid for by state taxes and perhaps foundations and be, presumably, for all reentering prisoners. The actual grounds and buildings could be as large as some city high schools, perhaps 1,500 "prisoners-in-training"—roughly 35 percent of returning prisoners. Perhaps this could work in conjunction with, or before coming to, the local county MPRI program.)

4. Julie DeRose went on to express a frustration about the need to "Get the prison administration to stop exploiting prisoner vocation programs, for their own institutional needs—e.g., horticultural program to get plants for walkways, custodial program to get maintenance of buildings, culinary arts program for the prison food service *only or primarily . . .* instead of more real vocational programs geared to the labor market."

5. She reported that, in her view, MDOC Correctional Education and prisons have fallen very short in the need to train prisoners. That reentering prisoner's need employment out there. And that there is a need to build bridges for the formerly incarcerated to transition, job-wise, to the labor market, in addition to the limited job support available through local MPRI Steering Committees. That there was a need for bridges to be built for prisoners to get the training and, as formerly incarcerated, get the training they need to get into jobs. (Again: Julie DeRose mentioned some kind of social enterprise that pays prisoners a little to learn trades, something like the Peckham Training Center in Lansing.)

There was a good round of applause for the fact that I had a rousing and critical opening piece for the "Legislative Forum," but the two hundred Lakeland prisoners probably did not feel reassured that anything positive would happen—what were the five legislators going to say?

#####

There has been good research on how, overall, getting some prison college reduces recidivism (return to prison). Some of the best research was done in the late 1990s by Stephen Duguid, from Canada's Simon Fraser University.

He and his colleagues broke down participants in that university's thirty-year prison college program (1970 to mid-1990s) (before prison college was eliminated in Canada) to find out "what's going on in the black box?" (the individual in the program). That is, how and why does prison college work for the individual? And for whom does it work and for whom does it not work? They found that, while prison college works for nearly all types of prisoners (murderers, serious assault, etc.), the profile of "28 year-old persistent property offender with a drug problem" did well in the program but then, after release, had a high rate return to prison (recidivism) (Duguid, Hawley, and Knights 1998; Duguid and Pawson 1998). The key to understanding this pattern lies in understanding how a brain disease such as alcohol or other drug addiction is a chronic relapse disease. Here is a representative prisoner story.

#####

Prisoner Essay 4.8

"Caught Up on the Drug Thing" (Parnall in 2009)
As a child growing up in Detroit, I really liked and enjoyed grade school. The educational factor played a big role in my life because both my parents did not have an education; they always wanted me and my sister to go to school. And with what I had learned I taught my mom how to write and my father when he was not working. I came to be incarcerated at age twenty four. I was at Cassidy Lake Technical School, doing three years for larceny from a building. I went to school while I was there, and received my GED in 1972. I also enrolled in Washtenaw community college taking up a few classes. I also attended other programs like small engine repairs at the Egeler Factory. I entered a program in math while incarcerated at Northern Michigan University called night-owl. I completed in two years later in machine tools. Yet after getting out of prison I never followed up on getting a job. I always looked for drugs, or got caught up on the drug thing.

#####

So, we could conclude that prisoners need both PSCE and prison-based substance abuse treatment.

REVIEW AND DISCUSSION QUESTIONS

1. What percent of Michigan state prisoners enter prison without a high school diploma or GED?

2. What are some reasons state prisoners enter prison without a high school diploma?
3. Do you feel that "working toward a GED in prison" should be a condition of parole? Why or why not?
4. What kinds of in-prison vocational certificates are typical in Michigan prisons?
5. Does getting PSCE help prisoners? Why or why not?
6. Make an argument for reinstating prison postsecondary (prison college) programs, and how would it be paid for?
7. What kind of social enterprise does the director of Michigan's correctional education department advocate for reentering prisoners?

5

The Individual and Crime

What predicts crime? Farrington and Welsh (2007) review the research on individual, family, and community levels of explanation of crime. They find evidence-based factors that predict crime at each level, and factors that prevent, or protect against, crime at each level (table 1.1). Farrington and Welsh found that at the individual level, a child is more at risk to be drawn into youth crime if there are certain factors in his or her life such as high impulsiveness, low empathy, certain types of personality and temperaments, and low educational attainment, along with, in some cases, low intelligence. The presence of these factors doesn't mean an individual will automatically gravitate into crime, but the research shows they increase the potential for an individual to gravitate into crime.

How can these individual level predictive factors be overcome? In their review of the prevention research Farrington and Welsh find that at the individual level the most effective crime prevention approaches are "preschool intellectual enrichment and child skills training programs." In reviewing the Farrington and Welsh findings it becomes apparent that protective factors for individual predictive factors are to be found at the family and community levels. That is, the school district, state education revenue sharing, and the federal "Head Start" program—family- and school-focused programs as well as community-level programs—must lend support. These crime prevention factors are not "individual" but rather "micro-system" (family and family support systems), and also "macro-system" (political, economic, and legal systems and policies).

The micro-system reality is that families do not stand alone. The proven protective factors have to be set in motion, for instance that the parents get their child in early childhood enrichment and child skills training (or that child protective services or foster care makes sure this happens). In examining cases where children get into the juvenile justice system or adult crime, the question can be asked: "Why wasn't the child involved in the proven protective factors early in life?" The answer may well be: "Because the parent was not involved enough in the child's welfare." This lack of parental caring about, or ignorance of, the child's welfare is known as child neglect.

#####

Prisoner Essay 5.1

"Child Neglect—Left to Raise Self" (2/18/09)
Growing up in my family was easy, and in my life now, I can see how that had something to do with my life of crime.

I had a father and a sister for parents. My father worked at GM so that means he was always gone, but I grew up with a lot of money. Everything I ever wanted, I was given, to make up for family time spent together that never happened.

With school, if I did not do good, so what? If I did not pass a grade, who cares? My sister acted as a mother to me but as far as school, she had her own life to worry about.

By the time I was 13, we moved to a bigger town and I was given everything needed to pass time, and have a blast, and raise myself. Kids with nothing to do and a lot to work with always found something to do.

As I got older, I spent my time going bigger and pushing the limits of the laws. At first, I did small crimes. With the family it was always a "Oh well don't do it again." So I would be smarter every time I went out. A kid left to control himself.

No matter what I did in home, at school, or on the streets, the money, time, and nothing to do, and no one to tell me not to do it, was an everyday reality for me. If someone did say "No," it was not anything I have dealt with so I said who are you to tell me that I cannot, or should not.

That there became part of my grown up thinking. Who can tell me not to do this or that? Wrong or right? I grew up making choices on my own. By this time I am grown—that was who I became: "My family factors are the lack of."

#####

In thinking about chapter 4, "Prisoners on Education: Selling Drugs and Dropping Out," many personal stories had common themes: "drugs, sex, and crime. Running the streets and hanging out with the wrong crowd." In prisoner essay 5.1 above the prisoner says, "I grew up making choices on my own." Where were the parents? The research cited by Farrington and Welsh shows individual predictive factors can be moderated through the involvement of a parent, mentor, or guardian (see also Higgins 1994). Such mentoring can intervene as a moderating factor to prevent low attainment by signing up the child for intellectual enrichment (Head Start, pre-kindergarten, etc.) and enrolling in short, "child-skills training" programs. But for these prisoners many of their parents taught them criminality.

#####

Prisoner Essay 5.2

"What a Child Is Learning: Parents Taught Criminality" (2/18/09)
As I look back at growing up the way I did it is obvious that I was raised wrong. But to me it was life. In other words I never had any other life. I grew up in the projects. My father was addicted to alcohol. My older brother was murdered during a robbery that went wrong. My father was very abusive, both physically and mentally. And my mother and I was his favorite victims. I grew up in the era of time where crack was destroying the black community. Not only did I see the change, I personally felt the effects.

My parents had no idea of how to raise children. And their personal habits interfered with any desire they may have had to learn. I watched them, and learned from them. I learned how to be compulsive. I learned how to be irresponsible and the abuse only feed my insecurities. I had no self-love and no confidence. And to make matters worse the school was telling my mother that I had a learning disability. My parents seen that as an opportunity to scam the state as a means of getting checks and it worked. Everything I was told about me I believed. It was not until maybe 5 years ago that I realized that I actually don't have a learning disability. I just was not being taught. I can still recall being in the fourth grade and not knowing how to tell time. Nor did I know left from right—because no one had taught me.

But I knew how to steal. Because someone had took the time to teach me how to steal and I picked up on it fast. I knew what drugs looked like. Everything I was learning in my home was only preparing me for a life of crime. There was no interest took in my education, instead my father sat me down and showed me how to steal crack. My mother taught me how to deal with the cops if I was ever questioned about a crime. I do not know anything, I have not seen anything, and I have not heard anything.

There was a lot of time and interest spends in assuring I know how to be a criminal. And no time spent in teaching me how to live right. I do not blame anyone for the decision I made. I just understand how important it is to pay attention to what a child is learning, and the benefit of having good role models. And I am the outcome of not having good role models—and when no attention is paid to what the child is learning.

#####

Consider the questions of "free will" and "determinism" in prisoner essay 5.2. Can we consider such a neglected child who, at age three or four or five received no "preschool intellectual enrichment" or "child-skills training programs," an adult? Do they "choose" their life? Yes, but without access to enrichment or training. They can only choose from the context they are presented with.

From the perspective of child developmental psychology and ethics, is a child an adult at ages nine, ten, or eleven? Is a child fully adult at twelve, thirteen, or fourteen years of age? Clearly there are *degrees* of maturing and free will.

Our justice system is separated into two systems based on these degrees of maturing and free will—an adult (either seventeen or eighteen and over) and a juvenile (sixteen or seventeen and under). This separation is based on the assumption, derived from advances in knowledge about child developmental psychology around 1900 to 1925, that began to consider children and youth as different from adults. Children sixteen and under are assumed to be still developing and not fully mature. This led to the juvenile justice system, first initiated in Illinois in 1899. The idea is that children under seventeen are not fully adult and have the developmental right to learn from their mistakes. Thus they are treated differently in a juvenile justice system rather than as an adult in the adult system.

Consider three- and four-year-olds: the research is conclusive— "childhood enrichment" and "good parental supervision skills" are relevant for preventing later crime. One thing that is developing in the child is the capacity for rational thought. At what age do children develop enough rational thought to be considered an adult under the law? Most states choose the age of seventeen to be treated as an adult; that is, going to adult jail instead of juvenile facility, sentenced as an adult, adult probation, prison. Criminal law requires, in the elements of a crime, that there be "criminal intent." Where does criminology fit into this legal concept? Much of criminology theory studies "influences" that shape individual behavior. Children under seventeen are assumed to not have a full and clear capacity for criminal intent.

The phrase "crime is a young person's game" summarizes the known fact that most crime is committed by fifteen- to twenty-five-year-old males. Figure 5.1 indicates the relationships between types of crime and age of offender.

Are youth and very young adults, emerging from developmental stages as children fully rational? The law has to draw the line somewhere, and has chosen seventeen or eighteen, but recent research suggests people are not fully adult until ages twenty-eight or so.

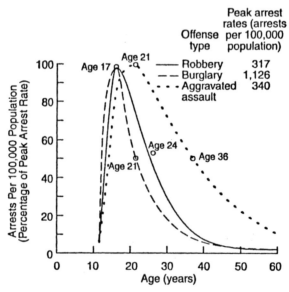

Figure 5.1. U.S. Age-Specific Arrest Rates (arrests per 100,000 population of each age for 1983). *Source*: Alfred Blumstein and Jacqueline Cohen, "Characterizing Criminal Careers," *Science* 237 (August 28, 1987); reprinted with permission from the American Association for the Advancement of Science.

RATIONAL CHOICE, THE INDIVIDUAL, AND DETERRENCE

Formal criminology theory begins with the *classical rational* school of thought. Cesare Beccaria, writing in 1764, views people as "free agents, pursuing hedonistic (self-interested) aims, and able to rationally decide on all or most courses of action." This historical era of "rationalism" emerged before the advent of scientific psychology and child developmental psychology. In the feudal period and in the revolutionary transition into rationalism, children were considered as "little adults." As Trojanowicz and Morash describe,

> The punishment was supposed to fit the crime and such factors as offender age or background characteristics were not to be considered. . . . Succinctly stated, the classical school said that "Crime involves a moral guilt, because it is due to the free will of the individual who leaves the path of virtue and chooses the path of crime, and therefore it must be suppressed by meeting it with a proportionate quantity of punishment." (1992: 40–41)

It is true that in good parenting there is discipline and consequence for bad behavior. The contemporary assumption is that family processes are learning contexts and children are assumed to be developing their will-training and abilities to be responsible. Children are not considered as little adults but, rather, as developing in their maturity. But for the "rational choice" early crime theorists, their focus was on the emerging critique of feudalism, the prior social order. They "were primarily concerned with legal and penal reform rather than with formulating an explanation of criminal behavior" (Akers and Sellers 2009: 17). That is, they were concerned with designing a more rational adult world. They were revolutionaries overthrowing the ancient regimes of feudalism, wiping away kings and lords and arbitrary justice. They would, in the American Revolution (1776) and Constitutional Convention (1787) and in the French Revolution (1789) establish *elected* legislatures and *public* law, rationally debated in deliberative bodies.

The assumptions about behavior of these political, economic, and legal philosophers primarily reflected the rationalism of that period. Their perspective reflects a philosophy of free will rather than determinism. By reforming the "arbitrary, biased, and capricious" law of those days into publicly enacted laws, where the severity of punishment fit the crime, and the certainty and speed of punishment was assured, this theoretical orientation—assuming a rational individual—emphasizes that the would-be-criminal will "think twice," assess the punishments and certainty of punishment and, by choice (free will), will adjust his or her behavior. The laws, thus reformed, would act as specific deterrent for that person and as a general deterrent for others.

In reading these life stories and the prisoners own reflections on the causes of crime does free will and careful consideration of the consequences figure strongly in their life histories? Recall prisoner essay 1.1, "Children are living an illusion, tricked into thinking they're full grown," Al's house was the rendezvous place for his oldest brother's friends to divide up the spoils from stealing and robbing. Al grew up during the years when he was younger than twelve, being rewarded for being tough, answering the door, giving directions to older people. In prisoner essay 1.2 the two brothers and sister grew up with alcoholic mother and a household of serious neglect: no food, lack of cleanliness, no clean clothes, no parental supervision. They were "used to this. In fact, they didn't know any different." Were these situations "rational" lifestyles for children?

Prisoners learned from the way they were raised and, when they get to prison, find it hard to change. You, the reader, have grown up with a "way of life" learned in your family and among your neighborhood peers. Assume you were moving to a different country, a different culture. You would feel strange. It would be hard to learn the new culture. Would it be easy for you to change?

It is not easy for some of the prisoners, having grown up in homes of abuse and neglect, to change (Newbold 2003).

#####

Prisoner Essay 5.3

"Cops Killed My Father—I Have Lived On the Edge Ever Since" (2/18/09)
As I were younger I'd always felt as though I'd end up in prison because I became rebellious for reasons I cannot go into and in part that I had a very grudging dislike of police once I found out they killed my father. So I wasn't getting enough grades in school when I went. That was the problem, I didn't go enough. School wasn't no longer exciting to me. Stealing, robbing and just being in the streets became exciting to me. I have lived on the edge ever since, even when I know what I'm doing is wrong. It's exciting! Now I have to find something else in life.

#####

Prisoner essay 5.3, reflects an elemental rejection of police and the legal social order, an attraction to the excitement of stealing and robbing (Katz 1988), making a living by doing economic crime (Tunnel 2000), and being stimulated by hanging on the corner, spending money on the party-life, and of "just being on the streets" (Milton 2012). In *Burglars on the Job: Streetlife and Residential Breaking*, authors Richard T. Wright and Scott Decker (1994) interviewed ninety-five active burglars in the St. Louis area. They note that

> nearly three quarters of them—68 out of 95—said they used the money for various forms of (for want of a better term) high living. Most commonly, this involved the use of illicit drugs. . . . For many of these respondents, the desire to break into a dwelling often arose as a result of a heavy session of drug use. The objective was to get money to keep the party going. The drug most frequently implicated in these situations was "crack" cocaine. (38–39)

Lemert argues that once locked into such events (keeping the party going), participants experience considerable pressure to continue, even if this involves breaking the law. He labels situations like these "dialectical, self-enclosed systems of behavior" in that they have an internal logic or "false structure," which calls for more of the same. Lemert, as quoted in Wright and Decker (1994: 202), observes: "If midway through a spree a participant runs out of money, the pressures immediately become critical to take such measures as are necessary to preserve the behavior sequence" (1953: 303–4).

From my own observations in high crime neighborhoods, I believe Lemert's explanation of "the crime spree" is a good one. So, does "keeping the party going" strike you as a rational lifestyle? Is extending the concept of a one-night, once-in-a-while party into a three or four-day party each week, throughout the year seem a rational "adult" pattern? Or does it seem more like an "adolescent-prolonging" pattern—a juvenile, not yet grown up, not yet rational adult choice of lifestyle?

#####

Prisoner Essay 5.4

"Need Parental Mentoring of Thrill Seeking Teens in Midst of Social and Economical Plague" (2/11/09)

Having been raised in a diverse cultural neighborhood bordering poverty on one side and mild housing and conformability on the other, youth's from both sides of track frequently commingled. What brought about this coexistence in my estimate was by-and-large excitement, experiment, curiosity, rebellious-ness and civil disobedience.

The demarcation line (between neighborhoods) was not etched in stone, it was more visible by the character of the individuals in relation to night clubs, liquor stores, dope houses, etc. . . . which were clearly visible as opposed a more quiet and family structured hood just blocks away where many of the curious youths such as myself came from.

During the summer months when school was out, we would sneak across town by using alleyways and short cuts through abandon buildings to reach our destination. In retrospect, it was if we were walking through an enemy mine field. On some occasions we would carry large sticks and broken bottles to fend off some of the wild hoodlums that roamed these grounds. Beside that, our biggest fear was the Detroit police.

I was introduced to this journey by a friend, a junior high school honor student whom I never suspected smoked cigarettes and drank wine. We would travel in a group of no less than six. Our objectives were the "Bamboo Bar" to see strippers perform. The thrill of making it though this labyrinth of destructions was 10 times greater than riding a roller coaster. The shock of being chased was more stimulating than diving in a fresh swimming pool of ice water.

The rush and thrill was my introduction to civil disobedience that ulti-mately leads to my life of crime. Ordinarily, only two to three weeks during these summer months did our community actually provide us other means of investing our time. Having time on your hand—that is what I honestly believe contributes to 50% if not 75% of the reasons why many youths go on to crime, the teenage thrill seeking venture, that increases more and more as the older they get.

Spending time is one of the most valuable keys parents, sibling, communities, teachers' etc. must diligently invest in all children. Timing the investment of attention to children—their entry into teenage years is the most critical and substantive portion of their lives in which these so-called turning points occur. In an attempt to minimize these acts, there must be a sound base of communication established between that child and his community. A sense of trust beyond truthfulness, but more so, a meeting of the minds between a father/mother and their son or daughter.

Another critical factor is that the community, teachers, clergy and like must all take part in this transformation. And despite all popular opinion, it can all change for the better or the worse in the blink of an eye.

No matter what community you come from, whether its Beverly Hills, CA or Harlem, NY, it's the mentality of those governing that community moral duty to ensure that each child is educated on the values of life. Only then, even in the wake of many of the immoral and attractive thrills that he or she may crave, this thrill-seeking phase will pass like the wind.

These few concepts are just the tip of the iceberg in assessing whether a child is capable to comprehending the nature of his conduct at such a young age. And yes, the community plays an integral role in saving this child as well as destroying this child. The failure of any given child is not only in part blamed upon the parents or lack of. It is a social and economical plague that also contributes to a child dysfunctional behavior resulting in incarceration.

#####

At the heart of the classical rational perspective in criminology is the concept of deterrence—the expectation that people will, in considering crime, "think twice" because the penalty is greater than the crime and/or an example has been made of others (those corrected). However, many youth and adults engaging in crime don't think about the punishment. In prisoner essay 5.3 the prisoner reports that "School wasn't no longer exciting to me. Stealing, robbery and just being in the streets became exciting to me." In prisoner essay 5.4 the prisoner recalls the thrill of going through the alleyways to the "Bamboo Bar" and that "The rush and thrill was my introduction to civil disobedience that ultimately leads to my life of crime." It may seem understandable that youth will be affected by excitement rather than rational caution, but adult criminals also choose in nonrational ways. As Shover and

Honaker (1992) report, in their interviews with active burglars, most did not think about getting caught. They note:

> If the potential legal consequences of crime do not figure prominently in crime commission decision-making by persistent thieves, what do they think about when choosing to commit crime? Walsh (1980; 1986) shows that typically they focus their thoughts on the money that committing a crime may yield and the good times they expect to have with it when the crime is behind them . . . (saying "I didn't think about nothing but what I was going to do when I got that money, how I was going to spend it, what I was going to do with it, you know"). (21–23)

Shover and Honaker thus emphasize that, in contrast to overly rational choice theories of crime, the decision making of persistent property offenders occurs "in the context of the lifestyle that is characteristic of many of their ranks: life as party." Some prisoners agree with this analysis, but other prisoners disagree.

#####

Excerpt 5.1

"Selling Drugs, Robbing—It's Not 'Life as a Party,' It's a Job"
I'm not condoning or siding with the criminal, but I find it difficult to say or agree with the "life as party" concept. The criminal in his mind has a job— selling drugs, robbing, etc. . . . and the money he earns from his "job" he will, like another human being, buy the best he can with his "paycheck"

#####

This economic type of thinking—"the criminal in his mind has a job"— reveals that *some* adults engaging in criminal behavior may be somewhat rational. There is money to be made selling drugs, robbing. Even going to prison can be seen as "part of the job." So some of the adults sentenced to an adult prison may be seen as rational within criminality chosen as "the life"—the risk (prison) is still worth the benefit (the money to be made from criminality). As one incarcerated individual said: "I took a gamble with my life and lost." But for other adult prisoners, criminality may be better seen as part of an irrational lifestyle—"life as a party."

Consider a young teenager. Is he or she choosing criminality in a rational sense? Trojanowicz and Morash observe that, for teens

> the *effect* of punishment is marginal in comparison to the *effects* of the availabil-ity of delinquent opportunities, the absence of censure from significant others,

the presence or absence of moral inhibitions, and the involvement in legitimate activity.

Aside from the issue of multiple influences on delinquency (there are) several other considerations (in understanding deterrence). First, it is not so much the objective level of punishment that is used in a family, court, or correctional setting, but the youth's *perception* of the speed, certainty, and severity . . . (of punishment).

A second problem . . . is to measure the deterrent effect accurately. . . . Perceived risk that is measured at some time period before the offense occurs can be changed dramatically through interactions with peers and experiences in breaking the law. Thus, the finding of little or no connection between perceived risk and delinquency may be a result of a sudden change in perceived risk just before the offense is committed. (1992: 52–53)

If you were a young teen and your parents were economically strapped, both working, and not giving you supervision, and your family was without the funds for the "more stuff" you wanted, and the older kids gave you a way to make money, what would you do? Probably you would say "No" to these "friends." But did that responsible decision come from your parents help along the way, raising you to "make good choices?" In this story below and other stories in this book the parents are not there to help develop maturity—"Most of the work for that (developing maturity) was left up to us (kids)."

#####

Prisoner Essay 5.5

"Older Kids and Friends Gave Me Way to Make Money" (2/11/09)
When I was growing up my family was somewhat poor but not poor. Everyone that could work had to work. That left even less time for the grown up's to raise the kids—so most of the work for that was left up to us. We were sent to school not so much as to learn as it was a for sure, cheap, babysitter.

In school you had three groups that stood out to me, the rich kids, poor kids and the not so much of either. Like I said I was down towards the lower half of the groups. So things didn't come so easily to me. You have to work extra hard to make even.

By the time I hit my early teens I was wanting a better life already. So when the older kids gave me and some friends a few ways to make money and have people think we were cool, it was the best anyone has offered us so far.

By the time I hit 20 most of my friends were locked up, dead, or just gone. I found myself looking at a prison sentence for selling drugs and stolen goods.

My family had turned their back on me long ago, so I was on my own. My only wish was that I could do it all over again, turn back time and start all over.

#####

Parents work with both free will and determinism models when they say: "Don't stay out late. I'm raising you to make good choices, to be a responsible young man—and who are those friends you're hanging out with?" The child is learning to be responsible (developing will-power through enhanced free will to know when to come home) but the bad friends can influence him (influences are a kind of determinism).

Sometimes the individual's capacity for free will is altered before birth (fetal alcohol effects), or by later life traumas (post-traumatic stress disorder [PTSD]: emotional memories, obsessive thinking, and flashbacks). Addiction, for instance, starts out as a choice but often becomes a chronic relapse brain disease. Birth defects, life traumas, psychotic-like drug reactions (e.g., PCP) and addiction are biopsychological individual level causes of behavior, including an increased potential toward criminality.

THE INDIVIDUAL, BIOLOGICAL THEORIES, ADDICTION, AND CRIME

Biological criminology emerges out of the turn toward "positivism" and science (1820–present) that occurred in the Western world after the "age of rationalism" (1740–1820). In the early nineteenth century the legal reforms connected to the American and French Revolutions had been accomplished. Penal reforms replaced the bodily tortures of the feudal period with the penitentiary (Clear, Cole, and Reisig 2009; Foucault 1979). Crime, it was now thought, could be studied by scientific methods.

Einstadter and Henry note, unlike the philosophic assumption of a (free will) rational person—a view characteristic of classical rational criminology—that, from the biological or positivist perspective:

Social phenomena, including crime, can be studied scientifically using methods, techniques, and rules of procedure derived from the natural sciences with the aim of identifying the key causes and making predictions about crime patterns with a view toward prevention (Muncie, 2001: 212; Gottfriedson and Hirschi, 1987: 10). Reviewing the positive philosophy of one of its founders, August Comte, Kolawoski (1972) asserts that:

[Positivism] asks how phenomena arise and what course they take; it collects facts and is ready to submit to facts. . . . It's sole aim is to discover invariable universal laws governing phenomena in time and for this purpose, it makes use of observation, experiment, and calculation. . . . The positivist mind presupposes a deterministic interpretation of phenomena. . . . The essence of positivism in criminology was well expressed by Barnes and Teeters (1943: 174): "Not until we recognize the fundamental truth that the individual is made a delinquent by forces beyond his control operating on his structure, can we make much progress in understanding such behavior and correcting it."

Clearly positivism allows for such forces to emanate both from within and outside the individual. We shall discuss the ideas of sociological positivists who see these forces emerging primarily from outside the body/mind as part of a pathological social context in later chapters. Here we're concerned with those theories that see predisposing criminal forces primarily located within the individual. (Einstadter and Henry 2006: 75)

For instance, we've mentioned "fetal alcohol effects" as an example of biological roots to later criminal behavior.

So, a person may be affected by a biological process (fetal alcohol effects, an alcohol-related neurodevelopmental disorder involving the central nervous system) developing some degree of mental retardation, and behavioral and learning problems (Abadinsky 2008: 122–23). These biological effects then produce a child who is more *predisposed* to school failure and the dropout process (see chapter 4). Such a child may frustrate teachers more, and tire out their parent(s), leading to a predisposition to be influenced by peers "in the street" and gravitating toward crime. Protective or prevention factors would include involved parent(s) who understand the fetal alcohol effects and take special care and more time with this child.

Addiction

The parent(s) of such a child, however, may themselves be affected by biological influences, such as addiction. (Why was the mother drinking during pregnancy? Because she was an alcoholic.) While the choice to take an addictive drug may be an example of free will, once the body is addicted to the drug, a degree of determinism takes over, and the body may develop a hypersensitivity to stress. Abadinsky observes that

Drug addicts . . . can often resist the cravings . . . for months. . . . But then there is a sudden relapse that addicts explain with statements such as "Well, things weren't going well at my job" or "I broke up with my girlfriend." . . . That they often relapse, apparently in response to what most people would consider mild stressors, suggests that addicts are perhaps more sensitive than nonaddicts to stress. . . . Chronic use of heroin, however, may increase hypersensitivity to stress and trigger a cycle of continued drug use when the effects of heroin wear off.

Research has shown that during withdrawal the level of stress hormones rises in the blood, and stress-related neurotransmitters are released in the brain. These chemicals trigger emotions that are perceived as highly unpleasant, driving the addict to take more drugs. Because the effects of heroin last only four to six hours, addicts often experience withdrawal three or four times a day. This constant switching on and off of the stress systems of the body heightens whatever hypersensitivity these systems might have had before the person started taking drugs. The result is that these stress chemicals are in a sort of hair-trigger release, surging at the slightest provocation. (Kreek, in Stocker 1999) (Abadinsky 2008: 94–95).

The toll that developing a chronic relapse brain disease like addiction has on even a highly educated person is made clear in prisoner essay 5.6, below. Those in prison for drug-defined (possession and sales) and drug-related (larceny, home invasions, robbing to support an addiction) crimes represent up to 40 percent of federal prison and up to 34 percent of state prisoners (21 percent of Michigan 2007 DOC). Yet, because the United States is so drastically punitive, criminalizing street drug addiction, addicts who've sobered up in prison are still seen as "criminals" (Terry 2003).

#####

Prisoner Essay 5.6

"Hopeless Desperate Addict When Sober a Pretty Normal Guy" (1/25/09)
During the course of my life I've worked numerous jobs and graduated with honors from Temple University in Philadelphia. When not caught up in hopeless desperate addiction I'm driven, benevolent and rarely am guilty of a traffic violation. Objectively, if you viewed my accomplishments and failures they would directly correspond to periods of sobriety and relapse. In no way am I without character defects but isn't it mildly conceivable that a large percentage of the modern prison system is filled with individuals who, while not sick, would be considered normal (i.e., un-criminal) by any reasonably intelligence person. However, now clean and imprisoned these people assume a position of guilt, shame, finger pointing and implication. "He is in prison" so the assumption is that there is something wrong with him; he is of weak normal fortitude, etc.

My own imprisonment has given birth to incalculable introspection. This soul searching has taken me from inconsolable rage and the feeling of profound failure to blaming a justice system that I feel has fundamentally declared war on its own sons and daughters by instituting bogus drug policies and treating addiction (a treatable medical condition) as a crime. The drug addict today is the modern leper and the prison the new leper colony. For lack of better solutions, concrete and fence create abject misery as a solution to the disease of addiction. It is the asylum, the chains, and electro-shock before the miracle of anti-psychotic medications. Prisons today are the futures' shame primarily because we live, more often than not, in fear, indifference and lack of empathy. Drug policies cause crime. Literally, drug laws cause acts of desperation in people addicted, who, after suffering the shame and humiliation of their disease are then further subject to irrational stereotypes, stigmas and prison.

I'm blaming, or so it may be read, yet I can't but conceive there must be a better way. Impulsive, yes, excitement seeking . . . of course, risk taker, etc. those traits may be a precursor to addiction. The factors highlighted in the chapter can be harmless, even likable qualities yet one step away from being declared of law morality, weak minded . . . sick. When you apply the factors of the chapter to addiction the behaviors they explain need further explanation. Those pre-disposed to addiction most often display the attributes of criminal behavior and of the "individual factors" when sick and distinct irony lies in that those behaviors predominantly disappear at the onset of sobriety.

When reading the chapter (on individual factors and crime) I feared at any moment to see Farrington and Welsh present stats of defined brow ridges, deeply sunken eyes and caliper readings of cranial dimensions as determining of future behavior. The statistics were mindless inconclusive data, that though numerically accurate failed to consider the sickness that causes most modern crime. Each crime has a context, a social aspect, a victim and a perpetrator but when the individual who commits the crime is delusional and sick it neglects away data on individual factors because that person is no longer sick or delusional and nonetheless becomes a data point in research that then assumes his actions while high are indicative of his sober, rational self.

#####

Another consequence of drug-taking behavior can be a "bad reaction." For instance, PCP use can alter the brain, producing (in a drug reaction) progressively disorganized thinking, even violent behavior, if not diagnosed and treated. Abadinsky notes: "Phencyclidine (PCP) is a "dissociative anesthetic . . . and (as a street drug) . . . is most commonly applied to marijuana . . . and smoked. . . . PCP is sold on the street by such names as 'angel dust,' 'ozone.'" (Abadinsky 2008: 162–65; Lerner 1980: 13)

Prisoners report that they "woke up" from a drug-induced daze to find themselves in prison and not remembering what happened. Other types of biological influences include PTSD and attention deficit hyperactivity disorder (ADHD). A young person growing up with chronic exposure to poverty and violence can develop PTSD from violent episodes in the home and the streets (Green 1993). Such rough experiences growing up can create a "trauma module" in the brain that, through exposure to violence and degrading experiences, develops a hard-wired network of neurons— an "emotional memory" (or a set of them), which can lead to behavior difficulties.

There is a set of causes working in sequence: environment-brain-behavior. The criminogenic environment of the youth has created a biological response in the brain (traumatic emotional memory) that now shapes the youth's behavior. Thus chronic exposure to poverty and violence is both a sociological determinism (growing up in a crime-infested inner-city neighborhood) and a (later) biological determinism (PTSD). In this "environmental case," the body is not born with predisposing factors, or develops criminal potential because of drug addiction, but becomes an individual who is crime-prone due to subsequent childhood traumas through family and neighborhood influences.

With regard to drug addiction, a similar progression from a free will state to a "determinist" state-of-being occurs. It is free will to choose to take a drug, but "prolonged drug use causes pervasive changes in brain function that persist long after the individual stops taking the drug." Once addicted the brain is altered. Addiction is a brain disease characterized by compulsive drug-seeking and use. As Alan Leshner, of the National Institute on Drug Abuse, notes:

> Not only does acute drug use modify brain function in critical ways, but prolonged drug use causes pervasive changes in brain function that persist long after the individual stops taking the drug. Significant effects of chronic use have been identified for many drugs at all levels: molecular, cellular, structural, and functional. The addicted brain is distinctly different from the nonaddicted brain, as manifested by changes in brain metabolic activity, receptor availability, gene expression, and responsiveness to environmental cues. . . .
>
> That addiction is tied to changes in brain structure and function is what makes it, fundamentally, a brain disease. A metaphorical switch in the brain seems to be thrown as a result of prolonged drug use. Initially, drug use is a voluntary behavior, but when that switch is thrown, the individual moves into the state of addiction, characterized by compulsive drug seeking and use.
>
> . . . Addiction is not just a brain disease. It is a brain disease for which the social contexts in which it has both developed and is expressed are critically important. . . . Not only must the underlying brain disease be treated, but the behavioral and social cue components must also be addressed. . . .

. . . [A]ddiction must be approached more like other chronic illnesses—such as diabetes and chronic hypertension—than like an acute illness, such as a bacterial infection or a broken bone. . . . Viewing addiction as a chronic, relapsing disorder means that a good treatment outcome, and the most reasonable expectation, is a significant decrease in drug use and long periods of abstinence, with only occasional relapses. That makes a reasonable standard for treatment success—as is the case for other chronic illnesses—the management of the illness, not a cure.

. . . An accurate understanding of the nature of drug abuse and addiction should also affect our criminal justice strategies. For example, if we know that criminals are drug addicted it is no longer reasonable to simply incarcerate them. If they have a brain disease, imprisoning them without treatment is futile. If they are left untreated, their recidivism rates for crime and drug use are frighteningly high; however, if addicted criminals are treated while in prison, both types of recidivism can be reduced dramatically. It is therefore counterproductive not to treat addicts while they are in prison. (Leshner 1997: 46–47)

On the other hand, ADHD appears to be genetically transmitted (inherited from parents). Unlike addiction, PTSD, or PCP reaction, some kinds of learning disabilities and ADHD are not acquired diseases.

#####

Prisoner Essay 5.7

"A Friend Finds out He Has a Learning Disability" (2/11/09)
I had a friend that went to the same school that I did when I was young. He was always getting bad grades and being held back. It got to the point that he gave up and started to get into trouble. He was called to the office at least once a week and had to stay after almost every day. Whenever I talked to him about it he would tell me he wished they would kick him out and get it over with.

From what I knew of his family things weren't much better. He had a single father who was never there for him. And a mother that passed away while he was still at a young age. The only time his father was there was when the school or police called. He opened up to me once and told me his father always made him feel like he was a failure and a waste of space.

No one ever took the time to sit him down and talk to see where the problem is. It wasn't until after he dropped out of school and he done some time (in prison) he found out he had a learning disability that with help and the right medication things could of turned out different for him. With the early detection he could of learned how to live a normal life and not been such a "waste of space."

So now (that he is in prison) the state has to dish out money to house, feed, and raise him. The cost for schools and meds that would of changed his life wouldn't cost a 10th of that. The need for early detection and treatment is a must. Also, community programs that can help where the schools and programs leave off. For that to work they must have programs for every student in every city and town. Not just rich white schools or out of the city counties. No Child Left Behind should stand for just that and go for everyone.

#####

Environmental Toxins

In a 2013 article titled "America's Real Criminal Element," in the magazine *Mother Jones*, Kevin Drum presents research evidence that charts the rise and fall of U.S. crime rates from the 1940s to 2010 and shows that it matches the rise and fall of lead in gasoline:

> The biggest source of lead in the postwar (post WWII) era, it turns out, wasn't paint. It was leaded gasoline. And if you chart the rise and fall of atmospheric lead caused by the rise and fall of leaded gasoline consumption, you get a pretty simple upside-down U: lead emissions from tailpipes rose steadily from the early '40s through the early '70s, nearly quadrupling over that period. Then, as unleaded gasoline began to replace leaded gasoline, emissions plummeted.
>
> Interestingly, violent crime rates followed the same upside-down U pattern. The only things different was the time period: crime rates rose dramatically in the '60s through the '80s and then began dropping steadily starting in the early '90s. The two curved looked eerily identical, but were offset by about 20 years. (Drum 2013: 31)

Kevin Drum further reports in his article on how several different researchers, including economist Rick Nevin (*Environmental Review* 2000, 2007*)*, Jessica Wolpaw Reyes (Harvard dissertation, late 1990s), Tulane University's Howard Mielke and Sammy Zahran (2013), all confirmed

> an astonishing body of evidence. We now have studies at the international level, the national level, the state level, the city level, and even the individual level. Groups of children have been followed from the womb to adulthood, and higher childhood lead levels are consistently associated with higher adult arrest rates for violent crimes. (Drum 2013: 32)

Drum explains that even miniscule amounts of lead affects the brain, increasing "the odds of kids developing ADHD," and "lower IQ."

> Needless to say, not every child exposed to lead is destined for a life of crime. Everyone over the age of 40 was probably exposed to too much lead during childhood, and most of us suffered nothing more than a few points of IQ loss. But there were plenty of kids already on the margin, and millions of those kids were pushed over the edge from being merely slow or disruptive to becoming part of a nationwide epidemic of violent crime. (Drum 2013: 33)

All of the biopsychological conditions that can predispose toward crime, whether genetic (fetal alcohol effects, learning disabilities, some mental illnesses) or acquired (trauma and PTSD, drug reaction, some mental illnesses, environmental toxins such as lead), are examples of determinism. That is, crime prevention research finds these conditions are a *predisposing factor*—a deterministic factor that increases the individual's potential for criminality.

Compare classical rational choice perspective, where everybody is assumed to be calculating rationally the benefit and the cost of doing a crime, with the psychobiological perspective, where there is a type of determinism, such as from a brain disease such as addiction (a chronic relapse disorder) that is also in the social or legal *context* of criminality or prisonization (Terry 2003). There are professional roles involved in the treatment of genetic and acquired biopsychological criminality—addiction counselors, professional counselors, mental health counselors, and psychiatrists who can prescribe appropriate medications. Most prisoners are in the "normal" range of psychological functioning. Yet, 16 to 20 percent of state prison populations are mentally ill and there are many people on probation, in prison, and on parole who are affected by genetic or acquired biopsychological conditions that may have been related to their crimes.

THE INDIVIDUAL PERSONALITY AND PSYCHOLOGICAL THEORIES OF CRIMINALITY

While biological determinism looks to chemical imbalances, birth defects, traumas, addiction, or environmental toxins effect on neurological functioning, psychological theories explain crime as an outcome of individual characteristics, such as personality development. Einstadter and Henry note:

> The central idea of psychological and psychiatric theories of criminal personality is that people are shaped by the developmental processes occurring

during their formative years, particularly their early childhood (age one through five), in ways that predispose them to crime (2006: 106).

In this view, most people receive effective socialization. They are "adjusted" to their society.

Some children, however, are considered to be inadequately socialized or undersocialized; some are thought to have experienced significant traumatic events resulting in disturbed perceptions that alter "normal" personality development. A "disturbed" personality predisposes those who have them to develop tendencies toward criminal behavior or to act in situations in ways that produce harmful outcomes for themselves or others. Some of these children are ineffectively socialized because of inherent learning difficulties stemming either from biological defects that affect their capabilities of mind, or from mental illness. Others are considered to suffer from defective patterns of socialization as a result of their parents' own defective past socialization, or from the stresses currently on the family from external social environmental problems, such as poverty, unemployment, and so on (2006: 104).

. . . Whatever the causal process (emotional dysfunction, maladaptive cognitive thinking patterns, etc.) for most theorists of abnormal personality the response consists of intervention to treat the offender, usually through some form of therapy, with a view to correcting the defect and changing his or her personality. . . . The form these therapies take varies depending upon the particular theory informing the diagnosis. This can include drug therapy, psychoanalysis, group therapy, family therapy, resocialization, reprogramming thought processes, and counseling. (2006: 106)

In addition to professional roles involved in personality and psychological treatment and corrections (therapists, counselors, social workers), both adult and juvenile correctional facilities will have "interventions to treat the offender, usually through some type of therapy." Prisoners have reported in their essays a variety of stories about inadequate socialization and/or trauma, as the following excerpts 5.2 reveal.

Prisoner Excerpts 5.2

- *Parental Criminality.* It all started in elementary school. I remember when my dad came home from prison, which was when my life changed. My dad played a very big part in "the game" in my city and had an even bigger influence on my life as a role model.
- *Exposure to Violence.* My grandfather was a police officer when I was younger and I used to look up to him. My father was just the opposite. He was a hustler and a street guy. He also was well respected. He would often teach me and my brother about the street life, as he understood it. The community that we lived in at the time was tough, and being that I was bullied around by other children in the neighborhood

. . . my father taught me how to fight . . . (on a trip to a local convenience store) the same car that my father's friends was in came down the street and a gun came out of the window . . . the first shot made everybody run but us. I saw my father fall. I look right in these guys face . . . I was covered in blood and my father's brains . . . when we got home (after being handled roughly by the police at the scene) my mother went crazy with the news. Me and my brother sat around with bloody clothes on all day cause the house was in an uproar from what just happened.

- *Parental Addiction.* I was born in '79. My father at that time was addicted to heroin, and my mom she enjoyed a drink every now and again. As time went on my dad dropped his addiction, for this new drug crack. And my mom started to drink more. As a result of their addiction, raising children became secondary. They lost touch with reality, they became increasingly unable to properly pay attention to what train of thought their children were developing.
- *Drug Dealing and Child Abuse and Neglect.* From my earliest childhood memories crime was present. Many of my family members in some way or another was involved in crime. From my uncles who sold weed, to my older brothers and cousins was selling crack; my father was addicted to crack. This activity was not shielded from us children. Violence was also present, from my father abusing my mother, and later abusing me and my older sister. My family didn't look down on criminal behavior. And in so many ways they encouraged it. So I learned right from wrong from those who did wrong and made it appear right.

Free Will and Determinism in Psychological Personality Theories

Humans, of course, are mammals, different only in degree from the other primates—monkey, chimps, and apes. Psychological criminology sees

personalities that are shaped by childhood developmental experiences in their family. Human behavior reflects the combination of biological attributes and early socialization experiences mediated through the neurochemical processes of their mind and played out in a variety of situations.

. . . [T]he brain is seen as a highly complex electrochemical organ, which is controlled both by its own chemical and genetic constitution and by the experiences of human development in a specified environment (107). Implied by these assumptions is a vision of mental health as a normal biochemical capability, and normal cognitive processes with their basis in an alleged consensus among qualified experts about what constitutes serious abnormality. (Einstadter and Henry 2006: 110)

There are, however, some psychologists who feel that most prisoners have the same psychological makeup as nonoffenders but have been subjected to life traumas or crises. Urban inner-city youth undergo chronic exposure to poverty and violence in their lives and may have a sense of hopelessness, anger, and rage, acting out with violence and assaults (Green 1993).

Dissociation from Empathy with the Other

> Particularly significant in these life course traumas is the post-traumatic stress disorder (PTSD) that has been associated with victims of wars and major disasters, rape, sexual harassment, and domestic violence, either as a child or a spouse. The effect of these events is to change the personality into an abnormal one characterized by "flashbacks," recurrent dreams or nightmares, or painful intrusive memories of the traumatic event. A diminished responsiveness, a don't-care attitude, and psychological "numbing" to the external world are common. . . . Feelings of alienation or detachment from the social environment are also characteristic, a pattern that leads to difficulty in developing close, meaningful relations with others" (Bartol and Bartol 2005: 218). Clearly, in this psychological state of diminished normality, the possibility of committing acts that harm others is increased, if only because of the disassociation from empathy with the other. While trauma experienced by an adult who has a fully developed personality results in PTSD, the impact of trauma on a child whose personality is in development can be dramatic and long-lasting. (Einstadter and Henry 2006: 111).

#####

Prisoner Essay 5.8

"PTSD from War—Flashbacks and Alcoholism" (3/24/10)
My "pathway to prison" was not fully set into motion until I became an adult even though as a juvenile I had a number of negative conflicts with law enforcement for minor violations of law, mostly for consuming alcohol while under 21 years of age.

At the age of 18 and my senior year of high school I enlisted into the military. Only 2 weeks after graduation I was sent to a place where my mind was altered forever. A world where I was trained to do things that throughout my life I was taught were wrong. The conflicts I faced were several and enormous but the tried and true brainwashing techniques of the military I overcame them. Trained to be ultra aggressive I was ready to be a soldier.

By late 1991 I was on my way to a foreign land to do my duty. Thrown into a culture I had never seen before I was told that I had to defend the interest of the United States. This consisted of using the power of any weapon at my disposal. I was made responsible for the lives of others while I spent the next 3 years bouncing around the Middle East with my nerves on edge. The sounds of automatic weapons and explosions haunting even the few hours of sleep I was able to achieve.

Becoming extremely hateful and disenchanted I drudged through the routine of monitoring radar screens and endless patrols. I took control of situations and gave orders that every person in a leadership role must do. Some of those decisions even today try to haunt my sanity and make me question if I was right.

After my time suffering in the scorching hell that I was forced to call home for 3 years that I finally came back here diagnosed with PTSD and disinclined to reenlist. After completing my enlistment contract I moved to work with the National Environment Service. Within a year I went ballistic over a matter that should have been left to law enforcement and found myself in prison.

While incarcerated I became extremely anti-governmental and antisocial, refusing to be compliant to laws. Becoming even more hate filled and prejudiced, I continued to fall into aggressiveness from untreated PTSD. At times being so lost to traumatic memories that I would cage myself in my cell and not associate with anyone.

Upon my release I still held my antiestablishment views. I worked odd jobs until things started working in my favor. I got married and finally after many long weeks of 100 plus hours I got my business off the ground and successful. Unfortunately along with success in my life came more problems dealing with my buried problems related to my PTSD. Soon I developed or should I say redeveloped a drinking problem. These problems lead to problems in my marriage and more drinking then more problems creating an endless loop of negativity ending in yet another stay in the prison system.

Again being denied treatment and being told literally that "PTSD does not exist" I deal as best as I can retreating into myself when needed to try to suppress memories that I would rather not deal with, I have adapted to self medicating since it is so much easier than dealing with a psychiatric administration that doesn't care.

Now, with nothing to look forward to inside these fences but more time and stress from both prisoners and staff, I spend my days in a monotonous routine of trying to keep my sanity while dealing with drudgery, negativity and pessimism.

In three years I lost one man and had six injured.

#####

Psychological Theory Views Society as the Outcome, Not the Maker of Minds

Personality theories focus on the "creature features" of the individual human being. This is a perspective that emphasizes "kinds of people." However, biopsychological and personality theories exclude the social level of reality—the "kinds of places" analysis of "*where* we grew up" that is so characteristic of many prisoners reports (see chapters 1, 7–9). Einstadter and Henry note:

> As in biological theory, most psychological theories of personality give little attention to society and culture, and their "concern for the environment is only as a source of stimuli" (V. Fox 1976: 155). . . . [S]ociety is, at best, reduced to "social factors" that influence. Where society is considered, most "tend conservatively to take for granted the existing social order" (Hagan 1986: 417). Freud . . . saw society as a "masses in motion and nothing else" (Freud 1985: 369). Indeed, the very assumption that humans are hedonistic presumes a society as little more than an aggregate of discrete and oppositional particles.
>
> Even those more sociologically aware psychologists assume that society is made up of individual personalities. They fail to consider that human nature may be an outcome of the kind of society that exists in any particular historical era. (2006: 111)

For instance, many state prisoners come from a handful of inner-city neighborhoods in their state, and those neighborhoods are full of factors influencing the youth growing up there toward crime: for example, loss of manufacturing jobs creating jobless ghettos with high homicide rates (Parker 2008), federal, state, and local government policies fostering jobless residential racialized ghettos (Wacquant 2008: Ch. 2), loss of educated community leaders and aggregation of dysfunctional and strained individuals (Agnew 1999; Wilson 1996), the illegal drug economy (Abadinsky 2008), chronic exposure to violence and poverty (Green 1993). The individual in the family does not stand alone—they are connected to schools, the local city labor market, government housing and development policy, and neighborhood parent networks (Sampson 2002, 2011). The individual psychological level of analysis is not sufficient, therefore, to understand most crime. Einstadter and Henry note that

> a recent development known as "community psychology" takes seriously the role of environment in shaping human minds and behavior by relating the individual to community and social structures (Dalton, Elias, and Wandersman, 2001). Indeed, "community psychology shifts the focus from individual to multiple levels of analysis . . . individuals are studied within a broader context of influence" (Livsey and Davidson 2005: 81). (2006: 112)

So, while it seems natural enough to see individual psychological factors related to crime, Urie Brofenbrenner argues that a better approach is one of "community psychology." He notes:

> The first level, the individual, is studied by community psychologists in terms of its relationship to the other levels. In other words, how do individuals influence their environments and how do environments affect individuals within them? The second level, the microsystem, includes systems with which an individual has a direct, personal, ongoing interaction. Examples would include families, support groups, school classrooms, and employment settings. Finally, macrosystems are large systems that influence a vast group of members. Societies, cultures, and governments are examples of macrosystems. (Einstadter and Henry 2006: 112)

We began this chapter discussing individual predictive and protective factors related to *Saving Children from a Life of Crime* (Farrington and Welsh 2007: Chs. 3, 7) (see table 1.1). Those authors found evidence for crime prevention through "preschool intellectual enrichment and child skills training programs."

> Individual-based prevention programs target risk factors for delinquency and later offending that are found within the individual. As we discussed . . . these risk factors include low intelligence and attainment, low empathy, impulsivity and hyperactivity. These programs are targeted on the child.
>
> These programs help society's most vulnerable members. They have as explicit aims the betterment of children's immediate learning and social and emotional competencies, as well as the improvement of children's success over the life-course. In addition, they are implemented at a time when children are most impressionable and hence receptive to intervention. (Farrington and Welsh 2007: 105)

The federally funded Head Start program, as a pre-school intellectual enrichment program, for instance, improves school readiness and reaches nearly half of children in poverty. It provides cognitively stimulating and enriching educational experiences that some parents under the stress of poverty do not provide.

> Social skills training or social competence programs for children are generally targeted on the risk factors of impulsivity, low empathy, and self-centeredness. As noted by Carolyn Webster-Stratton and Ted Taylor, this type of individual-based program is designed to "directly teach children social, emotion, and cognitive competence by addressing appropriate social skills, effective problem-solving, anger management, and emotion language" (2001: 179). (Farrington and Welsh 2007: 106)

Earlier in this chapter the question of degree of free will and degree of determinism led us to consider that *degree* of free will that a three- or four-year-old possessed. At this "most impressionable age" a lot of "the child's social, emotional, and cognitive competence" is determined by what intellectual enrichment and child skills the parents are, or are not "likely to provide at home." Looking at a child who is eleven or twelve—how much free will do they have as compared to how much of their life is determined "by what others think?" Who's eyes do they want to see themselves through—parents or peers?

#####

Prisoner Essay 5.9

"A 12-Year-Old Wants Peer Recognition" (2/11/09)
Before I came to prison I used to hear, "If you keep on doing what you are doing you're either going to end up dead or in prison." The word that was being spoken was going in one ear and out the other. I wasn't brought up without guidance. My family tried to teach me all they could about life. The main thing they tried to teach me was that "Education was the key to my future."

I grew up in Detroit going to Detroit public schools. Most of the lessons that I was being taught I tried to keep with me outside of the house, but in my eyes at that time it got me nowhere but being called "lame." Growing up for me if you were getting good grades, studying all the time you was considered a square. I didn't like being talked about and I wanted everybody to look at me the same way as they seen themselves.

At an early age (11 or 12) I joined a gang, which I thought would give me some type of recognition. I began to fight, steal cars, and tried to sell a little weed. I say this was in my middle school days. As I got older I left that little gang banging thing alone—it got old. And also it was really something I didn't want to do it was just something to become known.

I stuck with selling the weed because the money got me the females that I thought I wanted but in doing so it also brought me a lot of trouble. I began to carry guns which made me feel "better than them" and that began to be a problem. My family didn't know too much of what I was doing until I got into a little altercation with an individual and pulled my gun out and took his car. Somebody called the police and they came and picked me up for carjacking, whoever called the police never came to court so I got out.

Once I got out I thought that I couldn't get caught up like that again but I thought wrong. I got locked up again and got right back out. My family used to try to lecture me but I felt them sermonizing to me didn't do too much. I didn't care what they thought—all I cared about was what others thought of me.

The situations that I got myself into wasn't based on any type of factors. My problem came from me not looking at myself though my own eyes, because I knew right from wrong. I'm 21 now and those that are around my age are going though the same thing I was going though. Looking at themselves though the eyes of their friends, and that to me is a big problem.

#####

The Adrian College honor student, Nolan, and the author were discussing this prisoner story and the concepts of free will and determinism. Nolan said, "He knew right from wrong . . . but chose incorrectly." I responded: "He's now 21 and looking backward from prison . . . so: he's joining a gang at 12? I'd like to argue with you about the degree of free will a 12-year-old has. Because he was 12. . . . He wants to be recognized by his 12- and 14-year-old peers who are in a gang. Was this completely free will or was there a community subculture or peer influence? It's a matter of *degree* of free will. That's why we have a separate juvenile justice system and the child developmental rights (to learn from their mistakes). The prisoner says that when he was 12 'his family tried to lecture me,' 'I didn't care what they thought—all I cared about was what the others (peer-age gang buddies) thought of me.'"

Every culture recognizes the problem of eleven- and twelve-year-olds or young teens needing peer recognition. And each nation has developed answers: Nazi Germany had "Hitler Youth," the USSR and China had "Red Youth," and the United States has "Boy Scouts" and "Girl Scouts" (or the Boys and Girls Clubs). These organizations are developed to guide the youth in prosocial, positive direction at a time-of-life they are vulnerable to peer influence. Instead of Red Youth or Boy Scouts, the U.S. inner cities and some deteriorating suburbs have the oppositional culture of street life and gangs (Anderson 2008; Milton 2012).

The classical rational choice model assumed free will and choice—but three- and four-year-olds need child skills and intellectual enrichment to help them function as a *more* "social, emotional, and cognitively competent" person. So, too, does the eleven- or twelve-year-old need societal guidance to "shape" their intense interest in peer recognition. Parents may encourage sleepovers with friends. Parents in more stable neighborhoods may hope to channel young teens into music, sports, youth clubs, camping, hunting or fishing, or hobbies instead of gangs. Activities such as sports put young teens in contact with the young teens of other families where the parents get to know each other and the kind of values the other families have. This is the supportive parent network "behind" the teen-to-teen activity. With gangs it's just the teens leading the teens.

Child developmental psychology would assert that three- and four-year-olds, and eleven- and twelve-year-olds are "different types of persons" than full-grown adults. On the other hand, the classical rational view of criminal choice see all people as the same:

> It should be clear from the discussion above that classical thinking does not consider the criminal as a special kind of person. Those who commit crimes are rational, hedonistic, free actors, no different from non-criminals, except that they break the law. Beccaria believed that all people are "by nature self-seeking," and therefore, "all people are liable to commit crimes." (Einstadter and Henry 2006: 56)

But what classical criminology thinking does not consider is the *degree* of freedom. The Adrian College student, Nolan, is a bright twenty-one-year-old. The impact of determinisms for him, *in his life now*, seems way less important than free choice. He is a philosophy student with a double major in criminal justice. Many college students think the same way: crime is a choice. But what about the three- and four-year-old? What about the young teen being influenced by peers? What about some of the biopsychological conditions—mental illness, addiction, PTSD, trauma, and so forth? Raising issues of the limits on free will or assessing the degree of determinism is a very different discourse than the "rational crime model" which has, according to Einstadter and Henry, a causal logic like this:

> Free choice, lack of the fear of punishment, ineffective criminal justice systems, available unguarded targets, and opportunistic situations provide the components of causality under this model. Crime is the outcome of the reasoning process of rational calculation, purposive self-interest, and low-cost opportunities. . . . According to Meier (1989: 92) . . . "the decision to commit crime . . . is similar to deciding to undertake conventional actions, such as starting a new career or choosing a college. Motivation may stem from a number of different sources or needs, including greed, revenge, envy, anger, lust, thrill-seeking, or bravado" (Siegel 1989: 96). (2006: 56)

A lot of male prisoners the author has met in thirty years of teaching in prison are often *raised* to undertake criminal enterprise. This fact puts the question in a more realistic context.

Another way of looking at this for adults is to consider the insight that degree of free will—moments of free will—come and go, and that as an adult one's past and present can affect degree of determinism, taking over our "decisions." Here are some excerpts from prisoner stories exampling "degrees of determinism."

#####

Excerpts 5.4—Degrees of Determinism

- *Desperate Addiction.* My name is Erik and I am 2½ years into a 8 year sentence for armed robbery. Acts of desperate addiction brought me here to be imprisoned—read on with an open mind. What I do remember is despair and an almost animal drive to maintain my state and not come "down." . . . The girl behind the counter handed me some money. Leading up to that moment had been weeks of continuous drug abuse, Cocaine, crack, liquor, pills, everything. A breakup of a long-term relationship combined with (a drug) relapse set me spiraling down. Fundamentally, it comes down to this: I do not identify with that aspect of myself that commits crime to satisfy a drug habit. If you left your family, home, car and bank pin number with the man that writes this today, I would defend your family if I had to, would carefully watch your personal belongings and you would return just at rich or poor as you had left. However, none of these assertions or assurances could I make when I was using. Ultimately, then, I must be blamed or held responsible for that first drug usage. But is that realistic. You see, I am just as confused as you are. Maybe I am selfish, impulsive, or any amount of other things but, and here is the kicker, I feel when I am sober, I am inherently good, likeable and profoundly social.

    It is my belief that, had my desperation been heard, the series of events that lead to my crime would not have happened. I was scheduled to enter rehab (a decision I had to make on my own) shortly after I was arrested. It is unfortunate that that never came to pass but I have got to move forward.

- *Low Empathy.* By school age I became accustomed to just going along with what everyone else was doing.

    The coping mechanism in my father was to hit, punch, and throw things. My mother would beat us with extension cords, dish rags, razor straps, belts, two by fours, and other objects. This well learned aggressive script played in my head throughout life. I enjoyed watching violence and taking a back seat role in it being carried out. School fights were a major attraction to me and frequent topics of discussions. I enjoyed hearing and watching parents argue, silently saying to myself, punch him or her. Feeling my heart rate increase and my palms getting sweaty the intensity to see or hear violence manifest grew. So participating or watching violence being perpetrated upon someone else by an acquaintance or peer became the norm to me. I lacked the ability to prevent or intercede whether I understood it to be right or wrong.

    This progressed into my involvement in criminal behavior. I could watch a person being beaten or shot without much empathy. Oh hell, who felt sorry for me when my parents beat me? Most often everyone in the neighborhood could hear my screams and pleas for help. No one came to my rescue, so I developed low cognitive empathy, poor role taking—I didn't work at seeing a situation from another person's perspective.

In this, I have spent the last 25 years of my life in prison for aiding, and abetting to murder. I've never shot anyone in my life, but the traits of my childhood have lead to this life sentence, due to being present to "induce, encourage or assist" in the crime of murder.

- *Parents Taught Criminality.* My father often times took me with him to commit crimes. And when I was caught for committing some crime, I wasn't really punished.

  When I was fifteen I caught a drug case that was my first actual felony. I ended up having to go to the Wayne county youth home. My parents borrowed money from a loan shark to get me out and I was not punished. My parents had expected my desire to be a criminal so much so that my father was the person that showed me how to sell drugs. My mother went for whatever my father wanted, so if my father told me to do something that was illegal she wouldn't encourage it verbally. She just wouldn't say anything. Their action's prepared me for a life of crime.

  So, children's identity is not only *formed* through parenting (for good or ill), but also it is important to start out earlier in their lives to find out *who they are*. Each child is different—an individual. Yet what if an entire *community* such as the oppositional culture of street crime expected and encouraged criminal behavior? We might get an entire set of individuals who are, in fact, what we *do* get from the many neighborhoods represented in our prisons.

#####

EXERCISES 5.1–5.3

Exercise 5.1

Compare rational choice with biological determinism. How would you describe the difference between these theoretical orientations?

Exercise 5.2: Policy

What kinds of crime prevention social policy do we need for biopsychological logical determinism? Give one or two examples.

Exercise 5.3

1. Explore the following excerpts and locate where issues of free will and determinism occur
2. Pick one excerpt and explain how a program (mandatory and/or voluntary, formal or informal) could lessen the degree of determinism and raise the degree of free will and better choices

DISCUSSION AND REVIEW QUESTIONS

1. What is child neglect? Give an example.
2. What does figure 5.1 reveal about crime? Explain.
3. Describe rational choice theory of crime. What is the classical rational school of thought?
4. What are Trojanowicz and Morash criticisms of classical rational school of thought?
5. What does it mean for criminology that stress chemicals in a heroin user are in a sort of "hair trigger release"?
6. What is psychological theory's view of society?
7. Describe "community psychology." How does it differ from conventional personality psychology with regard to criminology?
8. What social skills do early childhood enrichment programs such as Head Start deliver to three- to five-year-old children? How does this relate to later crime prevention?

6

The Family and Crime

Most people understand the family influences whether a child will get into crime or not. Many of these family predictive factors show up in prisoner essays and excerpts in chapter 4 such as:

- "Things were good until after my mom got incarcerated halfway through 6th grade year."
- "With five kids and me the youngest my parents said: 'By the time for my education, they were wore out, therefore the discipline was absent.'"
- "My home life wasn't too strict. My parents divorced when I was 15. I remember that's when I didn't even make it to school anymore."
- "My parents were having marital issues, then divorce, then single parent—I had stress with schooling."

THE FEMINIZATION OF POVERTY AND CRIME

If the goal is to reduce crime a major focus should be upon single women with children. The link between neighborhood, family, and urban labor market is important. Single women need jobs. The working poor mother is stressed. African American women were impacted by labor market changes from manufacturing to services. There has been a

> deleterious effect of the economic transformation on minority women (Browne 1997; Browne and Askew 2005). Although deindustrialization increased the number of jobs in female-dominated service occupations (Jones and Rosenfeld 1989), black women lost rather than gained with the expansion of service-based industries (Browne 2000; Kletzer 1991). . . . Three . . . economic trends occurred. . . . First, like black males, black women were more likely to work in the manufacturing sector than white women were (Bound and Dresser 1999; Glass, Tienda, and Smith 1988), leading to higher levels of dislocation for this group when compared to others (see examples in Tienda, Smith, and

Ortiz 1987). Second, although the economic transformation was undoubtedly characterized by growth in the service industry, much of the growth was in administrative, information-based technologies (see Kasarda 1921), which did little to increase the employment opportunities or advance the economic status of minority women (Browne 1997; Ihlanfeldt and Sjoquist 1989). Third . . . as deindustrialization was in full swing, the disabling of welfare and the elimination of federal welfare entitlements such as AFDC to black women with children who were disproportionately represented (U.S. Department of Commerce 1993) removed any safety net to protect this group from the approaching deprivation. (Parker 2008: 88)

Some low-income women may be addicted and engaged in illegal activities, contributing to the criminality of her children. Many prisoners describe growing up in a single parent female-headed low-income household. While the growth in the service sector provided women, in general, with more jobs, black females actually faced employment decline. African American women have, as parents, faced *less* economic opportunity in the last thirty years in *both* manufacturing and in service jobs. Many of the inner-city community areas had

a reduction in low-skilled service and retail occupations . . . (see Goldin 1990; Hsueh and Tienda 1996; McCall 2000). Black women workers have been losing ground in both manufacturing and service-based economies since the 1980s, and joblessness has increased steadily. In fact, even though black women experienced gains in professional and managerial jobs, this growth in employment did not absorb a sufficient number of displaced workers to counteract job dislocation among black females over time. (Parker 2008: 88)

Parker concludes her review of the impact of the city labor market occupational restructuring by noting that black female-head housing and black children living with one parent increased over 15 percent, and divorce rates increased by 87 percent.

The single woman with children has a hard time in U.S. society. Oftentimes she may have had two or three children during or soon after high school and not have pursued postsecondary education. Her job does not pay much and, in fact, she may need two jobs to keep a roof over her family. Many women have such low income, even when working, that they qualify for welfare. The data on "concentrated disadvantage"—that is, high poverty areas characterized by chronic unemployment and racial segregation—reveal the single female-headed household as typical. Wacquant notes:

The consequence of this threefold movement—the outmigration of stably employed African-American families made possible by state-sponsored white-flight to the suburbs; the crowding of public housing in black areas already plagued by slums; the rapid deproletarianization of the remaining ghetto residents—was soaring and endemic poverty. In Grand Boulevard, a section of the South Side, containing some 50,000 people, 64 percent of the population lived under the poverty line in 1990, up from 37 percent only a decade earlier, and three out of every four households was headed by a single mother. (2008: 59)

Research has shown that a single-parent family doubles the risk for later troubles for that family's children. Some impoverished women may, themselves, be dysfunctional with addictions and mental health problems, and be engaged in criminal activities (e.g., dealing drugs, prostitution, larceny). Their children grow up and repeat the cycle. But remember, "the cycle" is part of community psychology (Brofenbrenner, in Einstadter and Henry 2006: 112). The micro-system (family) is affected by the macro-system (community, society).

There may be domestic abuse. The woman may be fighting the child protective services for custody of her children. Many women are not "into drugs and crime" and are just having a hard time making it. They represent the "feminization of poverty." If the United States wants to reduce crime it should have better "family policies" and find a way to help single moms. This would involve family policies at the macro level, such as a better job or more income, better housing, deconcentration of poverty, and so forth. Women raising children without adequate social support may try their best, but the children can "fall through the cracks" into the culture of street crime. Parent(s) are just not giving the proper support to their children on the individual level, or the parent of this child may evidence child neglect out of selfishness or ignorance. Their children often go to prison or are under supervision by the correctional system (probation, parole).

Throwing in the Towel—Lack of Warmth and Support

As discussed in chapter 4, it is clear that there was not very much help from the parents for most of these prisoners. Parents appear to not be there in helping the child focus on school, or stay in school. School failure and dropping out become a process that, for these prisoners, is not corrected through parental guidance.

At-risk youth counselors—childcare workers in the juvenile justice system or boys and girls club staff—will often say that "We can't fix these kids unless we can fix the parents." For police and Sheriff's deputies participating in a Lenawee County survey the author conducted about their experiences as "First Responder to Youth Calls" their unanimous response about "the problematic youth call" was to ask: "Where are the parents?"

As a prison teacher, the author learned that 83 percent of Michigan prisoners were themselves victims of child abuse and neglect (MDOC 1996).

In interviews with criminal justice research professors they often describe how "Family is the most important variable" in understanding crime, accounting for "37 percent of the variance in multi-factorial studies of crime causation." In other words, there is a strong finding in the research literature for family as a cause of crime.

It is commonsense that certain features of family life can predict children's offending. The best researchers on this topic agree. David P. Farrington's review of "Families and Crime" in the handbook *Crime and Public Policy* (Wilson and Petersilia 2011) notes, quoting Carolyn Smith and Susan Stern (1997: 383–84):

> We know that children who grow up in homes characterized by lack of warmth and support, whose parents lack behavior management skills, and whose lives are characterized by conflict or maltreatment will more likely be delinquent, whereas a supportive family can protect children even in a very hostile and damaging external environment. . . . Parental monitoring or supervision is the aspect of family management that is most consistently related to delinquency. (130–48)

However, this warmth and support and protective nurturance has to be available at every step: one to five years old, six to eleven years old, twelve to sixteen years old—all of the childhood years require parental attention. Teenagers sometimes, in the United States, receive less social support than they need. Instead, by the early teenage years, or earlier, parents "throw in the towel." (This is an old boxing phrase: the boxing trainer throws in the towel to indicate giving up on the fight—and giving up on the fighter.)

FAMILY FACTORS RELATED TO CRIME

Several family factors are shown to be related to crime causation by Farrington, including: criminal and antisocial parents and siblings, large family size, poor supervision, poor discipline, coldness and rejection, low prenatal involvement with the child, physical and/or sexual abuse or neglect, parental conflict and disrupted families, and other parental features such as teen parent, substance abuse, stress, or depression (2011: 131).

Farrington is known for careful methodological considerations in the effort to establish that a factor really does predict crime. Doing a study of a sample cohort over time (a longitudinal study) is a method with the highest reliability and validity. Farrington states: "The best method of establishing that a family factor predicts later offending is to carry out a prospective longitudinal survey, and the emphasis in this chapter is on results obtained in such surveys" (2011: 131). All the findings (see table 1.1), were obtained mostly through a review of high quality, longitudinal surveys.

Explaining Crime: Statistical Evidence versus Personal Anecdote

When my graduate school professor said "Family is the most important variable—it can explain 37 percent of the outcome of crime in a cohort, that is a greater strength in predicting delinquency and crime than any other variable" what did he mean? What he was talking about was "statistical significance." The six "family factors" presented by Farrington and Welsh have a "better than chance" association with predicting later crime. For instance the "strength in predicting delinquency and crime" is greater for a family factor such as "criminal parent" than comparing whether parents have brown eyes or green eyes. Brown eyes or green eyes have "no association" with whether the brown-eyed parent(s) children will be delinquent or go into youth crime. But "parental criminality" is a very strong predictor—way better than just "happenstance" or chance. "Parental criminality" is a *consistent and replicable* predictor. The six factors are also consistent and replicable predictors: large family size, poor child-rearing methods, abuse or neglect, parental conflict and disrupted families, and other parental features such as youth age, substance abuse, stress, or depression.

On the other hand, everyone knows of a child whose parents had a large family size and where the child did not go into crime. The statement: "I know the Smiths, a large family, where none of their kids became delinquents," is an anecdotal fact. It is not a statistical fact. It is a statistical fact that a large family has a better than chance association with predicting youth crime, but many children of large families will not "go into crime." Just as everyone knows that it is possible to be a cigarette smoker and live into one's nineties, there is a very strong association (consistent and replicable predictor) between smoking and cancer.

#####

College Student Excerpt 6.1

"My Cousin Has Been in and out of Prison—What Will Happen to His Son?" (2/18/09)

There is one story that I have realized matches these factors. Like my cousin, who has been in and out of prison, his son has now begun to start acting out. The title "crime runs in families," fits this story. My little cousin Kyle looks at what his dad does and thinks that this is the right way to live.

He is mimicking his dad because he thinks its okay. So far, he had gotten suspended from school for fighting and has caused problems at the home. This doesn't seem too bad, but how far will it go?

#####

Crime Runs in Families

Being raised in the context of parental criminality affects the child. In studying the Cambridge Study in Delinquent Development, a prospective longitudinal survey of four hundred males from childhood to late middle age, Farrington found "having a convicted father, mother, brother, or sister predicted a boy's own convictions. . . . For example, 63 percent of boys with convicted fathers were themselves convicted, compared with 30 percent of the remainder (2007: 56).

Farrington sketches out six possible explanations of why offending shows up in certain families or is transmitted from one generation to the next.

- Each generation in a family may be trapped in poverty, have disrupted family lives, live in deprived neighborhoods, and/or may experience single and teenage parenting;
- Female offenders tend to cohabit with or marry male offenders (or vice versa);
- Younger male brothers imitate antisocial older brothers, or older siblings encourage younger brothers to be antisocial;
- Fathers who are more frequently arrested tend to have delinquent sons "because they tended to impregnate young women, to live in bad neighborhoods, tend to use child-rearing methods that did not develop a strong conscience in their children (Farrington et al. 2001);
- Genetic mechanisms may be at work: twin studies show identical twins have more crime than fraternal twins (Raine 1993), and "adoption studies show that the offending of adopted children is significantly related to the offending of their biological parents (Brennan et al. 1993);" and,
- "[C]riminal parents tend to have delinquent children because of official (policy and court) bias against known criminal families, who also tend to be known to official agencies because of other social problems" (Farrington 2011: 132–34).

From our prisoner essays we have the following excerpts on "crime runs in families":

#####

Prisoner Excerpt 6.1

"Don't Get into That Angel Dust Stuff" (2/1/09)

Growing up in the city of New Orleans LA and in the "Magnolia Projects" in the late 60's and 70's I found it very easy to stay in trouble. You see, my mother sold drugs—weed, pills, and so forth—and by the time I was in the 4th grade, not only was I smoking weed, but I had learned how to roll my own joints. Now as far as I am concerned this put me in the child abuse and neglect category. This is not to mention the fact that I grew up in a one parent home, with a mother who was sent to prison for a five-year bit. Please keep in mind when my mother was with us she had no problems whipping our ass when we got into trouble. Even with all that it was my mother who turned me on to smoking that killer red-haired "sinsemilla" weed.

You see one day she sat me down and said something like "son this is weed and people smoke it." She also told me that people were mixing weed with angel dust smoking it and going crazy permanent. She said "Son, I know you are going to try it, so you may as well try it with me. So you don't get into that angel dust stuff." Little did my mother know, I had already tried it. You have to keep in mind that my mother was hoping that I didn't like weed—but I did.

So I started stealing weed from my mother's stash and not only smoking it but also selling it. Yes that is right I was selling while in grade school, 3 joints for 5 dollars. Yes you are right, what a damn shame!

But hey I was doing what I saw in my household. Besides that it felt awesome being the kid with the most candy, gum and pies. This also gave me more access to the girls. By the time I went to the 5th grade my mother was on her way to prison. This is also the time I became very bitter and developed a mean and violent streak.

#####

Prisoner Excerpt 6.2

"Growing Up around Crime—It Was All I Knew" (11/8/08)

My grandpa got sober before I was born in 1974, but the stories I heard of him beating my grandma, and uncles; and then heard that when she was 15 he molested my mother. But the effects of his alcoholism were inbred into the rest of the family, which resulted in both my uncles (all on my mother's side. I've never met my dad, but have recently started corresponding with him through letter and he's a recovering alcoholic/addict). My aunt and my mother having addictions and dysfunctional issues. So I grew up with "family fights" often. Seeing my uncles, mom and aunt smoke pot, drink, shoot heroin. In addition, I grew up around criminals in the neighborhood.

So, my family as well as my social geographical factors did have an impact upon me. It was all I knew until I became a later teen and started dating girls from the suburbs and the upper-middle class areas. But I learned from my mother, her boyfriends, my aunts and her friends how to use drugs, and indulge in illegal matters to receive financial and material gain. Fortunately, I've yet to have children of my own and maybe with my children this "vicious cycle" will be broken and I can show my children a different life.

#####

Prisoner Excerpt 6.3

"Shit, Yes: My Mother Went to Prison" (1/25/09)
[T]the first time I ever really broke the law, I was in something like the 4th grade. I was on my way to the local grocery store. I was one block away from the store and I spotted this kid on a nice shinny bike. Without even thinking I walked up to the kid pushed him off the bike and rode away in a hasty manner . . . within an hour the people who saw me sent the police to my front door. That was a very low point in my life. You see my mother was in prison by this time and I was living with my dear sweet aunt Jessie.

Okay back to the bike thing. The neighborhood in which my aunt Jessie and uncle Willie live in was a upper middle class neighborhood. In fact this was the first time I had ever seen black people who own their own homes, cars, and all that kind of stuff. . . . So what I am saying is: "Shit, yes. My mother went to prison for 5 years and I was smoking marijuana by the age of 10 and I was selling by 11." At the same time I was on the honor roll from 5th grade all the way to the 12th grade. Once living with my aunt I went to the best schools from 5th to 7th grade. Once my mother returned home we moved from New Orleans, LA to Baton Rouge, LA. Yes back to the hood. This is also when my life of crime somewhat came into play.

#####

Prisoner Excerpt 6.4

"No Guidance in the Home—Mother Seen as Hoe" (2/1/8/09)
I have to say last year, around May, I asked a guy that I was cool with: "Why is it that he shown so much disrespect towards women? And he asked me: "Why should I?" Man when he told me that we fell into a heavy debate. He broke down his life and told me that his mother did not teach him anything about respect or anything else of that manner. The way he viewed his mother is the same way he viewed females and he viewed his mother as a hoe.

He said when he was born he stayed with his mother for only 4 years and then child protective services came and picked him and his brother up. He stayed in a foster home for 3 years and then his mother ended up getting custody again.

He explained to me that when he was with his mother all he seen was men coming in and out of the house and his mother shooting up. . . . He told me never in his life have he ever heard his mother say, "I love you son." He had no guidance in the home so his guidance came from the streets, which led him into a path of destruction.

#####

Prisoner Excerpt 6.5

"My Decision to Follow My Brother and His Associates into Crime" (10/27/08)
During school hours my older brother would come to my high school and encourage me to skip class and drive him around. We had built a strong bond during our adolescence years that my decisions to follow my brother was not that difficult after all, he and I grew up doing most everything together. So my progression into crime with my brother and his associates was not that uncommon. It started out skipping class and drinking—then moving on to stealing cars and robbery. It was not considered antisocial behavior to us, but just having fun.

#####

Prisoner Excerpt 6.6

"My Father: An Unemployed Hustla with 'Bad Streets' Smarts" (10/27/08)
From my earliest childhood memories crime was present. Many of my family members in some way or another was involved in crime. From my uncles who sold weed, to my older brothers and cousins was selling crack; my father was addicted to crack. This activity was not shielded from us children.

Violence was also present, from my father abusing my mother, and later abusing me and my older sister. My family didn't look down on criminal behavior. And in so many ways they encouraged it. So I learned right from wrong from those who did wrong and made it appear right.

I knew that my father wanted to be a good guy, but his addiction overtook him, leaving him unable to make rational decisions and I learned from him. And in many ways I reflected him, I didn't have his addiction, but I inherited his obsession. I always saw myself as a reflection of the men in my family.

An unemployed hustla, with a lot of children by different women, uneducated, "Bad Street" smarts. I was cool with that. Most of my family really left
the city limits of Ecorse and River Rouge, and those who did always found
their way back.

So I never wanted to leave. That was my world, Visgar road was my
Sunset Blvd. Now, those who were 30 years ago throwing up the black fist,
was still there, with their hand out asking for change. And many of them had
high school diplomas. Some even certified in various fields. But the misery
of being denied equal opportunity was too much. They found peace in their
drug of choice. I found myself seeing their vision, so I never gave myself a
chance.

#####

Large Family Size

The size of a family, the number of siblings, as a variable all by itself, has
strength in predicting delinquency and crime. Farrington, drawing on the
Cambridge longitudinal study, notes that

> if a boy had four or more siblings by his 10th birthday, this doubled his risk of
> being convicted as a juvenile (West and Farrington 1973: 31). . . .
> . . . Generally, as the number of children in a family increases, the amount of
> parental attention that can be given to each child decreases. . . . Another interest-
> ing theory suggested that the key factor was birth order: large families include
> more later-born children . . . (who have more) exposure to delinquent siblings.
> Consistent with social learning theory, large families contained more antisocial
> models. (2011: 134–35)

From our prisoner essays we have the following excerpts on the effect of
family size on criminality.

#####

Prisoner Excerpt 6.7

"Family of Six Kids—Mom Goes to Work, I Gravitate to the Street" (2/11/09)
Growing up in a large family of 6 children during the 70's through to my ado-
lescent years beginning in the 80's was something. Not having enough money
to support a large family, mom soon had to go to work too, which left my
teenage brother and sister in charge. Ha! What a great idea—letting the teenage "hippies" delegate authority to the younger siblings. I soon found myself
fading and fending for myself. Not long after, the street became my family

and way of life. I found I got more discipline and praise from the hoodlums on the corner than I did from anyone in my biological family. After proving my worth to my street family and my well-toned theft skills, I became an asset to keep around. I soon could afford the finer things that my working parents couldn't.

Such as the $100 gym shoes all the kids my age were wearing as well as the $50 pair of jeans and all the while no one at home even noticed my new duds. I felt like I got away with the crime of the century. As I grew older, 13 or 14, I moved up to bigger and better things—pot, acid, anything that I could get my hands on that would sell and sell fast. I actually purchased a car even before I had my license. Sure, we were always stealing a car here and there just for kicks. But now I had my very own, bought and paid for with the almighty green, cash! Woo wee! I tell you, having a pocket full of the green stuff makes you feel on top of the world. But having it wasn't nearly as fun as spending it. And once it ran out, it was just as fun making more, it didn't make a difference whether I was selling drugs or hitting licks, robbing and stealing—cash was king.

Prisoner Excerpt 6.8

"No Curfew—Running with the Older Kids" (2/1/09)
Family Factors? Well, let's see. First off the matter is I was born into a large middle class family, 3 girls, 3 boys and I was the middle boy and 5th in line only to be short changed by my younger brother, the baby of the family. It seems I was always competing for my parents love and appreciations but always losing to the whiney brat in the corner. So as I grew older I found that I could win attentions not only by being good but also by being bad.

So begins my criminal life. I started fighting, bullying other boys in school, hoping to get in trouble. As time went by, my parents gave up—washed their hands of me, so to say.

I was 12 years old, I can't recall—and say I had a curfew. If I did, it sure wasn't being enforced. Unfortunately only the older kids were around outside late at nights. I soon found myself running with a new crowd. We were into everything from smoking to drinking—stealing anything, and everything that wasn't bolted down. That included cars.

At age 13 I had my 1st involvement with the police and landed my ass in the youth home, my first taste of structured living. And so it begins.

#####

Child-Rearing Methods

Many researchers have focused on child-rearing methods of parents as contributors to subsequent delinquency. Farrington argues that the most important dimension of child-rearing is supervision and monitoring of children. Also important is discipline or parental reinforcement "harsh or punitive discipline (involving physical punishment) predicts a child's delinquency . . . erratic or inconsistent discipline also predicts delinquency . . . and so can cold, rejecting parents."

Finally, Farrington notes,

> *Low parental involvement* in the child's activities predicts delinquency. . . . In the Cambridge study, having a father who never joined in the boy's leisure activities doubled his risk of conviction (West and Farrington 1973: 57), and this was the most important predictor of persistence in offending after age 21. (2011: 135–37)

From our prisoner essays we have the following excerpts on parental child-rearing methods.

#####

Prisoner Excerpt #6.9

"Stealing Dad's Music, Abused by Step Dad" (1/25/09)
Because my parents were so self-absorbed, during the years when I needed it most, I had almost no parental supervision. . . . You have to lead by example. My parents were not equipped to raise stable children.

My parents divorced when I was ten years old. . .

The breaking point in all of that for me was all of the abuse I suffered at the hands of my stepfather years later, that neither my mother nor my father took any act on to thwart or avenge. I ended up in foster care and the estrangement between my family and I began. I had been physically, emotionally, mentally and sexually abused and neglected by the time I was twelve years old.

#####

Prisoner Excerpt 6.10

"Parents Never There" (1/25/09)
I am impulsive. I always just do stuff on impulse. I never think it though until it is too late. My parents were never there to teach me right from wrong.

That was most of my problem. I would do stuff for their attention. When I would get locked up I had their full attention. When I come home I lost their attention. They had me put on medication and it made me worse. They made me hyper instead of slowing me down. Then I started to do drugs and drink. Now I am locked up again. I am 24 and been to prison twice. I always fall off my horse and get back in trouble. I have an 11th grade education. I like to work and stay busy. So I can stay out of trouble.

#####

Prisoner Excerpt 6.11

"Not Taught to Be Patient and Responsible" (10/27/08)
I grew up in the projects in River Rouge, Michigan. Me and a few of my friends were all poor, all from broken homes. All shared one goal, somehow getting out of the projects. Me, Gabe, and Ken choose to go up on Visgar road and sell crack. My friend Chester stayed in school.

Every Sunday during football season I watch my childhood friend Chester Taylor on TV he is a running back for the Minnesota Vikings jersey number 29. His housing project was just 2 down from me so how did he get there (pro-footballer), and I got here (prison)? The answer involves individual personality. I was never taught how to be responsible; I was never taught how to be patient. I was not taught self-confidence, I couldn't play sports, I was good at boxing but that didn't excite me. I hated school so I didn't stay there. I dropped out in Jr. high never seeing high school. I was impressed by the criminal life style. Most of my family members was somehow involved in crime, so it was crime that was held out for me as what life was.

Nobody shielded me from the violence, so I never really learned empathy. I learned how to give up. I learned how to not care, and not to be compassionate. I was a slave to my impulsive reacting.

#####

Child Abuse and Neglect

Many people have come to realize that child sexual abuse and child physical abuse and neglect, especially persisting abuse into adolescence, contribute to later offender (Farrington 2011: 138).

From our prisoner essays we have the following prisoner essays on child abuse and neglect.

#####

Prisoner Essay 6.1

"My New Step-Dad: An Individual's Story" (2/1/09)

It's amazing to look back now and see that there was a time in my life when I was happy and carefree. Playing catch with my dad in the yard, mom baking in the kitchen, countless family outings and the thrill of so many Christmas mornings. It was like something out of a 1950's television show. Now, it all seems like a vague memory of someone else's life.

I can't be sure where it all went wrong. Maybe it was the affair my mom was having. Maybe it was the affair my dad was having. Either way, the marriage was over long before it ended. I was witness to a number of physical altercations between my parents. Then my mom would pack us up and leave. And in short order, we'd come back. I welcomed the divorce. Up to this point, I was still your everyday kid. But once my parents officially split, my life became a nightmare. My dad put very little effort into being a part of my life. And my mom re-married. That's when my life fell apart. My new step dad was a severe alcoholic. I didn't know it then, but he was a lot of horrible things. Over the next two years, I watched my little sister, my mom and myself, all become victims of this man and his abuse—mental, emotional, physical and sexual. I can't explain how terrible it is to be as young as I was and so afraid to come home after school because I never knew what sort of abuse awaited me. But eventually I mustered up the courage to report him to the authorities.

My mom ran to my step-dad's defense. After I testified against him in court, I was shipped off to live with my dad. And quickly I was made to feel like an imposition. Even worse, my step-dad got off with a six-month sentence in the county jail. During the time I lived with my mom, I had too much freedom. Living with my dad, I felt like a prisoner. His justification was that I couldn't get into any trouble if I stayed indoors. I was also turned into his little slave. I had to cook fancy meals for him and his girlfriend, while I was stuck eating hotdogs and macaroni and cheese. And as soon as the girlfriend showed up, I was banished to my bedroom. I had been a victim, yet I was the one doing hard time. To top it off, my dad committed a crime and instructed me to take the blame for it. Had he been caught, he might be in prison himself. It all came down to a fistfight between father and son. And shortly after that, he dropped me back into the custody of my mother and stepfather.

It was at that moment I knew I had no home. Within months, my mom put me on the street because my step dad had told her that either I went or he went. So, once again, I was looked over and left to fend for myself. Fourteen years old and homeless. I reached out to a friend and he contacted social services. I ended up in a foster home and my parents lost their rights to me. They couldn't have been happier.

My foster parents were good people. But they weren't my people. So I felt alone in the world. I experimented briefly with drugs and alcohol, but I quickly knew that wasn't my style. My parents weren't into drugs or alcohol. That's not where I came from. And I was not a violent person. As a teenager I was lonely and depressed a lot. My outlet was girls. Lots of unprotected sex with anyone that came along. I was lucky enough to never have contracted anything. One girl did end up pregnant, but her parents talked her into an abortion. I was playing with fire. I took far too many chances. But these girls filled a void for me. They were my people, my family. But all it really ended up being was sex. Yet it filled that empty space in my life.

I was going to school and working while I was in the foster home. I figured the busier I stayed, the less likely I would be able to do something stupid. That's when I met my best friend, Jeff. He was almost twenty years older than me, but we had so much in common. He became my boss and went on to be family, my big brother. I am convinced that kept me grounded. I might have been a juvenile delinquent, if not for Jeff. At the age of seventeen, I was emancipated and moved out of the foster home. By this time, my mom, dad and sister were all living in other states. From the time I was born my paternal grandmother and I were real close. I was her pride and joy. So I decided to move closer to where she lived. My grandfather died a few years before and I thought it would be good for both of us. There I was, not even eighteen yet, and I had my GED, my own apartment, a full-time job and my own car. I was on top of the world.

But I was miserable. The only person I knew was my grandmother. I loved her with all of my heart, but I needed more than that. Those feelings landed me in the company of too many of the wrong females. I wasn't keeping a job. I was moving all the time. Losing all of my belongings. Having to borrow money from my grandmother. Jeff and I had lost touch and nothing I did made me feel any better. Eventually I ended up in financial ruin and that led to a series of bounced checks, which led me to prison in the end.

I wasn't down for long, but when I was released on parole, I vowed to change my life. Throughout that whole ordeal, I had a woman in my life. And she stood by my side the whole time. My thought was that the best thing for me to do was settling down and marry her. So I did. Had I thought it all through first, I could have avoided heartache. She and I had a lot in common. We had a good physical chemistry. But emotionally, we were on different planets. We were together nearly three years. The marriage lasted just over a year. I was devastated. And I felt myself plunging into another downward spiral. I went and stayed with my grandmother, while I tried to pick up the pieces of my shattered life. Then I landed the best job I ever had. My self-esteem shot through the roof and I was ready to take on the world. Grandma and I were closer than ever. We needed each other. And that made things seem right again. Slowly I managed to get back to where I had been. I had a car. Then I rented a room. I had my own money. But as usual, I had a void. How could I swear off women? I just needed to try someone different, maybe an older woman, and sixteen years older, to be exact. We were co-workers and she seemed so well put together. I thought that if I went with an older woman, someone more mature, that I would experience a longer healthier relationship. Maybe that void would finally disappear. I thought wrong.

We had some things in common. And I thought we wanted the same things. But even early on, I was miserable. I broke it off on several occasions and always went back. I didn't want to be alone. And by the time I was ready to call it quits, I was too invested in our life together to pull out. I would lose too much. Because I was so miserable, though, eventually I had no choice. I couldn't fool myself anymore. And just as I had feared, I lost nearly everything I had. I was living in a motel room I couldn't afford, then lost my job and eventually ended up going back to grandma's. One month later, she died unexpectedly. I lost all self-control.

Most of my life, my primary emotions had been sadness, loneliness and depression. But at the moment I realized I had lost my grandmother forever, I became angry. Consumed with hate. And no one was exempt from my feelings. God, my family, friends, but it was my dad who took the brunt of it. We were brought together by my grandmother's death. A lot of years had passed since he and I had last seen each other. And my resentment toward him boiled to the surface. I wanted him to know my pain. I wanted to show him what true loss was all about. Possessions had always meant more to my dad than people, especially his music collection. So one day I drove over to his apartment, kicked in the door and took it all away from him. And it was all an impulsive behavior. To me, it was never anything more than a domestic situation. Unfortunately, the courts saw it as a "home invasion—second degree" and you better believe that my dad took full advantage of his status as the victim. It was a role he knows far too well.

So here I am, 30 years old, and in prison for the second time in almost 10 years. But I'm lucky. I have received my parole. I have been given yet another chance. And a lot of things are clear to me now. I don't need anyone to feel complete. I can look back on all the things I have accomplished in my life. I can look back on all of the adversity I overcame. I can see my determination, my strength, and my intelligence. All of that comes from within me. And while I've been in prison this time, I have been able to regain three things that I lost touch with years ago—pride, dignity and self-respect. Again, all things that come from within me. You can't get these things through other people or drugs or alcohol or money or whatever else you might use to compensate. At the time, you think you're getting what you need. But then one day you look in the mirror and you no longer recognize the face staring back at you. And your only hope for redemption is that you recognize the problem before it's too late.

I know that there are certain factors that can be traced to my criminal behavior. My family life, my personality, and I have no doubt that had there been some preventative steps taken in my earlier life, I probably could have avoided trouble with the law altogether. But I can also see where, as a society, we have a structural problem with our justice system. Convictions equal dollars. Convictions also fuel political careers. Individual cases get lost in the haze of generalization. Innocent people go to prison. People who just need some basic help go to prison. So it seems to me that if the courts could start seeing people as individuals that would be a good start to lowering our prison population. But it's also necessary to take the necessary steps to prevent criminal behavior at the earliest stages. I just don't know where it would start or end. If one is to prevent factors on the family level, for instance, we would have to invade privacy, and to do that, we have to be willing to give up our own privacy. And even with intensive therapy, we can't always peel back the layers of a child or an adult. Until everyone agrees to work together on this epidemic, there won't be any widespread results—from the police, to prosecutors, to the judges, to the prison system. From the parents to the children, yes, I believe there are times when we can trace behaviors back to a certain event or factor. But sometimes, the only solution comes from within. I am living proof of that. Sometimes, people have layers that can't be peeled with scientific data. There is no master blueprint that connects us all. Each of us is an individual being, with specific ideas, faults, feelings and actions. The sooner we will accept that, the sooner we can actually make a difference.

#####

Prisoner Essay 6.2

"My Past—The Fuel That Made Me a Monster" (10/14/09)
Where I come from, it's not uncommon to see children grow up without fathers. I don't know what that's like. But if I had a choice, I would much rather not had a father then to have had my father.

My father single handily destroyed and distorted both my perception, and any positive view I had about life.

I don't think I've hated anyone as much as I've hated him, if so, it was probably me I hated as much.

Courtesy of my father, I grew up in a very violent and chaotic world where abuse was common, and varied on the individual. Between me and my mother it was psychical and mental, with my older sister it was physical, mental and sexual. And I grew up as a witness to everything.

Often times when I look in the mirror, my attention goes straight to the healed scar above my left eye brow, and the scar above my lip leaving a slight gap in my mustache, and my mind takes me back to the moment in time when I earned them. It was around 11:00 at night when my father came home, and he was drunk, usually that is a bad sign. From my bed I could hear him yelling at my mother, followed by a rumbling sound, and her screaming. I laid in bed praying that it would stop.

At that moment my mother did something she had been doing a lot lately, her and my sister came up with a horrible way to stop my father from beating on them, and that was by focusing the all of his attention on me. And that's exactly what she did, I heard her saying how I wasn't going to school, and or how I was messing up in school, just anything to get him off her. As soon as I heard his voice screaming my name, I knew what time it was.

I tried to play like I was asleep, but that didn't do any good. He came into my room, turn the light on and stated: "Get your ass up!" As soon as my feet touch the floor I was knocked on the ground from his fist crashing into my face, he stood over me, the alcohol on his brain was as obvious as his anger, slurring his words, but I understand every hateful thing he said.

"Stand the fuck up," he stated, while stepping back to give me room, but he was not walking away, cause as soon as I got up, I was knocked back down. This action was repeated until I can't remember. I just remember waking up on the floor, there was blood coming down my face, and my lip was starting to swell.

I sat there dumbfounded not knowing how I got there, and I heard his voice in the other room, and it started to come back to me. I climbed out of my second floor bedroom window and jumped down, and that was the first of the many times I ran away from home. I would either wander the streets all night, or I would go sleep in some broke down school buses behind a private school.

At 12 years old, I found the streets were safer than my home.

This type of upbringing left me very insecure, and my views about life was damaged. In my home, and in my community, violence was looked at as a remedy. I learned how to use violence to establish fear, and demand respect. And the more I seen, the darker my heart got. And hate became the center of my fantasies.

Not only did I hate my father, but also I started to hate all of my classmates, because thanks to them, school was hell for me. I grew up in a somewhat middle class black suburb, many of the kids I went to school with lived in nice homes, and their parents had jobs. And they were very materialistic. I lived in the projects, my dad was a crack head, and my mother was an alcoholic. I wore pretty much the same clothes to school every day. I can even recall a time I didn't have gym shoes. I had to wear church shoes to school. So I wasn't very popular, and even one of my teachers seemed to enjoy seeing me hurt. On one occasion my teacher was mad at me about something, so she had me stand in the middle of the class and encouraged all the other children to make fun of me. I never felt comfortable in school, or around people again.

Of course that made me hate school even more, and I knew I was not going to graduate. I made it to the 7th grade, with a 2nd grade reading comprehension level, and a 3rd grade understanding of math. I dropped out and never went back.

My father had came into a little money, and instead of giving me some money he gave me some crack, and showed me how to sell it. And that was my introduction into crime, despite the fact that crime and violence had been a part of life to me. It went all the way back to the 80's, when crack was pretty much hidden from the public view, those who got high did so inside a house, and our house was one of those houses. The bedroom I had shared with my sister was taken over, and her and I started sleeping on the living room floor. My dad and other strange men would be back there getting high all night.

Quite naturally chaos broke often, as a result of something being stolen, or something stupid being said. On one night in particular, my dad was arguing with some guy, and as a result he went to grab a gun, the guy tried to make it out the door but couldn't so he grabbed me, and used me as a shield, he carried me outside, and half way down the block, and let me go.

These are my memories. A series of misfortunes is what shaped my attitude. Hatred got in my heart and corrupted it. Compassion was lost. Insecurity caused me to hate myself. So I looked for ways to hide. Weed and alcohol gave me a false sense of confidence. It gave a feeling that allowed me to smile, and I became addicted, not to smiling, but to the substance that manipulated it.

The only people I had any sympathy for was children especially my little brother, little sister, and my nieces. I couldn't care for anyone else.

It's important that I mention that the guy I talked about in this story was not my biological father, but I grew up thinking he was until I was 13. My mother used to trick this dude named Raymond, she didn't really like him, but he was willing to pay. As a result I was conceived. I had the opportunity of meeting him, shortly thereafter he died of a heroin overdose.

By the time I was 15 years old I had already had a felony drug conviction and numerous misdemeanors. The police at the River Rouge Police knew me and my family well.

As a result of violating probation for the drug conviction, I was committed to be a ward of the state. I went to a boy's home in Houghton Lake MI, which I only stayed for 84 days, and I was back on the streets.

I went to see my mother one day; totally unaware of the revelation she was about to drop on me. She sat me down and told me straight out, my dad had AIDS and she was HIV+. I couldn't accept that as being true. She showed me some papers, but I couldn't read that well, and I never seen an AIDS test before. So I refused to believe it.

It wasn't even a full year that went by before my father had died. 2 years later, I was 17, in prison, 3 months into my life sentence, thinking life couldn't get any worse, and then I was told that my mother died. She was 40 years old.

In the beginning of this story I mentioned that I used to hate my father. I don't hate him anymore, and I don't blame him for any decision I've made. When it first came to a decision that I wanted to change the way I think, I realized I had to go back to the root of those thoughts, my father is responsible for a lot of thoughts that were planted in my mind, but my actions, and the consequence they produce, are all mine. I can only blame myself.

There are many scars that remain with me. I can't trust people, I've never been in love, and anytime someone acts as if they care about me, I become cautious of them.

I have one child, a son he is 13, and he seemed to love me dearly, but I'm bracing myself, preparing for the day that he will walk away, and not love me anymore. For some reason I find it extremely hard to let anyone get close to me, without thinking they are eventually going to abandon me.

[This story continues below, in a second installment, from 10/14/09]

Let me first acknowledge that my life was different. For many years I had a hard time accepting that. I don't know if it was out of shame or ignorance, or just a combination of the two. I just learn to deal with life as it was. My home was hell and masquerading as my father was "Satan" himself. There was no love, just rage and violence. Many of the scars are still with me—not only emotionally, but also physically. The mirror bear witness to some of his rage. The scar above my lift eye brow, or the one above my upper lip, that one I remember vividly. I was thirteen years old. My dad came home drunk and angry, which was usually a bad sign, and this night was to be no different.

From my bed I heard my mother screaming. And I knew exactly what was going on. My heart dropped from every burst of noise that sounded like something or someone hitting the ground.

I prayed for it to stop. Wondering would this be the day he killed my mother. So many times she'd been rushed to the hospital or I'd awake to find blood on the walls and both my parents gone.

Not this night, she had a plan, a clever little trick to get his attention off her. I was to be her diversion. From my bed I heard her saying my name, something about me not listening to her, this was not her first time doing this, so I knew what was to come next. I laid there paralyzed by fear, unaware of exactly what was to happen next. I heard him scream my name. I tried to play like I was asleep, but I could have been dead for all he cared. He came into my room and turned the lights on, the alcohol on this breath was just as loud as his voice stated, "Son, get yo ass up."

Talking wasn't going to do me any good, so I just obeyed the order. Just as my feet touch the floor, Bam! His fist crashed into my face, sending me flying backwards to the floor. He was not satisfied; he demanded I stand up again, warning me not to attempt to block his punches. Again I was knocked back down. And so this routine continued, until I don't remember it ending. I just remember waking up on the floor, my lip throbbing, and apparently swollen. I reached to feel my lip and felt blood trickling down. I had been knocked unconscious. I sat there trying to remember all that just happened, then I heard his voice, and it all started to come back to me. I jumped out of my bed room window which was two stories high, and that was the first of many times I ran away from home. Often I had nowhere to go, so I slept in school buses behind some school.

Just recently I started to understand exactly what my past has done to me. All my life I've been insecure, I've been pretending to be something I'm not. All because I had no idea who I was. My household didn't allow individuality. There was no love, and all respect was governed by fear.

Fear was the atmosphere in my home. My mother, my sister, and myself, we all was afraid of him. I always felt like I didn't belong there. Like I was kidnapped and made to live with a family that wasn't mine. I was constantly uncomfortable there.

I know my father destroyed me. Tearing to pieces any self-pride, or worth I had. I remember being called stupid so much that I thought it was some birth defect I had. That's probably why I struggled in school; I was told that I had a learning disability. And I believe it.

I'm just now discovering that there is nothing wrong with me. I reached a point in my life where I wanted to be better, in doing so I realized that my past was hindering me from any progress, I had to face it, and expect ugly truths. I carry with me not only my own secrets but also my older sisters. I know of her scars. She is 34 yrs old and she has been an alcoholic for over ten years. I think it started after my mother passes; I was in prison so I'm not sure.

Later in life I discovered that this guy was not my real father. My real dad was a trick; him and my mother had an arrangement, money for sex. I don't think I was supposed to be a part of the package. I often wonder what my mom's thinking as she carried me, did her desire for an abortion seep into my sub-conscious mind? Creating a situation for self-hatred.

I did have the luxury of meeting my biological father; he was also an addict, his drug of choice being heroin. The month after we met he over dosed and that was the end of that. I will not attempt to justify any of my actions, and there is a great deal of shame that comes with my past. I don't blame anyone, but I don't understand how my upbringing played a major role in my decision making. I was a follower. I wanted to be accepted, I wanted to be loved.

Although all of these experience's had a negative effect on me, it's one thing that I learned from my mother that I consider to be a good quality. Because my mother stayed though all that pain, I learned not to give up, and that's why I never turn my back on people. I'm still confused about love. Everyone that claimed to love me either abused, or abandons me. So I always expect love to end, I don't expect people to be there for me. These are the scars of my past, the fuel that made me a monster.

#####

Parental Conflict and Disrupted Families

Many people believe that divorce and conflict inside the family have negative effects on children. Farrington reports that

> [In 1951, John Bowlby] argued . . . that (to grow up properly) a child should experience a warm, loving, and continuous relationship with a mother figure.
> . . . If children are separated from a biological parent (they) are more likely to offend. . . .
> . . . (if) separated from a biological parent (they) are more likely to offend than children from intact families.
> . . . Homes broken while the boy was between birth and age 4 especially predicted delinquency, while homes broken while the boy was between ages 11 and 15 were not particularly criminogenic. Remarriage (which happened more often after divorce or separation than after death) was also associated with an increased risk of delinquency, suggesting an undesirable effect of stepparents.
> . . . [C]hildren who witnessed violence between their parents were more likely to commit both violent and property offenses according to their self-reports.
> Explanations of the relationship between disrupted families and delinquency fall into three major classes (Trauma theories, Life course theories, Selection theories). . . (Research) results favored life course theories rather than trauma or selection theories. Life course theories focus on separation as a sequence of stressful experiences, and on the effects of multiple stressors such as prenatal conflict, prenatal loss, reduced economic circumstances, changes in parent figures, and poor child-rearing methods. (2011: 139–41)

From our prisoner personal stories on disrupted families and parental conflict we have the following excerpts.

#####

Prisoner Essay 6.3

"Learning How to Jail with Grown Men" (2/1/09)

My family life or upbringing, has affected my life in many ways. But the one family aspect that led me to my criminal lifestyle would have to be the fact that my mother was a single parent. With her being that only parent in the home she was at work most of the time—which left me home with no supervision.

One good example of the lack of supervision would be the weeknights that I was supposed to be home in bed for school the next day, I would be out and about running the streets. While most of my peers were home doing the normal things, I was out running the streets, which became my family—due to the amount of time I spent there and had grown close to the life in the streets. It's not my mother's fault because she was just trying to provide for us. But I got most of my guidance from there (the streets).

So eventually I start asking as I've learn from the environment that, as strongly as I am influenced by, and pulled to my family, yet I got kicked out of my mother's house because I'm very rebellious to authority. On the streets there was no real authority, just a certain cycle to go by. After a while that lifestyle is what I become, and makes me who I am. While on them streets I feel as though I get the acceptance and respect that, at such a young age, seems so important to a young man. I start to take risks to maintain that lifestyle, so I end up getting caught doing things that go on in that environment. So now you have a young influenced man, living and learning how to jail with grown men from basically the same environment and upbringing that he has had. So naturally he starts to soak up every bit of information that he can. Just to keep living that lifestyle that he was now became comfortable with. Also now he is looking for ways to avoid paying the consequences of his actions. So now you not only got him learning to do things that in societies eyes are against authority but now he learning to avoid the consequences also.

These days knowing and experiencing the things that I have—my honest opinion is that strong supervision of your children is a main priority, and major way of prevention of them ever being placed in a environment such as prison. Now with me being a convict and having children the statistics say they have a good chance of being convicted of some type of crime. But strong and caring supervision of our children would prevent more than what people realize. With that supervision we know exactly what our children are doing and what they are involved in. Once we know what's going on in their lives we can get involved and guide them in the right direction.

#####

Other Parental Features

There are several other parental features that predict crime and delinquency, including young age (teen pregnancy), substance abuse, stress or depression, working mothers, low income, welfare, single parent using poor child-rearing methods with children characterized by "low school attainment and delinquency. . . . "Boys born to unmarried mothers aged 17 or less had an 11-fold increased risk of chronic offending compared to boys born to married mothers aged 20 or more" (Farrington 2011: 141–42).

And Farrington and Welsh note that studies show that "parental stress produced parental depression, which in turn caused poor discipline, which in turn caused childhood antisocial behavior (2007: 71–72).

#####

Prisoner Essay 6.4

"My Father's Depression" (2/1/09)
My family factors contributed greatly to the development of my criminal nature. Despite the several positive contributions, the negative family factors impacted me greatly. The factors, which affected me, the most were having a criminal father, physical abuse, and my father suffering from a mental disorder.

My father had an extensive criminal background before I was born. Even though he has never been arrested since I was born, he could never truly hide his nature. He grew up on the eastside of Detroit. Coming from an impoverished neighborhood, he found himself surrounded in a world full of drugs, guns, and fast women, which he indulged in quite frequently. My mother told me stories of guys pulling pistols on my father, or him smuggling drugs to Canada, and how he enjoyed fighting. He had several run-ins with the police and eventually was sent to jail. He made great strides to avoid breaking the law once I was born, but his anger problems were clearly present at home.

My father would have always have problems with anger. He would allow his anger to overcome him, and he would react without thinking. He began disciplining my brother and I with a belt. But discipline shouldn't turned into physical abuse. He would often times punch and slap me when I did something wrong. He would sometimes even attack me even if I had done nothing wrong. He would take his anger out on me and my brother. I suppressed a lot of animosity and anger towards him growing up. Since I was not strong enough to fight him back, I would take my frustration out on those around me. I would try to get into fights so I could make someone else feel the way I was feeling. I always had no respect for authority or those around me. I felt that my father took advantage of the fact that he was my father and that he had authority over me. I began despising those in authority and any rules that they attempt to put upon me. I later learned that part of the reason behind my father's anger problems were that he suffered from bi-polar and manic depression.

Discovering that my father was bi-polar helped answer a lot of questions that I had. Growing up I never fully understood the reason why he was so angry a lot of the time. He could go from the most loving father in the world, to the worst in minutes. One minute he could be laughing and playing and the next he would be yelling and screaming. Even though he would always apologize after one of his outbursts or after beating me, his words did little to mend the mental effect that it was having on me. A criminal nature was already instilled in me.

These are negative family factors that contributed greatly to my life of crime. If I would have some type of early intervention, I could have avoided breaking the law and the penitentiary.

Prisoner Essay 6.5

"When Fourteen Year Old Sister Had Baby Family Fell Apart" (1/25/09)
Me and my sister were problem child's as you could say, we had a problem with any kind of authority and we always expressed how we felt no matter how we was feeling at the time. Me and my sister have always had a problem in school ever since we were enrolled into school. My sister dropped out of school when she was fourteen because she had a baby and that's when everything fell apart in my family. My mom and dad had already divorced about three years before that, but that didn't affect the family because it's what everybody wanted. After the baby was born that's when everything went downhill and we started to go our separates ways, it was like we wasn't a family anymore. It took about ten years before we became a real family again.

#####

Family-Based Crime Prevention

Farrington reviews the possibilities for preventing delinquency. For example, among our six predictors of delinquency and crime (runs in families, large family size, poor parental supervision, child abuse and neglect, parental conflict and disrupted families, and other features such as substance abuse, stress, depression), some of them are open to intervention, such as "educating or training parents to use more effective methods of child-rearing." Are there effective parenting methods? Farrington and Welsh are encouraged by the behavioral parent management training developed by Gerald Patterson

(1982) at the Oregon Social Learning Center. " The parents of antisocial children used more punishment (such as scolding, shouting, or threatening), but failed to make it contingent on the child's behavior" (2011: 147).

At the Oregon Social Learning Center, Farrington found "Patterson . . . (trained) parents in effective child-rearing methods." What are these methods? "Noticing what a child is doing, monitoring behavior over long periods, clearly state house rules, making rewards and punishments contingent on behavior, and negotiating disagreements" (2011: 147).

CONCLUSION

Can effective parent training be delivered to the type of families described in our chapter 6 prisoner essays? If so, how? How can the parents in such stories become educated? Effective intervention with these types of families must ask *why* these predictors are so strong.

> Many theories have been proposed to explain these results. The most popular are selection, social learning, and attachment theories. Selection theories argue that relationships between large family size, poor prenatal supervision, disrupted families (etc.) and delinquency are driven by the fact that antisocial people tend to have large families, poor parental supervision, disrupted families (etc.) as well as antisocial children. . . . Social learning theories argue that children fail to learn law-abiding behavior if their parents provide antisocial models and/or fail to react to their transgressions in an appropriate, consistent, and contingent fashion. Attachment theories argue that low attachment to parents (recreated, for example, by cold rejecting parents or by separation from a parent) produces cold, callous children who tend to commit delinquent acts. (Farrington 2011: 147–48)

Family-based prevention methods such as parent training (in how to do effective parental supervision) could be mandated for parent(s) who come into contact with the courts.

What many of the prisoners say is that their parent(s) didn't know how to raise them, and that often their parent was engaged in substance abuse, selling drugs, prostitution, or various crime, and/or were stressed or depressed. The result was the child or youth was left to "raise myself."

#####

Prisoner Essay 6.6

"Parents Addiction Leaves Son with No Plan" (10/27/08)

I was born in '79 my father at that time was addicted to heroin, and my mom she enjoyed a drink every now and again. As time when on my dad dropped his addiction, for this new drug crack. And my mom started to drink more. As a result of their addiction, raising children became secondary. They lost touch with reality, they became increasingly unable to properly pay attention to what train of thought their children were developing.

As I grew, so did my impulsive action of bad judgment. The voice that you hear that tells you; don't do that, that wrong, was ignored. Originally my first thought was a good thought. After ignoring that thought (I went on) to encourage the evil thought (that had been) resisted. Evilness became impulsive. My heart was corrupted; the seeds of wrongdoing had been implanted in my brain, to grow and bear it's fruit. There was no thinking about what I'm about to do. There was no plan. There was only survival. Animals live off instinct I guess that's what I became, because my first instinct was to react off what was forced in my conscience mind.

My family—I have only one biological child. A son his name is Da'ron and he is 13 years old. However I've always been like a father to both my little brother and sister. And my nieces, I sometimes feel like I have 5 kids.

#####

Family-based prevention programs are available (see Colorado Center for the Study of Prevention of Violence) and take either psychological or public health approaches.

> When delivered by psychologists, these programs are often classified into parent management training, functional family therapy, or family preservation (Wasserman and Miller 1998). Typically, they attempt to change the social contingencies in the family environment so that children are rewarded in some way for appropriate or prosocial behaviors and punished in some way for inappropriate or antisocial behaviors. (Farrington and Welsh 2007: 121)

With regard to parent education, Farrington and Welsh note that home visiting programs are popular:

> The main goals of home visiting programs center around educating parents to improve the life chances of children from a very young age, often beginning at birth and sometimes in the final trimester of pregnancy. Some of the main goals include the prevention of preterm or low-weight births, the promotion of healthy child development or school readiness, and the prevention of child abuse and neglect (Gomby, Culross, and Behrman 1999, p. 4). Home visits very often also serve to improve parental well-being, linking parents to community resources to help with employment, educational, or addiction recovery.

Some parent education programs include daycare. Farrington and Welsh note that:

> Patterson attempted to train these parents in effective child-rearing methods, namely, noticing what a child is doing, monitoring behavior over long periods, clearly stating house rules, making rewards and punishments contingent on behavior, and negotiating disagreements so that conflicts and crises do not escalate. (2007: 126–27)

These family intervention crime prevention programs require moving a family beyond its social isolation, connecting to community programs. This is a reminder of the value of the "community psychology" point of view. Karen Parker (2008) found the transformation in city labor markets with deindustrialization impacting on African American women and men. As Loic Wacquant (2008) observes, the "communal ghetto" of the industrial era transformed into the "hyperghetto" of the postindustrial economy. The community-level variables such as strength of parent networks on the block (in neighborhoods) are weakened by these city transformations. The "hustler class" and youth gangs come to dominate in the most affected neighborhoods. In this atmosphere, the triage for families is vital. These parent education and parent management training support programs are effective—but would it not also be good to improve the living conditions of the "hyperghetto" to lessen parental stress in the first place?

The proximate causes—what causes the family to become criminogenic, for instance the feminization of poverty—could also be reduced by greatly reducing poverty in the United States, e.g., through incomes policy (guaranteed income), housing policy (help with homeownership), and improved skills training and education. This *level* of crime prevention requires a *community-level* criminology.

In addition to all six of the family factors we have reviewed, there is the fact that part of growing up means that from an early age kids go out of the house and play or interact with other kids and the other households in the community-area, or set of nearby neighborhoods. A different level the neighborhood effects we address in chapter 7.

EXERCISE 6.1

"Anecdote versus Systematic Study." What is the difference between criminological findings from a systematic forty-year longitudinal study of 1,500 subjects from age eight to forty-eight and a personal story about yourself or your cousin's son? (Use the Farrington and Welsh Cambridge Study in Delinquent Development to answer this question.)

DISCUSSION AND REVIEW QUESTIONS

1. What is meant by the feminization of poverty? What social policy could help?
2. What explanations are given for the fact that crime runs in families?
3. What explanations are given for the fact that large family size predicts crime?
4. What child-rearing methods are associated with crime?
5. What is child neglect? Why do you think child abuse and neglect are associated with crime? (Be sure to draw from the prisoner essays when writing your answer.)
6. Why would parental conflict and disrupted family be a predictive factor for later criminality?
7. Give an example of a "family-based crime prevention policy."

7

Community and Crime

Many observers would say that "Growing up in *that* neighborhood was a predictable path to being either dead or in prison by the age of 21." Prisoners often say that "the way things were in the community" as they grew up acted as a pathway for them to crime and prison. Farrington and Welsh say:

> Peer, school, and community prevention programs target environmental-level risk factors for delinquency and later offending . . . some of these risk factors include association with delinquent friends; attending high delinquency-rate schools, which have high levels of distrust between teachers and students, low commitment to the school by students, and unclear and inconsistently enforced rules; and growing up in a poor, disorganized neighborhood. (2007: 77) (See table 1.1.)

A POLITICAL AND ECONOMIC DECISION: TO ABANDON THE JOBLESS GHETTO

It is crucial to connect macro-level sociological and political analysis along with critical criminology perspectives to understand criminogenic neighborhoods. Farrington and Welsh, in their 2007 book *Saving Children from a Life of Crime*, do not address the question: Why are there so many unsafe neighborhoods to grow up in? Why do we have the *degree* of inequality, concentrated disadvantage, segregation, and power arrangements in the United States that help cause criminogenic conditions such as the extensive "social disorganization" in so many major city neighborhoods? Loic Wacquant (2008) argues that the sources of the jobless hyperghetto have both economic and political causes. Farrington and Welsh, for their part, talk about *proximate* levels of explanation of crime such as unsafe neighborhoods, individual factors, family factors, delinquent peers, and bad schools, and growing up in a poor, disorganized neighborhood. But the sociological fact is that all of these "levels of reality" are located within community areas (sets of neighborhoods) that, in turn, are "nested" in larger macro contexts such as city labor markets and national power, politics, and policies. Rueschemeyer, reporting on Charles Tilly's book *Durable Inequality*, observes that the study of inequality that takes off from the ideas of Marx and Weber

> focuses on social categories that profoundly shape social arrangements and that separate people with different life chances, categories such as gender, race, ethnicity, religion, and stable class position. It is social organizations, including economic corporations, that build and maintain categorical inequalities. (2009: 252)

Living in a nation that has a high degree of inequality, such as the United States, where there are already several hundred inner-city jobless ghettos, and where a "tide of social disorganization" is sweeping over nearby community-areas means *some* people are going to be an "absolute surplus population" (Wacquant 2002) because the corporations have moved out of the city to the suburbs or to other states or other countries, and economic corporations, as Rueschemeyer emphasizes, "build and maintain categorical inequalities."
Loic Wacquant argues:

> Instead of repeating or extending previous analyses of racial domination in the Fordist-Keynesian era as if it were some timeless institutional contraption, we must *historicize the state and function of the ghetto* in the U.S. metropolis and reach beyond its physical perimeter to elucidate its fate after the climax of the Civil Rights movement. Dissecting the economic and political forces . . . reveals that ghettos are not autonomous sociospatial constellations that contain within themselves the principle of their evolution. . . . (Ghettos are) not the simple mechanical result of deindustrialization, demographic shifts or of a skills or spatial "mismatch" between the supply and demand for labour. . . . Rather, it is the product of a novel *political* articulation of racial cleavage, class inequality and urban space. (2008: 47)

In short, Wacquant is saying that the abandonment of U.S. inner-city ghettos is a *political decision*.
Reuschemeyer's 2009 book *Useable Theory* introduces analytic tools for social and political research on macro contexts by observing that:

> Individuals, groups, social networks, organizations, and social identities exist within more comprehensive social environments These macro settings include cultural templates, overarching institutions regulating social, economic, and other spheres of life, as well as factual, nonnormative conditions such as power relations, conditions of war and peace, population composition, horizons of available knowledge, available technology, and past accumulations. Such encompassing social conditions are in many ways causally relevant for the lives

of individuals and small groups, while they themselves are often beyond the reach of smaller social units and their dynamics.

There tends to be, then, a rough asymmetry in the causal relations between the micro and the macro levels of social life. This asymmetry is not without significant exceptions; but to anticipate its likelihood when developing hypothesis is important because it runs counter to our common sense, which tends to neglect macrostructures.

Emphasizing the asymmetry may also seem counterintuitive in view of the axiom that ultimately all social structures are the result of actions and interactions of individuals. Yet this axiom can be upheld only if we admit of complex indirect effects on the actions and interactions that shape stable relationships and structures. It certainly does not entail that individuals and small groups—and even large organizations—can *on their own* change comprehensive institutional complexes, broad economic conditions, or wide-ranging established power relations. (143)

#####

Prisoner Essay 7.1

"This Jungle That You Call a Community" (2/15/09)

Today is a great day for today I have learnt a new word—socioeconomic. Personally I find such words to be nothing more than a conundrum or a game by the powers that be. In fact, where I come from people rarely encounter such words. So a sense of curiosity was all I need to encourage me to look this word up in the dictionary. Simple! A combination of two words.

Well these days there is not much socializing especially in my part of the jungle. Everyone seems to be sociopathic, no one is friendly they all have a fear of one another. Concerning this economics—is not the word based on predictions, concepts, theoretical and hypothetical? Or perhaps it does boil down to making the best choice or are we solving the economic problem the best we can with what we have. The most important word in my neighborhood is survive.

For some reasons we rarely use the word community. We say the hood, the set, or we represent with colors and numbers. They became our own little kingdoms that are controlled and patrolled by what some call a gang, or criminals. My gang is my family and I would gladly kill and die for them because they are all that I have in this jungle that you call a community. And what they call criminals we call heroes, providers, businessmen and entrepreneurs. This is my life and my reality. Today I paid the rent and all the bills. Today I made sure my mother had enough dope to last her. Today I went to a close casket funeral for my best friend because someone blew his face off; today murder is on my mind. Today I wonder if I will be murdered. Today is my birthday and I am only 15 years of age. I live in a third world that they call a community of the USA.

I have a combined word that I would like to share with my reader—social promotion. School was very hurtful for me because how could I be in the 10th grade? I can barely read and write. The teachers only saw a lost cause and the students that could read and write indirectly made me feel that low-self worth.

So school became my social club and my fashion show and occasionally my war zone. School offered me math. Keep your math because I make over 1,000 dollars a day. School offered me science, why? I already hold a degree as a master chemist. School offers me the history filled with lies and history refused to show me who I am. They offered social studies yet you do not socialize with me. I have no need for your religion for I have many gods—all-powerful, people, power, pussy, and politics. So again, I say to my reader judge me not for I was created. Home grown they call it these days. What do all human beings have in common? A natural instinct to survive. So while our new president puts together a plan, I be here surviving as only a 15 year old can in a third world, filled with socioeconomic.

#####

Urban Abandonment and Punitive Containment

In Loic Wacquant's *Urban Outcasts: A Comparative Sociology of Advanced Marginality* he analyzes the

> *institutional transformation undergone by the African-American ghetto* caught in the undertow of the wave of riots that swept the metropolis in the 1960s, in the wake of the reorganization of the regime of racial domination, the capitalist economy and public policy in the United States . . . (2008: 3).
>
> He talks of the "sociospatial relegation and exclusionary closure (in Max Weber's sense) that has crystallized in the post-Fordist city as a result of the uneven development of the capitalist economies and the recoiling of welfare states . . ." (2008:3).
>
> I retrace the historic shift from the *communal ghetto* of the mid-twentieth century, a compact and sharply circumscribed sociospatial formation to which blacks of all classes were consigned and bound together by a broad comple-ment of institutions specific to the group and its reserved space, to the . . . *hyperghetto*, a novel, decentred, territorial and organizational configuration characterized by conjugated segregation on the basis of race *and* class in the context of the double retrenchment of the labour market *and* the welfare state from the urban core, necessitating and eliciting the corresponding deployment of an intrusive and omnipresent police and penal apparatus.

. . . In the final analysis, however, it is *the collapse of public institutions,* resulting from state policies of urban abandonment and leading to the punitive containment of the black (sub)proletariat, that emerges as the most distinctive cause of entrenched marginality, in the American metropolis. In contrast with Wilson's (1987) *The Truly Disadvantaged*, which prioritizes the role of the economy, and Massey and Denton's (1993) *American Apartheid*, which stresses the weight of racial segregation, this book highlights the gamut of racially skewed and market-oriented state policies that have aggravated, packed and trapped poor blacks at the bottom of the spatial order of the polarizing city. (2008: 3–4)

Economic and Political Roots of Hyperghettoization

The collective urban disorders in American ghettos, some in the 1960s, others in the 1980s and 1990s are motivated, Wacquant argues, by a protest against *ethnoracial injustice* and a "class logic pushing the impoverished fractions of the working class to rise up against *economic deprivation and widening social inequalities*" (2008: 22).

In the first decades of the twenty-first century the U.S. social order has 11 percent poverty and 18 percent working poor. Thus, more than 29 percent of the American people are just above, at, or below the poverty line. When I was an instructor in sociology at Lansing Community College, Michigan (1983–1996), I was asked to help organize and lead a "Forum on Welfare" in the fall of 1995 protesting the elimination of welfare assistance for unemployed men and cutbacks in welfare for women with children—for example a new rule forbidding women on welfare from attending postsecondary education "while on welfare." The Clinton "end of welfare as we know it" reforms occurred during the economic boom of the 1990s and assumed people could get off welfare and that there would be no more deep recessions. The subsequent recessions of 2000–2001 and 2008–2009 exposed the bottom one-third of the U.S. workforce to extreme hardship. Wacquant argues that the urban riots of 1992 in South Central Los Angeles were demanding

> decent jobs, good schools, affordable or improved housing, access to basic public services, and fair treatment by the police. . . .
> . . . [The 1992 riots] were also . . . against grinding poverty and the severe aggravation of daily living conditions brought on by economic recession and cutbacks in government programs. (2008: 23)

However, it is not only periodic but temporary recessions that expose the low-wage worker and the unemployed to hardship but also the ongoing

> polarization of the class structure which, combined with ethnoracial segregation and welfare state retrenchment, has produced a *dualization of the social*

and physical structure of the metropolis that has consigned large sections of the unskilled labor force to economic redundancy and social marginality. This violence "from above" has three main components.

1. *Mass unemployment*, both chronic and persistent, amounting, for entire segments of the working class, to *deproletarianization* and the diffusion of *labour precariousness*, bringing in their wake a whole train of material deprivation, family hardship, temporal uncertainty and personal anxiety.
2. *Relegation to decaying neighborhoods.* . . .
3. Heightened *stigmatization.* . . . (Wacquant 2008: 24–25)

The ghetto of the 1980s and 1990s (and continuing to today) is, according to Wacquant, a hyperghetto characterized by "accelerating physical depredation, street violence and endemic insecurity, as well as by levels of economic exclusion and social hardship comparable only to those of the worst years of the Great Depression" (Wacquant 2008: 52). In describing the Woodlawn area of Chicago, Wacquant notes fewer than ninety commercial establishments remain, none of which employ more than a few workers.

> Yet the most significant brute fact of every daily life in the fin-de-siecle ghetto is without contest the extraordinary *prevalence of physical danger and the acute sense of insecurity* that pervades the streets . . . such internecine violence "from below" must be analyzed not as an expression of the senseless "pathology" of residents of the hyperghetto but as a function of the degree of penetration and mode of regulation of this territory by the state. It is a reasoned response (in the double sense of echo and retort) to various kinds of violence "from above" and an intelligible by-product of the policy of abandonment of the urban core. . . . (2008: 62)

Wacquant is saying that since the mid-1970s there has been a "policy of state abandonment and punitive containment of the marginalized fractions of the black working class" (2008: 91). This analysis fits in well with Jonathan Simons political sociology notion of "governing through crime" discussed in chapter 3. (For a critique of the narrow way justice reinvestment has occurred through the Council of State Governments since Wacquant wrote in 2008, see Austin et al. [2013]; also see chapter 10 in this book).

Prevention: Fundamental Change or Proximate Causes?

Wacquant's policy recommendation is that the United States institute a guaranteed income (see chapter 10). This would be, he notes, as fundamental a change in social life as the end of slavery and the right of a citizen to vote.

Most policy recommendations stay at the micro-system level, such as the individual or families. These proximate causes of crime were part of a focus by Farrington and Welsh to theorize an empirical basis for a national crime prevention program (2007). They argue that at the community-level, evidence-based programs of *peer mentoring* show promise to reduce the influence of delinquent friends and increase the influence of prosocial friends.

> Teaching children to resist antisocial peer pressures that encourage delinquent activities can take many forms, including modeling and guided practice. Peers must be older, preferably in their later teens, and influential; such peers are sometimes known as high-status peer leaders. (Farrington and Welsh 2007: 138)

From Farrington and Welsh's review of well done evaluation studies they find an effective protective factor in "after school and community-based mentoring programs." Many cities, for instance, have a Boys and Girls Club as an afterschool program sometimes combined with a "Big Buddies" mentoring program. The author helped to start the Boys and Girls Clubs of Lenawee (BGCL) in Adrian, and has researched the local club more than eight years comparing juvenile courts records with club attendance, and found that youth from the same set of nearby neighborhoods that went to the BGCL had fewer contacts with juvenile court and when they did have contacts were treated more informally (going through Teen Court). The National Research Council and Institute of Medicine's panel on juvenile crime "cautioned against the practice of grouping deviant or high-risk peers together during early adolescence." On balance it seems better to have the preventive mentoring available at the club than to eliminate the afterschool program because of "grouping deviant or high-risk peers together during early adolescence." The club offers the intervening factor of long-term paid mentors.

Breaking risk factors into individual, family, and community is somewhat arbitrary, since any one person is always in some relationship to themselves, their family, and their community—the sets of factors are always in a context and are a set of reciprocal or interactive influences. In chapters 5 and 6 we reviewed individual and family prisoner essays on criminology. Recall in chapter 4 that Joy Dryfoos's main point was that, while school failure was one of the first flags for youth troubles such as substance abuse, early sexual intercourse, and trouble with the law, there was *a need for multiproblem comprehensive prevention programs* tackling all four (and other) factors. Farrington and Welsh emphasize the same point and present evidence-based programs at all three levels—individual, family, and community, and argue for a *multiple factor intervention program*. However, it is helpful, for analysis, to focus on each "level of reality." What do prisoners think about community level variables?

At the community level, Farrington and Welsh's predictive factors include growing up in a low socioeconomic status household (see table 1.1). This is different than another of their community level predictive variables, "living in deprived areas." For growing up in a low socioeconomic status household, recall the chapter 4 prisoner describing social class differences at school:

> Fellow students made school hard: 90 percent of student's households were considered upper class . . . my parents managed to scrape together enough to rent a decent house on the edge of town. I hated school. Every year I was treated worse and worse (by fellow students).

Also at the community level is the predictive factor "associating with delinquent." This is a frequent theme: "I began running the streets, hanging out with the wrong crowd."

In writing their personal stories it is clear that many prisoners identify the nature of their community as consequential in the development of their criminal life. The Graterford prison long-sentence prisoners (LIFERS, Inc.) that developed out of the prison college program there, analyzed the typical prisoner involved in the culture of street crime in the following way:

> Unemployment, living costs, and an intense desire for material wealth drive the first major component of the street crime culture. These economic influences entice those within the culture into drug dealing and violence . . . (including) drug dealing, drug wars, and disputes between drug dealers that end up involving possession and use of hand guns. On the other side, it also causes those who purchase the dealers' products to commit crimes such as robberies and burglaries to get fast money to buy drugs. Moreover, most of those who are driven by this part of the culture *have less than an adequate appreciation for wealth earned by labor or the traditional aspects of employment.* Because members of this culture desire more than what traditional employment can provide, they turn to hustling. . . . They also crave the power, influence, and respect hustlers in the street crime culture receive from having expensive cars, the latest fashions, and flashy jewelry. (LIFERS Public Safety Steering Committee 2004: 58) (emphasis added)

Note that the first word in this succinct description is "unemployment." Certainly the transformation of the communal ghetto into the hyperghetto that Wacquant describes includes the shift in the economy away from manufacturing and toward services, and the rise of chronic unemployment. This is a major macro-context causal mechanism, that is, economic influences.

However, the analysis of the long-term prisoners in LIFERS, Inc. has a weak grasp of the *changes* in the urban labor market toward there being an *absolute surplus* labor population. The hyperghetto "culture of street crime" hustler has "less than an adequate appreciation for wealth earned by labor or the traditional aspects of employment" because of the deproletarianization Wacquant describes. As Wacquant argues:

> such internecine violence "from below" must be analyzed not as an expression of the senseless "pathology" of residents of the hyperghetto but as a function of the degree of penetration and mode of regulation of this territory by the state. It is a reasoned response (in the double sense of echo and retort) to various kinds of violence "from above" and an intelligible by-product of the policy of abandonment of the urban core. (2008: 54–55)

#####

Prisoner Essay 7.2

"I Acted Out in the Neighborhood" (2/18/09)
However, having a supportive family does not mean that a child will be protected from a very hostile and angering external environment. Because I have a family who encouraged me, throughout school being involved in glee-club, supporting me in track and field and football, yet I sought the inner-argument of my environment. I was influenced by my brothers at the same time it was a lot of frustration and conflict because I imitated their behavior. . . . But there are no parental restrictions once you are away from the home, so I acted out in the neighborhood, because I saw and understood the struggle that I was being sheltered from inside the house.

#####

Prisoner Essay 7.3

"Pushing Pounds of Weed through Hole in Screen" (11/8/08)
Early in life I realized that it is very unlikely that people will turn down help, and it really doesn't matter what form it comes in, plus, I was always looking to help my mother out, who had four children to raise on her own, fake-ass husband who left and offered no support.

When I was around 12 years old I ran into a guy that had a big bag of weed. He told me that if I gave him 15 dollars he would make it worth my while. So I did, he was right, I took what he gave me and rolled 60 joints out of it. The way I saw it was like this, I sell these joints; I make a nice 45-dollar profit. And so selling weed became my new forte. I would sell to anyone, because everybody that I knew smoked weed, including my mother, it was not bad or dangerous in the eyes of those around me. By the time I was 13 in high school I was selling over 100 joints every morning before school started. The entire school seemed to be looking to catch me before I ran out. Back at home it got so bad or good depending on how you look at it, that people knocked on our door past 12 midnight. Needless to say, my mother was pissed! She told me that I must tell everybody not to come by the house that late. I did, but they would come anyway. They would say things like; oh, I didn't know it was that late, or I didn't remember or somebody told me that it was okay. Well, before you know it I was selling pounds of weed, and I moved operations to my bedroom window behind the house. I put a hole in the screen and people would roll the money up and push it through the hole and I would push the product back though. It was a big operation, plus I had to get up and go to school in the mornings. I always split the profit with my mother; in return she would support me and help me make the right decisions concerning problems that I ran into.

As I stated, everyone smoked weed, this included my grandfather who was very picky, he only bought weed from me when it was good and potent. Sometimes he would take me to his connection and I would buy the expensive stuff. The only problem was, other people that weren't real weed consumers, but rather novelty smokers, wanted quantity not so much quality. But for the most part people seem to treat me with respect and would encourage me to keep it up.

Expert researchers claim the poor parental supervision is a strong replicable predictors of crime. Now, although I was doing crime according to established law, the funny thing is, why would a family (mother, grandmother, grandfather, uncles and aunts), encourage it? When money is tight, and it was, providing a service (fair and professional) seems to be the American way. But, I do agree that this type of behavior so early, can lead to being mislead to the point that if not corrected it will be a problem.

#####

High Crime Neighborhoods Surrounded by More Violence in Neighboring Areas

The big picture cause of crime not only includes concentrated disadvantage (chronic unemployment and poverty, family disruption, ethnoracial residential segregation in poor housing) but also the social isolation of the high crime community. Ruth Peterson and Lauren Krivo's 2010 book *Divergent Social Worlds: Neighborhood Crime and the Racial-Spatial Divide* is instructive. Kurbin provides an overview of Peterson and Krivo's analysis:

They ask: How much do the distinct spatial contexts in which white, African American, Latino, minority, and integrated neighborhoods are located contribute to varying levels of crime within these communities?

They argue a common feature of many African American neighborhoods, whatever their internal character, is proximity to communities with character- istics typically associated with higher crime rates, such as disadvantage and residential instability. In contrast, white areas are often surrounded by neigh- borhoods where crime-promoting conditions are relatively absent and factors that discourage crime, such as external community investments are prevalent. In the final set of analyses, we encounter the key finding: White neighbor- hoods benefit from the dual privileges of low internal disadvantage as well as embeddedness within a context of other white and advantaged areas. African American, Latino, and minority neighborhoods suffer a double jeopardy: They are at risk of greater violence stemming from their own internal—often highly disadvantaged-character and they bear the brunt of isolation from violence- reducing structures and processes because they are surrounded by disadvantaged areas. (Kurbin 2012: 120)

Peterson and Krivo, in their own words, note:

Neighborhoods are likely to be part of a broader system of linked territories that affect one another. Janet Heitgerd and Robert Bursik (1987: 776) made this point over twenty years ago when they argued that the greatest shortcoming of traditional social disorganization theory lies in "an overriding emphasis on the internal dynamics of local communities that ignore(s) the external contingencies that may be important in shaping the nature of these dynamics. . . ."

. . . Their finding that delinquency rates in Chicago neighborhoods were affected by conditions in adjacent areas supported the argument that the situa- tion of communities relative to one another is consequential.

. . . More recent studies support this conclusion by showing that violence is greater in local areas when there is more violence in neighboring communities.

. . . George Tita and Robert Greenbaum (2009) specifically compare how Pittsburgh neighborhoods with rival gangs affect one another's rates of gang violence to the way bordering neighborhoods influence each other's experience of this type of violence. (2010: 91–93)

The prisoner essay below shows the "communal ghetto" of the 1960s and 1970s in which the prisoner grew up and the beginning of the "hyper- ghetto" on 12th Street in Detroit five blocks away. Chris Sower, a Michigan State University (MSU) sociology professor, studied the 1967 Detroit riots centered around 12th Street and found that nearby neighborhood areas that were *organized* (block clubs, neighborhood watch, etc.) did not riot, but that neighborhood areas that were disorganized did have rioters and build- ings vandalized and burned. Out of his studies the MSU School of Criminal

Justice started a version of community policing studies in the mid-1970s that was tried out in Flint starting in 1975 as that Michigan city was reeling from auto plant shutdowns. Peterson and Krivo point out that since the 1960s U.S. racially segregated neighborhoods have increased and the high crime areas are surrounded by *more* racially segregated high crime neighborhoods. Contemporary children in the inner cities do not live in stable areas *and* they are *surrounded* by unstable, socially disorganized neighborhoods.

#####

Prisoner Essay 7.4

"Five Blocks Over on Twelfth Street" (11/8/08)
The neighborhood in which I grew up in the sixties and early seventies, was socially motivated, family adapt and each basically looked after each other. Our community leaders played a small role along with our teachers. But twice a year during the summer, our neighborhood families would chip in, cook and organize a block party. Many of the young boys such as myself would collect large bricks and help build small fireplaces for B-B-Ques.

Two days before the celebration, we would pick large apples, pears, plums and berries from some of the neighbor's backyards to make jelly, pies doughnuts fillings. Every neighbor from five blocks away would bring their family. With the help of several local ministers, both Baptist and Muslim would gather together and take part in the gala. Aretha Franklin's father had his church several block away, he would stop by and say a few prayers and bless every one there.

These people didn't discriminate against anyone; they just asked that no one bring any liquor or drugs. Occasionally, there would be a fight, which was immediately broken up. Sometimes the police would walk or stand guard hoping to catch some one doing wrong and make sure the teen-age curfew would be honored. After every one had ate, music played and everybody danced and sang together.

There was no killing, robbing, raping or extreme drugs being sold in this area. The black Muslims at the time had control of this area and would not allow them to deal. But five blocks over on 12th street were the 67 riot began was full of corruption, prostitution, drugs, etc. . . . some nights when my father was asleep, me and two of my friends would venture into this area. Unable to buy wine, we used to pay a wino to buy it for us.

We were extremely careful as to who was in the area because people from our closely knitted area would certainly without any reservations tell our parents. We were drawn into this area by rumors of seeing naked girls sitting outside this nightclub after dancing. This rumor came from another boy two to three years older than us. A friend of mine named Wilbur didn't have to worry about any one telling his mother because she was an alcoholic and didn't care about anything but drinking.

When I escaped from the youth center, his mother allowed me to sleep, eat and hide at her home as long as we went out and got her something to drink. In order for her son and me to provide her with wine, we started skipping school and raiding local newspaper stands. After the newspaper carrier dropped off a load of newspapers from Cunningham drug store and several other stores, we would take them before they could pick them up.

We would then go down and stand in front of the General Motors building and sell all the papers by hand. On a good day, we would earn ten to fifteen dollars apiece. Later that day, we would bring his mother two bottles of wine and a bar-bq dinner. If we attempted anything such as this is our own neighborhood, we would have been immediately caught and driven home by our neighbors.

Besides hiding out from many of the adults in our neighborhood, we had to also be aware of some of the boys and girls as well. They were a greater threat, because they knew most of the hangouts outside our neighborhood. For over a week, I hid out a block from where my father lived. One day I saw my older sister coming from school. She cried and begged me to come back home. I told her no and to tell our father that I was all right and I would come back home when our mother came back. I had my friend's mother ask my father where was my mother was at. And my father would always tell her he didn't know and I believed him.

Growing up in a social isolation in a high crime neighborhood that is surrounded by other racially segregated high crime neighborhoods reinforces the "magnetism of street life." The culture of street crime is (seemingly) everywhere (within walking or bicycle distance).

#####

Prisoner Essay 7.5

"Crime as Survival Numbness" (2/18/09)
Many factors can be considered in my reasoning for choosing to commit crimes. I do not think I could point to one thing in particular but more so a combination of events is what shaped my perception and caused me to look at life the way I did. The street life fascinated me, the money, the drugs it was all alluring. I seen guys I grew up with living the American Dream. Nice cars, plenty of girls, and they seem to always have money. I was not stupid; I knew crime provided that lifestyle for them. They either was stealing, selling drugs, or robbing people. Now, this is consider wrong, but I just could not agree. Especially since I was looking in the refrigerator, and seeing nothing

but baking soda. My little brother and sister crying to me because they are hungry—that is wrong. Committing crimes is survival because that is what it was all about. Everything we did was for a profit. The down side of it all is that you become numb; you become less and less compassionate.

What is worse than selling drugs to your friend's mother? If your heart can allow you to do that, it is because you do not have a heart. And if you don't care about your friend's mother, whose mother do you care about? Where I come from people justify wrongdoing this way—"If I do not sell this crack to my friend's mom, someone else will. It's better that I get the money." I had no idea I was enabling her. I did not even know what enabling mean. I just got use to ignoring my conscience. Whenever I felt bad about something I did, I would just go get drunk or smoke some weed and forget all about it. Eventually I just stop feeling bad. I became my environment. I became as heartless as the people I at one time feared. Since fear was not going to help me, I transformed that fear into anger. And the meaning of life was lost.

#####

Prisoner Essay 7.6

"Differences among Community Leaders" (2/25/09)
Being raised in what many described in the sixties as a melting pot, which was a small community of blacks, whites, Mexicans and gypsies. Each nationality despite our close contact maintained its own cultural values. Such as traditional holiday meals, holidays, etc.

At the time, there was a great division between our community leaders in reference as to whom we should seek guidance in.

On the black side, we had the black Muslims and Black Panther committees urging each and every black teenager they could find to reject that status quo of our Baptist minister and other community leaders that they claimed were misguiding us.

On the far left, you had dealers and other hustlers manipulating some of us into drugs and prostitution. In the middle were our schoolteachers, whom after school disappeared. 70 percent of the teachers were white that in retrospect I gathered drove from distant suburbs to teach us. From time to time, I recall seeing police officers guarding our junior high school and high so that their cars would not be stolen. During school, they provided basic minimal education, beyond the classroom, they were non-existent.

Our parents on the other hand worked during the days and based upon the barriers between them and our teachers forged a gap that in my personal estimate, if it had been prevented, may have prevented a lot of us from coming to prison.

Unlike some of my friend's parents, my mother and father refused to allow me to attend the black Muslims and black panthers summer youth rally even though most of our school black teachers attended them. And contrary to popular opinion, they personally saved a lot of children's lives from a life of crime.

A friend of mine named Wilbur, had a mother that was on drugs, their house was full of roaches. Wilbur dropped out of school in the fourth grade. Sometimes for days he would never see his mother. He would come get me and he'd ride my brother's bike while I rode mine and together we would ride all up and down 12 and 14th street in Detroit, where most prostitutes and drug addicts applied their trade.

With no food at home, and shamed to ask any one because of the others kids would tease him, Wilbur would go out to the local supermarket, open a thing of bologna, cheese, bread, crackers and eat. He would pick an apple or peach off the fruit stand, eat a few bites, and flip it over making it look like it never been touched.

At age 12, Wilbur's mother died. The local church turned him over to the police. They placed him in foster care. Three weeks later I saw him hiding in his mother old home. The black Muslims took him in. That was in 1969.

Wilbur came to prison, used drugs, robbed or killed anyone like most of the other boys like myself ended up engaging in. If it wasn't for this class, ("Social Science and Personal Writing"), I would never recognized the substantive value of our communities to prevent our children from exploring a life of crime and corruption. And in my personal belief, our communities, schools, parents etc. plays an integral role in developing or structuring the social economical values all youth need to survive.

It is a collective effort by all governing factor of any community as a body to formulate a cohesive bond to bring about awareness and preventive programs geared at providing our youth with alternative means in solving their problems rather than simply seeking refuge in drugs, crime, and corruption.

In my community, if our leaders spent more time working together, than arguing maybe they could have saved me.

#####

COMMUNITY AND VIOLENCE

#####

Prisoner Essay 7.7

"Becoming Hyperviolent in Order to Feel Safe" (2/24/10)

On a cold winter morning the last remnants of my childhood were shattered by the rapid burst of gunfire. Like a crystal decanter exploding into tiny shards of glass my life was broken in pieces.

It was March 8, 1990 and nearly twenty years later the memory replays in my mind like a syndicated television show. I can still feel the frosty air dancing over my teenage flesh. And the coppery smell of my life-liquid gushing from my body is forever embedded in my olfactory system. The most prominent thing I recall from that day is the intense heat that raged though my body as the first bullet met its mark. It reminded me of the fire that leapt from my flesh as my mother beat me mercilessly. I was in familiar territory because violence was something I had known since childhood.

My skin sizzled like bacon and my shin bone cracked like chapped lips when the first of three bullets hit me. The Nike Cortez running shoes I wore filled with blood that sloshed around with each step I took in my haste to escape my assailant. To this day one bullet remains lodged in my foot as a reminder of how fragile this thing is we call life.

The scene of my shooting plays in slow motion. I see the brown "Cavalier" pulling up to the corner where I stood talking to my friend Bo. When I looked up and saw the fire in the eyes of the driver I knew something was wrong. We exchanged warrior glares like warring tribesmen before I invited him to get out of the car to fight. A sinister smile crossed his face as he reached down and retrieved a nickel plated 380. My reaction time was slow, and before I could turn and run for shelter he squeezed off several shots. The first two bullets hit me in the leg splintering my shin, and the third bullet hit me in the foot as I fled for safety.

My heart pounded like an African drum as adrenaline coursed through my body. I pumped my legs like pistons while zig-sagging back and forth, dodging the fusillade of bullets he unleashed in a fury. As I ran I prayed none of the bullets hit me in the spine or worse, in the back of my head.

I ran around the corner into this lady's house named Lisa. She witnessed the whole scene play out and was mortified when I approached her. She begged me not to come to her house, but I ignored her request, my only concern was survival. I ran past her and entered the front door of her home. Once I gathered my composure, I fled though her side door. When I saw the coast was clear I ran back around to my street.

My emotions boiled and raged like a turbulent sea storm. The initial fear I felt was replaced by a deep abiding sadness. I felt lonely and confused. I couldn't comprehend why someone would attempt to kill me over a senseless argument. As I thought about what had just occurred I started to feel dangerously angry. The emotions I was experiencing festered with the poison of revenge. I wanted someone to feel the pain, fear and sadness I was feeling.

When I reached my street my oldest sister Tamika was the first person I saw. She raced down the block and embraced me when she saw I was still alive. Her eyes filled with tears as we walked back to the house. I took off my jacket and shirt so I could inspect my body for more bullet wounds. I was sweating and bleeding profusely and my mouth was dry as though someone had stuffed sand in it. My sister urged me to put my clothes back on, but I ignored her. I pulled out a pack of Newport's and was about to light one up when I was struck with a surge of anger. I jumped up and ran in the house to get a gun. I wanted to shoot someone so bad it nearly drove me insane. I hated being a victim and the only thing I felt would restore balance was getting revenge.

My sister pleaded with me and asked me to think about my nephews who were watching and had witnessed the whole scene. Her words coupled with the image of my nephews crying calmed me down. I fired up my crumpled cigarette and waited for an ambulance that never came. It wasn't a surprise to me. I was used to ambulance and police who never came to the rescue of black children. It was the reality of living in the hood. Finally after waiting nearly half an hour my friend Bo drove me to Mt. Carmel hospital on Detroit's Westside.

When I arrived at the hospital I felt like I was being moved through an assembly line manned by robots. For the staff at Mt. Carmel a child being shot was business as usual. The staff there had long ago divorced themselves from emotions that would allow them to feel compassion and empathize with boys like me, boys who were destined to die before the age of twenty one.

Once I was identified and it was determined I didn't have any weapons on me they gave me a shot of Demerol. Moments later I was rushed into x-ray in a drug-induced fog. When I came out of x-ray and woke up the room was full of police.

They bombarded me with a deluge of questions about the shooter. They were mean, callous and confrontational. They treated me like I was the perpetrator. They made me feel like I was the cause of my own shooting. In response to their questions I told them I didn't know who shot me. My response incensed one officer. He told me I deserved to be laying in the bed suffering. My ignorance coupled with my refusal to give him an answer seemed to upset his sensibilities. He hurled a few more invectives at me before he left the room in a huff.

I felt cold inside. I felt like I had just been victimized by an officer who didn't give a damn about kids like me. He knew what it was like for us growing up in a neighborhood that was a virtual war zone. There was a code we lived by and there was no way I was going to violate the code. We couldn't count on the police to solve our problems, so we did what we felt was necessary to solve them ourselves.

When the doctor arrived I felt a sense of relief. For the first time I felt like I could be a child and express my fears. But I was quickly reminded that we lived in an apathetic world. The doctor reviewed my chart and left without saying a word. He returned moments later with a pair of needle nosed pliers. He dug the pliers into my flesh and wrenched a bullet from my leg, puling bits of meat and bone with it. He irrigated the wound before leaving to write a prescription for antibiotics. After that I never saw him again.

An hour later I was awakened by my father, step mother, and mother. In my father's eyes I could sense the feeling of helplessness that poured from his spirit. And my mother appeared to be paralyzed by the fear of one day seeing one of her children killed. Sadly I was the third one of their children to be shot.

Unfortunately it wouldn't be their last trip to the hospital. A few years later my older brother was shot and paralyzed. My parents were at a loss for words. What could they really say to me? There were no parenting manuals that gave directions on how to handle your children being shot in the streets like rabid dogs. We talked briefly before they left. They were angry and frustrated by my refusal to come home. They knew I would return to the scene of the shooting. I had long ago given up on going home to either of my parents. I had long also accepted the streets as my home—if not before, surely after the shooting. When they left my bedside I could see the defeat in their eyes. Like many parents in our community they felt helpless when it came to disrupting the cycle of violence that had lead to countess deaths.

No one hugged me or told me that everything would be okay. No one came to talk to me. No one explained the cocktail of emotions I was feeling. No one told me I was programming myself to be a shooter in response to my fears. In my mind I would rather victimize someone else than to be a victim. No one explained to me that cars weren't death chariots that carried the grim reaper. So I became hyper-violent in order to feel safe. If I shot first I would no longer have to fear being shot. It was a very distorted way of looking at the world, yet it was the only way I knew how to cope.

When I left the hospital I returned to the streets deadlier than the man who shot me and killed the last hope I had of being a child. The anger I felt combined with the alcohol I consumed gouged out the eyes of my soul. I wandered the streets blind to what was going on inside me. Instead of crying tears I cried bullets, screaming in semi-automatic bursts every time I found myself in a conflict. Anger became my mask and carrying a gun with me everywhere I went became my shield.

Reflecting back, I know I am responsible for my reaction to being shot. For years I blamed everyone for my response to my fears and anger. However I now realize no one can make me feel anything I don't want to feel. However, I can't help but wonder how different my teenage years would have been if I would have gotten psychological counseling in response to the trauma I experienced at the age of seventeen.

Black children get shot, maimed, and killed every day and very few receive psychological therapy. So they grow up living in fear which eventually manifests into destructive behavior. Every day I ask myself why we are considered the dregs of society. "Columbine" children-shooting-children tragedies have been going on in the hood for years and very little is done about it. Sometimes we march or hold candlelight vigils, but this does very little to solve the problem of teenage gun violence.

No child should ever have to live in fear of being the victim of gun violence. And no child should ever feel like their only option in life is to be the victimizer of someone else's child.

Today I can proudly say I am healed from the pain of the teenage years. And hopefully by sharing my experience I can help others heal. We deserve it and more importantly our community deserves to have healthy, happy children.

Prisoner Essay 7.8

"Community Adults Taught Way of the Streets" (2/25/09)
A lot can be said about the socioeconomic background of my upbringing. As I previously stated, I was raised in a single parent home and my mother's social standing was like every mother's social standing in my neighborhood. She was the breadwinner who worked a blue-collar job for low wages. My mother knew about my drug dealing and although she never condoned it, she never turned down the cash I made from it, either. Back then, as I examined every teenager in my neighborhood, I realized that there were two types: those who had all they wanted were the drug dealers and I decided to be a part of that group. It was cool, because all the attention was on us. The other teenagers who weren't making money-dealing drugs were laughed at and considered weak and soft. They were the ones who eventually started running errands for us for a few dollars here and there. But for the most part, the teenagers in my league kept all the money and control. The community played a part in my lifestyle because they never encouraged me to do something positive with my life. In other words, they turned a blind eye to my illicit activities. Don't get me wrong, a few people here and there tried to steer me in the right direction, but the money outweighed their positive advice. Besides, some of the adults in my community were giving me the drugs to sell and they were teaching me the way of the streets; so why not maximize my potential and make a living and name for myself?

#####

Abandoned Hyperghetto and Social Disorganization Means Changing Neighborhoods

In this section we expand on Wacquant's macro-level abandoned hyperghetto view and add the more proximate level "social disorganization" theory. Prisoners like social disorganization theory, but are also angry about how they grew up. The more "political" prisoners would agree with Wacquant's "institutional" theory that emphasizes how the power structure ("urban elites") abandoned the jobless ghetto. More mainstream sociology talks of "social disorganization."

What are socially disorganizing processes? How does social disorganization affect families and neighborhoods? What are the proximate causes of social disorganization? Wacquant has shown that the jobless ghetto is really a political outcome of decisions by urban elites and the federal government, as well as business disinvestment. And Peterson and Krivo have shown us the high crime neighborhoods are surrounded by other high crime neighborhoods. But what does the local neighborhood effect look like? Prisoner essays and excerpts from prisoner stories show why, in their own sometimes vivid observations, they analyze this community-level theory as to be judged: "best theory." The social disorganization theory explains, in the prisoners' view, the reality of being criminally socialized as they were coming up, that is: "It was just the way it was growing up."

Why do urban neighborhoods decay, generating high rates of crime? How is growing up in such areas seen by prisoners? Several disciplines study urban problems including economics, sociology, urban geography, and criminology. Sociology emerged in the nineteenth century out of the responses to the social problems of the newly industrializing cities in the Western world. By the early 1900s sociologists were researching how crime and delinquency resulted from social disorganization. Emile Durkheim, who was appointed to the first professorship of sociology in France, worked in the 1880s and 1890s to produce foundational scholarly works, including a sociological study of crime and law. Barlow and Kauzlarich note:

> Durkheim was a functionalist . . . he was concerned with how societies attempt to regulate behavior for the purpose of stability, control, and solidarity. Law, Durkheim believed, should ideally represent the collective will of the people. . . . Punishment . . . was necessary to reaffirm the collective conscience so that all members of society would understand the wrongfulness and immorality of criminal behavior. This, he explained, increases social solidarity (2010: 242–43)

As the U.S. federal government built the interstate highway system (1958–1975), some businesses previously located in industrial districts in the city, and on downtown business streets, relocated to the suburbs, some being built just outside the city, some being built in outlying "edge cities" (Garreau 1991). In later trends some of the "subs" were springing up along the rural highways and roads. In this uneven development characteristic of capitalism the "capital flight" and "white flight" continued into the mid-1970s as a shift in the economy away from manufacturing and to both high wage and low wage services was occurring. At the proximate, close-up level, working-class white and black saw their neighborhoods change, reducing social solidarity. The norms of the community weakened and became unenforceable through the parental networks of informal social control.

#####

Prisoner Essay 7.9

"Utopia Vanishes: Changing Neighborhood Affects Community, Family, and Individual" (3/17/10)
Since I came to prison, I have always looked back upon my life to find where I went wrong. What, in and around my life, were factors that influenced me in any way, to lead me down the paths I have traveled.

On my own, I have found many factors, and have used the knowledge I gained, to change everything about me to make sure I stay on the right path. Now, with this class, and the reading materials, I have even more tools and insight to make my changes permanent. Each factor ties in with many other factors that build into a bomb within ourselves, that may go off if not diffused in time.

It's hard to tell a story about the variables in my community, and taking a look at myself, without showing the correlation between all factors. Family, and how it is and does, affect how our community grows. Then again, our community affects our families and communities affect an individual and the factors surrounding them. Sounds like merry-go-round in hell that I want to get off of.

My community helped to shape my family and I in many ways. My neighborhood and the era that I lived in, has just about every factor talked about in our reading material that I don't know where to start.

1. Where I grew up, was a well to do (or comfortable) community. Everyone had most all they needed and more.
2. We were a tight-nit community. Everyone knew each other, and looked out for each other. One example; a neighbor who became a good friend of my mothers, was chosen to be my sisters god-mother.
3. The closeness in turn, was like our own built-in neighborhood watch. Anyone new, moving into, or just hanging out in our community, was on the radar of everyone.

4. That also results in a neighborhood of babysitters. Us kids know that everything we did in and around our neighborhood would most likely get back to our parents, or we would be corrected by the neighbors.

These are some of the good factors that may have been influential in keeping brothers and sisters out of the big trouble. But in most of my life, this utopia vanished. Many of the reasons for this are in the following factors.

1. The well-to-do General Motors' shop workers, were starting to move out of their small homes that were almost built on top of each other, in search of bigger and better.
2. That type of housing sells cheap. So, as the better paid families left, many who bought into the neighborhood were the not so well-to-do-people. Also there were those wanting to buy low, and rent cheap, which brought the poor families, many of whom were nonwhite.
3. Racial tensions began. More white families sold their homes and moved. More black families moved in. Racially motivated threats forced others to flee. We were a changing neighborhood.
4. The crime rate increased, so those that could leave, did.
5. What eventually were left in the community were the ones who liked the criminal life, and saw it as an opportunity. Then there were those who wanted to leave but could not afford to.
6. General Motors' decided to finally shut down the plant in that area. So the lack of good jobs, crime and drugs, and others factors made the community undesirable.

So during the many years this was destroying a pristine community, it was also taking its toll on families that were trying to stick it out, hoping for something better. Like some of the following.

1. When a community is going though these kinds of changes, those factors tear at the bonds that hold a family together. Children turn against their parents, siblings against siblings, spouse against spouse, and even turn them away from their religion and beliefs.
2. This stress, can in turn, lead to a divorce, as it did with my parents.
3. Which in turn leads to less parental supervision, and remember, since the tight knit community fell apart, no supervision from the neighbors either.
4. It leaves open the door for a child, through peer pressure, to become deviant and go down the wrong path.

Now we get to the individual, which in this case is me. Which led to some of the following factors.

1. I learned many wrong and possibly criminal things from those in my community.
2. Again, supervision was lacking because of the divorce and other factors, but I must add, my mother did a real good job with the hand she was dealt.
3. My parents divorced, which is a factor that had a huge affect on me.
4. The crime and racial factors caused me to withdraw from the community, into my home, and within myself.
5. Which led to antisocial behavior. To quote from Sampson's book, page 241, "antisocial children tend to fight, steal, become truant, drop out of school, and drift in and out of unemployment, live in lower-class areas and go on to commit adult crime." This quote sums up my life.

These and many other factors helped lead to me committing my first crime at the age of 19. Two of my friends and I were arrested and convicted of commercial breaking and entering. We were to meet some girls on top of a parking ramp in downtown Flint, Michigan. They did not show up, and we were drinking, we were bored, so we stupidly decided to cross the top of the walk bridge, to the roof of the old Montgomery Ward building, just to fool around. We slid down a pole to a lower section. We joked about going inside through a hatch on the roof. We lifted up on the hatch, and it opened easy, rotted wood. We went inside thinking it was an abandoned building. Nope, it was a Perry's drug store, and of course, the police showed up quick. We were busted. We all got a good deal, a program that let us do one year probation, and upon completion, our records were expunged.

Now, enough is enough. I am older and wiser now, and do not want that type of life ever again. This time I hurt the ones I love the most, especially my children who lost their dad to prison and his bad choices in life. All that I have learned and implemented has helped me to change and made me a new person. My past will not guide my life or who I am any more. I have a new life with my loved ones, while in here, and when I get out. Goodbye old. Hello new!

#####

As suburbanization contributed to uneven development (Darden, Hill, Thomas, and Thomas 1987) some corporations moved to other states establishing "greenfield" plants in small city areas. Changing business organizational form and strategies were driving community change also. This included the switch to stockless production and just-in-time inventory, which allowed large manufacturers in the 1980s to close internal parts divisions and outsource parts to small factories or shops in rural cities. These smaller plants and suburban office complexes and shopping malls that sprang up nearby shifted business investment away from the many bigger cities, especially in the "rust belt" upper Midwest and Northeast. Due to these trends the large metropolitan inner-city residential districts declined. The former communal ghetto that, though a residentially segregated black district, had all the black social classes now became the politically abandoned, advanced marginality hyperghetto (jobless apartheid). The Los Angeles area Watts Riot of 1965, the Detroit Riot of 1967, and many urban tensions in 1968 signaled that "stability, control, and solidarity" in the "rough" areas of U.S. cities was being lost. But there was also the abandonment by federal, state, and local government (Wacquant 2008: Ch. 2). It was both the weakening of community norms (social disorganization) and the actions of uneven development and political abandonment (social power).

Disruption of Community and Family Life: Crime and Divorce Rates

Then the illegal drug economy moved in. Over the last forty years "regular" work in the increasingly *jobless* urban ghettos disappeared (Wilson 1987/ 2012 and 1996). For prisoners old enough to have witnessed these changes, the influences on their lives growing up in this shift from communal ghetto to this "advanced marginality" were criminal influences.

#####

Prisoner Essay 7.10

"Crack Hit Our Neighborhood with the Force of a Runaway Train" (3/3/10) I recall climbing high up in the pear tree next door to retrieve the delicious fruit it offered. There was nothing I loved more than sinking my teeth into the sweet juicy flesh of a yellowing pear. It's one of my fondest memories from my childhood. No matter what was going on in my small world I looked forward to the fruit of one of the many trees that were in our backyards; whether it was the plum tree in my backyard, my neighbors' peach tree, or their pear tree, I could always count on the succulent fruit to erase the pain of the moment. And then one day the trees no longer gave fruit. It was then I realized my neighborhood had died, leaving in its wake an iniquitous skeleton that no longer resembled this healthy, vibrant place I once called home.

The neighborhood I grew up in embodied the American dream. Our tree-lined street on Detroit's east side was rich with diverse culture, laughter, dancing, and the aroma of exotic foods. Summer days were spent playing freeze tag, leaping in the water from the fire-hydrant and eating juicy pears plucked from our neighbor's Miss Moore's tree. She was a sweet woman with a pleasant smile and frosty white hair. Out of my mother's six children I was her favorite. Whenever she made her homemade pear preserves she made sure to send me a mason jar full. In turn I cut her grass and ran small errands whenever she called on me.

The house on the other side was occupied by a festive Italian family. We shared a grape vine that draped across our backyard fence. When the grapes were purple and plump our families would go out back and pick them. We laughed and joked, and shared food and music. We gave them collard greens, Mac n' cheese and Marvin Gaye, and they gave us Linguini, lasagna and opera. They had a peach tree in their backyard and we had a plum tree. Whenever we picked fruit we shared it with our neighbors. I loved to eat and my neighbors delighted in filling my fat belly with fruit and cookies. On any given day you could find me in the backyard with juice from a peach or pear dripping down my chubby cheeks until the day I got stung by a bee. After that I enjoyed their offerings from the safety of our closed-in patio. Sharing food and merriment was an everyday experience—it was the way life was meant to be.

Back then we slept with our doors open and took care of each other. Our neighbors were like family and they made us feel welcome even though we were the first black family on the street. Back then I didn't know that racism existed because we never experienced it. Underneath it all we were the same. My parents wanted for us what I imagined my childhood friends parents wanted for them, a good education, a good job and ultimately a family of our own.

Sadly the cultural and moral fibers of our neighborhood slowly began to erode. My parent's American dream unraveled like ball of cheap yarn. The changes rolled out inch by inch. First the Dodge and Chrysler car dealerships relocated away from our neighborhood. People who took pride in caring for their homes were now being replaced by transient renters, who thought nothing of destroying the property of others.

The mom and pop stores were replaced by liquor stores that sell alcohol to children, turning their brains into mush. The comforting diners that once provided us with healthy food made by local people now were replaced with fast food chains that sold diabetes-inducing burgers and cardiac arrest fries. The once manicured lush green lawns were now yellowing and unkempt. And the once friendly police who would stop on the street and allow children to play with their sirens were replaced by an occupying force who brutalized and shot unarmed men in the back.

The teachers, firemen, dentist, and factory workers that once nurtured and cultivated our neighborhood were replaced by out of work alcoholics, welfare recipients and drug addicts. But the final nail in the coffin was the arrival of crack cocaine.

Crack hit our neighborhood with the force of a runaway train causing it to implode, leaving behind the wreckage we now call the hood. The neighbor element which is an integral part of the community's success was destroyed. Leaving our doors open at night was like inviting death into our homes. The sound of laughter and children playing in the street was replaced by the rapid fire burst of AK-47 assault rifles and 40. Caliber Glocks. The trees that once fed our young bellies were now camouflage for bandits looking to prey on the innocent. The white men and women who now roamed our hood were unlike the whites from before. They were afraid and standoffish. Or worse they ventured into the hood to buy their illicit drugs or make perverted transactions before slinking back to the safety of their homes on the other side of Eight Mile road.

The childhood friends I grew up with were now enemies warring over drug turf. By the time I turned 21 half of my friends were in prison and the other half were dead. Instead of parents gathering to celebrate a child going off to college, they now gathered to mourn a child shot down in the streets. Today in this hood that was at one time pregnant with hope there is nothing left but pain and suffering. The children dream no more and the parents have surrendered their destiny. Teenage mothers are the norm, and young men don't expect to live past 18. Abandoned houses mar the land like infected scabs. Babies roam the streets at two in the morning hungry, and afraid, not knowing if their parents will return from their three day crack binge. The schools which at one time demanded academic excellence are now prisons with barbed wire windows and armed guards patrolling the campus. The antiquated books with missing pages and inoperable bathrooms, lower the students' self-esteem along with their standardized test score. Grocery stores which once provided the neighborhood with healthy food have given way to corner stores that sell as all the worst things at all the best prices—sugary concoctions offering us a sweet dose of diabetes. The fruit of a once pristine neighborhood had all but rotted away. And the trees that once gave fruit— give no more.

#####

Prisoners, in reflecting on the origin of their criminality, often report that their life of crime was "Just due to how I came up. It (crime) was just the way it was as we were growing up." These reflections by prisoners on neighborhood undergoing decay indicates the "kind of place" cause of crime we are exploring in chapter 7 rather than a "kind of person" explanatory perspective we explored in chapter 5.

Durkheim noted that every society has some crime and, in this sense, "crime is normal," and, as mentioned, punishing the crime acts to "increase social solidarity." But he also noted that "No doubt it is possible that crimes will have abnormal forms, as, for example, when the rate is unusually high" (Barlow and Kauzlarich 2010: 243). A decaying neighborhood is associated with an *increase* in the crime rate. In sociological criminology the analysis of kind of place has often rested on social disorganization theory. But there is also a social power dimension.

The urban conflagrations of the 1960s, symptoms of decaying neighborhoods, did not lead to the social reform of the city. Instead of effective state action to bolster these once stable neighborhoods (communal ghetto), political abandonment led to festering inner cities (hyperghetto). This trend has been going on for more than forty-five years now, with streets dominated by drugs, guns and violence. Barlow and Kauzlarich note that

[o]ne common understanding of the relationship between the city and social problems is that decaying urban environments generate high rates of crime and delinquency. Beginning in the early 1900s, sociologists at the University of Chicago published a series of studies of life in Chicago. Under the guidance of Robert Park and E. W. Burgess, these studies were designed to document the belief that problems such as crime and delinquency resulted from *social disorganization*. Simply put, social disorganization is the inability of a community to regulate itself (Bursik and Grasmick 1995). Social organization is maintained by a group's commitment to social rules; when this commitment breaks down, social control breaks down. Members of the Chicago School and many contemporary criminologists believe that this breakdown in social control could occur through ecological changes, such as when communities experience rapid population change through social mobility (in and out of the neighborhood) and migration (2010: 54).

. . . This can result in less community surveillance, more opportunities to engage in crime, and people who are disenchanted, cynical, or apathetic about their neighborhood. Neighborhoods that are dilapidated are also often stigmatized, Stark maintains, for they signify disorder and seem attractive to those seeking deviant opportunities. Furthermore, Stark (1987: 901–2) proposes that:

• More successful and conventional people will resist moving into a stigmatized neighborhood; and
• Stigmatized neighborhoods will tend to be overpopulated by the most demoralized kinds of people and suffer from lenient law enforcement, which may increase the incidence of crime and deviance. (2010: 54–56)

In the prison classroom the black man may say: "When I get out I want to move to a better neighborhood so I can raise my son not to be a criminal." How would one create a better neighborhood? If you look at table 1.1, Farrington and Welsh say that it is reasonable to target all these types of risk factors in early prevention programs. Such programs might seek to improve a family's economic status, discourage a child's association with delinquent peers or encourage association with prosocial peers, change the climate of schools or improve the social cohesiveness of areas. (2007: 89)

What are the causes of festering, crime-infested, throwaway neighborhoods? Why did we go from family dysfunction in *West Side Story* (a 1950s film) to community dysfunction in *Boyz in the Hood* (a 1990s film)? Farrington and Welsh say "Some aspects of an inner city neighborhood may be conducive to offending" and they quote Albert Reiss (1986) who argued "high-crime rate areas often have a high concentration of single-parent female-headed households with low incomes, living in low-cost, poor housing." But *why* are these types of neighborhoods *there* in the first place to be "coming up" in? The various kinds of "interventions" that target all these "types of risk factors in early prevention programs" are to be encouraged. But what about the *degree of decay* in the cities? If the *rate of social disorganization* has increased, how is that explained? The question then becomes: how to slow down the *creation* of such throwaway city, high crime areas?

Williams, Imbroscio, and Alperovitz in their book *Making a Place for Community* note:

> There have been numerous studies of the general social costs of dislocation. During the 1970s and 1980s, for instance, the deindustrialization of the Midwest and Northeast prompted scholars to examine the impact of plant closures and capital mobility on individual communities. Consistently, researchers found disruption of community and family life in the form of increased crime and divorce rates. In the wake of plant closings, there were demands on social services—at the same time that tax revenues dropped.
>
> . . . [C]reating truly stable communities will probably require much more localization of investment decision-making than that afforded by large, hierarchical corporations operating multiple facilities at different locations. (2003: 10–15)

For instance, the United Steelworkers, Mondragon, and the Ohio Employee Ownership Center have started a new union cooperative model: steel workers now have their own cooperative bank and can better anchor the capital of their *worker-owned* steel mills in the communities where they live (www.usw.coop) (*United Steelworkers News* 2012).

Prisoners' personal stories describe parents who have lost jobs and are living in poverty—"I looked in the refrigerator and there was nothing but an empty box of baking soda"—and how they started selling drugs, usually pot in middle school and then quickly moved into hard drugs and carrying guns.

Exposure to Illicit Drug Markets and Homicide Growing Up

The prisoners' stories are almost all about the drug economy. The academic researcher Karen Parker describes the effects of socially disorganizing processes this way:

> The nature and type of businesses found in segregated areas affect the community's level of collective efficacy (Sampson, Raudenbush, and Earls 1997), if not increased levels of public disorder (Greenbaum and Tita 2004; Wilcox, Quisenberry, and Cabrera 2004) because of the abundance of "liquor stores and currency exchanges" (Wilson 1996: 5). These conditions increase the attractiveness of illicit drug markets as an alternative source of income (Fagan 1992). And violence associated with illicit drug markets is related to the prevalence of homicide (Blumstein 1995). Evidence has linked illicit drug markets (especially the crack-cocaine epidemic), which peaked in the early 1990s, to homicide trends during this same period (Ousey and Lee 2002). Ford and Beveride (2004) found that visible drug sales only further diminished the ability of urban areas to attract more desirable businesses. (2008: 95)

The following two prisoner essays reveal how the cultural and moral fibers of a neighborhood erode to the point that the neighbor element is destroyed.

#####

Prisoner Essay 7.11

"Lawless Community Can Only Give Birth to Outlaws" (11/11/09)
It's been said that criminal behavior is as much personality as it is upbringing. As if some people are born criminals. I strongly disagree with that theory. I believe that some people are born rebellious and if not properly guided that quality can become criminal.

In no way would I suggest that everyone that comes from my community is criminal or just naturally rebellious. And I personally know people who grew up worst than I did, and did not turn to criminal behavior. Just like there are people that grew up in better community that still ended up coming to prison. Life style is a choice. The difference is a person's ability to make his/her own decisions, and influences are critical in every community.

My influences were from my mother, father, and older brother. Both of my parents were drug addicts, so their decision-making was not always the best. My mother just showed a little more concern for my future. She tried to keep me away from doing wrong.

When I was younger, my older brother and my aunt were killed. Both of their deaths, though happen separately, were indirectly the result of drugs. My brother's death was the result of someone trying to rob him; he was on a known drug street and the guys that committed the crime knew he had some money; my aunt supposedly stole drugs from a drug dealer and was beat to death with a hammer. My mother took me to her wake, she wanted to show me what that life style does to people. I remember looking at her, the thick make up on her face could not hide the bruises as the service was intoned. I was too afraid to cry, my mother made me promise her that I would never sell or use drugs, I agreed mainly because I wanted to get out of there. Around a year later my older brother was murdered. (This is my father's son by a different woman.) I went to his wake alone. This time I was not afraid just angry. My brother was my savior. I was always able to count on him. He just wanted the best for me, and his experience with the streets proved that it was not the place a real man wanted to spend his life. So he tried to encourage me to do right, and stay out of trouble.

There is an ugliness that exists in the drug world; you got to be in it to see it. If you're looking from the outside in, you'll never notice it. The violence is brutal, the people are unforgiving. It's nothing like what it appears to be.

Often times my brother would come and get me just to keep me company. Another fact about that life style is that it's very lonely. You find yourself surrounded by people who really don't care about you. They just want to use you for whatever they can use you for. I just enjoyed hanging with my big brother. And he knew that. It was those moments that he would talk to me seriously. And I would listen, but I also would notice the large amount of money he usually kept on him, or the nice car he would drive. I wanted what he had. Material things held my attention more than wise words.

My father was the total opposite; he didn't care what I did with my life. He was the first person to show me how to sell crack. And he encouraged me to be a drug dealer. My mother knew this, but she still was angrier with me than she was with my father. And she reminded me of the promise I'd made some year prior at my aunts wake. I ask myself what I could have done differently.

There are times we didn't even have food to eat. . . . My younger siblings would come to me saying they are hungry, so I would go out and do whatever I could to bring them something to eat. If I made three dollars that was enough to at least get some bread and bologna. . .

Because many members of my family either use or sold drugs, I never really viewed drug dealing as a crime. I looked at it as if it was survival—just another way to make a living. In my community, the guys that sold drugs are often the guardians of the neighborhood, and often very generous. Since they are not working for the money they really don't value it. As I arrived to that life style, the women, the clothes that seemed to make people look better, they sure did make me feel better.

A lot of us that grow up in lower class communities are materialistic. We spend all of our money trying to look rich. We become slaves to fashion. We look for happiness in superficial things. Our desires for riches are our primary finances; leaving us poor in our ability to make good decisions. Poor in our ability to be individuals, and these are lessons we don't learn at home.

Drugs are the gateway to more brutal crimes. The people that use these drugs become highly addicted, and they resort to crime to finance their habit. Some of them steal; some of the women sell companionship. Some rob people. I've personally seen a guy steal meat out of his mothers freezer, and sold it to me for drugs. I thought he was the worst person ever, but what about me? I later realize that I, as a drug dealer, was an enabler. I encouraged what I thought to be horrific behavior. And everything I hated, I started to accept. Just as I accepted drug dealing as being a way to make money, I started accepting the violence that went along with it as being a part of the business. That's the ugly side I mentioned earlier. Family members stealing from you, women playing games with your feelings, I began not trusting people, so often I would drive around my neighborhood alone.

My feelings for people were depleting, and I started to look at everybody the same. There was no love in my heart; the streets had devoured it a long time ago. I was like a robot, programmed to be emotionless, and designed to view the American dream as a fantasy. Preparing for death as I turned every corner; a lawless community can only give birth to outlaws. We are all taught that the system is against us. Some of us are strong to make it out. The rest are people I see every day, trapped inside a prison yard.

#####

The problem of "no love in the heart" as a sign of community disorganization is complex and weighty. What to do about it? How to intervene in it?

FOR PREVENTION, TARGET MULTIPLE FACTORS USING MULTIPLE ACTORS

Farrington and Welsh find that:

> Risk factors tend to co-occur, making them difficult to disentangle. Independent, additive, interactive, and sequential effects of risk factors need to be studied, to establish how many different underlying theoretical constructs are important. . . . This is an argument in favor of targeting multiple risk factors in interventions. (2007: 22)

Wacquant argues that the "urban elite" has abandoned the hyperghetto, and basically use police and penal institutions as social control. Prisoners themselves, in analyzing deviant community norms and "the culture of street crime," argue that instead of a "unidirectional" approach of only using formal criminal justice apparatus to fight crime, (cops, courts, corrections), that there should be multiple actors in prevention: community organization, criminal justice agencies, ex-cons making good and incarcerated grey heads. In the LIFERS Steering Committee (2004) Graterford Prison prisoner "think tank" group essay "Ending the culture of street crime" these prison grey-heads say:

> As an alternative to the aforementioned unidirectional approach, the more practical, multidirectional approach assumes that those who are included, and made a part of their community by personal investment, will be better motivated to work to sustain that community's well-being and act more concertedly and consciously to defend and adhere to its norms, values, and principles as opposed to rejecting them altogether. This would inevitably lead to less crime.
>
> Typically, it is those who are excluded, kept apart, or otherwise cast away from the majority who feel less compelled to abide by the norms of the society that rejects them. Moreover, these so-called outcasts are more likely to create a counter subculture—usually the antithesis of the larger, majority culture—wherein they feel accepted, embraced, and included. From this emerges a subsociety that breeds criminal activity. (2004: 50)

This prison think tank group emphasize that any serious efforts to address the problem of drug addiction needs to include drug users, who consume illegal substances, and drug dealers, who market them. "Therefore, the members of Long Incarcerated Fraternity Engaging Release Studies (LIFERS, Inc.) have adopted the mission of ending what we have identified as the culture of street crime, by starting with ourselves, with the institution, and expanding out into the community" (2004: 50–51).

In the volunteer prison classes I teach, the older prisoners read the 2004 LIFERS, Inc., essay and discuss it. The grey heads in the prison can help build up their community's ability to regulate itself. However, in addition to the movement coming from the ex-cons and prisoners still incarcerated, there needs to be more, and better, jobs in the urban areas. Looking closer at the urban jobless ghetto (high unemployment, racially segregated neighborhoods) reveals an economic and social cause-of-crime in this kind of place—long-term loss of good paying jobs, increased employment instability, and job location mismatch where the low-cost housing is in the inner city but what jobs are available are in the malls, office complexes, and factories of the high-housing-cost suburb (Garreau 1991; Holzer, Offner, and Sorenson 2005). Holzer advocates the establishment of buses from the inner city to the suburban mall jobs. Wacquant analyzes the hyperghettos residents as largely an "absolute surplus population" and, for his part, advocates a guaranteed income (2008: 254–56), a proposal to which we will return to in the conclusion (see chapter 10). Clearly there is a relationship between city labor markets and crime.

LABOR MARKETS WORK INDIRECTLY THROUGH THE FAMILY WHEN INFLUENCING RATES OF URBAN CRIME

Parker, focusing on the long-term dynamic trends in city labor markets, notes that the impact of recessions and their temporary increase in unemployment, as episodic phenomenon, are not able to capture the decade's long trends in industrial restructuring and the longer-run outcome of changes in the urban labor market. *Crime rates increased in the 1980s and have declined since 1991.* However, Parker notes there has been *an unequal crime decline*: black violent crime was higher than white during the crime rate increase (1980–1990) and has been higher than white rate during the decrease in crime rate (1990–2000) and continues to be four times as high as in 2013. Returning to what explains the unequal crime rate increase and unequal crime rate decline, Parker notes that

> black males were found to face the highest level of employment instability as labor shifted from the manufacturing sector to the service sector; further, there was considerable imbalance in the impact of industrial restructuring on black males during the 1980s and 1990s. . . .
> . . . To be precise, black male employment declined despite a booming U.S. economy (1990s) during this time. How might the disparities in the industrial restructuring among black males, specifically the dramatic change in black male employment between 1980 and 1990, correspond to the rise of homicide rates for this group during this period? (2008: 81–82)

Parker's study *Unequal Crime Decline: Theorizing Race, Urban Inequality, and Violence* (2008) aims to integrate better criminology theories with stratification theories. She notes that "all connects start with the local labor market characteristics of urban areas." That is, people in families need jobs. While the crime-reducing impact of *jobs in the local neighborhood* for mid-teens (fifteen-year-olds) has been documented by Mercer Sullivan (1989) and others, adults in the family get their jobs in the wider city labor market. Typically they travel outside their home, their block, their neighborhood, even their community area to hold down a job. There is a pattern to the city's labor market. Parker observes:

> Labor market opportunity structures symbolize the industrial mix in a given area, such as the proportioning of occupations in industrial sectors (e.g., manufacturing, service-oriented, professional, or managerial) within a city, and the shifts in

the industrial mix, or economic restructuring . . . race and gender inequality is evident in opportunity structures, where workers are often segregated and face dislocation or prosperity as occupational sectors shrink and expand.

. . . Job markets do not fall within neighborhood or community boundaries; rather, city residents are typically exposed to the same labor market dynamics. . . . Neighborhood conditions . . . are shaped by the larger labor market opportunity structures of an area. (2008: 87)

Prisoners often tell stories of dysfunctional families and criminal influence in the neighborhood. If a parent is working the prisoner may mention the job, however prisoners generally do not describe how their neighborhood characteristics are *shaped* "by the larger labor market opportunity structures" of their city. They often have a graphic description of the *local* illegal drug economy and its labor market positions (lookout, holder, deliverer, and seller) but no description of the *city* labor market. They may mention many liquor stores or "Arab store owners who fronted us drugs to sell," but they are not often aware of the structure of the city job market—they dropped out at fifteen and began selling drugs. They did not have relatives and family friends that could connect them up with a job. They did not go to a local vocational-technical school or community college to learn about the city labor markets. They did not go to college and have the services of a career planning office or internships to learn about the job market. Parker notes that

work not only helps to structure time (Wilson 1996) but connects people to other social institutions within the community (Crutchfield 1989; Wilson 1987). Work also plays an important role in life course criminology, where scholars propose job quality as a positive transition in one's life, contributing to crime desistance (Laub and Sampson 1993). (2008: 87)

The tendency of labor markets to expand or shrink would be reduced—and community economic stability would be increased—if there were more localization of capital investment decision making (William, Imbroscio, and Alperovitz 2003). But, instead, the trend is toward increasing economic insecurity due to the preponderance of decision making by large hierarchical corporations. Family stability is linked to stable jobs or income. For the family to play a crucial role in maintaining a viable low crime community, the family needs more, not less, economic stability. Parker notes:

During times of industrial restructuring, families are less able to maintain networks and participate in community organizations (e.g., sports, volunteer groups, etc.) that promote social control (see Kellam et al. 1982), leading to higher crime. Research on family disruption, for example, has found that divorced parents have less contact with neighborhoods than married parents

(Alwin, Converse, and Martin 1985) and maintain fewer informal networks that assist in supervising youth. The first connection, then, proposes that labor markets work indirectly through the family when influencing urban rates of violence. (2008: 88)

Again, many prisoners will write about their family but will be unaware of links between labor markets and the family. They almost never write of "community organizations (e.g., sports, volunteer groups, etc.)." Their families are not "able to maintain networks" and are distinctly isolated—often in addiction and domestic violence.

Many African American male prisoners describe single mothers who are working one or two low wage jobs, where the man (father) is not part of the family; however, many other black prisoners describe mothers who are unemployed and often addicted. The way the economy (urban labor markets) gets translated through the family (single parent too busy to parent or too addicted to function—both resulting in poor parental supervision) to youth delinquency and crime and violence is an important theme.

Climate of Economic Instability

The lack of informal social controls is central to the definition of social disorganization theory. Karen Parker notes:

> Transitions in local labor markets, such as the move away from manufacturing to service-oriented economies in many cities, created a climate of instability for workers as they were forced to seek jobs in other sectors . . . high levels of restructuring or shifts in the industrial mix in urban areas influenced violence by means of employment instability or dislocation or both.
>
> Theoretically, this process worked in a couple of ways. First, Wilson (1987) suggested that deindustrialization resulted in joblessness, reducing access to job networks and weakening attachment to the labor force, which increased urban violence . . . black male workers were unique in the degree to which the shift from manufacturing to service-sector occupations created a climate of instability—the percent change in industrial restructuring among black males was 596 percent compared to 22.3 percent among white males. (2008: 89)

Deindustrialization basically means that the mobility of capital to leave the area is more powerful in its consequences than the ability of localization of investment decision making that can anchor capital in a city or community labor market (Williams, Imbroscio, and Alperovitz 2003). As Karen Parker notes, the shift from manufacturing to service-sector occupations (deindustrialization) hit African American men particularly hard. And African American women were also hit hard by the shift to service sector since many of them had been in manufacturing, and they did not benefit from the shift to services. Because manufacturing generally had higher wages, this drastic increase in the occupational climate of instability translated also into family insecurity and an increase in poor parental supervision (informal social control) and consequently an increase in social disorganization and crime.

When people lose their job their communities become less stable. As Sampson notes: "Smith and Jarjoura (1988) concluded that communities characterized by rapid population turnover and high poverty have significantly higher violent crime rates than mobile areas that are more affluent or poor areas that are stable" (2002: 227). Sampson continues:

> Family disruption (e.g., divorce rates, female-headed families with children) has been posited to facilitate crime by decreasing networks of informal social control, such as observing or questioning strangers, watching over each others' property, and assuming responsibility for supervision of general youth activities (see Sampson and Groves 1989; Taylor et al. 1984). . . . For instance, youth in stable family areas, regardless of their own family situation, have more controls placed on their leisure-time activities, particularly with *peer groups* (Sullivan 1989: 178). Neighborhood family structure may thus influence whether neighborhood youth are provided the opportunity to form a peer-control system free of supervision by adults. (2002: 29)

A "peer-control system free of supervision by adults) means that gangs form. So, in this climate of economic instability, when work disappears (Wilson 1996), the illegal drug economy moves in, and gangs form, the struggle for respect among the youth becomes a "code of the streets" increasingly reflecting drugs, guns, and violence (Anderson 1999). As one of our prisoner essays said: "You better represent, little dog." This was characteristic of the 1980s, and especially during the crack epidemic of 1986–1991, and has continued to plague the festering inner-city neighborhoods of major U.S. cities.

Exposure to Social Disorganization Growing Up

#####

Prisoner Essay 7.12

"The Broken Down Hood" (3/11/09)
I will reflect upon crime-ridden community in which I raised.

The ideal that certain communities inherit crime rather than breed crime is twofold; Having lived in one small community that harbored their youth from drugs, crime, and prostitution as opposed another just blocks away does attest to the basic premise that one's behavior is in part the outcome of his environment.

In no way do I dispute the dynamic in which Shaw and Kay support their claims. In support of this assessment, many of the young men and women that lived just half a mile from the dilapidated drug infested area of 12th and Philadelphia (in Detroit) had a greater risk of using drugs than those that lived in modest middle-class homes a quarter mile away where lawn was kept, streets clean, housed painted etc. as opposed to run down homes filled with roaches etc.

By in large, economic also played a critical role in developing the moral stability within those living in these run down areas. Their clothing was sub-par; food, health care and other basic needs were far below—second hand, handouts—unlike several blocks away where churches engaged in sharing. The lack of human resources needed to bring this broken down hood into the present day was non-existence. The few stores within two-mile radius only offered poor grades of pork. Most people lived off welfare produce such as canned beef and pork.

Many clothing stores resold stolen clothes at bootleg prices. Drugs were cheaper than anywhere else which left many youths to seek refuge in drugs, theft and other criminal acts. The largest surplus commodities were alcohol, drugs and sex. Other areas could not compete with these social disorders. And while many people arriving from the south visited these areas for enjoyment and suddenly became hooked, many others traveled south to escape it.

So in part, some hoods breed crime by choice rather than by design. And in some area's it was inherited though its structure and lack of economical values, cultural bankruptcy and lack of identity and community efforts to rid these elements from their grasp.

In relation to the neighborhood climate as it relates to crime, it does in fact play a significant role. Many hard cold addicts that could not bear the harsh winter in Detroit running the streets hustling moved out west to Texas, Cali, Vegas, Miami, and other places to satisfy their drug addictions.

#####

THE SPATIAL ISOLATION OF RESIDENTIAL SEGREGATION

Many prisoners that came to my "Social Science and Personal Writing" volunteer prison classes were long-sentence prisoners, having already spent more than thirty years in prison, who had grown up witnessing the events of the 1960s, 1970s, 1980s, and 1990s. The economic boom of the 1990s helped to lower the crime rate, Parker notes: "As labor markets were booming in the late 1990s, in other words, the tie between labor market structures in the new economy and urban violence is modified as other sectors absorbed workers, reducing dislocation and the level of labor market discrimination along racial and gender lines" (2008: 92). Recall that during the 1980s "the percent change in industrial restructuring among black males was 596 percent compared to 22.3 percent among whites." That is, in the 1980s a dramatic negative impact of joblessness and community instability hit urban blacks. She continues:

> Deindustrialization contributed to the social isolation or residential segrega-
> tion of African Americans. . . . Wilson's term "concentration effects" reflected
> the continued reduction in employment opportunities and job networks among
> inner-city residents (Wilson 1987: 58), causing the disadvantage accrued by
> blacks to become increasingly spatially concentrated. (Parker 2008: 92)

Prisoners describe their neighborhoods in various ways, but African American prisoners almost always describe their neighborhood as a black neighborhood—and as a set of streets rife with poverty, addiction, and "death around every corner" due to rampant drug turf violence and power struggles between gangs. And, as Peterson and Krivo's study found, high crime African American neighborhoods are very often surrounded by other high crime segregated African American neighborhoods—increasing the overall social isolation and exacerbating crime rates and violence.

The urban housing is, according to the academic researchers, reflect-ing "the role of industrial restructuring in contributing to the spatial isola-tion of minority groups." The prisoners themselves talk of the dad or mom losing their good job at GM and the family and neighborhood going downhill. Parker discusses the relative impact of job losses and discrimination:

> Massey and Denton (1993), (while) agreeing with Wilson's concerns over
> deindustrialization, shift the emphasis to the role played by racial residential
> segregation in the concentration of disadvantage among blacks.
>   The isolation of blacks from whites residentially results in a preponderance of
> African Americans in specific industrial sectors (Boyd 1998), further segregat-
> ing labor markets (Ihlanfeldt 1992; Kain 1992).
>   This suggests that racially segregated areas are hindered when attracting
> potential employers, further disadvantaging black workers in the labor market
> (Bogard et al. 2001) and significantly limiting the types of jobs available. . . .
> Wilson (1996) made a similar observation . . . that the closure of manufacturing
> plants triggered "the exodus of the smaller stores, the banks and other busi-
> nesses that relied on the wages paid by the larger employers" (Wilson 1996,
> 35). (2008: 92–93)
>   . . . ([T]hese trends) heighten feelings of anger and frustration that result
> in aggression (e.g., violence). According to Blau and Blau (1982), when an

economically polarized environment is coupled with ascribed (racial) forms of inequality, the potential for violence increases (2008: 96)

Peter and Judith Blau summarized their 1982 study "The Cost of Inequality: Metropolitan Structure and Violent Crime," this way:

The analysis reveals that socioeconomic inequality between races, as well as economic inequality generally, increases rates of criminal violence, but once economic inequalities are controlled poverty no longer influences these rates, neither does Southern location, and the proportion of blacks in the population hardly does. These results imply that if there is a culture of violence, its roots are pronounced economic inequalities, especially if associated with ascribed position. (114)

As inequalities increased in U.S. society over the last forty years, and a "war on drugs" policing and penal control approach was taken, the state prison budgets became very large. Since 2008 some state legislators have been capping prison budgets and shifting some of the money saved to community corrections (probation, parole). Five states have actually reduced prison populations. Some criminologists are recommending that some of the money saved by capping and reducing prisons costs be reinvested in the jobless ghettos. This movement is known as "justice reinvestment." This would be one source of public capital to help anchor investment in local community economic stability.

Fundamental sociological crime prevention social change strategies, then, include increasing the localization of capital investment decisions, building up wider community processes of coalition-building such as "communities that care," social movement work toward guaranteed income, the revenue-neutral justice reinvestment thinking (cut prisons, invest in jobless ghetto) spreading among the members of the American Society of Criminology, and involving the grey heads in prison (LIFERS, Inc.) in a multiple group community justice crime prevention approach trying to reduce the impact of the culture of street crime.

HOW CHANGES IN THE LOCAL ECONOMIES OF U.S. CITIES LEADS TO CRIME

Because community economic stability is crucial to neighborhood crime prevention it is necessary to ask: Why do urban environments "decay?" How does a stable low crime community become an unstable high crime area? What kind of social mobility and migration (moving into and out of the community) is occurring and why?

In the 1920s and 1930s, University of Chicago sociology department researchers Shaw and McKay studied urban problems and launched the social disorganization perspective. The context was one of city growth, of a rapid industrialization and economic development.

Shaw summarized the links between ecological change, social disorganization, and the development of "delinquency areas" as follows:

> In the process of city growth, the neighborhood organizations, cultural institutions, and social standards in practically all areas adjacent to the central business district and the major industrial centers are subject to rapid change and disorganization. The gradual invasion of these areas by industry and commerce, the continuous movement of the older residents out of the area and the influx of new groups, the confusion of many divergent cultural standards, the economic insecurity of the families, all combine to render difficult the development of a stable and efficient neighborhood for the education and control of the child and the suppression of lawlessness. (1930/1966: 387)

One of Shaw and McKay's (1942) most important observations (of these high crime areas) was that the relative levels of delinquency and crime in a local community tended to remain stable over many years, despite changing ethnic and racial composition (Bursik 1988: 524; Bursik and Grasmick 1993, 1995). Shaw and McKay argued that delinquent values and traditions were being passed from one generation of residents to another; in other words, a form of cultural transmission was taking place. In Shaw and McKay's view, the only way to combat the tendency for areas to become permanently crime prone was to develop neighborhood organizations that could help promote informal social controls and encourage residents to look out for each others' welfare (Sampson 1986, 1987; Stark 1987) (Barlow and Kauzlarich 2009: 242).

However, instead of a *growing* city, such as Chicago in the 1870–1930 period of industrialization causing neighborhood change, starting in the 1970s, American cities entered a decades-long period of changing industrial mix: manufacturing jobs declined and information technologies and services jobs increased. Meanwhile much of the population moved out to the suburbs, businesses moved to greenfields in U.S. rural areas, or businesses moved plants to Mexico or China.

There is a countertrend of young, upwardly mobile professionals buying or renting in the downtown or central city areas—a trend known as "gentrification." However, several large cities, such as Detroit, have mostly been in *decline*, resulting in drastic decreases in good paying jobs in the inner city, as documented by Karen Parker (2008). Smaller cities have also lost population to growing townships around their perimeter, and the endless sprawl into U.S.

rural areas of housing development has also created losses of population for U.S. cities.

So, we have, over recent decades, a picture of urban decline leading to disorganized communities. Police efforts to flood officers into "hot spots" and to "stop-and-frisk" people on the streets appear to lower a city's crime rate (Gopnik 2012). However, do these newer policing strategies mean there is no need to solve the root problems of American cities? For one thing, we have built the world's largest prison system—and it's expensive. This raises questions about the ultimate effectiveness of ever greater prisonization. As Sampson argues:

> Public discourse on crime policy has traditionally been dominated by calls for the ever-greater penetration of official control—especially more police, more prisons, and longer mandatory sentences. Public-health approaches have begun to challenge this emphasis on reactive strategies by the criminal justice system, advocating instead crime prevention (Reiss and Roth 1993; Earls and Carlson 1996). In thinking about the prevention of crime, policymakers have turned to programs that attempt to change individuals (e.g., Head Start; job training) or families (e.g., child-rearing skills; conflict resolution).
>
> Although individual- and family-level prevention are welcome partners in crime control, there is another target of intervention that until recently has been widely neglected in public policy circles—the community. This level of social inquiry asks how community structures and cultures produce differential rates of crime. For example, what characteristics of communities are associated with high rates of violence? Are communities safe or unsafe because of the persons who reside in them or because of community properties themselves? Perhaps most important, by changing communities can we bring about changes in crime rates?
>
> . . . A community-level perspective also points out how federal, state, and local governmental policies not directly concerned with crime policy may nonetheless bear on crime rates. In particular, not enough attention has been paid to "noncrime" policies—especially on housing, families, and child development—and how they influence the link between crime and community. (2002: 225)

For instance, the city of Detroit has begun to relocate inner-city residents. A recent newspaper story describes this:

> Detroit, the very symbol of American industrial might for most of the 20th century, is drawing up a radical renewal plan that calls for turning large swaths of this now-blighted rusted-out city back into the fields and farmland that existed before the automobile.
>
> Operating on a scale never before attempted in this country, the city would demolish houses in some of the most desolate sections of Detroit and move

residents into stronger neighborhoods. Roughly a quarter of the 139-square-mile city could go from urban to semi-rural.

. . . Politically explosive decisions must be made about which neighborhoods should be bulldozed and which improved. Hundreds of millions of federal dollars will be needed to buy land, raze buildings and relocate residents, since this financially desperate city does not have the means to do it on its own. It isn't known how many people in the mostly black, blue-collar city might be uprooted, but it could be thousands (*Daily Telegram* 2010: A3)

The lack of informal social controls leading to crime and delinquency is the key insight provided by social disorganization theory. The major social policy response to the consequent increases in crime rate was a vast increase in the use of prisons. The impact of "imprisoning communities" is the weakening of the community.

#####

Prisoner Essay 7.13

"Going to Prison's Impact on Community" (3/17/10)
I can remember when I was young that there were older guys in my neighborhood that people as well as myself look up to. These guys had it all the girls, clothes, and cars. But most of all they had the money. They would give us money so we could go to the penny candy store or record shop to buy stuff we wanted. This was good cause a lot of times our parents didn't have extra money to give us for these things unless it was the first of the month when everybody expected their welfare checks.

When some of these people got lock up for crimes, it made it hard for us to get extra stuff that we wanted cause they was gone and the money left with them. Now we had to hustle for ourselves to get money and that meant we had to commit crime. Yeah we could had cut grass, but there was no grass. We could have even collected bottles, but those were all broken. Crime pay is much better cause all we had to do at that time was be a look-about, or take and package somewhere, and keep your mouth shut.

My father for the most part showed me and my brother how the streets can pay. I watch little by little how my parent's neighborhood was getting worse by the day when people started to get lock up on a daily basis. The neighborhood was largely a breeding ground for crime but when people started to get lock up it got worse. People who was alright in the neighborhood who had a little money all of a sudden didn't cause their father or brother was lock up who provided for the household in major way. People on the block would help each other out as much as they could but things was just tight, there wasn't a lot of jobs to be had let alone even be offered. So there was no networking about getting jobs, just hustling.

People who had jobs had to catch the bus or walk to work. People who had cars got lock up, so going to work every day was hard and in the winter was not even an option. I see how social disorganization in my neighborhood made it worse than it already was when people got lock up. When my father was killed I see how our household went down and the things I was used to having was now gone, so I did the only thing I knew to do at that time which was to commit crime to help out around the house and take care of myself.

When I got lock up this hurt my family as well as the community. I was someone that people knew and could trust for things. I wouldn't let people houses get broke in or their cars stole in my neighborhood. Prison changes that.

So when I got here and seen almost everybody from my neighborhood, I was like damn! This is almost like a neighborhood reunion, minus the fact that we all were lock up in prison.

How does mass incarceration makes disadvantaged neighborhood worse, because the people that keep it safe like myself are gone from the neighborhood. Trust me I have first-hand knowledge; I sit here talking to you. I was once part of the problem. There is hope though. We must first clean up our minds! Crime and violence isn't the way to provide for our community. Yeah a lot of money is made, but at what cost? I can write and read about the cost for a year or two and have a new issue every day, we see it on TV and hear it in our music.

I still believe that good can still be done by having after school programs and community meeting where everybody gets together to talk about making our neighborhood safe, having love for our neighbor so we can walk down the street safe. It's start with us, the adult. We tore the community down and the cleanup is on us. We owe it to the community and they look to us for guidance. Let's show them the right way because they are the futures. Let's stop the mass incarceration and start mass living. Because prison life isn't living life but wasting life.

#####

We've reviewed sociologists systematic studies of how the multiclass communal ghetto became the subproletarian hyperghetto (Wacquant 2008); how the postindustrial "oppositional culture" of street youth emerges (Anderson 2008; Milton 2012); how "social disorganization" and the impact of changing city labor markets affects families causing African American males to have four times as much homicide in the "unequal crime decline" of recent decades (Parker 2008). The black male comes to prison.

Academic researchers, reflect on "the role of industrial restructuring in contributing to the spatial isolation of minority groups." The prisoners themselves talk of the dad or mom losing their good job at GM and the family and neighborhood going downhill. As Williamson, Imbroscio, and Alperovitz in their book *Making a Place for Community: Local Democracy in a Global Era*, note:

> Consideration of each of the three principal threats to community economic stability in the United States . . .—the effects of globalization, capital mobility between states, and sprawl—all point in a common policy direction: the need to provide localities with stable economies that will not be blown away by changes in market conditions or in the overall economy, that do not run away when the next opportunity comes along, and that do not relocate to greenfields in order to escape problems at home. (2003: 99)

Capricious Economy and Faltering Economic Institutions

This same experience of "structural shift" or restructuring of labor markets—from manufacturing to services—that Parker links through its impact on families to crime, and to explain unequal crime decline, Williamson, Imbroscio, and Alperovitz link to the more general issue of community economic stability that affects most Americans. How to create stable communities when investment dollars are highly mobile? The Great Depression of the 1930s and fighting World War II brought Americans together to solve common problems. Then there were the collective movements of the 1960s and early 1970s (civil rights, antiwar, women's liberation, environment, etc.). Again, many Americans were struggling together—but by the mid-1970s there was a conservative countermovement.

Since the mid-1970s the broad "middle-class" experience in America has been more placid and an individualistic and family experience trying to pin down an "American Dream"—"work hard, get an education, and you and your family will get ahead." Prisoners, too, believe in the American Dream. However, Parker shows us how urban blacks were impacted by community instability due to the restructuring of industrial business. This same trend toward community instability has been hitting whites. Judith R. Blau reminds us how the American middle class are also in an increasingly *contingent* situation, an apprehension about economic insecurity that increasingly more Americans feel. She wrote that

> the rock bed of middle-class lifestyle—the suburb and, more specifically, traditional domestic life—is giving way. Increasingly in large cities, white-collar suburbs are populated by commuters—dual-income-earning families; single,

unmarried adults; and cohabitating adults—while institutional child care is increasingly prevalent.

... there has been a steady increase in economic inequalities, as a result of gains among the rich, deterioration of the economic conditions of the poor, and declines in the income of the middle class. (Blau 1995: 225–26)

Judith Blau notes this has been in part due

to a steady decline of full-time workers in core labor sectors accompanied by an increase in contract workers and in part-time workers in peripheral or secondary labor sectors.

... For the first time since the end of the Depression, the gap between the rich and poor is widening while the proportion of the middle declines. In the context here that means declining opportunities for upward mobility and increases in downward mobility.

... There are glaring contradictions between, on the one hand, a national middle-class culture that successfully spawned democratic institutions, egalitarian patterns of lifestyle and consumption, and an ethos that linked hard work with success and achievement and a capricious economy and faltering economic institutions on the other

... To the extent that hard work and achievement were core cultural values, the collapse of economic institutions could very well entail a major reevaluation and overhaul of these core values, which themselves are already contradictory.

... As Michael Kammen (1991) suggests, the American myth that mobility and success is a matter of individual striving rests uneasily in a democratic society in which there is little economic growth (Blau 1995: 227–28)

The trends described by Judith Blau, who was writing in 1994–1995, have continued to show up over the last twenty years in the broader American middle class—not only as the consequence of the eighteen-month "Great Recession" (2008–2009), deep recession and subsequent years of inability of the U.S. economy (at 7.3 percent unemployment in 2013) to produce much more than the 150,000 jobs a month needed to keep up with population growth, thus continuing to leave millions out of work—but even more so as a fast-paced *structural shift* due to the effects globalization and technology (and hierarchical corporate decisions) on the American occupational structure. Writing in late 2010, Fareed Zakaria notes:

Some experts say that in every recession Americans get gloomy and then recover with the economy. This slump is worse than most; so is the mood. Once demand returns, they say, jobs will come back and, with them, optimism. But Americans are far more apprehensive than usual, and their worries seem to go beyond the short-term debate over stimulus vs. deficit reduction. They fear that we are in the midst of not a cyclical down-turn but a structural shift, one that poses huge new challenges to the average American job, pressures the average American wage, and endangers the average American dream. The middle class, many Americans have come to believe, is being hollowed out. I think they are right. (2010: 31–32)

Zakaria notes that by using the new technology, companies have learned to do more with fewer employees. Also, more companies have gone global and are generating more of their profits outside of the United States, cutting jobs at home "where demand is weak" and adding jobs in the emerging markets. Zakaria concludes:

You can divide the American workforce in many ways, but any way you slice it, you see the same trend. People who get paid a decent wage for skilled but routine work in manufacturing or services are getting squeezed by a pincer movement of technology and globalization. David Autor, an MIT economist, has done an important study on what he calls "the polarization of job opportunities" in American. Autor finds that job growth divides neatly into three categories. On one side are managerial, professional and technical occupations, held by highly educated workers who are comfortable in the global economy. Jobs have been plentiful in this segment for the past three decades. On the other end are service occupations, those that involve "helping, caring for or assisting others," such as security guard, cook and waiter. Most of these workers have no college education and get hourly wages that are on the low end of the scale. Jobs in this segment too have been growing robustly.

In between are the skilled manual workers and those in white collar operations like sales and office management. These jobs represent the beating heart of the middle class. Those in them make a decent living, usually above the median family income ($49,777), and they mostly did fine in the two decades before 2000. But since then, employment growth has lagged the economy in general. And in the Great Recession, it has been these middle-class folks who have been hammered. Why? Autor is cautious and tentative, but it would seem that technology, followed by global competition, has played the largest role in making less valuable the routine tasks that once epitomized middle-class work.

. . . Technology is a much larger driver of the hollowing out than trade (2010: 31–34)

Karen Parker traces the effect of restructuring in urban labor markets and the effect on impoverished neighborhoods and families and the consequence of "unequal crime decline": more violence from African Americans hit harder that others by the labor market restructuring. Judith Blau and Fareed Zakaria describe large trends of globalization and business application of technology to jobs that is resulting in the *experience* of restructuring of the labor market for average working-class and middle-class Americans.

The 1950s and 1960s was the "discovery of poverty" and "war on poverty," and the assumption at that time was that the United States, as a nation, could "bring everyone up out of poverty." Starting in 1968 and continuing into the twenty-first century, we've lived through a period in which the nation acted like it could end crime and drug abuse through a "war on crime" and a "war on drugs." The United States has also launched four major wars in that period.

Now, Americans are worried about the impact of industrial restructuring, new technology to reduce jobs, globalization of both manufacturing and service jobs, and the increasing bifurcation of the American labor market into "good jobs," and "bad jobs." There is an apprehension that there is likely to be a deep change in the context for the American dream. The conservative countermovement to the 1960s progressive movement that started by 1980 has had its thirty-five-year run. It's hard to predict the future, but we seem to be at a turning point. Can the American people get more localization of capital to ensure community economic stability to improve peoples' lives and reduce crime? The fitful start of the "Occupy Movement" and efforts to revitalize the labor movement, the movement of American steelworkers in the Mondragon-style production cooperatives (Alperovitz 2013; Alperovitz and Bhatt 2014; Strether 2013), and other progressive social policies may only require a small input of additional effort to spark large scale change. As Wallerstein notes:

> The present is always a matter of choice, but as someone once said, although we make our own history, we do not make it as we choose. Still, we do make it. The present is a matter of choice, but the range of choice is considerably expanded in the period immediately preceding a bifurcation, when the system is furthest from equilibrium, because at that point small inputs have large outputs (as opposed to moments of near equilibrium, when large inputs have small outputs). (1999: 84)

EXERCISES 7.1–7.2

Exercise 7.1

Connect two or more quotes from prisoner essays in chapter 7 to the issues of the increasing climate of economic instability in the United States. Find a prisoner story quotes that are examples business disinvestment in a neighborhood. Connect this prisoner quote to Loic Wacquant's description of the transition from communal ghetto to hyperghetto. How does Karen Parker theorize linkage between labor markets and urban crime?

Exercise 7.2

Design a set of social policies that would respond to the situations as described in exercise 7.1.

DISCUSSION AND REVIEW QUESTIONS

1. Describe the transition from the communal ghetto to the hyperghetto (jobless ghetto) in the United States over the past fifty years.
2. Provide a description of the U.S. inner-city hyperghetto from one or more of the prisoner essays.
3. How does Loic Wacquant see the "political and economic abandonment" of the hyperghetto? Who makes the decisions to abandon the inner-city jobless ghetto?
4. Why have there been urban riots in the emerging hyperghetto of 1965, 1967, 1992 (and continuing) according to Wacquant?
5. Summarize the Graterford Prison LIFERS, Inc., essay—what is the culture of street crime?
6. According to Karen Parker, why do African American males have four times the level of violence as compared to white males?
7. What reasons do prisoners in the essays give for becoming "hard," "cold-hearted," and violent? How does this relate to selling drugs and the culture of street crime?
8. What reasons can you find in prisoner essays for "changing neighborhoods" (decay and decline)?
9. What is the relationship between disruption of community and disruption of family life and crime? How are they connected?
10. What is the linkage between urban labor markets and urban crime?
11. What is meant by a "climate of economic instability"? What is meant by "localization of investment?"
12. What is meant by "capital mobility" and "globalization."
13. How has technological change undermined family and local economic stability?

8

Social Structure, Social Process, and Alternative Criminologies

So far, the book has reviewed the individual, family, and community levels of explaining the causes of crime. In chapters 5, 6, and 7 an argument was built emphasizing that it is often necessary to examine the way macro-social realities influence crime rates. This chapter briefly reviews several sociological theories of crime: social structure theories, social process theories, and alternative critical criminological theories. Social structural theory takes the structures of society—the norms and values, the institutions, the power arrangements of the society—and sees in them the root cause of crime. For example, Robert Merton argued in a 1938 essay titled "Social Structure and Crime," that a misalignment between America's basic values ("work hard and you'll get ahead") and economic institutions (not enough good paying jobs) leads to a "structural strain" on the American lower class to engage in street crime.

Consider this: In America everyone is expected to "get ahead," but the structure of decision making over good jobs and pay belongs to corporations (our economic institution and power structure), unlike in Germany, where power over jobs is shared (Derber 1998, 2002). American corporate decisions lead to devastated cities with, for example, massive downsizing in manufacturing as depicted by Michael Moore's film *Roger and Me*, leading to more violent crime as demonstrated by Karen Parker's book *Unequal Crime Decline* (2008) and Elijah Anderson's "Against the Wall: Poor, Young, Black, and Male" (2010), and, because kids want stuff, this leads to a structural strain toward crime (Merton 1938) where youth become "innovators" through the underground and often illegal economy in the inner city.

The strained neighborhoods become places where "strained individuals" accumulate (Stark 1987) and have stresses in their individual lives that pressure them toward crime (Agnew 2010).

SOCIAL STRUCTURE AND STRAIN

Can the very social structure of American society help explain crime? Akers and Sellers note that "Anomie/strain theories provide an explanation of the concentration of crime not only in the lower-class urban areas but also in lower-class and minority groups in general, as well as the overall high crime rate in American society." Strain theory explains this. Akers and Sellers note:

> This theory leans heavily on the work of Emile Durkheim, one of the founders of sociology. Durkheim (1951 [1987]) used the term *anomie* to refer to a state of normlessness or lack of social regulation in modern society as one condition that promotes higher rates of suicide. Robert Merton (1938, 1957) applied this Durkheimian approach. (Akers and Sellers 2009: 183)

Regarding Robert Merton's "social structure and anomie theory," Trojanowicz, Morash, and Schram note:

> The main thrust of Merton's efforts was "in discovering how some social structures exert a definite pressure upon certain persons in a society to engage in nonconformist rather than conformist conduct." He built on the work of Emile Durkheim . . . (who) focused his attention on *anomie*—a situation in which individuals feel disconnected from any group and are isolated from the mainstream of interaction and positive peer support.
>
> Merton's explanation considers three concepts: (1) the cultural goals or aspirations that people learn from their culture, (2) the norms that people employ when attempting to achieve the goals, and (3) the institutionalized means that are available for goal achievement. When there is a discrepancy between the institutionalized means available and the goals to which an individual aspires, strain or frustration is produced, norms break down, and deviant behavior can result. For example, if a lower-class child is exposed by the mass media to success symbols and a lifestyle that are difficult to attain because of lack of institutionalized means—such as adequate schools and employment opportunities—this, Merton feels, will create strain and frustration that leads to illegal behavior. (Trojanowicz, Morash, and Schram 2000: 62)

Prisoners frequently describe wanting stuff as children when they were growing up, but having parents who were unable to buy them the things other children have. Merton's structural strain often shows up in "kids wanting stuff" and children, teens, and young adults having a sense of relative deprivation.

#####

Prisoner Essay 8.1

"I Need That Syndrome" (3/11/09)

Everyone always says it's the communities you grow up in that are a major factor in the making of a criminal. Maybe it's just me but I also think it's the communities that you don't grow up in that also have a major impact on why crimes are committed. A man grows up in a household where maybe the family bond is there, but the area where you live isn't as rich as the surrounding cities or towns. You go to school with these other kids from a better off sections and it triggers the "I need that" syndrome. A form of greed, because greed is wanting more when you already have everything. Now back to school, you're wearing hand me downs and in walks another student wearing the newest fashions, the best clothes, so on and so forth. This triggers that want, that eats at your soul to the point you are willing to do anything to gain what this student has.

Now this can be positive or negative. Also, unfortunately, the positive way takes a bit longer. The positive way is going out getting a job and working for what you want, you can do your best in school and get a good job and always have what you want. All the while you set a good example for others, and giving back to your community. The negative way you can take many paths on this point. You can go to a store and rob them, steal cars, run scams, sell drugs, the possibilities are endless and the results are instant and satisfaction guaranteed until you get caught. Basically I'm saying it's not the community you live in, but the one's you don't and then that's just to show them what's out there, everyone has the opportunity to do right, but they choose to do wrong.

#####

Prisoner Essay 8.2

"Social Comparison" (3/3/10)

When one hears the phrase, "The American Dream," the illicit within them imagines prosperity beyond comprehension. Whether these desires are material or idealistic, one who is achieving their prescribed goal is considered to be living the American dream. But does this gilded phrase have a dark side? A side that forces those considered less privileged to stop outside of the socially-acceptable behaviors and pursue criminal enterprises to achieve the pinnacle of success?

Whether we like it or not, and despite what the Constitution insists, all people are not able to pursue happiness though standard means. Being within a capitalist society we are subjected to various socioeconomic classes.

These range from those that are so far below that poverty line that they require enormous amounts of governmental assistance just to enjoy the basic necessities of life, to the ultra-affluent, whose philanthropic donations are the equivalent of most nations' gross domestic product. We as a society have chosen to place all value and honor based solely upon what one possesses in a bank account, or how many tangible things they own.

Allow yourself to imagine the following scenario; you reside within an over-populated, well known urban setting, a city once held in the highest esteem filled with opportunity and civility. However due to economic conditions and governmental mismanagement, this prosperous city has fallen into despair. Crime rates have escalated while employment ceases to be available. Despite your finest efforts within school, the district where you graduated couldn't afford to provide a quality education and your merits fail to allow for a continuation of scholastics. Each time you turn on the television or radio, you are inundated with the latest and greatest but realize that at this time those wants are far beyond what's practical.

As an escape you decide to explore the surrounding areas. What you see is astonishing prosperity seems to be falling off the trees. Curiosity gets the better of you and you request a tour of the local high school. Upon entering, you immediately become dejected by seeing everything that was unavailable to allow you to continue your academic career, available to many who are indifferent to its presence. The distance traveled may have been twenty miles, but it might as well have been a time-warp, thrusting you back to Plato's academy. Knowledge was literally in the air. The point of being under-privileged overwhelms you; you ask yourself, why am I less suited than these? Why do they have all possibilities at their disposal and despite excelling, you can only manage to acquire a part time, dead end job.

Leaving this proverbial paradise you become increasingly angry you vow to yourself that you will prosper regardless of what had to be done, with the utterance of that simple phrase, the seed of criminality become firmly planted within your heart.

This scenario exhibits how simple it is for environmental conditions to spur criminal activity. This person was a law-abiding citizen, willing to work doggedly for what was right, but circumstances and geography prevented that from occurring. It is clear that without a revamping of our collective ideals, aspirations, and desires, this process will continue to occur. The "real" American dream will only be accessible once equality to opportunity is insured. Without this conscious decision, crimes of status will plague and eventually destroy what all Americans hold dear, freedom.

#####

GENERAL STRAIN THEORY

Robert Agnew notes that "subcultural deviance theory argues that many of the community characteristics" found in socially disorganized neighborhoods (or the hyperghetto) contribute to "or are associated with the development of subcultures that hold values conducive to crime." Agnew writes:

> This article builds on previous theory and research and argues that those values conducive to crime are rooted in the "strainful" experiences of community members.
>
> In sum, social disorganization theories now dominate the current research on communities and crime. . . . It is next argued, however, that community differences in crime rates are a function not only of differences in social control but also of difference in the motivation for crime.
>
> General Strain Theory (GST) argues that strain or stress is a major source of criminal motivation. The theory explains community differences in crime by community differences in strain and in those factors that condition the effect of strain on crime. In particular, high-crime communities are more likely to select and retain strained individuals, produce strain, and foster criminal responses to strain.(2005: 51)

For Agnew, the theorists associated with the development of social disorganization theory "indicate that slum communities contribute to several types of strain, most notably the failure to achieve economic goals" (2005: 51).

#####

Prisoner Essay 8.3

"Welfare Is Our Way to Get Over and Hustle on the Side" (3/3/10)
I often wondered when I was a child that I sometimes thought being a hood was cool. Then I thought being a police officer was cool also. I can honestly say that my community had a lot to do with it. My community dictated how I acted as well as I thought. My parent's neighborhood was a lower class community where there was always someone hustling or some type of violence going on all the time. And the money that was made from this made the life-style attractive. When my father was killed I understand why I went back to my old community, where people felt the way I did at that time. Which was—"They don't care about us? They don't give a damn that we are being gun down." We don't have good jobs or no job at all. Welfare is our way to get over and hustle on the side. And this way of thinking was reinforced by the people who I was hanging with. The only thing that was expected of us in

my parent's community was to stay alive and get money so we could get out. We had parks and after school programs in my parents neighborhood. But going to the park was different because we had to watch out for broken glass and needles everywhere. People was always drinking and fighting and women half naked showing us young boys what we could have when we got older and had some money. Also when my grandparents moved out when I was young that had a huge effect on me. A lot of the positive values that I was learning left with them. That is not saying that my parents didn't want the best for me, cause they did.

I went to school, and as long as I didn't get D's and E's, I was good. My father loves us very much but he taught us what he knew. Don't get me wrong, I have been knowing the difference between right and wrong as a child. But I was also showed how crime pays and how being delinquent was cool and how it gain social status in the hood. I was taught that some laws don't apply to me. It was cool to carry a gun, just don't let the police see or catch you. If someone disrespected me I was taught to check them hard, and if that got into physical violence, so be it. Being respected was the goal. If that meant getting or giving a black eye it didn't matter. As long as I check people who I felt disrespected me I was cool. And we was taught to socialize in this manner. In my grandparent's neighborhood I was just the opposite. I wanted to fit in. Robert Agnew GST (general strain theory) is something I most identify with. I never got to achieve my positive goals as a child that was taken from me when my father was killed. What was reinforce to me was the street code. I now understand why I watched Scarface or the Miami Vice before I went out to commit crimes. The bad guy got away and was rich, and they didn't have jobs. What we call "social disorganization" was a way of life for me as a child, which I carried into adulthood that I struggle to correct to this day. I know that in order to change this way of life we must first change the way we think and our community, cause that is where it starts. As adults we must teach our children it's okay to do the right thing and facilitate positive places and activity. And get away from "do as I say and not as I do". Children look up to us because it us the adults that a child first learn from. Expect high grades from our children in school and show them the reward of this. Our community shouldn't be a deviant place to live that glorifies crime. Our lower class community should be afforded the same opportunity that upper class communities have. One of the main reasons for high crime and juvenile delinquency in lower class is lower class community aren't afforded the same opportunity as upper class community and this need to be fixed. By us the people of the community, let's save the children and give them a positive chance at life.

#####

One goal in understanding crime is to capture the social processes—the concrete day-to-day interactions—that are mechanisms leading from larger social structure to individual crime.

SOCIAL PROCESS AND CRIME

A mother may say: "I'm raising you to be a responsible person and am proud of your behavior, but I don't want you to hang around with those bad friends of yours anymore." On the one hand, she believes in the free will of her son and his will-training to be a proper boy. But, on the other hand, she believes in the determinism of the influence of his delinquent friends. Social process theories emphasize that criminal behavior is learned through interaction with others.

Edwin H. Sutherland, coauthoring with Donald R. Cressey (1974), put forth differential association theory, which consisted of nine propositions:

1. Criminal behavior is learned.
2. Criminal behavior is learned in interaction with other persons in a process of communication.
3. The principle part of the learning of criminal behavior occurs within intimate personal groups.
4. When criminal behavior is learned, the learning includes (a) techniques of committing the crime, which are sometimes very complicated, sometimes very simple; and (b) the specific direction of motives, drives, rationalizations, and attitudes.
5. The specific direction of motives and drives is learned from definitions of the legal codes as favorable or unfavorable.
6. A person becomes delinquent because of an excess of definitions favorable to violation of law (the principle of differential association).
7. Differential association may vary in frequency, duration, priority, and intensity.
8. The process of learning criminal behavior by association with criminal and anticriminal patterns involves all of the mechanisms that are involved in any other learning.
9. While criminal behavior is an expression of general needs and values, it is not explained by those general needs and values, since noncriminal behavior is an expression of the same needs and values. (Sutherland and Cressey 1974: 75–77; Barlow and Kauzlarich 2010: 75–76)

Obviously, this theory can explain conformity to the law as well as criminal behavior. For understanding our prisoners, we want to look at how differential association can explain variations in *group rates of crime.* . . . Thus, relatively high rates are predicted for people and places having extensive exposure to definitions favorable to law violations, especially when there is a high probability that such definitions will be learned by a relatively large number of people. Shaw and McKay's delinquency areas . . . would meet these criteria. (Barlow and Kauzlarich 2010: 77–78)

Additionally, behavioral learning theories emphasize that people tend to copy others when they see these others being rewarded. Daniel Glaser developed *differential identification* theory wherein a person identifies himself with real or imaginary persons that are behavior models (Barlow and Kauzlarich 2010: 79).

This process of differential identification would help explain the prisoner essays where they report fascination with adult gangsters in their neighborhood.

As social disorganization spread over fifty years in the central cities of the United States, and more recently in the inner-ring suburbs, more neighborhood delinquency area milieu occur. The uneven development caused by political and economic decisions creates more social structure of lower-class street-corner society. Within these criminogenic milieu, youth learn crime. Compare a typical law-abiding college student's growing up (college student 8.4) with a prisoner's description of learning crime through differential association (prisoner essay 8.5).

#####

College Student 8.4

"I Lived in a Sheltered World" (2/25/09)
While growing up as a child, I pretty much lived in a sheltered world. Whenever I was bored my brothers and I would go make up some game to keep us occupied. Also since I lived in the country there really wasn't that kind of peer pressure around me. In high school the only major thing that someone really tried to pressure me to do was to go out and drink. However, in high school I was able to say no and that was it. I felt since I was good at sports that people and young kids looked at me like I was a role model to them. Then when I got to college I started to experience peer pressure a lot more. Whatever it is to try and cheat on a test or to go out and smoke marijuana on the weekends. Most of the friends in college have smoked before and a lot of them are regular users. Personally I do not think drugs are the right things to do so I am always able to say no. Although my friends ask me to smoke every time they do it I am not really sure what the main reason is for not falling into peer pressure in these situations. I don't know if it is because the way I was brought up from my parents or if it was the DARE class we took

as kids. Another reason that I do not fall into peer pressure is because I am a strong-minded individual.

#####

Prisoner Essay 8.5

"For Late Teens: Peers and Buddies Are the New Family" (2/15/09)
When I was in my mid to late teen years, I did most of my crime with my peers. I was highly influence by my peers at that age.

I can remember numerous times when one of my "buddies" we'll call them or I would think of some crazy thing to do. In which we all knew that it was wrong. But still deep down within ourselves when we got truly honest with ourselves. Most of us went right along with whoever's crazy plan. Only because this was our "buddy," and in some way or form we just couldn't say no. Now being loyal to your friends is fine. It's a good thing to learn early. But just to follow anyone into harms way, first because they are your "buddy" is very reckless. Which truly is what our minds are at that stage in life. We feel, as though as long as we have our "buddies." Nothing in life can stop us. Which again are another reckless thought and probably the most elusive.

So what happen here is that, you have your young male usually more than young women, brought up in a low economic home, who hangs around a set of peers. Which he feels like this is his new family because his youthful mind is so influenced by his friends and what they are doing. This is where they get caught up in something to where society feels as though they own a debt to. So from there the vicious cycle of the penal system starts.

Now some may escape this vicious cycle, but really few do. Not until later ages in life. The reason for this being the fact that they find it hard to separate themselves from that certain peer groups that they not only get into the situation with, but also they become even more comfortable with these persons. For the simple fact that they've been through the situation (the crime) together. But as a person grows more mature mentally, they tend to find their own way in life. Finally then, they start to drift away from them peers for the simple reason that they just don't have the same concerns in mind. So as parents and adult reconciles it's our jobs to our youth, to notice the ones in our home and our communities that are traveling down this path and to help guide them towards a more successful one. We need to be witnesses in our communities that there are things that need to be watched for in our youth, so that we don't have a generation after generations falling into the vicious cycle that our youth continues to fall victim too.

#####

Prisoner Essay 8.6

"Peer Transition: From Nerdy to Trouble" (2/15/09)
Socioeconomic factors played a very significant role in my life. I spent the majority of my life trying to fit in with my schoolmates and those in my neighborhood. Instead of surrounding myself with those who were dong positive things in life, I instead gravitated towards who I viewed were having the most fun. I gravitated towards those individuals who specialized in breaking the law.

When I began attending Wayne Memorial High School in 1996, I did not have any black friends. As I black male, I was ridiculed for hanging with the white students. At first I just laughed off the teasing, but soon the taunts began to affect. I began to dislike going to school and would often skip school just to avoid my tormentors. After my freshman year, I decided that a change had to be made. I was determined to fit in with my fellow back students and make the teasing stop. During my sophomore year, I began hanging with a group of black students. I slowly watched as my popularity soared and the taunts began to subside. I enjoyed the change that I experienced but I noticed that there were some blacks that were still refusing to accept me. After my sophomore year in high school, I started change for the worst.

My first group of black friends was really dedicated to their schoolwork and were a little nerdy. I decided that a change of friends would give me the acceptance that I was looking for. I began hanging with the troublesome students at the school. I learned how to steal, fight, smoke weed, and sell drugs hanging with them. I was an honor roll student for my first time in two years in high school, but when I started hanging with them, I was eventually expelled three times from the high school. I felt like I was living the life that I had always wanted. I was finally accepted by those who used to shun me. But with that acceptance came my run-ins with the law.

In the summer of 2000, I was arrested and charged with 13 felony charges ranging from breaking and entering to fleeing and eluding. I've also been arrested for trespassing, retail fraud, and felon in possession of a firearm.

I've often looked at my extensive criminal record and wondered why I did those things. I never set out to be a criminal and I certainly don't enjoy it. I realize now that negative peer influences played a significant role I my development. If I had had an early intervention, I may have been able to avoid the criminal justice system and lived a productive life.

#####

Prisoner Essay 8.7

"My Choice, Context of Social Learning" (3/11/09)

I'll be the first to admit it; I'm a product of my environment. Now don't get me wrong, I do not fault my community or even blame my community, but I'm of my community. Do you understand what I mean when I say; I'm of my community?

Growing up, I had aspirations, dreams, goals and ambitions I wanted to obtain. I was in college, community college, but something is better than nothing. However, I wanted for my life to be easy, to me, going to school was enough, I couldn't work a real job. I did what was easy, what I was capable of, so I sold drugs.

In high school I played sports, basketball and track mainly, I did the football thing, but I got hit so hard one game, I said the hell with that. But while playing sports, I didn't sell drugs, my brothers did that, I didn't work hard in my classes because my coach took care of that; but when I tore my knee downhill all things went. I went from an athlete who did really nothing to now having to do everything. I had to attain, no scholarship coming, no one wanted the risk, but I had to go to college, to get ahead, but I followed the easy road, the new painted dream, of the American piece of pie, do it easy, get it easy!

I can't tell you one house in my neighborhood I know I got broke in, we didn't do this, my friends and I, we weren't in gangs but we called ourselves a "click" the two are really different in my eyes. But in my little five block area we did things we thought were fun; yes we sold drugs later in our lives, some early; we carried guns, but this was all learned, taught by others, which I do not fault nor blame, but I saw things they did and I followed.

Crime did occur in my neighborhood, but the guy's who I grew up with, we were somewhat committed to keeping things clean, or as fair as we could. We didn't kill or hurt each other, small fights—nothing a neighborhood barbeque couldn't fix or later night laser tag with everybody hanging on the porch. We did what we did, but we tried our way, low economy, told we wouldn't make it, no real equal protection in our communities by the police. We had to protect our own, govern our own, but somehow, greed overcame us all, mothers, fathers, sons and daughters. We lost dignity, self-assurance and self-esteem, all, which was formed by the American dream, the poor suffer the weak die, the rich live and live long.

I loved every second every day I lived in my neighborhood. I wouldn't change a day, I have no regrets, no pains, no hurts, I came from poverty, from nothing, but I got my son, a new house, I was a man at seventeen, I didn't dream to live longer than this!

#####

ALTERNATIVE CRIMINOLOGY THEORIES

Critical theories of crime stem from sociological conflict theory, which sees society shaped by conflicts between people with competing self- and group-interests revolving around money, power, and influence.

Emile Durkheim viewed society as fundamentally based on norms. As the social division of labor became an extreme division of labor due to industrialization and urbanization, the normative integration of societies weakened, leading to *anomie* (normlessness). As Merton showed, the norms of achievement in U.S. society could be frustrated and those without legitimate opportunity structures might use illegitimate opportunity structures to achieve common goals.

On the other hand, what if society is "glued together" not by common norms but, rather, structured by a tension of constant *power* differences and a web of social conflicts? As Akers and Sellers note:

> Conflict theory began to challenge consensus and (normative integration) functional models in sociology in the 1950s. . . . [T]his approach is . . . traced to the European sociologist Georg Simmel (1950), who viewed conflict as a fundamental social process. Its chief proponent in criminology at that time was George Vold, who, in his classic *Theoretical Criminology* (1958), proposed that group conflict explains not only criminal law and justice but criminal behavior as well.
>
> The whole political process of law making, law breaking, and law enforcement becomes a direct reflection of deep-seated and fundamental conflicts between interest groups and their more general struggles for the control of the police power of the state. Those who produce legislative majorities win control over the police power and dominate the policies that decides who is likely to be involved in violation of the law. (Vold 1958: 208–9, in Akers and Sellers 2009: 195)

This brings us back to the *political* view of "theorizing criminal justice" presented in chapter 2 and the "governing through crime" perspective in chapter 3. These early chapters went into some detail explaining the rise of mass incarceration from a social power or conflict perspective. Prisoners in my "Social Science and Personal Writing" volunteer class often wrote about power differences on a *local* level—the level at which they live their life.

#####

Prisoner Essay 8.8

"Three Neighborhoods: Power Differences" (10/28/09)

Like most inner city, improvised minority communities on the west side of Detroit, there existed invisible boundaries that imprisoned one and offered vast freedom to the other. The area in which I grew up had an unspoken demarcation line which bordered Linwood Avenue. On the west side, you had low income housing, prostitution, drugs, gambling, liquor and many home-less people and youth unrest. To the east, there lied an area called LaSalle Gardens where spacious homes with manicured lawns, peach, pear and other fruit trees littered their back yards.

On the far east, you had 12th street. Between two of the roughest drug and prostitute infested hoods on the west side. In the middle, you had the spacious gardens where rich and powerful people lived in 6 to 7 bedroom homes. Even the unoccupied homes were marvelous. The empty homes in our hood were used for dope shooting galleries, prostitutes, gambling and hangouts.

The gardens had garbage cans in the back of their homes as opposed most of the homes in my neighborhood where we had to drag garbage to the corner of the street. The garbage men refused to drive up the streets. Dozens of complaints fell on deaf ears. In the Gardens, garbage men drove straight up to these people's homes; some residents even offered them tips for picking up the garbage. There was no liquor stores, strip clubs, after hours clubs, gam-bling, drugs nor prostitution in the Garden area because the police guarded this area like it was Fort Knox. On the other side where I lived, police took hours to respond to an emergency.

One evening while we were sitting on the curb of Linwood Avenue; two junkies were wrestling with a white man that had just had sex with a prosti-tute. The whore, after seeing all the money the man had, tipped off two junk-ies to rob him. We sat there and watched the whole set unfold. Unfortunate for the junkies, an undercover police car had cruised around the corner. My buddy tried to tip off the junkies. But it was too late. Jumping out of the car; the man gave chase after the junkies. The police seen him and followed suit. One of the junkies, unaware of where he was heading, ran across Linwood into the Gardens. We could hear one of the police officers screaming into his radio that they had an armed and dangerous nigger heading into the Gardens. In less than 10 minutes, I saw over 15 police cars from two different precincts setting up perimeters to catch this junkie. Suffice to say, the other one that ran west, they simply let him go. Their main objective was to secure the safety of the Gardens.

From time to time, some of the resident allowed us to explore this quiet, clean and spacious area. On Halloween nights, under the watchful eye of some of the residents they allow us to run from house to house trick-or-treating after all of the children in the Gardens had finished. Only boys and girls under 12 were allowed. They would give us shopping bags full of candy. In my hood, you would barely receive a rotten apple and cursed and shot for walking up on a stranger's porch begging for candy dressed up in an old torn white sheet or over coats two sizes too big. But to us, it was simply the thrill. In a collective group, once we reached a certain point, we were guided back to the point of where we came. The police was always nearby patrolling the area.

During the summer, the Gardens had summer block parties and Barbeques. It was no use trying to sneak in to get a bite to eat because everybody there knew everybody. All we could do was sit a block away and savor the smell from the ribs they were cooking.

The Garden's close bonds were far greater than ours. In our hood, some sections and families looked out and took care of one another. But the Gardens, there unity was legendary and universal.

From a casual view, most of the teenagers from the Gardens never cursed, drank, smoke, fight or argue. Their behavior pattern was cut from a different cloth. We engaged in all of the above and more.

The small grocery stores in the Gardens sold fresh meat and vegetables. You never saw roaches in their stores. Nor did you ever smell or see dead rats, wild dogs or cats roaming feely. In our hood, they were everywhere. Most of the teenagers and adults associated with their own. From time to time, a few old men that lived in the Gardens would hang up at the Linwood pool hall talking shit.

The quality of life that separated us was in small part due to the police invisible demarcation line that had been drawn by blood. At any time, the police in our hood could have shut down all the drug houses, closed the illegal whore houses, stop the sale of liquor to minors and overall exploitation of our youth. It may have only made a small dent, but it would have been a valuable start.

The social disorders that affects us, was something comical to them. Our community's leaders in the area hands were tied. A few chosen ones lodged pickets and protests about our conditions as compared to how the police treated them. Still, nothing actually changed.

Unlike my hood, the Gardens were working class people. Even the teenagers like myself attending Northwestern High School, 99% of them drove cars to high school. We walked in worn down shoes because our mothers or fathers were unable to provide us with quality products due to unemployment.

The Gardens teenagers never wore the same clothes twice in one week. Their quality of life offered them a much better edge at survival. All the boys from the Gardens controlled Northwestern High School R.O.T.C. program. Our teachers even bowed down to their influence and wealth. If you complained, as a friend of mine did, we were transferred.

A lot of teenagers in my hood skipped school because they had no clean clothes to wear that day. Others dropped out to work odd jobs to help their mothers feed their family. A lot of teenage girls dropped out due to pregnancy.

I can only recall two boys out of the Gardens that I attended high school with that actually dropped out of high school. Both of them got turned out on heroin. A junkie and his prostitute named Mary tricked him into sex and drugs. Once they were strung out they drained them dry. I do recall dozens of my former elementary and junior high classmates dropping out of school like flies.

From time to time, we were just being mischief and trying to outwit the police. We used part of the Gardens as a short cut to reach 12th street. These turbulent and dangerous encounters was fraught with feeling and excitement, for we knew if we were caught we would be beaten by the police, arrested and charged with every unsolved crime over the past week.

Fueled by jealousy and rage for not having the luxury of what they had to offer, we ventured uninvited into the Gardens at night to raid their fruit trees. Once we were seen, the neighbors turned on their lights. One by one, houses began to light up. We knew that within seconds, the police would arrive. We always saw them before they saw us. The chase was on. Only once was a friend of mine caught. They knocked out all of his teeth and broke his jaw before they allowed him to tell about his associates.

Funny, I can only recall during the early 70's only one black police officer. Remarkably, 50% of the people living in the Gardens were black.

The bags of pears, apples, and plums we would raid. We would give them to a neighbor named Mrs. Meadows who would in turn would make everybody on our street a jar of jam; our weekly contribution to our hood.

#####

In conflict theory criminological theory is seen as needing to be shifted toward the explanation of criminal law and to explain the process by which certain behavior and individuals are formally designated as criminal. For instance, some interest groups were able to pass legislation to make the production and distribution of alcohol illegal (U.S. Prohibition 1920–1933). There has been growing disagreement over the "war on drugs." In the fall of 2010, California passed a law legalizing marijuana; in 2012, Colorado and Washington State did the same. However, the federal laws still prohibit marijuana. Unlike Emile Durkheim who saw society held together by common norms, conflict theory sees society's structure as mostly an outcome of power arrangements. Akers and Sellers note:

Chambliss (1975: i–ii) agreed: Instead of asking, "Why do some people commit crimes and others do not" we ask, "Why are some acts defined as criminal while

others are not?" Conflict theory answers that question: both the formulation
and enforcement of the law directly and indirectly are more likely to serve the
interests of the more powerful groups in society.

. . . [I]t is central to conflict theory (that) . . . [d]iversity and lack of uniformity,
not commonality of values, are the hallmarks of modern society. Conflict theory
portrays society in a more or less continuing state of conflict among groups
(Ritzer 1992: 262–71). Social structure is comprised of the working arrangement, coalitions, and balancing forces "in a shifting but dynamic equilibrium
of opposing group interests and efforts." (Vold 1958: 204, in Akers and Sellers
2009: 195–96)

For instance, in the contemporary United States there are different interest
groups with opposing views on such policies as drug treatment versus mass
incarceration for drug-defined and drug-related crimes. How does conflict
theory apply to the situation of so many people in prison in the United States?
Critical criminologists such as neo-Marxist and anarchist theorists have a
"view with an edge."

Neo-Marxist Criminological Theory

It's one thing to see conflicts between people and groups with competing
interests revolving around money, power, and influence. But what establishes
the *bases of power*? Writing in the mid- to late-nineteenth century, Karl Marx
saw the industrialization of society brought by capitalism as profoundly
affecting society.

Marx believed that a society's mode of economic production—the manner
in which relations of production are organized—determines in large part the
organization of social relations, the structure of individual and group interaction. Marx put it this way:

In the social production in which men carry on they enter into definite relations
that are indispensable and independent of their will; these relations of production correspond to a definite stage of development of their material powers of
production. The totality of these relations of production constitutes the economic structure of a society—the real foundation, on which legal and political
superstructures arise and to which definite forms of social consciousness correspond. The mode of production of material life determines the general character
of the social, political, and spiritual process of life. It is not the consciousness
of men that determines their being, but, on the contrary, their social being determines their consciousness. (1859/1970: 20–21)

Under a capitalist mode of production, there are those who own the means
of production and those who do not. This relationship affects law, and by
extension, crime. Laws are created by the elite to protect their interests at the

expense of the workers. However, the image of the law that is promoted to the masses is one that implies democracy and consensus. For example, nearly everyone would agree that killing another without legitimate reason should be criminal. However, what are those legitimate reasons? War? Corporate violations of safety laws that result in worker deaths? Marxists might point out that even presumably simple and well-supported laws may not work in the interests of the have-nots, though they may be perceived to be a representation of the collective will of a society. In this spirit, Marxist scholars have noted:

> The fact is that the label "crime" is not used in America to name all or the worst of the actions that cause misery and suffering to Americans. It is primarily reserved for the dangerous action of the poor. (Reiman 2004: 25)

It is not the social harms punishable by law that cause the greatest misery in the world. It is the lawful harms, those unpunishable crimes justified and protected by law, the state, the ruling elites that fill the earth with misery, want, strife, conflict, slaughter, and destruction (Tifft and Sullivan 1980: 9; Barlow and Kauzlarich 2010: 105).

#####

Prisoner Essay 8.9

"Class and Race" (3/22/09)
This essay will be an attempt to compare and contrast two sociological theories. My topics will be socioeconomic factors associated with crime and juxtaposed to that will be criminology theory, in particular, conflict theory.

It is my belief that the capitalist economic system should be abolished. The problems inherent in this type of system are intensified and proliferate because we are a racially unequal society. In the U.S. you cannot mention race without mentioning class. Racial inequality is just disguised class conflict. Those people who are poor, and often poor for social reasons, lack of work, peer influences, lack of educational opportunity and poor social environment. Capitalism favors the rich while maintains the poor often minorities in abject poverty. When a social movement or up-heave does occur, it is often seen and reported by the media as a racial issue when in reality it often has to do with social economic and class factors. Subjection of the lower class by the capitalist in the U.S. is done to a great degree by the continuation of bogus fraudulent drug policy. Without illegal drugs as a means of bare substance, many inner city or low income areas would have already exploded in revolt. The reason would be class conflict however, the interpretation would be racial. Socioeconomic factors in U.S. society cannot be discussed alone without mentioning the enormous divide and tension between classes. In the U.S. capitalism creates unfair distribution of wealth and opportunity; which alone breeds contempt and the potential for class conflict. However, these already existing conditions are assaulted by the unique racial atmosphere. All too often issues are seen as racial yet, underneath they are class conflicts. Socioeconomic conditions and environments are also often seen as racial but they are brought about by policies designed to sustain poverty, crime and the agenda of the elite—a prime example of this being the drug war.

Socioeconomic factors describing crime and theories of class conflict can be thought of as differing because it can be argued that one doesn't necessarily lead to the other. For example, there are societies in which the disadvantaged, though poor, don't produce much crime. Moreover, certain societies have strictly enforced caste or class systems that don't lead to much class conflict. Essentially, the poor can be poor and content. Once again, I need to stress that the U.S. is unique. The rich here are incredibly arrogant and the poor are teased, pacified by dreams of equality they may never possess. Issues are blamed on race and crime is an association minorities can't shake. The Marxist idea of revolution within capitalist societies would have already happened here if not for the pacification of the socioeconomically disadvantaged by absurd drug policies and the use of race to mask legitimate social issues. In conclusion, socioeconomic factors of crime cannot be spoken of without the mention of class though class divisions and socioeconomic divisions can exist with relatively little crime most often it breeds tensions and more crime. The U.S. is unique because race is all too often used as a scapegoat to explain class and socioeconomic theories about crime.

#####

Left Realism

British criminologists Jock Young and Roger Matthews began a critique of radical Marxist criminology in the 1980s and 1990s.

Young and Matthews proposed that the "left idealism" of the radical perspective be replaced by "left realism." According to Young (1986, 1997), left idealism has tended to downplay the severity of crime and the fact that it is most often intraclass and intraracial. As Matthews (2004: 9) explains:

> While not ignoring crimes of the powerful, new left realists have taken the position that the effects of street crime are both serious and real, that the criminal class is not revolutionary, and that critical (i.e., Marxian, conflict, feminist, and radical) criminologists must pay attention to it. What ties new left realism to Marxian criminology, however, is its emphasis on understanding crime within the larger political economy.

. . . To say that poverty in the present period breeds crime is not to say that all poor people are criminals. Far from it: most poor people are perfectly honest and many wealthy people commit crimes. Rather, it is to say that the rate of crime is higher in certain parts of society under certain conditions. (Young 1997: 30–31; Barlow and Kauzlarich 2010: 114–15)

Feminist Criminology

The author taught prison college classes in 1998–1999 at the Scott facility, a Michigan women's prison. The women prisoners themselves define feminism as "The fight for equality and civil rights," and emphasized that this sense of movement has been "a continual struggle in the lives of black women for hundreds of years in this country." In fact, historically, the African American woman "wasn't allowed to attend school or to be educated in any means except for those who needed it in her work therefore she was kept ignorant of the possibilities and opportunities offered by education such as the pleasures of reading and even writing her own name!"

Women prisoner students made points such as the fact that women are just as equal in the workforce to perform the same jobs as men, however, instead of "earning the equality we deserve for our efforts we are labeled as 'feminist lesbians' radicals by our prejudiced male counterparts."

Women prisoners were sensitive to the social (or gender) roles and said things such as "Many people have considered women inferior to men and less important, basically that a woman's place is in the home. Women were house cleaners and child bearers—when women were, in fact, the backbone of the family."

Politically, in the past centuries, women were less powerful. The women prisoners noted such things as "Women weren't allowed to vote or serve on a jury. Most institutions of higher learning and most professional careers were closed to woman. So a woman in the 1800s was nearly existing like now, but a lot worse, the world was considered a man's world."

The women prisoners identified strongly with the women's movement, noting that despite strong opposition "feminism grew in power during the (late) 1800s and 1900s and won a number of new rights for women." They felt that "the feminist movement and the resulting changes in the status of women were turning points in the history of society." And the shared sentiment was that "We fight until we win; we protect what is ours and what we believe in. Females do not give up as easily as the males."

EXERCISE 8.1

Present excerpts from two or more prisoner essays that represent two or more theories from this chapter.

DISCUSSION AND REVIEW QUESTIONS

1. What is meant by "The American Dream?" Describe Robert Merton's structural strain theory of crime. How does structural strain relate to "The American Dream" and trends in job creation and income?

2. Compare Merton's "Social Structure and Anomie Theory" of crime with a quote from a prisoner essay.

3. What types of individual "stress" does Robert Agnew see as related to crime?

4. Summarize Edwin Sutherland's "Differential Association" theory of crime.

5. Example Sutherland's social learning theory of crime with a quote from a prisoner essay.

6. Compare and contrast Durkheim's normative consensus view of crime and Turks, Simmel, or Vold's conflict view of crime.

7. Explain the neo-Marxist view of crime.

8. What is meant by "Left Realism?"

In-Prison Criminological Issues

Survival, Transformation, and Reentry

This chapter focuses on in-prison criminological issues, prisoner movements, and reentry and recidivism. Once people go to prison there are separate sets of criminological issues: survival, maturing, and transformational efforts peculiar to the prison setting and reentry to society.

One problem is lack of prison-based accredited skills training and educational opportunity beyond the GED, which reduces hope of ever getting a good job upon release. There are power and control dynamics among the prisoners. Coercive sex can be a problem. A Michigan prison for seventeen- to twenty-five-year-olds had so many power struggles and abuses it was called "Gladiator Prison."

An impediment to personal transformation for the entering and even the long-term prisoner is that the prisoner dynamics on "the yard" dominate: the yard is "the streets" in the prison setting—with cliques and gangs "in the mix"—and there is an expectation that conversation on the yard will be about "how to do crime better next time" (Owen 1998).

While the author gives MPRI workshops on "How to Go to Community College Upon Release" (and get Pell grants) (see chapter 4), if prisoners spend their time in prison without postsecondary educational opportunity, they are less likely to succeed upon release (CEA 2003; Tregea 1998, 2003).

Before we go further into the prison context it's good to remind ourselves that people may be in prison because of too many laws, or the wrong laws.

Prisoner Essay 9.1

"Too Much Criminalization" (2/1/09)
Though early prevention is a good goal, it should definitely not be done by adding more government and rules and regulations on the youth.

One example of how this could be counter-productive is, if you have more rules, it's easier to offend. Already our youth is bombarded with rules and regulations that far exceed the youth of the past. And in fact if you look historically, when there were more freedoms for the youth (which in turn would promote responsibility) we had less crime and less prison populations.

It is my observations that there are not more criminals but there is more criminalization because there are far more laws and forfeiture of common civil rights. History supports my opinion. Educations into common sense skills are important.

#####

Once there are "rules and regulations" (laws) and lawbreakers go to prison, there are now wardens who manage the prisons. The evaluation of prison wardens' job performance is based on institutional control: no riots, no disorders, or escapes. The evaluation of prison wardens is not about *maximizing* prisoner opportunities to do well upon release. For instance, wardens could be evaluated on success-in-reentry rates (lower recidivism). Regarding prisoner education and skills training, one midwestern state director of correctional education stated: "It is like turning a battleship around—it is hard to change prison wardens to focus on prisoner education." She said that even with a strong state emphasis on prisoner reentry "Prisoners are still treated on the principle of least advantage." That is, prisoners did crime and don't deserve any 'advantages.' This is hindering the development of good job training certificate programs," she said. Yet, 95 percent of prisoners are eventually released. There is a need for prison control ideology (punishment for bad behavior) to be balanced by remunerative approaches (rewards for good behavior) (Reisig 1998).

Prisons themselves can become "criminogenic environments." Prisoners are vulnerable to prison conditions that foster assaults, rape, extortion, and threats.

#####

Prisoner Essay 9.2

"Homosexuality at MR" (3/25/09)
Homosexuality in Michigan prisoners is and will be forever imbedded within its infrastructure, as is hotdogs at a baseball game. However, unlike the purchase of a hotdog while enjoying a baseball game, the introduction or breeding process for homosexuality has many ways. Years ago, as far back as the

mid seventies when I first arrived at Michigan's notorious reformatory (MR) it was a selected breeding process for sexual predators.

These predators ran in wolf packs, shared information about their sexual conquest among themselves in an effort to establish power structures to govern their actions.

Most of these small groups of men would target prisoners convicted of rape or child molestation, or child abuse. At the time (1977), these prisoners were the most vile and hated class among us. They had no one but themselves to depend on.

Each day, large caravans of prisoners arrived at the reformatory. Before each prisoner was processed, these predators, the most powerful ones would pay several packs of cigarettes to a trustee prisoner that worked in the prison control center. Having access to these prisoners file for processing, he would alert a member of their group as to a prisoner serving time for rape or molestation. Armed with this information, they would set their sights on him and began their games.

Their first port of call would be to use an undercover homosexual to lure the unsuspecting host into sexual stimuli by offering to issue the prisoner oral sex. Once the host engaged, the next port of call was to lure him into an isolated area while him and the undercover fag is engaged, and burst through the door demanding that since he has turned out their friend he has to now satisfy them. Armed with homemade knives, and nowhere to run and scream, they would rape him and leaving him crying in the arms of the undercover homosexual who would comfort him with drugs and treats, and promises not to tell anyone. If he agrees, which rate above 85 percent, they would have him.

And it is safe to say that, most of these young men had or experience one time in their life prior to prison, some homosexuality. Sometimes in the form of sexual abuse from family member, which in my personal estimate came from more than 70 percent of them.

The other percentage came from young boys experiencing sexual gratification among themselves.

As years passed and these techniques were disbanded by these predators, they advance like another group into a more elaborate and sophisticated operations. And like always, they would employ an already seasoned homosexual to pave the way for them in seeking out willing and unwilling participants.

The wealthier prisoners would use drugs to turn another prisoner into becoming their sexual slaves. These homosexual prisoners would be fed crack cocaine, heroin and other drugs until they are hooked and cannot afford to pay.

They would force the prisoners to perform sexual acts with other homosexual prisoners to loosen them up. Some of these prisoner, often times men that sold drugs on the streets and perfects these acts upon women would continue on with they special trades while in prison.

I have witnessed first-hand the immoral, heinous and shocking side effects of these men actions. I have come across some of them today, as they explain that 30 to 35 years ago, they were young, foolish and made some very bad choices.

And yes, I have seen some men so ashamed of what they had done, they killed themselves by taking large amounts of prescription drugs, or hanging themselves.

In the overall scheme, over 50 percent of the men that freely fell victims to these predators knew in advance the ramifications of their actions.

One young man whom entered prison with me while we were being processed asked another prisoner that was about 6 foot 4 to look out for him and he would have his girlfriend send him money. This prisoner accepts his offer. However, being a new arrival like us, he thought that his size would protect him.

A week later, he was stabbed six times, and his little friend was under the protection of another prisoner's crew. It happened that fast.

In the present day, with large influx of mentally unstable so-called prisoners under the influence of dozens of psycho-topical drugs have been the target of choice. Another factor that has eliminated these cliques of predators is the large numbers of rapist and child molesters that have taken over the system and many of them have now banded together and formed their own social groups and have now attempted to reverse the game in which the hunter now becomes the hunted.

These vile characters utilize date rape as you call it today. They offer a prisoner two bottle of home-made wine and sprinkle it down with several forms of psycho-topical medication. Once the prisoner is knocked out; they all rape him one by one.

In my personal estimate, over 50 percent of the prisoners that fell victim to sexual abuse in prison find it difficult to find a meaningful transformation back to a normal life after these encounters.

In Michigan prison systems there are very little, if any, that offer counseling treatment for these men.

The long term effect leads many of them to drugs, alcohol and other self inflicted wounds they create in their attempt to heal.

This ever-expanding sexual disorder is growing larger and larger each and every day. Failure to acknowledge this social, dysfunctional sexual revolution is sure to become one rude awakening in the future of Michigan criminal system.

#####

Prisoner Essay 9.3

"Increased Criminality by Being Housed with so Many Criminals" (3/22/09)
After reading various information on criminal behavior, social values, family values etc., I have found that my beliefs are that no one is protected from these traits. Whether one is born with these traits or not, I also believe that one who is incarcerated for a lengthy period of time may possibly begin to pick these instincts up.

I have observed while incarcerated that some individuals begin to show signs of increased criminal activity by being housed with so many other criminals themselves. In some, I see a very negative attitude such as "Yeah, fuck you all, I have been down 10 years" and many of these are still young men. Possibly it could be that these men have not took advantage of some of the opportunities available in prison, school, work, special activities etc. Their attitude is "I will just do my own time and hope for my parole."

I think the longer one is locked up the less chance he or she has to be rehabilitated. It seems to me that it becomes a way of life to some behind bars stealing, hustling, lying and other criminal behaviors.

Also homosexuality is more common in some prisons then others. This I can't figure out an explanation for.

Also what happens when one is released from prison after being housed with some hardcore criminals? What has he or she learned in that environment?

Will there be a job or opportunity for one with a felony record? Or will they go back to a quick and illegal way of survival as what they already know or what they have learned in prison. I think that psychological education is fine but is it really working? The one who teaches this is not the one behind bars.

I myself can only hope, as I am incarcerated, that I have not learned more of criminal behavior in here after being exposed to it 24/7 over a 1 year period of time, I can only try and overcome this obstacle I have encountered and work hard to start over at age 49.

#####

MANY PRISONERS ARE PARENTS

How to stay in touch with family is worrisome to some prisoners. Research shows that staying in touch with family lowers recidivism upon reentry. The mass incarceration era has removed prisoners from family for longer sentences.

#####

Prisoner Essay 9.4

"The Sons of Men in Mass Incarceration" (3/17/10)
It may seem that the most reasonable solution to crime is to simply remove the offender from society, but from my experience, it's surely not most effective way to prevent more.

I didn't grow up in an area known for crime. In fact, I was in the 6th grade before I knew someone who was sentenced to prison. It was a huge scandal. I remember seeing parents talking to each other about it in hushed tones, and many of them wouldn't allow their children to play with that man's kids, as if criminality were a communicable disease. It didn't bother me, however, because it didn't affect my life in any way. I still had my father. The only thing that intrigued me about the whole situation was that it was another house in which had no parental supervision during the day and a lack of repercussions from an overworked single-mom. But it wasn't until years later, after I got myself thrown in prison, that I realized who the victims of incarceration truly are.

I was sentenced to prison at twenty-one, leaving behind a four-year old son and a wife who just entered army basic training. She couldn't care for him then, and as circumstances unfolded, it would be several years before he was able to live with her. My parents took him without question, but they had thirteen other children to deal with. My son didn't receive the attention a hyperactive child struggling with the loss of both parents requires. He would grow up in an overcrowded house with a mother serving her country half the world away and a father serving a sentence that would last into his adulthood.

No matter the minutes spent on the phone or the hours in the visiting room, there was no way I could be there for all the things that a father should for his son. No playing catch in the back yard, no shouting encouragement from the soccer field sidelines, no fishing at that lake up north, no kitchen-table talks about slipping grades, no teaching him how to drive, or to shave; no setting an example of how a man is supposed to care for his family or how to handle life's mounting responsibilities. By the very act of conceiving him, being his father was my responsibility, my place in this world, but since I was not there, someone else would have to step in—or no one at all.

My son entered his teen years while living on an Army base, where most fathers took active roles in their children's lives. So, in an attempt to fit in, he told potential friends that his own father was still in the Navy. It is impossible to know how he escalated from telling such stories to attempting to cash checks he'd stolen from his mother's purse at the PX. Getting caught didn't dissuade him from continuing to act out. Not long after, he took off in his mother's car and got it stuck in the mud, only to ruin the engine trying to get out. Thinking a change in environment might help with his attitude, his mother moved off base; a month later he stole a golf cart from a nearby course and drove it to school. It resulted in felony charge, two years probation, and ultimately, after getting caught with a tiny amount of marijuana on his school bus, a three-month stint in a Florida correctional camp for boys.

To say that my son would never have gotten in trouble if I was there to guide him is hubristic at best, but I have no doubt he would have stood a better chance. He wouldn't be so far behind maturity-wise, he most likely would have graduated from high school, and he probably would have more ambition in life then to sit around playing guitar hero while getting high.

I'm thankful he's not in prison, especially considering that he was heading down that dark and treacherous road like so many of those with whom I'm forced to share my every waking moment. There are fathers, uncles, brothers, cousins, and neighbors who have done, or are currently doing, time. I can only imagine what it's like to grow up in a community with so little positive male influence. Without real men to show a boy how real men are supposed to behave. The more who are locked up, the less there are to instill values and realistic, attainable goals. Not to live for the moment, because there is no hope for the future.

Removing the offender from society may be a reasonable solution, but sentencing guidelines only account for the victims of the crime committed, never the victims such a removal creates.

#####

BEING CRITICIZED FOR IMPROVING YOURSELF

There is a price for some of the younger prisoners to come to the prison school building for a volunteer activity rather than staying in the yard. He may be criticized for assuming he can be better than those in the yard.

#####

Prisoner Essay 9.5

"Tension between Yard and School" (10/7/09)
For the past two years I would say; I've been mainly focusing on building self. Majority of my time is spent reflecting on what can I do to improve my community and how can I maintain a decent life style. When approached by the peers I tend to get criticized because of the fact that I'm not being what they want me to be. In their eyes I'm turning into a square.

At times I feel like I'm doing something wrong but then I realize that I'm not. I yearn for knowledge and in order to obtain knowledge I go to the older brothers to give me knowledge. I feel since they've been on this planet longer than me what they tell me is empirical, but my peers seems to think differently. They think they know everything.

Maybe not in this environment, where I'm at, but at another prison I might have a lot more problems with my peers. Jealousy seem to play a big role in here and when a person feel that you are better than them in which you're not, violence might come into the picture.

#####

Prisoner Essay 9.6

Resist the Yard—Become a Leader" (10/14/09)
"In contrast, the defendant is a high school dropout, unemployed with no marketable job skills or verifiable employment history. The defendant mother states that her son is a follower."

After reading these words from my Presentence Investigation Report (PSI), which led me to realize what my mother thought about me, I became agitated because I knew that I was more than a simple follower. I had to show my mother different, I had to show her that I am able to become a leader.

Since reading that PSI report and reflecting, I have spent the majority of my free time in this prison school building going to the library and participating in special education classes. I had to take myself away from what is to be expected by a young black male in the penal system. I had to replace ignorance with knowledge. Outside of the school building there's so much to get into by the minutes if you're not doing the right things. If you were to walk on this prison yard now you would see men in blue and orange coats sitting down at bench or walking the yard. From my experience the conversations that are taken place is either about money, drugs, women, or a guy. Oh and I forgot rappers and sport players.

It's hard for me to engage in any type of dialogue with some of my peers because mentally we are in two different places. If I was to ask somebody to put a kite in, (a request slip), to go the library with me, I would be looked at as if I was a clown. I would also become criticized because I'm not really interested in participating in their daily functions such as: playing cards, dominoes and basketball.

A few months ago I ran into a high school friend who I used to get into a lot of trouble with. When he seen that I wasn't into the negative he began to look at me funny as asked, "Why I am I trying to be something I'm not." That question he asked struck me hard because I seen how he looked at me. I no longer seen myself through his eyes or anybody else's eyes and that caused him to think that I thought I was better than him.

These types of situations happen all over the system and at times ends in violence. When a man steps away from the crowd that is following a false perception of the American Dream he will have problems, but in order to avoid those problems he must stay focused on becoming a leader. That's how you prove people wrong!

#####

Prisoner Essay 9.7

"Prison Is a Place Where . . ." (10/28/09)

Prison Is a place . . .
. . . Where morals and values become displaced,
When love come and teaches you hate.
Were hope and faith are your only true friend's
Where cons are created, fakeness is emulated.
Black heart's behind innocent faces.
Where vengeance learns patience,
A recipe for disaster.
Predators prey on guys that are passive.
Weak minded people don't survive.
Loyalty is extremely hard to find.
Trust is a razor wired fence with out-of-bounds signs.
You guaranteed to get hurt if you ever try to climb.
Some guys get smart and expand their mind.
Others get drunk off of prison made wine.
And time is how you tell them apart
A place where tough guy's cry in the dark.
Fishes get thrown in a pool full of sharks.
People start conflicts just to kill time.
Satan's workshop is an idol mind.
Prison is a place . . .
. . . . Where I close my eyes and envision her face,
I pray and ask god to keep her safe.
And she forgot I exist.
Where joy is seldom and pain is constant.
Acts of kindness have cruel intentions.
Spirits are crushed directly after being lifted.
Where love letters are stamped return to sender.
Nothing is forgotten, small things remembered.

#####

Prisoner Essay 9.8

"Prison Is Hell for Long-Term Prisoners" (10/28/09)
November 20, 1996. At just seventeen years old I walked into a prison better known as Michigan Reformatory, or as we called it M.R., the oldest running prison in Michigan, and one of the oldest in the world.

It was late fall, but this world was cold, not in temperature, but in reality. I quickly learned the on-goings of my environment. Every act was deliberate, and thought out. M.R. was also known as gladiator school, a place where warrior's were made and destroyed. There was no acting hard; you had to really be that, because you were going to be tested. And if you allowed anyone to get away with any form of disrespect, the prison would know about it, and your days of walking around safe would be numbered.

The average age of prisoner's was approximately 24/25 years old. At least half of the 1,200 prisoners was either surviving a life sentence or some outrageous term of years. Another portion of the prison population had come from lower level prisons and was deemed unmanageable. So they were sent to M.R. for punishment, not for the staff, but from other prisoners. At that time prisoner ran the prisons. All the guards could do is write a ticket, and or put you in segregation. The prison could kill you.

The prison yard was ran by the religious organizations, at least 75 percent of all the black prisoner's was a member of one of these groups. The white guys were split. Those with heart became members of the white supremacist group, the others were either in Protective Housing Unit (Administrative Segregation) or paying for protection on the yard.

Prison is a very racist environment, it's not as bad as it used to be, but it's still racist. I came in here without any hatred towards anybody, but as time went on, I became just as racist as everybody else. I was young and impressionable, and I wanted to belong to something. My mother had just passed away. So I was looking for some kind of support. I was searching for love and acceptance in a cold world.

I once wrote a poem about prison, titled "prison is a place." In this poem I state; "where love comes and teaches you hate." That line identifies my prison experience to a tee. My search for love enabled me to hate. This is a vital tool in dehumanizing a person. What that does is; you start to lose compassion for people. First I started to hate white people, and then I started hating black people for looking or acting like white people, or associating with white people. Before I knew I was hating everybody. But that's what prison was like back then. That was the negative thing about those organizations.

The positive thing about it was that it creates a chain of command. You couldn't just do what you wanted to do, you had to get permission, of course not everyone followed the rules, but if you didn't there were consequences. This chain of command kept things running smoothly, order is the first law of the universe. Without order, the world would be totally chaotic. Those organizations created order among the prisoners, enabling the prisoner to stay in control of what went on in the yard.

But as time went on, the prison administrators started destroying those organizations. Identifying them as threat groups and placing markers in the file's of all its members. The parole board has access to that information, if you are labeled an affiliate to a security threat group, you will not get a parole. The prison officials started holding every member accountable for something one person had done. The fear of being sent to level 5 caused some members to become informants. And slowly those organizations started to fall.

When I came to prison, I was approached by every organization, trying to get me to join, back then they had recruiters. Older guys didn't allow the young guys to just roam free on the yard; it was too many predators out there, so they offer them something better. Book's were passed and discussed frequently. Even if the books were just street novels, people were reading and learning. The young guys listened to their elders, prison was a serious place back then, and so you needed someone to guide you, and point out traps. This was their world, and it was wise to show them respect.

Now-a-days, the young guys are at odds with the elders and the lack of respect is the number one cause of threat division. Prison officials play this to their advantage. Division destroys unity. Now they are in control of what goes on. And that creates uneasiness with the population. Prison is all about punishment. We are constantly reminded of our confinement. If it's not because of the officers, it's the prisoners. At least once a week, a group of guys go home, and all too often you see at least one of them return. Whereas, before, you didn't see people coming in and out of prison. That causes problems with the prisoners because you have guys that are never going home, and they feel like the guys that are coming back don't value their freedom and in some way is responsible for them not being able to get out.

Some of the changes are necessary, and are responsible for prison being a much safer place, which is a negative in here, because some prisoners benefit off prison not being safe. With the guards having this fake sense of control, (I say that because they really don't have control, they just have informants that will tell them everything). Because of that, prison is a playground for short time prisoners, and hell for lifer's and long term prisoners.

#####

ENDING THE CULTURE OF STREET CRIME

A movement launched in 2003 by prisoners is spreading throughout the state prisons in the United States. The LIFERS, Inc., group steering committee at the State Correctional Institution at Graterford, Pennsylvania began this movement enhanced by the National Lifers Association (NLA)—both groups making efforts to educate prisoners. The movement was captured in the 2004 essay "Ending the Culture of Street Crime," which explores

> the problem of crime and violence, offering a new way to look at what motivates certain individuals who habitually engage in criminal activity. Explaining the concept of the existence of a pervasive culture of crime is the primary focus of this article. It also seeks to provide a multidirectional strategy for ending that culture, which includes the utilization of former members of the culture as part of the solution. (LIFERS, Inc. 2004: 48)

Segments in this chapter focus on how the personal transformation involved in ending the culture of street crime relates to the frequent prisoner view of their criminality that: "It was just the way it was, growing up" (social disorganization theory).

> The LIFERS, Inc. Public Safety Initiative was launched as a movement designed to help the public recognize the culture of crime and engage citizens to work toward eliminating it. When it is understood that those responsible for the bulk of street crimes are part of a unique group with its own values, beliefs, and behaviors, a more effective strategy can be initiated to eliminate it. (LIFERS 2004: 49)

This LIFERS group, having taken college classes and finished college degrees while in prison formed their own Graterford Prison "Think Tank," and after having sponsored an in-prison conference galvanizing long-sentence prisoners and community groups, have written a report, "Ending the Culture of Street Crime," that was published in *Prison Journal* 84, No. 4 (December 2004). They advocate a social process—a "multidirectional approach" going beyond traditional criminal justice agencies and including long-term convicts, ex-cons, academics, criminal justice leaders, and community groups to work toward *ending* the culture of street crime. As *transformed* prisoners, the long-sentence prison-based convict leaders of this movement have done a lot of "self-work"—reflections on and changes in their values and self-concept, away from crime and toward maturity: they want to help younger prisoners who are going to return to society.

LIFERS, Inc., stands for Long Incarcerated Fraternity Engaging Release Studies, which began in 1980 to focus on pursuing the possibility of parole for life-sentenced prisoners in Pennsylvania, through public education and legislative efforts. They held an April 2003 Anti-Crime Summit at Graterford Prison "Where more than 150 individuals representing the public attended, along with more than 100 prisoners."

At that time there were changes in the broader national outlook on prisoner reentry. President George W. Bush authorized $50 million in January 2001 to be spread between the fifty states to start prisoner reentry initiatives. The author organized a half-day session in June 2001 on prisoner education at the week-long National Institute of Justice (NIJ) sponsored "Prisoner Reentry and Community Justice" workshop held at the University of Michigan and Institute of Social Research in Ann Arbor. Academics, scholars, and members of think tanks were meeting to trace out the major issues in prisoner reentry (see description chapter 4). The State of Michigan started a 175-person Michigan prisoner reentry initiative (MPRI) steering committee to hammer out a better reentry approach in the state.

By 2003 early-adopting counties in Michigan had their own county MPRI steering committees. Prisoners in Michigan would now have a local county steering committee to line up services (housing, clothing, transportation, skills training, and education, etc.) for returning prisoners and an "in-reach group" to work with the reentering prisoners during their last month in the prison.

The "multidirectional approach" to ending the culture of street crime recommended by the LIFERS, Inc., essay worked in concert with the NLA, connecting with other state prisoner chapters within a state and spreading from state to state. In Michigan the NLA helped to organize workshops in the fall of 2010 at the Ryan Correctional Facility and spring of 2011 at the Lakeland Correctional Facility on prisoner issues, described in chapter 4.

The "Ending the Culture of Street Crime" essay emphasizes:

It is apparent that massive incarceration has failed to make crime-ravaged areas meaningfully safer. The imprisonment of hundreds of thousands of nonviolent offenders has served to exacerbate the problems faced by communities by effectively turning them into incubators for more poverty, crime, and violence.

. . . habitual criminals become desensitized to the adverse effects their actions have on the lives of their victims and society, not to mention their own families and loved ones. Likewise, the public and policy makers become desensitized to the adverse effects of the overuse of imprisonment on ex-offenders and the neighborhoods to which they return. Massive incarceration suggests a state of paralysis in the field of criminal justice. (LIFERS, Inc. 2004: 56)

As part of the broader movement in the states, and, in part, motivated by costly corrections budgets in the context of Michigan's long-term, continuing budget crises, in the fall of 2004 all of the Michigan Department of Corrections (MDOC) administrative personnel (wardens, assistant deputy wardens, housing unit managers), along with the parole board and MDOC headquarters administrators met at Michigan State University (Kellogg Center) in one big room—450 of the decision-makers and lead staff of the MDOC—to hear their new "marching orders." Henceforth the goal of the MDOC was to make sure as few prisoners as possible came back after release from prison. The culture of the MDOC was changing.

Nine years later, as of 2013, the Michigan prison population has been reduced from 52,000 to 43,000 and all Michigan counties are now part of an MPRI program. But the MDOC culture change was in part a values shift and in part a pragmatic effort to lower the corrections budget and save the state money. The shift has capped the MDOC budget. Unfortunately, the Michigan Corrections Budget has remained high due to employee costs such as health insurance and pensions, older prisoners' health costs, the need to revisit sentencing length (shorter sentences), instituting parole guidelines, and denying parolable lifers parole after many years of incarceration (CAPPS 2013). The kinds of changes the LIFERS wrote of in 2004 have begun in several states but are still unfolding. They wrote:

> Many of the destructive values and codes of the current street crime culture developed as a direct result of the gang system of the 1960s. . . .
>
> The present-day street crime culture consists of a group or groups of individuals who live outside societal norms. They have their own values, codes, practices, and principles that are oftentimes in direct opposition to the larger society, although many of the negative characteristics displayed by this culture, such as self-focus and greed, are also common to the mainstream culture. As was true with the gang system of the past, those who are a part of this street crime culture are loyal to the other members of the group and to their system of values, beliefs, and practices that are maintained in the streets, reinforced in prisons, and fueled by the antisocial lifestyle of each new generation lured into it either by circumstance or recruitment. (LIFERS 2004: 57)

#####

Prisoner Essay 9.9

"If Sports Stars Won't Step Up, Maybe Ex-Cons Should" (3/22/09)
I do believe that if we really want to put a dent in crime in our communities we must go back to programs like neighborhood watch and things like that. Let's face it, back in the days if you did something wrong before you got home your mother already knew about it. And if you lived in the country you would get your butt spanked by a Mrs. Smith or a Mrs. Ruth or something like

that. Yes, I know this was not true for a lot of neighborhoods in the city but still you could not just do a crime and totally get away with it.

I think once we learn how to bring back being proud of our neighborhood and the way it looks along with neighborhood centers and activities, we will be on the right track. I have ideas on how we can do these things, and I also have hope.

You see we talk about not forgetting where we came from. Well if the big time football, basketball, baseball and entertainers will not step up to the plate, well maybe the ex-cons should. I feel we have just as much if not more to give back to our community. Yes, I know money helps. At the same time to give hope is priceless. Not to mention to give a person an avenue to dream.

I think as a father of five, I will start with my own most beautiful children. All by the same lady I must point out. Then from my children I will continue by being a coach and installing new values in my team. For our values have become all twisted, if you know that I mean.

All in all the children see the common man/woman daily so this is where we must start. One child, and one community at a time. It can happen by all means remember the guy they call Miami who was born in New Orleans, LA and lives in Marquette, MI. One person can make a change. God bless always peace and love forever.

#####

Prisoner Essay 9.10

"Change the Mind" (3/22/09)
What struck me as the most profound aspect on the "ending of street crime" article was the section on the "transformational model." The model has distinct Eastern philosophical air to it. It speaks of teaching a person to view the world differently.

The current rehab models in our society are colossal failures. They serve to dig up the past and cast blame. They assume that there is something wrong fundamentally with the person. The transformational model, as well as Eastern philosophy more generally, seem to espouse that maybe it's how we perceive and relate to the external world. If that is corrected then a person can "see" free from delusion.

When a person no longer feels helpless and understands that it is how we choose to engage our external circumstance that determines our level of peace, he is then truly free. Not a thing in this world is permanent. Nothing. How then can you crave, attach to or desire that which is in transition? You cannot.

The transformational model seems sound because it is grounded in changing how a person perceives things. Change the mind, change the perception, and you change the man.

#####

Prisoner Essay 9.11

"America Could Do So Much Better" (3/22/09)
Concerning the input of the lifer's project and/or ex-offenders, I personally find that to be a no brainer.

Who better to motivate our young than the people they worship as gods. Why every state does not have many such programs is beyond me, for I would gladly assist, and lend my voice to uplift our young.

Perhaps this state will begin to take a serious look at such positive programs. Who knows; maybe I would not be sitting here with seven to life again.

Street crime is never going to end, but I truly believe America could do so much better with such programs as the Lifers Public Safety Committee.

Personally, I cannot think of any such committees in the state of Michigan. What a crying shame, for this correctional institution is the worst.

No programs, no trades, no college, and now no more money. What harm could it cause to encourage such programs in this state? It truly is a shame.

#####

Elijah Anderson describes the hierarchy of drug dealing in the culture of street crime:

In Philadelphia, the drug trade is organized hierarchically, in terms of "top dogs," "middle dogs," and "low dogs" (Anderson 1990), similar to a pyramid scheme. The top dogs are believed to make the most money, operating essentially as drug "king pins," but to local residents they are mostly invisible, known largely in the abstract or as urban legends. As aging babydaddys, homeboys, brothers, cousins, nephews, and sons, the middle dogs are more visible and often have an everyday presence in the community. Ranging in age from twenty-five to thirty-five, they visit the local street corner carryouts, clubs, barbershops, and car washes and drive around the neighborhood in a Lexus, Mercedes, or BMW, their flashy "rides" attesting to their financial success and drawing the attention of youthful wannabes. On their rounds, they "do their business," but also are on the lookout, or even an outright hunt, for young recruits to the trade. Their most likely prospects are financially strapped young boys in need of self-esteem. Typically, these boys lack a "decent" and strong father figure or other male presence in their lives, but the draw of the street is so powerful that boys from even the most intact families can be taken in.

Upon spotting vulnerable boys, sometimes as young as thirteen or fourteen, the middle dogs seek to cultivate them and turn them into "low dogs." By showing them attention, the middle dogs overtly or subtly court them, perhaps letting them "hold" (borrow) a few dollars or doing other small financial favors for them. The task, or the challenge, may be as simple as serving as a lookout. With each completed task, a bond is struck between the young boy and the middle dog, and mutual confidence grows. . . . As the young boy becomes increasingly dependent on this relationship, his street credibility is ever more strongly tied to his job performance as evaluated by the middle dog

. . . To seal the deal and initiate him into the drug trade, the middle dog may offer the young boy a "package" to hold, or even a corner to stand on and sell drugs

. . . The stage is now set for the boy to become a full-fledged low dog in the local drug trade. (Anderson 2008: 12–13)

#####

Prisoner Essay 9.12

"Street Life" (3/22/09)
Your sons, daughters, grandchildren, aunts, uncles, brothers, sisters, neighbors; they are today's criminals. These are the individuals who have been ostracized by the community because of bad behavior that was left without correction and is now deemed criminal. Those individuals now are in the hierarchy of the street-chain developed codes and rules that coincide with the same bad behavior displayed by your youth and they have now found acceptance in the street life (gangs).

Once accepted it is then embraced and loyalty must be shown. Chain of command is quickly established and you have now adopted a low-end form of new world order. Just as a child is eager to please his/her parents to receive a reward (bike, shoes, etc.) a teenager is just as, if not more, eager to prove their loyalty to the higher-ranking street veterans.

In order to tackle a problem of such magnitude, we must first make the street life an unpopular choice to have. It must be replaced with school as a place to be that's cool and with respecting others as a motto to live by. We cannot remove an individual from what they have become accustomed to without replacing substance and life values in its stead—just as a surgeon cannot remove a heart without first having a heart to replace in its core.

To find a solution we must look in every household to discover the problem areas first then respond. Once there are issues that have been discovered that can be categorized alike form each household, then there can be shared solutions. Parents and children must be prepared with the tools necessary to make adjustments in their homes and lives. Then the changing of the world can begin.

#####

Prisoner Essay 9.13

"The Fight Is Really with the Money That's Being Made off Crime" (12/6/08)
Fighting crime:

Fighting crime has always been approached with an eye on "tough on crime" as a way to actually fight crime. I think that they are really missing the point. Crime, in my eyes, has been the result of something and not the cause. I know that the topic should be obvious that people commit street crimes as an alternative to live the American Dream. Because let's face it, that's all that we really want.

The American Dream can typically be defined as a suburban housewife, 2 children, 2 cars, and a generous income. When the typical families in the urban areas are usually much different—single parent, 4 children, renting homes, used car, and low income. So, once again in my eyes, I think that society's inability to create jobs for able body people coupled with the American Dream advertisement wherever you look, you should be the starting point for fighting crime. I've said time and time again, urban philosophy is: "get money or sleep in the park." Which can be translated into do what you have to do to make it in this world (American Dream world).

Transforming the mind set:

Now, one thing that I believe could transform our future, as it related to crime in this country, is viable, relevant education, because, "to know is to do." I can't help but think that, if the goal is the American Dream, then there has to be many ways that you know, the less likely you are to commit acts that will jeopardize your freedom and in many cases you life. If this country is willing to invest in education, in the streets for those who can't afford it and education in the penal system for the so called criminal mind, then our community would experience less crime and we wouldn't be having this conversation as much.

People tend to think the most criminal behavior can be modified through therapeutic programs yet continuing to live in an environment that is totally contrary to this line of thinking. Sometimes the old way is staring you right in the face yet we refuse to acknowledge its success rate. Example: if we wanted a person to realize that the glass he is drinking from is dirty and potentially dangerous all that needs to be done is to set a clean glass besides him, and if history holds true to form, you get the picture.

In the end, it is going to take those who really care to begin doing instead of talking. We have the answers, but I will be the first to say that after that has been said; the fight is really with the money that is being made off of crime, which is another two-hour class session all by its self.

Prisoner Essay 9.14

"We Never Deal with the Primary Cause of the Crime" (12/6/08)
The Lifers Public Safety Steering Committee has some very interesting points on curtailing street crime. The primary cause of street crime through my experience is a breakdown in the relationship between the perpetrator and the community. Too often people feel that they are not a part of this capitalist society when they don't have the material possessions that everyone else possesses. Whether it is through the lack of opportunity to gain those goods or from a lack of willingness to do what's necessary to pursue or even the culture of a criminal mentality. Having several possible causes, the Lifer Project had the correct concept of a multidirectional approach.

The primary elevation and promotion of crime is generated through television and the news media. I've learned that many people get their information and ideals or concepts of what life's standards are through the television and news outlets. In a society of electronics, people do not effectively communicate with each other much anymore. Families with single parent homes and some with both parents working full time jobs to keep up with the "Jones" or too often just to make ends meet, leave today's children on their own to be taught by television programs. The warehousing of people in prisons which allows them to just sit around and watch television 15 hours or more a day is actually reprogramming their minds and teaching them that violence is the way of American life. It is acceptable to see the president of the United States go in and invade countries making all sorts of false claims to justify their occupation there. All of these are signals to the subconscious mind of our youths that's it totally acceptable to take what you did not earn. Street crime is just a smaller scale of the overall unspoken philosophy of the America Way.

We want positive role models for our children and encourage them to associate with people that have the potential of "going somewhere in life," but we allow them to absorb all the media violence and crime stories from the news and television programs not understanding the deeper effects it has on their psyche. As with the contrast of the LIFERS rehabilitation model that illustrates that residing in a hostile prison environment is counterproductive to therapeutic prison programs. Society expects the prison system to heal the ills of people being incarcerated at a rapid pace, but the elements of prison itself do not support rehabilitation or reward positive behavior or change. The majority legislators, prison administers, parole board members, and members of society all hold a person to the negatives of incarceration. Very seldom is the ability to overcome adversity and improved behavior celebrated.

The LIFERS, Inc. made a very unique analysis when they illustrated that "massive incarceration suggests a state of paralysis in the field of criminal justice." America is a land of symptoms. In the field of medicine America treats the symptoms of the ailments. If you have a toothache, the common remedy is to extract it. If we have a cold, we buy medicine to suppress the runny nose, the cough, congestion in the chest, etc. all of these treatments are motivated by profit rather than cures. Never does America sell medicine to cure the cold. They just sell us enough relief to get us through the cold period. The same holds true with crime and prisons. Law enforcement does not address the cause of crime; it merely treats the symptoms of crime by suppressing perpetrators through removing them from the so-called free society. In many cases you hear police, prosecutors, and others in the media say we don't have to worry about him/her for a long time. S/he is going away for a long time. Never do you hear them say we will be dealing with the primary cause of this crime. So the elements of what causes street crime or even corporate crime are still in place. It's just there waiting for the next unsuspecting citizen to recognize the opportunity to carry out its antisocial purpose.

Even in corporate America crime is acceptable. The only difference between street and corporate crime is that in street crime you have fewer victims. There's a direct face to who was actually wronged and who is to blame. In corporate crime there are many victims but the millionaire white-collar perpetrators have cronies to cover their trails. The prime example of this is with the latest banking and mortgage scandal under the Bush administration. The billions of dollars the government just has the U.S. treasury, under the supervision of Mr. Paulson to distribute to his cronies as he pleases. The ironic thing of that is, Mr. Paulson was the head of Sachs group who were competitors of Lehman brothers. Everyone may remember that Lehman brothers went bankrupt and ended up being brought by one of U.S. treasury Paulson's fellow corporate cronies. What difference is corporate cronyism than street crime partnership? One drug dealer become informant, snitches to law enforcement on his rival so he or his fellow man can get the customers after the competition is hauled off to prison. There were hundreds of thousands of family's victims to the mortgage crimes inflicted upon them by white-collar criminals. These perpetrators destroyed the entire U.S. economy robbing innocent people of their homes, lifesavings, and all of their worldly possessions. And what happens? They get the U.S. government to give them billions of dollars to continue business as usual. In the world of street crime, this type of travesty would be an outrage. Everyone the street perpetrator knew would be investigated and questioned concerning their role in the crime. In the culture of corporate crime, the gangstas just rides out into the sunset like the good ole boys do in television cowboy movies.

The economic factor of street crime doesn't start in the streets. It is a factor of institutional racism as well as other primary elements, the capitalist concept of the haves and the have-nots. Until the primary causes of crime is addressed which in my opinion is an equal opportunity for all, building stronger interpersonal relationships, a fair distribution of wealth and the implementation and enforcement of laws being equally distributed to all violators, antisocial symptoms of crime (overuse of incarceration, long sentences) will continue to be acceptable as the remedy to a safer America.

#####

As mentioned, this article, "Ending the Culture of Street Crime," has been making its way, as part of a prisoner initiative, in part led by the NLA, from state prison to state prison. Through formal educational seminars organized by the NLA and through informal networks (such as the eight-week "Social Science and Personal Writing" volunteer class), this movement is eliciting long-term prisoners to help those prisoners who are getting out, to end their participation in the culture of street crime. How is this done? They cannot be "rehabilitated" because the street crime culture and criminality they grew up within the family—and the streets—in the first place is not a place they want to return to. Instead, such prisoners need "habilitation," but even better—"transformation."

BECOMING INTERESTED IN OTHER THINGS

For some prisoners the prison experience represents rehabilitation, but for most prison presents the challenge of habilitation or maturing. For still others the path lies in transformation. For a good many—maybe 20–30 percent—prison is just "doing time" as part of a criminal lifestyle. For yet others, the law is not respected—for instance, selling pot where the law is not agreed with and the risk was taken to be a seller.

The typical state prison population is a "mixed bag." There are nine typical criminal offense categories: homicide, sex crimes, motor vehicle, assault, arson, weapons, robbery, larceny, and burglary. And then there are the unusually punitive drug laws (and drug-related crimes). What are the details of these different types of criminality? For instance, some criminals are "opportunist" and may do nearly all of these types of crime. Others may fall into particular profiles. What are the different recidivism rates for different profiles? For instance, in a thirteen-year study of 76,000 Michigan prisoners released between 1986 and 1999 in terms of what percent of each offense group returned to prison within four years, the 2009 CAPPS recidivism study found: homicide and sex offenders have a very low rate of returning to prison within four years after release, whereas burglary, larceny, and robbery (the "economic crimes") have a much higher rate of returning to prison (reoffending), especially when tied into drug addiction. Motor vehicle, assault, and drugs and weapons fall into the middle (CAPPS 2009).

In terms of return-to-society, what personal "self-work" is needed by the individuals in different statistical risk categories? This section briefly reviews prison programming as well as different restorative justice programs.

Joan Petersilia, in *When Prisoners Come Home*, recommends four reforms to parole and reentry practices in American prisons:

1. Alter the in-prison experience. Provide more education, work, and rehabilitation opportunities. Change the prison environment to promote life skills rather than violence and domination.
2. Change prison release and revocation practices. Institute a system of discretionary parole release that incorporates parole release guidelines. These parole guidelines should be based primarily on recidivism prediction.
3. Revise post-prison services and supervision. Incorporate better parole supervision classification systems, and target services and surveillance to those with high need and risk profiles.
4. Foster collaborations with the community and enhance mechanisms of informal social control. Develop partnerships with service providers, ex-convicts, law enforcement, family members, victim advocates, and neighborhoods to support the offender (2003: 171).

Petersilia has a thorough set of recommendations, including that "prison administrators should embrace the mission of prisoner reintegration," "implement treatment, work, and education tracks in prison," and that "prisoners should participate in comprehensive prerelease planning" (2003: 172–84). None of these 2003 recommendations have been thoroughly implemented, indicating how slowly "turning the battleship" of the prison system proceeds.

Cheryl Swanson, in *Restorative Justice in a Prison Community*, studied a prison "honor dorm" program in an Alabama prison and sketched out the elements of what makes special residential educational programs work. The honor dorm had several "semesters" of classes over a two-year period with curriculum such as: restorative justice, self-betterment as an individual responsibility, relationships, reinventing our lives, anger, mentoring, convict code vs. honor dorm code, crime victimization/trauma, the impact of various crimes on the community, anthropology, sociology, and the community (2009: 136–39). She notes the case for prison education:

Why should prisoners have educational opportunities? There are two lines of argument. One contends education is a necessary condition for rehabilitation. A second belief is education promotes safety and order in prison communities. The education-rehabilitation connection is not simple, and research findings are mixed. Barb Toews offers this explanation: "Individuals choose if and when they want to experience personal growth. It requires them to remove the cloak of offending and turn toward their inner, true self. For some, experiencing growth comes before accountability. For others, meaningful accountability triggers growth." (Swanson 2009: 126–27)

The psychology of "making good" is reviewed: how do those who are *desisting* from crime differ in their thinking from those who are *persisting* in criminality?

Shadd Maruna, in *Making Good: How Ex-Convicts Reform and Rebuild Their Lives*, explores this question. He notes:

Unlike active offenders, the long-time, persistent offender who tries to desist from crime has a lot to explain. The participants in the Liverpool Desistance Study (LDS) each spent around a decade selling drugs, stealing cars, and sitting in prison. Most critically, they have made repeated breaks with the life of crime and drugs (often announcing their "reform" to authorities and significant others), only to return to offending behavior. No one (including the speaker himself or herself) is going to automatically believe such a person, when they announce, "I am a new person" or "I have changed my ways."

If such an enormous life transformation is to be believed, the person needs a coherent narrative to explain and justify this turnaround. . . .

Perhaps most importantly, ex-offenders need to have a believable story of why they are going straight to convince *themselves* that this is a real change. It is easy to say one is giving up drugs and crime. Yet, when setbacks occur—and ex-convicts are likely to face many such disappointments—wanting to desist is not enough. The individual needs a logical, believable, and respectable story about who they are that "makes it impossible to engage in criminal conduct without arousing guilt reactions and feelings of shame that are incompatible with the self conception" (Cressey 1963: 158). The desisting person's self-story, therefore, not only has to allow for desistance but also has to make desistance a logical necessity. . . .

The life stories of desisting narrators in this sample maintain this equilibrium by connecting negative past experiences to the present in such a way that the present good seems an almost inevitable outcome. "Because of all that I have been through, I am now this new way." If this can be accomplished, desistance can be reshaped as a process of "maintaining one's sense of self or one's personal identity" (Waldorf et al. 1991: 222) rather than the "schizophrenic" process of rejecting one's old self and becoming a "new person" (Rotenberg 1978). This secure self-identity also helps protect the person from becoming overwhelmed with shame regarding his or her past self. (2001: 85–87)

LIFE STORIES: REHABILITATION, MATURING, AND TRANSFORMATION

One can see typical prisoners who come to the prison school building, for volunteer activities, as in a process of "self work" toward rehabilitation or transformation; whereas others (who stay in the yard) are doing time as part of the business (of crime). To repeat: prison is a mixed bag. In teaching the volunteer classes and asking prisoners to write stories about themselves, the role of the lifer as leader has been mentioned. The efforts to help younger prisoners are a way for the "grey heads" in prison to make a transformation, as described by Maruna. This section includes prisoner essays from different types of prisoner (with different offenses) and asks critical questions about "rehabilitation" and/or "transformation." These are linked to a continuing discussion of "free will and determinism," "society and subcultures," and "power arrangements."

The following "Life Story in a Few Pages" reveals a man who got involved in a robbery among drug dealers when he was young and is now serving a life sentence. One of the grey heads who came to my volunteer classes, the man in this story, represents a question of why many states in the United States have such long sentences. Convicted in 1977, he had been in prison thirty years when he wrote this personal story. The Citizens Alliance on Prisons and Public Spending advocates that lifers such as he get a parole or commutation review. In general, CAPPS argues against such long sentences and believes lifers should get a real parole board review at regular intervals (www.capps-mi.org). Here is a man's story—see what you think.

#####

Prisoner Essay 9.15

"Getting too Deep in the Dope Game" (12/6/08)
December 3, 2008 (Gus Harrison Correctional Facility) marks over (30) years of my incarceration.

In 1978 I was convicted by jury on two counts of (aiding and abetting) felony murder robbery. Prior to the trial, the prosecutor and judge noted on the record (attached exhibit) that I should entertain a plea to (10 to 20 years) based upon the evidence showing that I was unaware that my co-defendant was going to shoot the victims.

Ignorant of the law at the time, I took the advice of my attorney and proceed to trial. For the most part, I never thought that I would be found guilty of actual murder. Not based upon my innocence, but more so, my unconscious belief that since I never possessed a gun or shot anyone that my offense or minor culpability in the crime of robbery. I thought I would be acquitted.

On the fourth day of trial, the jury advised the court that they had reached a verdict on my co-defendant, but was having difficulty determining my guilt. The judge instructed them that if my co-defendant was guilty, and even though I never had a gun or shot anyone, under the law, since I aided and assisted him in the robbery, I was also guilty of murder under the state's aiding and abetting theory. Two days later, the jury found me guilty under the state's aiding and abetting statute of (2) counts of felony murder (robbery).

On April 18, 1979 I was sentenced by the judge to spend the rest of my natural life at hard labor in the states penitentiary. This harsh sentence was by in large mandated by statute. The recommendation for hard labor was based upon after hearing the jury's verdict, I called them a bunch of dumb ass motherfuckers. This wild outburst was borne out of anger and rage. Moments later I was wrested to the courtroom floor by seven sheriff deputies, chained down and placed in an isolation cell. The remainder of that day I cursed and yelled until a doctor and nurse escorted by several deputies came to my cell. They rushed in, stripped off all my clothes. The nurse pulled out a long needle and stuck it inside a small bottle of clear liquid. She handed it to the doctor. When he looked at it. He ordered her to put more in the needle. The deputy was choking me so hard. I couldn't muster a scream. She inserted the liquid into the needle. The doctor then shoved the needle in my left hip. I felt a burning sensation going all though my body. I woke up the next day with a hockey helmet tied around my head, a plastic mouth-guard inside my mouth shackled to a bed with a strait jacket on. I was so fucked up off the drugs inside my body, I was oblivious to the pain. Two deputies were posted inside the room. An elderly white nurse came by and asked me if I was thirsty. She told me to nod my head yes or no. She removed the helmet and mouthpiece and gently poured some ice water down my throat. This cold drink was the best feeling I had felt since being charged with murder. She told me that she would leave these items off my face if I promised to behave. I said okay. The next day they removed the jacket. I hadn't been fed in two days. The effects of the drug had me walking like a snail. Just lifting my arms felt as if they were tied down to fifty-pound weights. I made a promise to myself that I would never act a fool again while in Wayne County Jail. State of Michigan VS (redacted), Recorders Court for the city of Detroit. Case No. (redacted).

In relation to the crime in which I was convicted, I never actually witnessed the entire shooting, but I heard the gunfire from my associates and the victim's associates shooting. I'd imagine that someone might have been killed at that moment. But it wasn't until watching the evening news that highlighted "drug shoot out leaves two people dead and two wounded." After hearing this broadcast, I never felt so much pain and depression before in my life.

A year or so prior to this dreadful day, My associate older brother asked us to help him move a lot of drugs around the city of (Detroit) from house to house for his dealers to sell. He offered us $100.00 a day to simply drop off packages to certain individuals. We never had a problem. It was in and out; drop off the package and split, then on to the next spot. Each time, to avoid police or hijackers, we used different routes and decoys.

Everyone involved in this tragic comedy was cut from the same cloth. Runaways, high school dropouts, prostitutes, dope friends, hustlers, dope dealers, corrupt police, pimps and a host of other sordid characters that lived outside the limits of the law.

Although their circumstances as opposed to mine differed due to age, culture, and addictions or otherwise, we all sought after the same thing: "Money, excitement, power, lust and greed."

My associate's brother began falling on hard times when his drug connection was shut down by the state police, which forced him to buy lesser quality heroin from his competitors. It also reduced our five to six hundred dollar a week hustle down to two hundred dollars a week. In the mid seventies, this was a great deal of money to someone without a job.

Everyone in the area of 14th and 12th Street from West Grand all the way south to 8-mile was feeling the pinch, and liaisons that had been forged by greed soon lost their value and minor scrapes soon erupted into severe violent encounters. Rival competitors began hostile takeovers of certain areas. Without a consistent cash flow, the weaker drug dealers were forced under the thumb of many of their former rivals in order to survive.

My associate brother soon became engulfed in this madness. Since me and my associate were not familiar with the in-depth operation and structure of this drought, we laid low. But everywhere we traveled, you feel the tension in the air. The usual strip joints johns were being robbed. 85 percent of the hustlers that lived off gambling houses were shut down. The only people that seemed to weather this storm was the prostitutes and thieves that shoplifted out in Oakland county malls. Instead of selling their products on 12th street. They simply headed downtown.

On Sept. 19, 1978 my associate called me and asked me to pick up his brother and another man from his sisters apartment. When I arrived there they told me that they had bought some foul dope that was making all the addicts sick and they wanted me to drive them over the Webs spot to get their money

back. They wanted to use my car because the people in the area didn't recognize it as a competitor. My attitude at the time simply geared at returning
to receiving my weekly quota of cash. Although I personally seen up close
Webs knack for violence many of times, if I have knew before hand that it
Web that sold them the dope, and they were going to pay him a visit, I would
have never got involved. Once I got there, it was too late.

When we reached the area where Web and his crew operated, we cut
through an empty apartment building and came out facing the building where
Web and his dealers were stationed. My Associate and his partner pulled out
guns and ordered them all to empty their pockets or be shot. I was standing
by the curb shaking like a leaf because a few of the men that were sitting on
the stairs I had seen years earlier were without question men to be feared. My
associate ordered this female named Cat to collect all the dope and money
they had, place it in a shopping bag and gave it to us. When she did, I turned
briefly to leave and all hell broke loose. Gunshots rang out everywhere.
I ducked behind a green Cadillac next to Cat. The sound of gunfire amidst
her screams makes me sweat uncontrollably in a matter of 5 seconds. When
the shooting stopped for a second. I looked around and Cat was holding her
stomach screaming. I could see blood running through her fingers. I looked
between the cars and saw one of Webs associates running towards my associate. This brief second allowed me to escape back through vacant apartment
I came though.

Just as I was entering the passage way, though, I heard a man's voice
scream out. "Get that skinny motherfucker over there, he got the shit," refer-
ring to the bag of drugs and money that I had. I didn't look back, but I heard
several more shots.

When I reached my car, both associates seemed hyped and pumped up
as we drove away. No words were spoken. Once we returned to his sister's
apartment, I was issued some money and close to 200 small packs of heroin.
We then made a pact of silence. Less than 30 days later, another associate of
theirs turned us in to homicide detectives to escape a murder case he caught
and we were arrested and charged with felony murder. Cat has been shot
and killed and Webs brother had been killed. From witnesses' testimony
and the informant, it was obvious that one of my associates had killed Webs
brother. But it was unclear as to who shot Cat. The feud did not end in the
streets. It carried over to prison. Another more dangerous side effect that
I was unaware of. The two men that was shot kept true to the code of the
streets and refused to prosecute us or testify. They felt as if vengeance would
satisfy their pain.

Prior to this unfortunate event, even though I was not receiving as much
money a week as I did running drugs, I still had a nice apartment, car, food
and a nice girlfriend whom knew nothing of my hidden lifestyle across town.

About my background: At age 13, I was incorporated by several thieves and hustlers in this area to travel downtown to shoplift, pick pocket and break in to clothing or jewelry stores. Due to my age, in the event that I was captured, they told me to issue police a false name and number and they would have someone pretend to be my mother or father to get me out. On two of the dozens of times I was caught, the detectives that questioned me let me escape through the basement of the (local) police station.

Having intentionally dropped from high school in the 11th grade, at age 16 I was living with an older female prostitute before I got my own place that I use to bodyguard for. Armed with a hunting knife and a 22-caliber pistol, I use to stand outside her hotel room watching her back in case any of her tricks got out of order. Most of her tricks, or johns as they were called were mostly elderly wealthy white men that drove miles from the suburbs to seek out her pleasures. Mary, who stage name as a nude dancer was "Virgin Mary" because she would dress up as a nun, then strip naked and ask her johns to baptize her by inserting their dicks inside of her. This would drive them wild. Mary looked upon me as a younger brother. And I learned 90 percent of how to run the streets from her. She always advised me not to sell dope or get too deep involved in that game. She always stressed to me that I'd either end up dead, half dead or life in prison. Little did I know that her forecast would turn into reality.

Our paths crossed in the early seventies when this man was kicking her and dragging her down the alley. Me and several friends were hanging out in the area. She begged us to help her. Armed with broken liquor bottles, we forced the man to let her go. The man fought us back and I busted his head with a wine bottle. From that day forth, she gave me anything that I ever asked for. Money, clothes, shelter, food, plus, at the time, word spread about what I had done, and many other prostitutes and hustlers in this area treated me with respect. And from time to time, his girlfriends paid me for my protection services. 90 percent of the hoes out on the strip had pimps. Only a chosen few operated independently. Mary, Sheryl, Candy and a few personal hoes had earned that pleasure.

Mary never incited me into any sexual activity or drugs but we often talked about how I should please my girlfriend in bed. On an average night I would be paid 50 to 60 dollars for protecting her. Food, shelter and clothes were a bonus she would buy from thieves for me. I was never addicted to any drugs. I have tried heroin and weed. The effects it imposed on me such as weed, made me paranoid. I could not stand the feeling. Heroin had me slumbering, slobbering, spitting, scratching, throwing up and lazy, another factor that I hated. I tried them both about three times and never done them or any other drugs since. I did enjoy beer and an occasional shot of whiskey.

At age 17, my girlfriend was about to have our baby and Mary helped us get an apartment in a nice neighborhood. She knew the manager and told him that she would give him some pussy once a week to pay for the rent. To eat, I used the money Mary gave me to buy food stamps at half price from local junkies on the first of the month when people were picking up their welfare checks.

From time to time I would see some of my old classmates from high school. Sometimes my girlfriend would have them over listening to records and playing cards. On weekends, I would attend our high get-together while my girlfriend attended night school while her sister watched our daughter. My girlfriend's mother used to call me a black swamp snake, and always accused me of being a low life lazy nigger. Every Sunday, her mother along with her eight sisters and two brothers would go to church. Her mother would always invite me to attend claiming that she was going to remove the devil from my soul. I never went. I was actually scared of her mother's religious ramblings about the devil and Jesus. After church was over, I would always show up to pick her up. Her mother's eyes would be bloodshot red watching me walk out to the door with her daughter. She would just pray. One day when she visited our apartment, she did call me a nice father when she saw me changing my daughter's diaper.

By discussing my life style to my naïve girlfriend, her mother clearly saw through me. I always believed that her mother's younger brother whom I saw from time to time shooting dice and hustling, told her things about me.

Something inside me really missed being in high school. My girl friend used to beg me to go back to night school with her, but the streets was where the excitement was that I desired. Something that could not be found in high school. In the summer on 1975, I took my girlfriend to her prom. We were the toast of the town that evening. I had so much fun, I felt as though I was being split in half.

I was addicted to delivering payoffs to the police by prostitutes, numbers runners and drug dealers. I loved the power that I possessed at the time—not having to abide the curfew, drinking on street corners, shooting dice in the back alleys and hanging out at after hour joints. Entering strip clubs with no questions asked. Buying alcohol from liquor stores knowing I was under aged. Seeing naked women dancing and having sex. Driving without license, and driving right pass certain police officers without being stopped. Carrying a gun and knife and all of the above was a far more stimulating aura than anything I have ever experienced at this point in my life.

Of course, I was aware of wrong from right. And without question, I chose this lifestyle at first as rebelliousness that soon engulfed and translated my priorities and desires from reason to one of greed and lawlessness.

Out of a litter to four boys and one girl, no one from my family, cousins, in-laws etc. has never been to prison. My father was a very religious Southern man that worked 30 years as a laborer at General Motors. He instilled in all of his children that value of an honest day's work. We never went without food or clothes. He planted a small tomato, onion and lettuce garden in our back yard. And every weekend during the summer he would take me and my younger brother fishing. My mother would skin all the fishes and freeze the ones that we did not eat that evening. Every Sunday after church we would have a big family dinner. My father would be in the kitchen teaching my mother how to cook. We use to all laugh. It was always a special occasional for our family to get together.

At age 10, my mother left my father for another man. I was not aware of this during this time. My father was left to raise us alone, me and my two brothers and older sister. My oldest brother was drafted into Vietnam.

I was accustomed to being woken up each morning by my mother's soft voice preparing breakfast as she played her jazz albums. At the time, I had no ideal as to why she had left. And when I asked my father about it, he would say she left and when I become a man, he would tell me why. That very day, I just started hating him and blaming him for her not being there. I was a student at the time. Every day that I went to school, I refused to work unless the teacher called my mother. She could never find her.

The pain I felt then, I still cannot describe to this very day. The first time I ran away from home, my ultimate quest was to search for her. As time passed, I just couldn't stand being around my father, a deeply devoted Christian man that never smoked, drink, cursed or abuse any of us. He loved us all unconditionally. Fortunately, he was the kind of father any son would love. Unfortunately, I wasn't that son that could understand or appreciate that love based upon the pain I felt without my mother who drank, cursed and dis-respected my father. I didn't know whether she was dead or what. All I knew at age 10 that I missed her in my life. I refused to attend the community meet-ings that collected all the young boys and girls and had them cleaning out the empty houses in the hood before the adults painted them. Soul singer Aretha Franklin father, Honorable Reverend Franklin headed this community orga-nization. It was a close-knit community; every one took part and respected one another. And we were always advised to stay clear of certain areas east of our neighborhood.

If a family had not cooked or didn't have anything to eat that evening, each family would donate leftovers to ensure that they had something to eat. When our clothes got too small, my father would give them to people with smaller children to wear. The compassionate community I can safely say contributed to the success of many of the young boys I grew up with that went on the lead productive, loving and stable lifestyles as opposed to over a dozen that hung out across town that I ran into in prison.

At age 14, me and my mother crossed paths and we were reunited. I lived with her for a while. But me and her boyfriend had problems because I refused to work, and I didn't like seeing another man that was not my father with my mother. So I moved back in with Virgin Mary. Something I could never do with my father. My mother asked her to look after me. Never once did she tell me what went wrong after asking her dozens of times why she left. She would say that it's all history, and she was back to look after me. Never once did she blame my father for anything. From that day forth, we drank together. She smoked weed from time to time. Her man never smoked weed. He did drink on the weekends. I gave her money all the time. Her apartment was my second home whenever I needed to rest.

It wasn't until after my tenth year in prison that they both shared what had happened between them. None of my fathers were ever affected by what had happened. Two are retired now and one is still working.

Me and my then girlfriend has since got married. She went on to obtain her B.A. in elementary education. We have two adult daughters and 11 grandchildren. She is also studying to be a pastor. Throughout my incarceration, both my mother and father has visit me together often. They are now both in their late 80's and are the best of friends.

#####

Among her recommendations for prisoner rehabilitation and reentry, Joan Petersilia mentions postsecondary education, and especially to have ex-cons help with counseling. This next essay, "Transformation," reveals a prisoner who is on this track.

#####

Prisoner Essay 9.16

"Transformation" (1/25/09)

I write this essay from my heart and from my 30 years of experience as a criminal and mad scientist, for I too have studied the mindset, movements and the behaviors of the criminal. Since I lived in such dismal world I have no choice but to learn the ways of the wild or shall I say the anti-social.

I have come to respect and obey these unwritten laws of the wild. I understand the practice, the concepts and the philosophy of this social class. Better known as the street code. This essay has three parts, past, present, and future. I shall express my opinions and disclose self with very little detail.

I read Chapter Three (Farrington and Welsh 2007: individual factors) more than once, an interesting analysis to say the least. As I continued to read I found myself in an emotional state, for the truth does hurt! I even got angry a few times. However a great deal of relief was upon me to know that all of my pain and behaviors defects were not totally my fault.

The Past:

At the tender age of three I was placed in foster care. My mother was young and unfit to raise me in the slums of Detroit. While in foster care I was exposed to sexual abuse, verbal abuse and extreme physical abuse. Even outside the home I was antagonized and beat by the bullies. Back then even the teachers were allowed to hit children. To me, the world was dog-eat-dog. I knew nothing of compassion, love, affection or peace. Often times I would run away only to be returned as victim of abuse. In conclusion to my childhood past, let me say that I was created to lack compassion, concern, empathy, love. And temperament. By the age of 15 I had join a well known gang of stone cold-killers. By 16 years of age I had begun my police record. By the age of 20 crimes for me was A through Z and everything in-between.

The Present:

Today at this hour I am unfolding and developing into a mature mindset for positive change. They call it the recovery process. Here is where I address my issues, be it anti-social personality disorders such as low intelligence, temperament, empathy or impulsiveness. This process allows me the golden opportunity to develop the social cognitive skills to intersect in the pro-social world.

After living most of my life on the animal level I have blessed to receive the gift of enlightenment, which did not come easy for me. That is to say. After 14 years being locked up, in and out of treatment centers among other heart breakers such as being shot 11 times and watching my friends die, I give up. I acknowledge the fact that I must remain diligent in this life long process for I will have to dig deeper, work harder and fly higher. I accept this challenge and a mission for it is vital. MY LIFE DEPENDS ON IT.

The Future:

It has been said that as a man thinks then so he is. Today I work diligently to change my perceptions and outlook on life. I was programmed to think, feel and react a certain way. Now I am de-programming in order to reprogram my mind. Only with the help of others who are serious and committed to the process can I grow into such mature insight. I have come to realize that my empowerment lies in education concerning such subject matters as social science, criminal science, and 12 step programs. This education process takes time and effort on a daily timetable. This is my only way out of the enslavement of my insanity and my enslavement to the system. I am enrolling in college upon my release. And I plan to help others as a motivational speaker and I will be a Certified Addiction Counselor, CAC I and II. I have a passion for it and I'm very good at it. That is my future and I claim it before man and before the God of my understanding.

#####

CRIME PREVENTION VERSUS WAREHOUSE PRISON

Prisoners can offer some good insights on crime prevention, as the next two prisoner essays reveal.

#####

Prisoner Essay 9.17

"Invest in Youth: Prevent Crime, Rather Than the Warehouse Prison" (2/24/10)
It is evident by the populations of today's prison system that this state's crime prevention programs have failed en masse. Some of this can be blamed on individual and family factors but also a very large percentage comes down to community influence such as antidrug/anticrime programs. With the effort of a few members of any community and a relatively small amount of money invested a large percentage of problems with the influenceable youth could be avoided.

It should be noted that if only 25 percent of the annual 2 billion dollar Michigan Department of Corrections budget, or a mere 500 million dollars, could be put each year into programs to prevent crime rather than being used to warehouse the forgotten lost victims of an uncaring society it would greatly reduce the overall cost of corrections in the long run.

Also a thorough review of the laws would help reduce incarceration rates since some, if not most, sentences are disproportionate to the "crime" committed. By offering more rehabilitation and/or community programs to first time offenders to help solve the underlying problem rather than incarcerating them for many years and forcing a stigma onto them, a great deal of money could be saved and lives could be rescued from despair.

The justice system and society in general need to work together to find or develop, a rehabilitation program that can be applied to drug, alcohol, and sex offending such as the "Our House" program out of Ottawa, Ontario. It must be a rehabilitation program not a treatment program which only "treats" the symptoms but doesn't really ever address the cause of the problem to begin with.

Rehabilitation is not simply "getting clean" but also breaking the physical and psychological patterns that even short term abuse of drugs/alcohol can quickly establish. Yes, it is good to detoxify the body but it is only a small part of the overall experience. This is not possible in a 30 or 90 day program but can only be achieved in a long term (one year or more) residential setting with intense (12+ hours a day) group therapy with a well qualified therapist that has experience what they are trying to teach.

Community members need to work together to try to avoid letting problems get to the point of needing rehabilitation by offering alternative activates and educational programs that not only teach but are enjoyable at the same time. Also offer youth places they can "hang out" and not have to worry about the influence of antiproductive individuals such as drug dealers and gang members.

By offering activities such as basketball, baseball, and martial arts it not only occupies time but also offers physical exercise. This in turn helps reduce medical cost caused by childhood obesity. These areas should not only be posted as drug free/gang free zones but strictly enforced as such.

The influence of parents of children can never be stressed enough. Most parents seem lost when trying to help guide their children. This is why classes will be offered for parents and potential parents on how to direct their children's activities and thoughts.

This state's educational system especially in the inner cities has broke down. No longer are students passed on their merit but about by their age. Teachers are so afraid to hold a child back that we are ending up with high school graduates that can't read or write. This is such a perversion of the educational system that some teachers have quit teaching in protest. This must stop, make children learn, base teacher pay on performance, send problem children to special classes to assist them with learning. Much more money needs to be spent on educational system not cutting the budget every year to support an already over inflated prison system. Also more classes need to be offered on life skills.

#####

Prisoner Essay 9.18

"I Need to Fix Me, Not the System" (2/1/09)
I'm sorry but people are sick and tired of listening to the excuses. When someone you love is injured or killed, when the madness of the neighborhood you live in makes you afraid to let your kids out of your sight you really don't want the excuses. You just want it to stop. Whatever it takes, stop it.

Victims and victim's families of violent crime don't want to hear about how little Jonny grew up in a bad part of town had a dysfunctional family, a mental illness or problem with drugs.

I'm a product of society and the place I grew up in. I'm sick of listening to these excuses. If you lack empathy and little control over your emotions or impulses and are as ignorant as a box of rocks, you are still accountable and responsible for what you choose to do.

I had poor supervision growing up. This does not absolve me of accountability to the choices I made. Kids with the same background and worse chose not to go as far as I did. I chose to commit a violent crime while others chose not to. It's just that simple. The parole board does not want to hear how wrong the system is. The system is bad, will get worse and I'm not going to see how I'm going to fix it. I need to fix me not the system so that I don't commit another heinous act and so that I pass on to my children what the system will not—pro-social morals.

I was in a very sour mood when I wrote this. When you mentioned today that statistically, the negative result attributed to a particular group, it is important to know, and understand why and pay attention, so you can reduce risk. I was reminded that we want to prevent this stuff in our children and stop it at the roots. I must understand these risk factors if I do not want to re-offend. Call me frustrated.

#####

In statistical analyses of recidivism, it is possible to predict different reoffending patterns in different categories of prisoners, as a group, but it is not possible to predict individual behavior. While it would be good to reduce the degree of poverty and family dysfunction through structural policy's (e.g., guaranteed income, family supports), there is also a need to fix individuals and families. The police role, the prosecutor, even the probation and parole roles are not directly involved in structural-level policy. This is a political role for those making policy, and social movements. However, probation and parole agents can act as "brokers" of social support services and various criminal justice system "case managers" need to have empathy with several different interest groups. From the prisoner himself, it comes down to the individual transformation, as this next essay reveals.

#####

Prisoner Essay 9.19

"I Am Tired of Living the Life of a Criminal" (2/19/09)

I lived with my parents and my three sisters. We had a good family until my parents got divorced. My dad chose the drug life. My mom kept on working.

When I was 11 years old I got in to trouble. I broke into a house. My mom would never let our dad know this. So when I didn't get in trouble I kept on doing it. Finally, it got caught and I got locked up.

My mom and dad came to visit me; I thought that would change me. I was always getting in trouble in school and I was always kicked out. My sisters never got in trouble. So I felt that they were getting all the attention. So I would do stuff to get my parents attention. My mom would always love my sister and my dad had me.

My dad was an alcoholic and I thought that was cool. When he would get drunk we could bond better. We would go fishing; I would go work with my dad.

Then I started to smoke meth at fifteen. My dad was smoking it too so I thought that it was OK. That is when they got divorced. Mom let me get away with everything. I hoped on getting locked up and she would be there for them then. Every time I would get in trouble mom was there. My dad is in prison now, 41 years old and in prison for the first time. Mom, I don't know where she is. Sisters are in Florida and Georgia.

Now I go home (next month), I am thinking about calling on my Christian family. I know they will help me, and they will be there for me no matter what. I think that it will be a good experience for me. I love more than life; my real family only cares for themselves. I found this out with I went to Florida. It was always them they talked about. When I needed them they were not around. I would try to get them to go to church with me, but they wouldn't come because they said they had nothing to wear.

I want to finish school. I want to go to college. I want to be a teacher. I am tired of living the life of a criminal. I am done.

#####

THE CRIMINOLOGY OF RECIDIVISM AND REENTRY

There is a "criminology of reentry and recidivism" that attempts to locate causes of success and failure in reentry and reviews emerging state and local "prisoner reentry initiatives." The prisoner reentry process involves local resources working in a monthly steering committee meeting to wrap services around reentering prisoners. These issues of reentry and recidivism are reviewed in this section through integrating prisoner essays and essay excerpts on prisoner views and concerns on reentry, and the fear of returning to prison. Prisoners can be scared of returning to the streets, knowing how easy it is to fall back into the old "set"—the old ways of life—as this next prisoner's essay reveals.

#####

Prisoner Essay 9.20

"Why I'm Scared of Going Back to the Streets" (1/25/09)

My life growing up was OK for the most. My pops wasn't around very much you could say—he was doin' a bit for the bank robbery. My mom and my grandma was there, you know, that was good for me. I grew up with mostly women in the household. All them hoe's was crazy, it was me and Tyrone. I was about 10 years old when I joined the street gang back in 94. A day I would never forget how my ass got jumped in just to prove a little guy like me could take the beat down. But my boys, my good ole friends nasty Nate, a little puppet, they wasn't down till about 2000. When girls came more into play for'em. I mean life was good, I mean I didn't really need much from nobody. My mom was work'n hard then as a teacher my grandma was gone at work too. I had the house till midnight some time especially when my mom left on dates. Boy like in 2000 was my best years. I was makin a little dough enough to gain attention and the girls loved me and I knew all the right people when a party was to go down they knew I was the king who the best for day bangers. Damn I lived well. Why, they called me and my life style that of a rock star!

Then I got locked up in for accessory to murder. I had to go to Green Oaks and Maxey Boys Training Center till I was proven innocent of the crime. In '04 I was found not guilty due to a technicality. I went home, tried to leave that life style alone—it was hard for the most part, and the first 8 months I stayed away from certain blocks and stores. I was tryin' to not get noticed by my ole' homies but none of that lasted long. I was in college by then and ready to have my first son in '05. He and my girl was trying to do the right thing. I started selling dope again to make that fast cash. Then I bump into Nate and my crew. Before I left they found me shit. Never seem like anything strange after me being gone for a few years. So I never let them know. All them brothers too. I took my team, we started to get that fast cash buying a new cars, getting fine apartments, parties. But I thought to myself, the power I have now is good once again. I found myself back in the old behavior. I scared, OK?

#####

The MPRI Steering Committee for each county assembles twenty to twenty-five of the most active, relevant, knowledgeable people in that county (or three-to-four county district). The steering committee then designs a county or multiple-county districtwide plan that mobilizes social support resources to "wrap around" reentering formerly incarcerated persons in that county or district, such as: housing, transportation, clothing, job placement, advanced skills training and education, health, and other needs. There is also an "in-reach" committee that meets and talks with prisoner during their last month or two before the day of reentry, and working out a plan for them: "On the first day you will be connected to housing here, and you have an appointment with the Department of Human Services. By the second day you need to report in to your Parole Officer," and so forth.

The author has been on the Lenawee County MPRI steering committee (2007–present), and for three years prior to this (2003–2006) was a guest member of the Lenawee County Community Corrections Advisory Board (CCAB). The local CCAB searches for ways to reduce jail and prison bed-space at the front end (people coming into the corrections system). The MPRI seeks to lower the recidivism rate at the backend (formerly incarcerated people coming back into the community).

More than 700,000 prisoners return from U.S. prisons to society each year. The *policies* driving massive prison growth have set up the problem of planning for reentry. Imported from the policy world now grappling with success in reentry is a "prison binge growth culture hangover": the criminal justice network (community corrections probation, prison, parole) now have a set of issues and tensions related to a change in the organizational culture of the prison system that began about 2001 and had become very real by 2003—instead of "sending them back to prison through a revolving door of (necessary to be tough) parole enforcement," how do we now "increase the (necessary to save money) success in reentry?"

The new, emerging policies are focused on capping prison growth and, hopefully, downsizing the prison (Austin et al. 2013; CAPPS 2013; Jacobson 2005; MPRI 2008). However, this new "organizational culture of reentry success" and the beginnings of "Justice Reinvestment" must address the set of values, fears, and oppressions that are representative of the "old organizational culture" of state departments of corrections—a culture that emphasized control and enforcement *more* than prison rehabilitation and reform (Sykes 1958).

#####

Prisoner Essay 9.21

"Persistence, Planning, and Never Relinquish Your Goals" (2/10/10)
Imagine a business that has invested $1.8 billion developing a product, but fails to provide for its launch into the marketplace; this company would

most likely fail, right? Ironically, this very scenario is occurring in Michigan prisons. In FY 2010, the state legislature appropriated this amount to operate the Department of Corrections without a single dime being allocated for college education programs. It is appalling that the entity championing for an increased education employment pool, prohibits those in most need, from accessing the services that would virtually insure a successful reentry to the community.

My quest for societal reentry began in 2007 when I made the decision to increase my education. With federal and state financial assistance unavailable, I was forced to research for private grants and scholarships. After several months of investigation and countless rejections, I stumbled upon a distance learning program from a prominent private university that provided limited financial aid. Applying for aid was somewhat frightening; for I knew that this may be my last chance at furthering my education while in prison. After months of waiting, an award was granted, and the long journey toward a college degree was embarked upon.

Over the past three years I have been awarded nearly $2,500 worth of scholarships and endowments. In addition, to facilitate an easier admissions process post-incarceration; I increased my college entrance exam scores by 52 percent. Although I know that it will be a difficult process reentering society, I stand in a far better position today than I was in 2007.

Persistence, planning, and never relinquishing one's goals is imperative to the reintegration process. Everyday decisions are made with this in mind, and with each successful step toward my goal, self-esteem increases and positive opportunities present themselves. If a mental key possesses the power to lock a prisoner inside a cell, then an advanced education is the key to granting freedom and prosperity.

#####

Prisoner Essay 9.22

"Reentering Society from Prison Is Hard" (2/10/10)
Re-entering society from prison is a very hard task. The best way to make sure the transition is smooth is to prepare for society and make a plan prior to being released. The plan will be the beginning of a new lifestyle that will reduce the chances of recidivism. Although the transition to society is hard it can be done though dedication and determination.

Being accustomed to a regular schedule for a certain amount of years will be hard to tune out. Then the fast pace of the outside world will be a jolt to an ex-inmates mind state. The whole demeanor of the ex-prisoner would have to be adjusted to lift into what society considers regular. To add to the complications it's extremely hard for an ex-inmate to get a job with felonies on their record. They lack the socializing skills and have the gap in employment history.

While inside prison there are a number of things an offender can do to prepare for society. Having outside information about the place you plan on paroling to is a great start. You also have to leave the prison mentality and adopt a more trusting attitude. You should try to obtain a Michigan I.D., birth certificates, and social security number to get on a productive path. Keeping an open mind is also beneficial because you have to start over which means everything may not be as it once was.

Once you're released you have to make sure you maintain your freedom. Keeping a job and staying focused is one of the main things to do. You can also report to a parole officer, attend self help classes, such as N.A. and A.A. and having good influences. You also should have good clean fun like sports or other healthy hobbies to keep from sliding back into old patterns that landed you behind bars in the first place.

Reentering society from prison is a very hard task to complete. You have to start planning and changing prior to being released to start on a productive path. Once your released you have to maintain a job, change your way of thinking, and be more social to reduce the risk of recidivism. Although the transition to society from prison is hard it can be accomplished though preparation, motivation and dedication.

#####

Prisoner Essay 9.23

"A Missile Struck the Hull of My Life" (2/10/10)
Navy General Quarter's drills often include an exercise in which one must brace for shock. First, you grab hold of the nearest stanchion, bunk head, or doorframe, then open your mouth wide, and slightly bend your knees in anticipation of a violent collision. I've often wondered how silly this must have looked: myself and two dozen shipmates from repair locker 3 in sweaty flash gear, placed like extras in a scene from Down Periscope, waiting for the boatswain to yell "boom!" over the 1-mc, then hustling like ants over spilled sugar to repair imaginary damage. Silly perhaps, but I'd seen enough grizzly training footage to know what could happen if any of us weren't prepared to handle whatever the enemy threw at us.

Back in 1993, the enemy could have been one of several saber-rattling remnants of the Cold War, but now, for me at least, it's clearly and unmistakably time. One frigid, unforgiving swathe of it.

It's been sixteen years since I slipped into the dark void of prison, and it will be nearly two more before the parole board will decide if I'm worthy of release. That uncertainty doesn't frighten me. In fact, I don't recall ever feeling frightened of prison itself, on a conscious level that is. Sure, I dreaded walking into a place filled with men who'd cut your throat for your dessert. But prison wasn't a wholly new experience. I knew what is like to live in close quarters with other men; my ship had been smaller than most exercise yards. Even the fabled totalitarianism of the Department of Corrections harbored vestigial echoes of the Uniform Code of Military Justice and an adamant chain of command. Pecking orders, politicking, intimidation; I was prepared to deal with it all. I figured I'd slide though with minimal complications; I'd cause little notice, and soon after my first parole hearing, I'd walk out the gate unblemished.

I've never been so wrong.

I had no hubristic crash and burn, but I surely underestimated many things. Whether it's from staff or inmates, trouble will find you here. Some of it will be your fault—temptation will present itself every day—but most often, it won't be. Simple misunderstandings can bubble into an all out blood vendetta. Even something as innocuous as a $1 bet on a football game can result into sixty days in segregation, an increase in security level and, to punish you yet again years later, the parole board declines to release you. The last decade and a half, assaults, manipulation, robbery, burglary, outright racism, sexual perversion, and an overall lack of compassion have been a part of my daily life, coming from the freshest-numbered prisoners all the way up to the Director of the DOC. Of all the chaos, however, none of it, distilled for every sticking drop of fear, measures up to the terror oozing from the membranous veil of darkness separating me from the world in which I once lived.

I don't pretend to have been blind. I've had access to television and radio, newspapers and magazines, yet media isn't experience. Twenty dollars for a fifteen-minute phone call to my out-of-state family for the majority of my sentence has made regular communication tedious at best. I only know what I'm told.

When I came to prison, computers still filled rooms the size of basketball courts and cell phones were the providence of doctors and drug dealers. The internet was only just crawling from the primordial ooze. If you had to go to the bank for more than a withdrawal, you stood in line with everyone else, and you were thankful if you got out before your lunch hour ended. Many aspects of today's daily routine are quasi science-fictional to me: touch screen phones, hybrid vehicles, text-messaging lexicon, flocks of tweets that seem to darken the sky with their ubiquity, high-definition everything . . . I'm half expecting to parole into a liquid-electric Gibsonian universe where everyone, from earth to the Jovian moons, communicates telepathically. Basically, Moore's law has run amok of my life. And not just in terms of technology.

If I were released today, I can honestly say that I don't know what to expect of the people I know. My personal life is riddled with rifts, and the spaces of familiarity grow narrower every day. I fear that soon the people I love will be as alien to me as my next cell mate. It may sound like an exaggeration, but the facts are that my son was four years old when I came to prison, he's now married. My wife left me, and then came back eight years later although, if my situation doesn't soon improve, she might very well leave again. She hasn't said so, but I know she's sick of waiting. And why should she wait? It's my fault I'm here. She hasn't deserved the pain, the anger, or the guilt she may feel if she does decide to go. No one could fault her for it. Aside from that she has trouble moving around; my father now wears two hearing aids and bifocals. Four of my siblings have been to war; three of which are still fighting. Did I mention my wife served too? I have nine nieces and nephews I've never met. And friends? I count myself blessed to have one left.

I recognize the rifts for what they are, though I don't yet know which are bridgeable and which are un-crossable chasms. Either way, as long as the caustic agents of time continue to erode the walls of the rifts, all I can do is brace for shock against something firm (hope, faith, most likely) until the day the Control Center officer keys the final door and waves me though. Only then will I be able to scramble out and assess the damage. A missile struck the hull of my life sixteen years ago; the longer I have to wait, however, the less that will remain for me to repair.

#####

Prisoner Essay 9.24

"Back to Prison? It's Ok—I Know the Ropes" (2/10/10)
My name is (redacted) and this is my story. I'm from Detroit, Michigan and a father of two girls, 15 and 6. I have a high school diploma. I have job skills in welding, auto mechanic, and home repair. Also I work in print shops and factories as a laborer. When it comes to job skills I'm real good with my hands and physical labor. Like a jack of all trades.

Coming back to prison (the joint) really wasn't that hard or mentally difficult. For several reasons, First, I wasn't committing crimes that carried a lot of time. Mostly stealing cars and stuff like that. I knew that if I got caught I would get a year or two and be out. Second, doing time wasn't hard cause I seen and knew so many people from my hood and the Westside of Detroit; it was like a block reunion. Also I seen people that I was cool with or seen from all over the Detroit area. Sometimes there would be situation where

I had to fight because people in prison are going to try you. But I fought, win or lose because it brought respect. And that is a must. Without respect I wouldn't have made it. I live by the code. There is no snitching. My name is and always will be good.

When it came time to go home and get back into society I would be greeted by my family and friends, with clothes and money go get back on my feet. I would even be hooked up with jobs. Also I knew that if I messed up I would be straight because my family had my back. If I went back to prison I would be alright because I knew the ropes and this cycle repeated itself. This is my story.

#####

The prisoner who wrote the following essay "A Transformed Life Hangs on a Hearing with the Parole Board" was finally granted parole. He has published two books and reflects for us here on what it's like to have your fate depend on what the parole board decides. His case brings up what had been a problem for Michigan prisoners—getting access to mandatory programming in a timely manner; and starting the reentry initiative at the beginning of a prison sentence instead of later.

#####

Prisoner Essay 9.25

"A Transformed Life Hangs on a Hearing with Parole Board" (2/10/10)
Nearly nineteen years into my prison sentence I am preparing to see the parole board for the third time! I am excited, anxious and a bit afraid. I am excited because there are so many positive things I plan to accomplish when I am released. I am anxious because this window of opportunity continues to shrink with each day that passes as I grow older. And I am afraid because I don't know if I can handle another year in prison with my sanity intact. With each flop my internal light of hope diminishes and resignation threatens to sink in. I could die in prison if the current MDOC policy of punishment isn't replaced by a policy of rehabilitation.

Prior to my first two parole board hearings, I held out hope that I would be released when I completed serving my minimum sentence. I believed that in accepting responsibility, I would be given a chance to redeem myself. I was nowhere near the model prisoners that advocacy groups hold up for the public to see. When I first entered the volatile world of prison at the tender age of nineteen, I was bitter, angry, afraid and emotionally confused. And I reacted to the violence, racism, and chaos of the Michigan Reformatory and subsequent facilities based on my distorted feelings and thoughts. The first eight years of my incarceration was marred by multiple misconduct reports that resulted in several trips to solitary confinement. However over the course of the last ten years I have worked tirelessly to transform my life from an uncaring thug into a principled man of purpose. Despite these self-inspirited efforts the parole board has refused to look at the entire picture. Instead they chose to focus only on the snap shots that fit the fear-based politics of the day.

My first parole board hearing was a farce that lasted twelve minutes. The succinct interview was unprofessional and unpleasant. Instead of determining if I was prepared the interviewer sought to emphatically crush the hopes out of me. She was antagonistic in her responses to my answers. She cut me off midsentence anytime I tried to explain what was going on in my nineteen year old mind at the time of the crime. And on several occasions she mocked me as my father looked on helplessly. And when he was asked to speak she cut him off after a mere thirty seconds. We were both devastated. We had been forewarned by others about some members of the parole board, and had both chalked the rumors up to urban legend. There was no way we would have imagined that my father would be treated with a lack of respect after traveling nearly 12 hours from Detroit to attend my hearing. To us it was clear from the onset that she had made her decision prior to me walking in the room. And when the interview was over I felt like I had been pummeled by Floyd Mayweather (a boxer).

When I received notice of my denial two months later I wasn't surprised. She said her reason for denying me a parole was due to the lack of insight I had into why I had committed the crime. She also said I needed to complete AOP (Assaultive Offender Programming). My family and I were grandly disappointed because we had spent nearly a year and half trying to get me into (the AOP psychotherapy) group. And when I was finally placed in group before my first hearing it was canceled a week later. Yet the onus of respon-sibility for programming fell on my shoulders despite the fact there was nothing I could do.

The more I thought about it the worse I felt. The state had it all backwards. Instead of making AOP a requirement at the end of my sentence it should have been offered when I first entered the violent world of prison. Programs like re-entry and AOP should be part of the rehabilitative process from the very beginning. In order for any of the programs to work there has to be a holistic approach to rehabilitation that encompasses the entirety of our sentence. Great consideration must be given to all aspects of the individual. Criminals aren't born in a vacuum; they are manufactured and nurtured in dysfunctional and abusive households, underfunded foster homes, ill equipped juvenile facilities and broken neighborhoods.

Most of the men I grew up in prison alongside came from hard-scrabble backgrounds. We were the victims of physical child abuse, experienced gun-violence early in our development, and abused drugs and alcohol as teenagers. We learned early on to use violence primarily as a defense mechanism and secondarily as a tool of power to ascertain the things we desired out of life. Most of the men I know entered prison with a third grade education and suffer from the lasting effects of post traumatic stress syndrome. And most will leave with a fourth grade education and super post traumatic stress syndrome unless there is a dramatic shift in policy.

Most of us grew up in hoods that are brutally violent and unforgiving. Gun violence is so commonplace that we grow up expecting it around every corner. Not only did it foster in us a deep sense of dread, it also devoured our innocence and humanity. From early on we learned to be reactionary. We reacted to the violence from our formative years with hyper violence in our later years. We reacted by abusing alcohol and drugs to escape our painful existence. We reacted by abusing each other in the most vile and vicious ways imaginable. Degrading and dehumanizing each other became second nature.

We learned to call each other niggas and bitches which was the foundation for the pathology that stripped us of our humanity. By seeing each other as niggas (people who by definition are unworthy of respect and honor) it made it easy for us to shoot and kill each other. By seeing women as bitches and hoes instead of women made it easy for us to objectify them and treat them inferior. It meant nothing for us to ejaculate into them, produce babies and walk away as though they are meaningless, creating another class of victims who will ultimately replace the prisoners who are currently being released.

Waiting until the end of the sentence to address these issues is criminal. Thirty and forty-five day programs cannot undo twenty-five years of distorted thinking. There must be an integrated process that involves the family community, and correction officials. Everyone from officers, counselors, volunteers, educated inmates and the like must be used in the reentry efforts. It is the only way we will see considerable changes in the parole board practices and a reduction in long-term recidivism rates.

There has to be a concerted effort to destroy the prison industrial complex which feeds the fiduciary greed of corporate shareholders. It has to be replaced by a human rehabilitative complex that serves the developmental needs of the men and women who will be reentering society.

These were my most pressing thoughts as I prepared for my second parole board hearing. I was hopeful that the next interviewer would take the time out to look at where I came from and what I had been though that molded and shaped my teenage world view at the time of the crime. And I was hoping they could consider the work I had done to transform my life. And I was prepared for a chance to prove myself worthy of being freed.

The weeks leading up to my second hearing were stressful. I thought about what another denial would mean for me and my family; the thought of telling my son and daughter again that I wouldn't be home was too much to bear. I had no desire to break their hearts a second time around. But all I could do was pray and hope for the best.

Finally on May 20, 2009 I went to the parole board for the second time. It was a beautiful spring day as well as my father's birthday.

When I arrived in the control center where the hearing was to be held I embraced my father, I wished him a happy birthday and he gave me a few words of encouragement. I was the first one on the docket for the day. I was a bit nervous when I entered the room. We were told to wait until the parole board interviewer appeared on the screen before us. I marveled at the technology that allowed us to converse with each other even though we were in different cities. It reminded me of the Jetson's cartoon I used to watch as a child. It also reminded me of how much life had changed since I left the streets in 1991.

I recall how amazed I was when I first heard people talking about Google, gigabytes, online profiles, applications, machines that talk like humans and teckies from India who can fix your computer from thousands of miles away. Listening to them speak this new language was like listening to someone speak Mandarin. I felt like I needed a modern day Rosetta Stone to decipher what they were talking about. If I were to be released I knew I would be entering a world very different from the one I left.

Finally after a brief wait my interview began. The interviewer asked me if the information in parole eligibility report was accurate. I assured her that it was. Then she got down to business.

She allowed me to explain my actions and what was going on in my mind at the time. She didn't cut me off and seemed genuinely interested in hearing things from my point of view. I accepted responsibility for my decisions and explained what I had learned regarding my cognitive process. When I was finished she asked if I had completed AOP. I was excited to tell her I had. She retrieved my termination report from an email and we went over it together. When she finished reading it she asked a few questions for clarification. She then went on to say that it was clear from my AOP report that I had been doing the work I needed to do in order to return to society. When she finished going over the report she then asked what I had done to prepare myself for release.

I responded by telling her that I had taken it upon myself to atone for the crime I committed. As a man I realized saying I was sorry would never be enough. I realized that true remorse and atonement would only come at that point in which I used my personal experience and god given talents to reach out to other at risk youth. So I embarked on a personal journey to reach as many children as I could. I started writing articles and essays for newsletters and newspapers both locally and nationally. The most prominent being the *Michigan Citizen* and *Spreading Hope* the newsletter of Helping Prisoner's Elevate. As a result of my contributions to these publications I was given an opportunity to organize the writing of a children's workbook entitled *Building Bridges: A Workbook for Children with an Incarcerated Parent.*

I told her about the introduction I wrote to an anti-gang book entitled *windows 2 my soul* by Yusef Shakur which is now part of the Wayne State University curriculum. I informed her of the release of my debut novel *crack vol. 1* which is a cautionary tale centered in Detroit which is now part of the recommended reading for the University of Wisconsin-Platteville social science and human relation class. Written in the gritty voice of the streets it's a story that addresses the far reaching consequences of the drugs and violence that ravage our community. In addition to the aforementioned writings, I showed her two of my essays which had just been published in the follow up to *chicken soup for the prisoner's soul* entitled "Serving Productive Time."

She listened intensely as I enumerated my accomplishments I shared the countless support letters I had received from people all over the country who were eager to work with me upon my release. They ranged from professors at UNC to newspaper publishers and community groups. I told her of the college level correspondence courses I had taken for writing and other classes I had taken though the University of Michigan. And finally she listened as my father told her of the response he had received from the children's book and all of the organizations that sent him emails requesting I mentor their teenagers. After nearly forty-five minutes the interview was finally over I felt good about my chances of being paroled after serving eighteen years.

I waited anxiously for two months before the parole board returned with a decision. When my counselor called me in her office I could sense from her body language the news wasn't good. When she told me they denied me for the second time it knocked the wind out of me. My thoughts raced to my children and my father. I knew they were going to be crushed and that was the hardest part of it all. In getting incarcerated I had imprisoned my family and everyone who loved and cared about me.

A few weeks after my parole board hearing I received a copy of my case summary report and discovered that the woman who interviewed me had voted to parole me. The decision then went to a second parole board member who voted against me despite the fact he had never seen me. Due to it being a split decision my file went before a third board member. The third board member voted against all logic. How could they be more informed than the women who interviewed me? What if the roles were reversed. What if she would have voted against me after the interview, but her partner had of voted to release me? Who would the third voter gone with, the lesser informed individual? Many questions with far too few answers.

How is it that some men with no education, no job prospects and few life skills being released while others continue to be warehouse? Why aren't parole board hearings made public like trials? Why are our families denied real answers regarding our release? And how can one parole board member say the following: "completed AOP with above average remarks, several other significant programs listed, has college credits. Has helped write a book for children, continued with other self help programs, has strong community support with parents and other family members. Has potential and used his time to better himself" and two others see something entirely different?

In order for true justice to be served there must be transparency when it come to parole board hearings. And in order for rehabilitation to reach its apex the efforts of the offender has to be met with the efforts of the community.

As the date of my third parole board hearing nears I continue to fight to hold onto the flickering light of hope at the end of the tunnel. But more importantly I continue to raise critical questions for those who are willing to listen. And hopefully through this process we can effectuate change!

#####

Prisoner Essay 9.26

"Two Mink Coats and Recidivism" (10/7/09)
The two mink coats interview/report.

Antonio: Are you a parole violator?

Anonymous inmate: Yes

Antonio: Did you come back with a new sentence?

Anonymous inmate: Yes

Antonio: If you don't mind me asking what were you first incarcerated for?

Anonymous inmate: 2nd degree murder

Antonio: Are you back for 2nd degree murder? If not, what for?

Anonymous inmate: No I'm not back for 2nd degree murder. I'm back for receiving and concealing two mink coats.

Antonio: Why in the heck are you back for two mink coats?

Anonymous inmate: Because I purchased them for $1,000 apiece the person sold it to me got caught and told on everybody he sold coats to.

Antonio: so you bought the coats from a Booster?

Anonymous inmate: yes

Antonio: Wow! You are the first person I've met in prison that back for buying two mink coats. How much time did you get sentenced with?

Anonymous inmate: 1 year

Antonio: Ok! You have to tell me your one year story

Anonymous inmate: I came from Chicago to bring my daughter back to see my parents. My mother told me that my uncle had been sick, so I went to see him. While I was at my uncle's house my cousin pulled up with a friend of his. His friend showed me some mink coats that he wanted to get rid of. I didn't see any harm because my cousin was hanging with him so I thought the coats were his. Anyway, the guy gave me a deal; two coats for $1,000 a piece, the guy ended up getting caught up and gave the cops names of all he sold coats to.

Antonio: How many years did you spend in prison your first bit?

Anonymous inmate: 14 years.

Antonio: upon release from doing 14 years, what type of support did you have when you got out and how long did you stay out before catching this case?

Anonymous inmate: I had the support of my family and numerous amounts of church bishops and ministers that knew me personally. I also had the support of both my children's mothers and friends. I was home for 2 years, 2 months.

Antonio: if released today how would you go about finding a job to support you and your children and what will you be doing to stay out of prison?

Anonymous inmate: I'm glad to say, the same jobs that I had before I left are still available to me. To stay out of here, I won't try to take anymore shortcuts to acquire things I want. If I want them I'll save money to purchase them legally! The guy that I work for in the church ministry and juvenile programs is flying here to Michigan in November to attend my parole hearing.

Antonio: I hope that you're sincere and true in staying out of prison and remember, a man is as strong as he pushes himself to be and as weak as he let himself be. Don't let your want for material things take away your freedom. Thanks for the interview.

Anonymous inmate: You're welcome.

Synopsis of our take home handout and interview:

I'm 22, I've been here in prison for only 4 years and I have 6 more to go. Upon my release I do not plan on coming back. The interview that I had with this anonymous inmate was interesting. Majority of individuals that I've seen come back to prison on parole violations were those who either sold drugs or robbed somebody. Many of whom do return to prison say how they came back was because of circumstances, so they say.

The Michigan Prisoner Reentry Initiative I find to be helpful to many prisoners on their getting out based on the comments I've read in the Detroit Free Press. A lot of people, who was a part of that program that came back, were because of lack of patience. Circumstances in my opinion have little to do with anything. Before I came to prison I was in Juvenile. In 2003, I spent 5 months in the detention center for joy riding and was released on probation. I was also put on tether for 2 months for assault. The next year 2004, I was back in juvenile for carjacking, that case got dismissed. I have to say the choices I've made were my reasons for going back. I had a strong support group and I was involved in special programs that were for me to be a part of while on probation but I had to be ready to change my way of thinking in order to not re-offend again and I wasn't ready.

Reentering back into the community without making a complete change within oneself will increase a person's chances in coming back to prison. The FGDM (family group decision making) program could help bring about change in a prisoner. If that program was active in Michigan our crime rate and recidivism rate would be lower than it is now. Internally a man or women would feel loved because of the fact that their family is completely involved in their reentry.

Family and friend support plays a big role in a parolee life. Family at times can influence some of the decisions a person makes sort of like the anonymous in mate. His cousin hanging around the booster so the anonymous inmate felt that was OK. Him coming back to prison really doesn't make any sense, but according to the research done by CAPPS, it does. Recidivism is defined in the Webster dictionary as a relapse in criminal behavior. CAPPS defines recidivism by whether the person returned to prison in Michigan within four years of release.

The man bought a coat from his cousin friend and now he's back in prison. He didn't relapse into criminal behavior; he did what anybody else would if they run across a good deal on something.

#####

Prisoner Essay 9.27

"Recidivism and Reentry" (10/7/09)
The Reentry programs in Michigan have brought new hope and disappointment for some men and women in the prison system. I have been incarcerated for 25 years and it has been my experience that the reentry program has different results depending on what county you are from.

As illustrated in the *Warehouse Prison* by John Irwin (2005), I've seen that the disorganization of prison life contributes substantially to a parolee's failure in reentering society. They have become dependent on others doing almost everything for them. Providing food, shelter, tell them when to sleep, when to wake up, when to make their beds, where they can and cannot go, how to do this and that. What the routine of the day really is, how to act and what they can or cannot say. Further, in the Detroit area, where I am from, upon release, many of them men and women find it difficult to find jobs and housing because a very high percentage of parolees never had a home prior to coming to prison. They may have been in a child protective services program (like foster care), a ward of the state (in juvenile facility), or just plan homeless due to the mortgage crisis nationwide. Their families may have had a home but lost it during the time of their incarceration. In many of those mortgage crisis cases families have moved out of state and a parolee leaving the penal system may not be approved to leave the state. So they are left to count on the Michigan Prison Reentry Initiative for commercial (home) placement. Often times this will delay their release to the Detroit area due to the lack of available placement.

In other instances, you have sex offenders who find it difficult to find acceptable home placement. The many restrictions on a person convicted of a sex crime hinders their ability to be in areas where children may reside or the commercial placement may be near a school which is prohibited for a person convicted of a sex offense. These are situations that delay release and add to the prison budget crisis we face in Michigan.

One parolee had completed a fifteen year sentence. He was originally sentenced to 8 to 20 years for second degree murder. He had written several children's books, established a nonprofit organization with his family to give the proceeds from the book sales to underprivileged children. The parole board had given him several flops (continuous) in spite of the fact he had made this transformation while incarcerated. In 2008, he was instructed to enter into the MPRI program prior to release. While in the program, he discovered that many of the programs and training offered for parolees in the Detroit area were minimal or inadequate for anyone to genuinely seek employment. He was so disappointed in what the program offered that he voiced his opinion in a platform the National Lifers of America Inc. had set up with state legislators in a town hall meeting. It was one of the first-of-a-kind where elected officials came into the prison setting and heard the opinions of the prisoners in an open forum. During the town hall meeting the parolees that were scheduled for release in two days made his complaints known. He spoke of the job seeking training of filling out a resume, how to conduct yourself in an interview, how to account for the years spent incarcerated and other issues of this nature. His complaints really upset many of the prison administrators as well as the legislators in attendance. Many legislators had no clue that the program was not meeting the standard and requirements of the people it was designed to serve. Following the town hall meeting several emails and phone calls were made to prison officials concerning the allegations put forth. Needless to say, there were no other programs of this magnitude held. The primary organizer of the NLA program was transferred and all programming at the facility was halted for years to come.

The ideal of the MPRI program is a wonderful concept. The primary downfall is the bureaucratic process it takes for the funds to reach their intended goals. In Macomb County the MPRI has been successful in providing a vehicle for parolees, and apartments with expenses paid, and meaningful employment. In Monroe County, the MPRI program provides apartments, minimum utility usage, and cell phones for parolees to seek potential employment. But often time, you have parolees who are not accustomed to the mainstream way of life. It is just not their intentions to utilize the programs offered or available to them though any program. I have known some parolees to get money from social security, the chance of a life program, and still return to the street life. They use the initial large sum of money to purchase drugs and return to destructive behavior. Upon their return to prison, they attempt to justify their illicit drug and return to saying life is fast and they had to play catch up. I've learned that most prisoners returning home are less prepared for reintegration, more likely to have had health or substances abuse problems in the past, and typically are not as connected to community-based support structures. I've seen that it is their desire for material possession that dominate their very existence and overwhelm their commonsense.

So in short, it had been my experience that what county you reside in plays a larger role in the Michigan Reentry Program as to what services are available and your chances of success with those programs. According to an Urban institute, Prisoner Reentry report by Amy L. Solomon, Gillian L. Thomsom and Sinead Keegan who examined prisoner reentry in Michigan, at the end of 2003, 17,449 people were on parole; during that year 3,806 parolees were returned to prison. About one-third (34 percent) of those released in 2003 were released to Wayne county. Of those, 80 percent returned to Detroit. Ultimately, it is an individual decision and the choices one makes that determines their success of becoming a productive member in society.

#####

In assigning prisoner essays to college students as reading assignments in a "Criminology and Prevention" class, the author got many types of responses. Here is one.

#####

College Student Essay 9.28

"An Adrian College Student's Take" (10/7/09)
It seems that environment plays a large role in the rates of reentry for felons. They are charged once with what is perceived as a minor crime and then get back out and fall right back into old habits. They spend time with the same people, go to the same places, stir up the same kind of mischief as before. Only this time the minor crime has already been committed. Such crimes hold no more interest and so they're out committing a larger offense. Without the environment they went back to, they very well could have turned out completely different.

I also believe negative community perspective keeps felons as felons. Granted in some ways the perspective of felons as a black mark on society, some people and organizations take it too far. How are they to even improve themselves and become a functioning member of society if they are cut off from opportunities at every corner?

Together these two aspects keep felons in their own sort of social class where they learn criminal association. That is, they are told they are criminals and grouped together with worse offenders and so begin to see themselves as criminals with that mind set how are they to reform themselves? They're told they're criminals, they believe they're criminals, they are criminals. In their minds this is the most they can expect out of life and if they should remain out for a couple months between sentences, lucky them.

#####

Prisoner Essay 9.29

"I've Matured" (10/7/09)
My childhood was much like a lot of other guys, where at a young age (ten) I caught my first felony and I didn't stop there—it got worse. Basically I didn't have any authority figure at home to tell me what to do or how to do things. My mother and father were on drugs and still are, so as you can see, I raised myself.

Me and my brothers raised each other the best way we knew how and after getting somewhat older one of my older brothers caught a murder case at sixteen. He has been incarcerated going on thirty years. You would have thought that would have woke the rest of us up. It didn't. We started, or rather continued, to do crimes to land us behind bars. Here I sit writing this essay but also my story about my life. I'm glad though I've matured from a boy into a man, it has been hard by no means, but I'm still here.

#####

Prisoner Essay 9.30

"Why I Went Back to Indulging in Criminal Activity" (10/7/09)
Since this is not my first time being incarcerated I choose to write about my own return to confinement, and express my opinion on why I went back to indulging in criminal activity.

This is my first and only prison sentence; however at age fifteen I was confined to the jurisdiction of the juvenile courts. I was sent to a boy's camp in Houghton Lake, Mich. In all, I spent a little over seven months locked up there. That experience made me really consider my future, and I attempted to make plans for success. I was young, and I had no idea of how life could turn out, or what circumstances we can face tomorrow.

The place I was at was called Camp Nokomis Challenge Center. The program was designed to place young men in trying situations with the attempt to bring out the best in them. Our daily itinerary for activity was always full. From waking up in the morning and working out, to working in the kitchen serving the other prisoner, and lastly going to some class which taught sex education, and other academic studies.

On seven separate occasions we went on camping trips, including one to Baraboo, Wisconsin, where we had to rock climb at a real rock climbing site. Which was rather unique due to the fact that I was a young dude fresh out of the projects, and never seen life outside of an urban city.

I had no idea people had cows and horses in their front yard. I didn't even know that Michigan had bears or any other wild life except for squirrels, and stray dogs and cats I seen often, not to mention the rats in the city. So the great outdoors was kind of fascinating to me. One can argue that that was not jail. To confirm that it was, every night our room door were locked, and when we went on camping trips we were usually way up north somewhere. The staff would jokingly say, "We've never had a black guy escape before." Of course not, why would I go? I was a little too far from River Rouge, Michigan.

While there I actually started to make plans to change my life, but my options one in the same, so I choose the lesser of two evils. Instead of going back to River Rouge to live with my parents, I arranged to go live on the east side with my uncle. Both of my parents were addicts and it wouldn't be much discipline at home. My uncle sold weed, and his house was a house where people came by to buy weed, but between him and my father, he was the better role model, or so I thought.

Upon my release I made several plans . . . I was not to go back to selling drugs, I was not going to smoke weed or drink, and I was going to get some kind of job. And just stay out of trouble.

I was released on May 7th, 1995. My first day out, my uncle's girl rolled up a joint and brought it to me, she said, "Jamie, you want a hit of this?" It smelt kind of good, and since scent is the strongest sense tied to memory, I instantly remembered how good it make me feel, so I took her up on her offer. That was the beginning of a downward spiral.

I later attempted to get a job at McDonalds, but since I didn't have any form of I.D. they would not hire me. So I asked my uncle to give me some weed. And he obliged.

Then June 9th came, and I was told that my father passed. Since he was the real reason I didn't want to go home, his death was my excuse to go back. I tried to convince myself that my mom needed my assistance with my younger brother, and sister, which was true, but I still really just wanted to go back to my old neighborhood.

I went home the day of my dad's funeral. Later that day a couple of my homies came and gave me some crack to get on my feet. That night I was back to selling drugs. Ten months later I turned seventeen, ten days after that I was in the county jail on my way to prison, and I have not been free since.

There are many factors that helped bring about my return . . .

1. I had no education, prior to coming to prison the highest grade I completed was the 5th. But I had a first grade reading/comprehension level. I was literally stupid.
2. I had no real plan, I just didn't want to come back to jail, so that's why I wanted to do right, but I didn't consider failure, and road blocks, or relapse, I just hoped that things would work out.
3. I really didn't change, I was the same person, I just had acquired some life skills and experiences, particularly being locked up, which made this prison transition rather smooth. I knew what to expect.

Because of these experience's, I know what to avoid once I'm free. In the 14 years I've been in prison I've seen numerous people come back and the reasons for doing so varies from person to person. But what is true is this: if a person really valued freedom he wouldn't put himself in situations that would bring him back here. Obviously we value other things over freedom.

#####

The author brings his Adrian College students to the local prisons to participate in the "Social Science and Personal Writing" class (see Appendix). Oftentimes students who are attracted to a criminal justice major will have known someone—in their family, or among friends and acquaintances—who went to prison. Often the story involves drugs.

#####

College Student Essay 9.31

"Adrian College Student's Friend: Prison, Then Got Clean—Finishes B.A." (10/7/09)
Someone close to me, got into drugs heavily, and it affected everyone around him.

When he was a teenager he was arrested and thrown in jail for a few months. When they released him at first he was fine and stayed away from it, but later on he found himself in the same mess as before. This time, though, he was thrown in jail because one of his friends overdosed, and since the person found his friend, the police thought that he had something to do with it. The person ended up having an alibi for his whereabouts and then it became clear it was just an accidental overdose.

My friend said he would never do that again but when it came around to it, he ended up in jail for another time. This time he was tried as an adult for he was over the age. He spent several months in jail, and while in prison, he worked hard to get clean, and has been free from drugs for several years now.

The factor behind it was because he had help from his family and friends and once he was out he did not return to the group of people that he normally hung out with. He stayed away from them and ended up going back to school.

He now has his high school diploma and his bachelor's degree in English. The prison that he was in also helped by giving him counseling sessions and helping rehabilitate him, and he thanks God for even the mistakes that he has made and lives by the morals he now has.

#####

Prisoner Essay 9.32

"Remember: Most Prisoners Will Be Getting Out" (2/10/10)
This is my first time in prison, and I have been locked up almost ten years now. This has given me plenty of time to think on re-entry into society, and recidivism, making sure I don't ever come back in any way. Especially now that I have only two years till I have my chance for parole.

Re-entry into society from our prison system in Michigan has gotten better in the last few years, just because of a few new programs. Before these new programs that help one transition into society, what they did have, helped no one at all. This resulted in a higher recidivism rate. Since implementation of these new programs, like M.P.R.I. (Michigan Prisoner Re-entry Initiative), a lot less people are returning to prison, even on simple P.V.s (parole violations). I am glad that I am witnessing this for myself. It gives me even greater hope, not just for me but many of my fellow prisoners here.

As for me, re-entry into society should go easy, although I still have my reservations about it. I have the love and support of my family, which not all have. I will have a place to live and the essential necessities, until I can get out on my own again. I also have some of my own things that were stored for me still out there. Anything else that I will need, again, family will help me with. My biggest worries are that work will be harder to find with having a criminal record on top of our bad economy and unemployment. I should do fine though; I don't have high expectations, and will accept whatever jobs there are. I am pretty sure that I will fit back into society okay. Yes, it can be a hard transition from here to there, but I have made sure that this place did not change me for the worse. If anything, I have used my time here to better myself, with no help from the MDOC. So, besides for some anxiety, it should be all happiness, excitement and enjoying my freedom.

The problem is, not many in here have the love and support that I do. Since they don't have that, not much about them has changed while being in here, let alone getting out. So it needs to be up to the MDOC, and people in society, to help the prisoner re-enter properly into the real world upon his release. This is why programs are needed in here and out there. Otherwise he will be back. That brings my thoughts back to recidivism.

There will always be those who commit new crimes after being released from prison, and those who return because of parole violations. It is just inevitable. Not all will, or can be changed—they like the criminal life. But that is a smaller percentage than what society thinks it actually is. Let me put it this way, if ten prisoners are released from prison, only four returns because of committing a new crime, should we throw all ten back in prison because of four persons crimes? I would hope your answer is no, but this is what the people in our society are asking of the MDOC when they say to just keep them all locked up as long as possible, just because of the few that got out and committed a new crime.

As an individual, I have no control over what another person decides to do, so don't punish me longer than needed, because of another's actions. Instead, as more prisoners are needing to be released, put some of the savings of money from that into programs that work to lower recidivism as much as possible.

Remember, most of the prisoners will be getting out some time, so society needs to decide what kind of person they want to have re-enter into their neighborhoods.

Next, help by getting the state to implement the programs needed to promote a good re-entry and lower recidivism.

As for me, just thinking on re-entry and the chance of recidivism, has helped me so I will be successful when I am released. I will always hope and pray, that the MDOC and our state, will make the changes needed to trim our oversized prison system, that consumes more money than need be, which does not make our communities any safer.

#####

RISE OF CONVICT CRIMINOLOGY

Many people who are convicts change and mature. Once released, between 30 to 70 percent of those leaving prison do not recidivate (return to prison). This varies by state; for instance, Michigan's recidivism rate is close to 32 percent while California's recidivism rate is close to 70 percent.

A handful of ex-cons have been "making good" in the academic field after getting some prison college, being released, and going on to graduate education, attaining the PhD, and becoming professors.

The late John Irwin, professor emeritus at San Francisco State University, author of several books long used in criminal justice classes, was himself an ex-felon. He told the story of growing up in his younger days in the late 1950s that, among some in his neighborhood, it seemed cool to be a safecracker. Irwin decided to be a safecracker. Then, he reports, "They made it harder to crack a safe." He moved on to robbery—a big mistake—and he went to prison for five years. He was, of course, labeled a criminal.

But convict John Irwin got the opportunity to take some college courses while in prison. He began to affiliate himself as a student. Upon his transition after release from the prison in the early 1960s, and with this new "student" identity, Irwin went on to complete a PhD at the University of California–Berkeley, publishing his doctoral dissertation, *The Felon*, in 1970. John Irwin subsequently became a professor at San Francisco State University. The key to his life story was the availability of prison college.

Over the years 1972 to 1995, about 10 percent of prisoners in the United States had access to prison college through the Pell grant program. Then, in a punitive turn, Congress ended prisoner eligibility for Pell grants in 1994 and the prison college programs ended.

However, a small number of ex-felons who had been imprisoned mainly for drug or drug-related crimes, and who had taken some prison college while it was available, hit the academic trail upon release to continue their higher education. In 1996, Chuck Terry, one of the academic ex-cons, finishing his PhD at University of California–Riverside, organized (with help from Joan Petersilia), the beginnings of a movement that would subsequently develop as "convict criminology." This network of ex-con academics, leaving prison and entering the nations' universities and colleges, has gone on to have an influence on academic criminology. Several ex-con academics now mentor new "convict criminologists" coming up through graduate education (see *Journal of Prisoners on Prison* 21, Nos. 1 and 2 [2012]).

The ex-con criminologists made it out of street-drug culture and crime to higher education, professional academic jobs, personal transformation and health. They often have a critique of the U.S. incarceration binge. Teaching at various colleges and universities in the United States the convict criminology professors have written books, book chapters, and journal articles analyzing the prison system from prisoner and ex-con perspectives. As Ross and Richards, as editors, say in their "Introduction" to the reader *Convict Criminology*:

> The outlines of the new school of convict criminology's mission and purpose emerged as writers shared the experiences they have had with prison and academia. This represents an effort to revitalize the criminological literature with research validated by personal experience. Together, these academic authors critique existing theory and present new research from a convict or insider perspective. In short, they "tell it like it is." In doing so, they hope to convey the message that "it's about time" (Austin and Irwin 2001)—time served, time lost and time that taught us the lessons we share (Ross and Richards 2003: 9)

EXERCISES 9.1–9.2

Exercise 9.1

In reading the story about "Homosexuality at MR" about the "Gladiator Prison"—what prison policies could reduce the sexual predation described?

Exercise 9.2

Analyze the "Life Story in a Few Pages" prisoner essay. Apply three or more criminology theories to this story.

DISCUSSION AND REVIEW QUESTIONS

1. Compare the stories about "Being Criticized for Improving Yourself" with the section "Becoming Interested in Other Things" (and the Honor Dorm). How could an "alternative community" to "the yard" in prison be created and sustained? What would such an alternative community consist of?
2. Many prisoners are parents. How could they see their kids and be a part of their family more often? In Sweden, Norway, and Finland they have

"family leave" where selected prisoners can go home on weekends. What do you think of this idea?

3. Describe the "Ending the Culture of Street Crime" movement by the LIFERS group and National Lifers Association (NLA).
4. Describe the reforms for parole and reentry practices advocated by Joan Petersilia.
5. What does it mean for prisoners to do "self-work" and to "become interested in other things"?
6. Why would having ex-cons, people returning from prison, help in drug counseling program or crime prevention programs be a good idea?
7. Why would a prisoner be "scared" of returning to society?
8. Do you know of anyone who went to prison? Describe what you know of his or her story and relate it to this book.

10

Conclusion

Like many Americans growing up in the 1950s and 1960s, I experienced the racism present in American life—incidents of prejudice and discrimination I encountered as a young, white, early 1960s university student. When I started teaching at Jackson Prison in Michigan, in 1981, I knew little about prisons or prisoners, but I learned over a thirty-year period about prison teaching. When the prison college programs were ended in 1995, prodded by former prison college teachers now out of work to help create a movement for reinstating prison college, I started to study the issue.

During the mid-1980s, I witnessed the new mandatory minimums (long-sentence) laws impact on my Michigan Reformatory prison college classes. "War on Drugs" prisoners came into my classes. Then, in the 1990s, I witnessed the scale-up of prison building that took Michigan from fourteen to thirty-four prisons. In 1998, I joined the start-up, statewide Citizens Alliance on Prisons and Public Spending (www.capps-mi.org), which was forged to reduce sentence length and shift resources to prevention.

THE GEOPOLITICAL DIVIDE

I studied the basic problems causing "the prison state": racism; punishment rather than health care approaches to drugs; punitive law with overly long sentences; and the politicization of crime, cops, courts, and corrections. And, underlying all of this, the fifty-year transition from "communal ghetto" to "hyperghetto" attendant to the change in industrial mix from manufacturing to services, the disinvestment in the city and the subsequent political abandonment of the ghetto poor. Commenting on Detroit's bankruptcy in 2013, former U.S. labor secretary Robert Reich notes:

> [T]here is a more basic story here, and it's replicated across America: Americans are segregating themselves by income more than ever before.

Forty years ago, most cities—including Detroit—had a mixture of wealthy, middle-class, and poor residents. Now, each income group tends to live separately, in its own city, with its own tax bases and philanthropies.

Those support, at one extreme, excellent schools, resplendent parks, rapid-response security, efficient transportation, and other first-rate services; or, at the opposite extreme, terrible schools, dilapidated parks, high crime, and third-rate services.

The geopolitical divide has become so palpable that being wealthy in America today means not having to come across anyone who isn't.

Detroit is a devastatingly poor, mostly black, increasingly abandoned island in the midst of a sea of comparative affluence that's mostly white. (Reich 2013)

As an outcome, and reinforcing all these developments, as outlined by Jonathan Simon, the 1967 Safe Street Act developed a new "governing through crime" political formula.

For twenty years I have been teaching college criminology courses and out of that experience and joining the "Convict Criminology" movement, I have been encouraged to develop publications that bring out the prisoners' voice.

I have tried to listen to what prisoners have to say—about their lives, about what caused them to go to prison. So I've asked them to write on their lives giving, in informal stories, responses to "how the criminology theories" relate to their lives.

In order to write this book I have had to read both classic criminology works and recent academic books on crime and select from these readings handout material for prisoners to consider (see the appendix).

Over the twelve years I have been doing this (2002–2014) this book gradually took shape. I have also been using the prisoner essays in my criminology classes for several years, and learning from the Adrian College criminal justice students whom I teach.

I used Farrington and Welsh, *Saving Children from a Life of Crime* (2007) as one of my sets of criminological handouts for the prisoners, as well as using the book as a text in my main-campus criminology and prevention class. I constructed table 1.1, "A Public Health Model of Early Childhood Prevention: Early Risk Factors for Offending and Effective Interventions," to summarize Farrington and Welsh's work. Their book introduces conclusions from the best prospective longitudinal studies on crime and prevention. The book reviews individual, family, and community level factors (predictive and protective). Chapters 5, 6, and 7 of *Prisoners on Criminology* has been structured around Farrington and Welsh. I have used several other criminology textbooks and research studies in this book as well.

The more psychological approach that Farrington and Welsh take has a strength at the individual and family level of criminogenic factors, but is weak at the "community" or sociological level factors. In particular, they do not ask the questions: Why and how does the United States wind up with so many deprived areas *within* which to "grow up in a low socioeconomic household," "associated with a delinquent," and "attend a high delinquency rate school." Why do we have the degree of poverty we have and what are the consequences?

Thus I have made a special effort in chapter 7 to answer these questions. Farrington and Welsh are strong on the *psychological* and *social psychological* levels of crime and prevention explanations, perhaps because their book is recommending a *national crime prevention program* that is *politically feasible* if there were to be a U.S. congressional bipartisan vote.

But the question of why we have so many jobless ghettos from which the United States has built the world's largest prison system demands a deeper analysis. *Sociological criminology* as examined by Karen Parker's linkage of change in urban labor markets and crime rates, cause Williamson, Imbroscio, and Alperovitz to believe that the United States needs more localization of investment to anchor a stable community economy, and Loic Wacquant's "institutional" analysis focusing on federal, state, and local governmental political decisions as the appropriate domain level of analysis needed to further a policy of guaranteed income—these and other "solving root problems" are a necessary "level of analysis" that too many criminology textbooks fail to include. And it is the prisoners' voices that have brought me to this conclusion.

Urie Brofenbrenner's "community psychology" alerts us to the need for micro-system (individual, family, and peers) analysis to be linked to macro-system realities (community, urban labor markets, localization of investment versus corporate disinvestment, regional and federal policy, etc.) (Brofenbrenner 1979). As Robert Reich concludes:

> While the Detroit city population fell by 62 percent between 1950 and 2012, metropolitan Detroit grew by 42 percent during the same period. Detroit's wealthy and most of its middle class moved from the city to the suburbs.
>
> Much in modern America depends on where you draw boundaries—who's inside and who's outside. Who is included in the social contract?
>
> If Detroit is defined as the larger metropolitan area that includes its suburbs, it has enough money to provide all its residents with adequate—if not good—public services, without falling into bankruptcy.
>
> It would come down to a question of whether the more-affluent areas of this Detroit were willing to subsidize the poor inner city through their tax dollars and help it rebound. That's an awkward question that the more-affluent communities probably would rather not face
>
> . . . In an era of widening inequality, this is how wealthier Americans are quietly writing off the poor. (Reich 2013)

If, with the jobless ghetto, comes a "new social type"—the contemporary poor black male with an oppositional culture—and if the prison system has 50 percent of prisoners being African American from these jobless ghettos, then we need to do something about these jobless "hyperghettos."

Because the politicization of crime, cops, courts, and corrections has occurred through the "governing through crime" noted by Simon, we've had to detour through chapters 2 and 3 of this book to sketch out in some detail where the nation's political culture over prisons and the ghetto is right now.

PUTTING THE BRAKES ON PRISON GROWTH

State corrections budgets are high. However, there is a growing interest in a harm reduction approach to drugs and a gradually increasing interest in a public health model for crime prevention.

> In the summer of 2013 U.S. Attorney General Eric Holder announced that "low-level, nonviolent drug offenders with no ties to gangs or large drug organizations will no longer be charged with offenses that impose severe mandatory sentences. . . . A vicious cycle of poverty, criminality, and incarceration traps too many Americans and weakens too many communities," Mr. Holder will say, according to excerpts of his remarks. . . . "Too many Americans go to prison for far too long and for no good law enforcement reason," Mr. Holder plans to say. "We cannot simply prosecute or incarcerate our way to becoming a safer nation." (Holder 2013)

The brakes are beginning to be applied on the growth of U.S. prison populations but without revising sentencing lengths, justice reinvestment in high impact communities, and major social policy shift on jobs or income to alleviate U.S. urban poverty, it will be hard to bring the prison populations down and shift resources to prevention.

Effective crime prevention programs must recognize the interactions of individual, family, and community (Farrington and Welsh 2007: 88). If street life is more ordinary than 9-to-5 jobs in these abandoned inner-city neighborhoods, if the youth of these jobless ghettos are marching into illegal activities, and if the magnetism of street life continues to influence youth growing up within a rising tide of social disorganization, then there will need to be a program of *community level crime prevention*.

The pieces of community-level crime prevention need to include both metropolitan-, regional-, state-, and national-level policies to move beyond the "drug crime era." In a handful of states the percentage of prison admittance for drug crimes has begun to fall. One report has Michigan falling from 21 percent to 8 percent for new admissions for drug crime in the period 2008–2013. This was accomplished through efforts by FAMM, and some enlightened Michigan legislators. In Michigan, people with drug problems that have not been involved in violent crimes are handled increasingly in community corrections (probation, mandatory treatment in group homes with case management) and drug courts.

Still, concentrated disadvantage, which is the intersection of economic deprivation and family disruption concentrated within particular racial groups, persist and grows. The United States has become an increasingly unequal society. The rise of a *prison incarceration binge culture* has made the prison experience inside harder—more warehousing than rehabilitative—although the new prisoner reentry initiatives are helpful. Still, entire urban ghetto neighborhoods are being incarcerated (Clear 2007).

Racial disparity continues in U.S. prisons with 50 percent of the prison population being African Americans. In terms of offense categories, prison is a mixed bag, but the root problems of urban cities have festered to such an extent that, as mentioned, Detroit has declared bankruptcy.

The prison build-up movement for many years tended to neglect the possibilities of community corrections (probation, tethering, house arrest, day-reporting centers). In recent years these "community corrections" approaches have begun to be used more. However, fundamental community problems remain.

ADDRESSING THE STRONGEST PREDICTORS OF CRIME RATES

The strongest predictors of crime rates are factors related to "concentrated disadvantage" which is the intersection of economic deprivation and family disruption, concentrated with particular racial groups; long term chronic unemployment; and stingy social policies that undermine levels of social support for citizens. (Pratt 2009: 67)

Pratt, in noting the "get-tough punitive womb has begat such fine crime control offspring as jails that are tent-cities in Arizona, the chain gang in the South, television programs like the ineffective 'scared straight,'" concludes that policy makers like such programs because they seem tough and cheap and the media like them "because they simply make good TV."

Instead, effective crime control policy first requires targeting the factors that are actually related to crime. . . . This means policies aimed at ameliorating the effects of economic deprivation and family disruption—especially in community contexts with large proportions of racial minorities. . . . These policies could come in the form of social support efforts on the part of public or private entities to help families stay stable in the face of economic hardship, such as early intervention programs for at-risk families and youth; financial, housing, and transportation assistance; and quality health care and education programs (Currie 1998). Some scholars have also suggested that directed efforts at job creation, systematic efforts to upgrade working wages, and greater support for labor organization in communities characterized by economic deprivation may help to reduce crime (W. J. Wilson 1996).

It is important to note that these approaches to crime control do not require a radical transformation of the existing social structure. For example, Pratt and Godsey's (2003) cross-national analysis of 46 countries found that those that devoted a greater portion of the GDP to health care and education experienced significantly lower rates of violent crime (in particular, homicides). . . . Thus, increases in levels of social support in these areas are capable of producing concomitant reductions in crime, even in the absence of a social and economic revolution—the impossible task that policy makers have often invoked for ignoring the recommendations of academics. Still, this approach does require a shift in a fundamental assumption of human behavior, to one that says crime may be more effectively reduced by doing something *for* a person rather than doing something *to* a person (see, e.g., the discussion in Cullen, Wright, and Chamlin 1999).

. . . [A]dopting a more progressive crime control policy agenda that specifically targets the multiplicity of negative effects associated with concentrated disadvantage is much more likely to result in a substantial reduction in crime. (Pratt 2009: 101–2)

Better education in the inner-city neighborhoods and more postsecondary educational opportunity in prison would help. Alienated, undereducated, unemployed kids just hanging out feed into the state prison systems. Child neglect and parental criminality feed new recruits into prison, along with addiction. Families are seemingly the greatest contributor to criminality in their children. Addressing the feminization of poverty, single poor women with children need much more social support.

This book presents many prisoner stories that focus on dysfunctional families. However, to repeat, the micro system of individual and family are connected to the macro-system level of community, urban labor markets, and corporate and governmental decision making and policies.

The institutional transformation that Wacquant describes from communal ghetto to hyperghetto has involved mass unemployment, deproletarianization, increasing labor precariousness, relegation to decaying neighborhoods, and heightened stigmatization (2008: 24–25). The economic and political roots of this hyperghettoization need to be kept in focus. Even as Detroit entered the economic and political semiparalysis of official bankruptcy in the summer of 2013 there has been fifty years of economic and political causes, rooted in racism and uneven development that has affected Detroit as a city and as a southeast Michigan region (Darden, Hill, Thomas, and Thomas 1987).

The divergent social worlds of well-off suburb versus jobless hyperghetto urban outcasts signals a historically specific "development of underdevelopment" in the city. This trend has resulted in incarcerating whole communities and leaving the high-impact neighborhood with people going to and returning from prison.

Meanwhile, the "magnetism of street life" amidst the "rising tide of social disorganization" in the high-impact neighborhoods reveals the growth of the *hustler class* as youth, despite high levels of incarceration, continue to march into illegal activities.

As the overall crime rate has continued to fall every year since 1991, it is nevertheless, an unequal crime decline with African American violence four times greater than white violence—and this has fueled the prison buildup.

Abandoned hyperghettos and increasing social disorganization mean urban and inner suburban ring areas characterized by "changing neighborhoods." The disruption of community and family life brought by changes in the industrial mix (from high pay/high stability manufacturing to low pay/low stability service jobs) has impacted on family stability, increasing the divorce rate, family dysfunction, and crime.

Exposure to illicit drug markets and homicide growing up recruits the young into the hustler class and "the ugly, cold side of the drug world"—and leads to early death or prison.

To prevent such a criminogenic community there is a need for prevention policy to target multiple risk factors using multiple actors. And, because of the linkage between labor markets and urban crime, there is a need to develop "jobs or income" programs at the city level. That is, as Parker emphasizes: "Job markets do not fall within neighborhood or community boundaries, rather city residents are typically exposed to the same labor market dynamics. . . . Neighborhood conditions . . . are shaped by the larger labor market opportunity structures of an area" (2008: 87).

Parker found four aspects of the local urban economy that influenced homicide rates over time and for specific groups: (1) industrial restructuring from manufacturing to administrative, professional, and information services, which directly influenced black males; (2) both African American men and women got most of the *low wage* service jobs; (3) in areas where extreme black residential segregation exists the homicide rate is higher; and (4) immigration producing multiethnic cities has actually reduced homicide.

Parker does not have much to say about policy beyond better enforcement of the fair housing act and searching for a way "to address the historic and long-standing inequality that looms large over black males" (2008: 124).

The climate of economic instability in the hyperghetto and increasingly in the inner-ring suburbs and small blue-collar cities needs to be analyzed at the appropriate domain level: the disinvestment of corporate capital and the policy questions of how to increase the localization of investment. The changes in local economies (reorganization around the hustler class or "social disorganization") require attention to the structure of investment. Barlow and Kauzlarich note:

> In Shaw and McKay's view, the only way to combat the tendency for areas to become permanently crime prone was to develop neighborhood organizations that could help promote informal social controls and encourage residents to look out for each others' welfare. (2010: 242)

A criticism of Shaw and McKay's view is that it doesn't include an analysis of the ownership structure and the *degree of localization of investment*. That is, as Judith Blau notes, the American middle class and working class are increasingly in a capricious economy and among faltering economic institutions. There has been

> increasing economic inequalities, as a result of the gains among the rich, deterioration of the economic conditions of the poor, and declines in the income of the middle classes. . . . This was due in part to the economic conditions already summarized (shift in industrial mix from manufacturing to series, globalization, technology) and also to a steady decline of fulltime workers in core labor sectors accompanied by an increase in contract workers and in part-time workers in peripheral or secondary labor sectors . . .
>   . . . To the extent that hard work and achievement were core cultural values, the collapse of economic institutions could very well entail a major reevaluation and overhaul of these core values, which themselves are already contradictory. (Blau 1995: 225–28)

For Loic Wacquant and William Julius Wilson, the only solution when jobs disappear and there occurs a deproletarianization of the lower working class, is to guarantee jobs or guarantee income through a massive governmental policy effort, which would mean a massive change in cultural values: everyone should have a guaranteed income floor (instead of income being based primarily on hard work and achievement). There could still be "The American Dream," but it would rest on top of (or in addition to) a guaranteed "right to life" (federal and/or state government providing jobs or income). To some extent this would look like Germany as described in "The European Dream" (Rifkin 2006), or look like Sweden, Norway, and Finland. These countries tax heavily and thus are able to provide a livable income and welfare floor. But it would have to be a national social income policy that applied to everyone, like Social Security, Medicare, Medicaid, and the Affordable Care Act. Wacquant offers a website; see the Basic Income Guarantee (BIG) network at www.usbig.net for North America (Wacquant 2008: 255).

The "structural strain" that pressures the hustler class to "innovate" through crime could be lessened with a livable income *combined* with the various community-level programs to increase parental networks and informal social control proposed by Farrington and Welsh and the LIFERS project. There would be sufficient resources to answer the "personal stress" Agnew's General Strain Theory describes (Agnew 2010: 25–44). There would be a reduction in the "criminally socialized" to interact with, slowing the march into illegal activities.

Obviously this type of general social policy solution will not happen overnight. But one of the values of alternative criminology theories is that they alert us to the need to see where the progressive edge of the American mainstream is—to be as "historically specific" in our practice and thought as possible. Part of the understanding of conflict theory is the understanding of how social movements can change society. Part of *understanding power* in society is pushing to alter or dissolve the power "structure." To reiterate Emmanuel Wallerstein's insight on social change:

> The present is always a matter of choice, but as someone once said, although we make our own history, we do not make it as we choose. Still, we do make it. The present is a matter of choice, but the range of choice is considerably expanded in the period immediately preceding a bifurcation, when the system is furthest from equilibrium, because at that point small inputs have large outputs (as opposed to moments of near equilibrium, when large inputs have small outputs). (1999: 84)

In our many prisoner life stories about rehabilitation, maturing, and transformation we can learn from the prisoners about "self-work." In the choice between crime prevention versus the warehouse prison, prisoners can offer some good insights. In the difficulties of successful reentry and avoiding recidivism, some prisoners can offer examples of overcoming their "institutionalization" and fears. If the United States needs a guaranteed income to solve the hyperghetto-hyperincarceration cycle we are now in, a good way to push further on this issue would be to encourage more justice reinvestment. The study of criminology highlights several social policies or "protective factors" to reduce crime, but what the United States needs most of all is *social change*.

STATE BUDGETS, PRISON DOWNSIZING

This section shifts the focus from criminology theories and individual prisoner-student essays at the "front end" describing their coming up, and prison criminological issues and "back end" where prisoners describe issues of reentry, to a focus on the prison build-up movement itself. We traced the origins of U.S. mass incarceration in chapters 2 and 3. To review: the United States had a stable incarceration rate of 75 to 125 people per 100,000 of the population for more than one hundred years (from 1860 to 1980). Figure 10.1 shows the U.S. crime rate per 100,000 of the population from 1933 forward.

U.S. Unified Crime Report (UCR) crime trends and sentenced prisoners in federal and state institutions, 1931–2004, showing an increasing incarceration rate and a rising and falling crime rate. Rate of crime and rate of incarceration given are per 100,000 resident population. Over the last twenty-five years, however, the incarceration rate has rapidly shot up from 125 per 100,000 to 500 per 100,000.

During this recent twenty-five-year period there was a political momentum pushing for a build-up of state prisons. This prison build-up movement, unfortunately, has, until recently, had no brakes, and the United States became a "prison state"—with the world's largest prison system. In recent years and going forward to "put the brakes on" the prison build-up movement (Useem and Piehl 2008: 169; CAPPS 2013), there is the new context of state budget crises and recent recession with jobless or slow recovery. Another current trend is a growing re-examination of the war on drugs. There is continuing public interest in crime prevention and a growing focus on success in prisoner reentry (Jacobson 2005; Petersilia 2003).

But there is the need to build up the social supports in the jobless ghetto. Since it will take time for the United States to move toward a guaranteed income, in the meantime—and to help us get there—there is a need to continue to cap prison growth, downsize prison populations, and from this prison decarceration movement build support to *shift* resources, investing in the high impact hyperghetto.

THE JUSTICE REINVESTMENT MOVEMENT: STABILIZING CORRECTIONS POPULATIONS AND BUDGET VERSUS REDUCING THEM

"Justice reinvestment" has emerged among leaders of the American Society of Criminology and has been introduced in wider academic and policy circles. This is the idea of a revenue-neutral way to shift resources from the corrections incarceration budget and investing some of the money saved into evidence-based crime prevention programs and in the social support infrastructure for the jobless ghetto communities with high crime rates where up to 80 percent of state prisoners come from (Clear 2007). In a spring 2013 essay, "Ending Mass Incarceration: Charting a New Justice Reinvestment," James Austin, Eric Cadora, Todd Clear, Marc Mauer, and several others have given a critical overview of the current state of justice reinvestment.

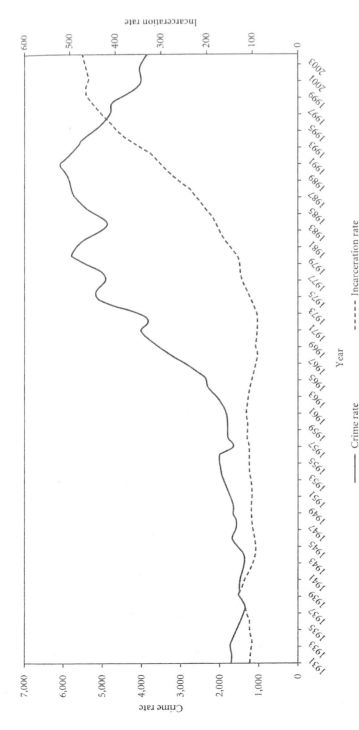

Figure 10.1. U.S. Unified Crime Report (UCR) Crime Trends and Sentenced Prisoners in Federal and State Institutions, 1931–2004, showing an increasing incarceration rate and a rising and falling crime rate. Rate of crime and rate of incarceration given are per 100,000 resident population. *Source: Unlocking America,* JFA Institute, November 2007, 4; used with permission.

In the decade since Justice Reinvestment was launched, much has been accomplished. With assistance from the Justice Reinvestment Initiative, around 27 states have participated one way or another in this data-driven reform, which has revealed previously unacknowledged realities about U.S. correctional systems. Throughout this paper, "Justice Reinvestment" connotes the concept and originating idea and the "Justice Reinvestment Initiative" or "JRI" refers to the formal implementation strategy spearheaded by the Council of State Governments (CSG) and its now principal funders, Pew Charitable Trusts (PEW) and Bureau of Justice Assistance (BIA). Of the 27 states that have participated in the JRI, approximately 18 have enacted JRI legislation for the purpose of stabilizing corrections populations and budgets. JRI has played a major role in educating state legislators and public officials about the bloated and expensive correctional system, persuading them to undertake reforms not previously on the table. Considering the country's four-decade addiction to mass incarceration and harsh punishment, the general refusal to acknowledge its failures and the monumental resistance to change, JRI's most enduring contribution to date may be its having created a space and a mindset among state officials to seriously entertain the possibility of lowering prison populations.

. . . (However) the Justice Reinvestment Initiative, as it has come to operate, runs the danger of institutionalizing mass incarceration at current levels.

The destructive effects of mass incarceration and harsh punishment are visited disproportionately upon individuals and communities of color. Justice Reinvestment was conceived as part of the solution to this problem. The intent was to reduce corrections populations and budgets, thereby generating savings for the purpose of reinvesting in high incarceration communities to make them safer, stronger, more prosperous and equitable. Increasingly, the formalized JRI has moved away from these progressive goals, seeking to reduce the rate of prison *growth* rather than reduce the *number* of prisoners. Instead of producing savings that enable reinvestments in high incarceration communities, in too many places we are likely to institutionalize our massive incarceration rates for many decades to come, largely ignoring its impact on communities of color in particular. This is not the future we want,

Some have argued that compromise necessitated by politics and the need to reach stakeholder consensus has meant that avoiding projected prison growth has become more feasible than achieving substantial reductions in actual prison populations. Possible savings in the form of "averted costs" for JRI work have been either returned to the general coffers or used to augment community corrections and law-enforcement budgets. By focusing on state-level political and administrative policymakers, the JRI process has too often marginalized well-established local advocates and justice reformers who bring knowledge of local conditions and politics to the table, and who have a vested interest in providing long-term implementation oversight and ensuring sustainability of reforms.

We believe this is an important moment to take stock of the JRI, especially within the context of an unusually favorable climate to challenge mass incarceration, and assess how to get a more ambitious Justice Reinvestment movement back on track. (Austin et al. 2013: 1–2)

In another press for change, it is also suggested that the time has come for a stronger focus on the "criminology of reentry." This trend, introduced through the convict criminology movement (Richards and Jones 1996; Ross and Richards 2003), has taken hold in the heart of academic criminology with many recent contributions that explore what the factors are for failure on parole and in prison-to-society reentry—failures that lead to return to prison in a now too familiar "revolving door."

WHAT ABOUT THE ONES COMING UP?

Jim Austin once remarked: "I'm not afraid of the older convict or ex-con, it's the young ones coming up that worry me." Returning to the policy recommendations of Farrington and Welsh (2007): Can we develop a national program to save children from a life of crime? What crime prevention programs work at the individual, family, and community level? How can socially disorganizing factors be countered? To answer these questions we have reviewed macro- and middle-level policy. To prevent the march of youth into the hustler class and beyond individual transformation, how can past individual, family, community, neighborhood interactions be transformed into a future way of life that—as a process—results in a personal shift away from the culture of street crime? What are good crime prevention programs for the nine different categories of criminal offending? What are good programs helping prisoners in their day-to-day process of "making it" (Maruna 2001).

Our conclusion has scanned the horizon for hope, tracing trends moving us toward capping prison growth, capping prison costs, actually downsizing prison populations by an overall reduction in length of stay, and shifting resources to prevention (www.capps-mi.org). We want *prisoner views* on all of this policy world. What do prisoners think?

We hope this book helps criminal justice and sociology students, and the general reader, to better understand prisoners as thinkers. And for the prisoners' voice to become a standard part of the way we think and discuss issues of crime causes, crime prevention, and the social supports needed for personal transformation and restorative justice. There is a window opening to push for justice reinvestment, a focus on the criminology of reentry, a strong push for evidence-based crime prevention, and a growing rethinking of the war on drugs. Perhaps, as we find ourselves in an increasingly unequal society, there will be a wider and more fundamental rethinking of cultural values to consider a U.S. national guaranteed income, and policies to anchor capital in local communities to increase economic stability.

Interest in crime prevention has grown. Farrington and Welsh, in their book, *Saving Children from a Life of Crime* (2007), propose to build upon the public interest in crime prevention. Working through the process of "growing up criminal" at the "front end," before children and youth get too far into criminality and go to prison. However, as Barlow and Decker note, "their (2007) proposal entered the policy arena during a closing of the window of opportunity" due to the Great Recession of 2008–2009 and its slow recovery aftermath.

Having now presented reviews of criminological theories and prisoner essays reflecting these theories, with exercises, and some longer prisoner essays, the reader doing exercises and answering discussion and review questions can ask when reading a specific prisoner essay, "How does this prisoner essay examine *this* theory? *How* and *why* does this essay reflect the criminology insights?" The reader who "has gotten into" the prisoner essays is challenged to "figure it out:" *where* in the prisoner essay does their life story (paragraph and line) reflect the theoretical concept(s) in that specific criminological perspective?

Most of the prisoner essays in chapters 4 through 9 have introductory remarks that help to ask theoretical questions appropriate to that essay and acts to guide the reader. Critical thinking exercises in each chapter and discussion questions appear at the end of each chapter, helping the reader to grasp the way the theory, and the way the prisoner essays, reflect free will and determinism, and assumptions about the importance of, and the structure of, society—and how society relates to the individual.

Everybody has a story, in prison, and the prison classroom is one place to tell these stories. In teaching the eight "Social Science and Personal Writing" volunteer prison classes, over five years, the author asked many prisoners about their lives. What does a typical prisoner classroom look like in terms of prisoner background. Are they parents? What is their education? What are their job skills and work experience? What is their life story? From excerpts and essays of prisoner writings, readers can learn a great deal about how criminology and social deviance theory apply to their lives, *overcoming the disconnect between the classroom text and lectures, and the prisoners lives "coming up"*—often in the streets.

#####

Adrian College Student Narrative 10.1 (3/17/10)

"Overcoming the Disconnect between Classroom and Streets," Nolan Gillespie

As a Criminal Justice student it is imperative to understand what our future efforts will result in. There is an extreme disconnect between the classroom and the streets. Yet, we should not simply aim at taking what we define as criminals off of the street.

Prisoners Are Human Beings. Many of the people sitting in prison made choices very similar to choices non-criminals make. One example is that some drugs are defined as legal and some illegal. People sitting in prison for drug crimes chose the illegal drug, which led them to prison. Many will have done other crimes besides drug-defined crimes, but my point here is to show that some criminals are not as bad as we think. For some reason people universally place the same negative views on most prisoners. Many prisoners have similar memories and lifestyles to us. This should be recognized when thinking about some of the people in prison.

Prevention Is Possible. It is hard to conclusively prove what the causal reasons are for crime, but that does not mean we should give up trying to learn. I believe it is fair to say that we know enough to at least save some people from criminal lifestyles, through prevention efforts. A considerable amount of criminologists and scholars write books about theory and prevention. Some arguments are better than others, but the point is that we have many theoretical tools and proven prevention programs when explaining and preventing crime. We can use their work to further our efforts and knowledge.

Think of Criminology as a Toolbox. We can also think about these reasons for criminal behavior as resulting from many different things. It is not necessarily true that all crimes are committed for the same reason. This thought should lead us to considering the explanation of crime as being described by many theories. It is safe to say that there are many causes of crime; consequently it is up to us to equip ourselves with the proper tools of understanding which theories can lead to practical solutions.

Practical solutions of crime prevention must be properly aimed at the factors that increase the chance for criminal acts or the causes of crime. It would not be beneficial if we blindly attempted to solve criminology problems. I believe we have the intellectual tools and proper motivation to successfully figure these sociological problems out. If we have the opportunity to study and learn we should take it very seriously. As a student I understand that some information can be dry and dull, but the passion for criminal justice pursuits should override any wearisome and boring features of class.

Look Inside Yourself. If this passion is troubling for some and they are serious about pursuing some form of career in the criminal justice field my best advice is to look inside themselves. This introspection, if properly aimed at what matters (in my opinion), then they should become motivated enough to care about some criminals and their lives.

The Potential to Become Transformed. To put it simply, when we become practitioners or criminologists, we have the opportunity to not only make the world a better place, but to save people who are in a less fortunate situation. Protecting the innocent has always been an aim for criminal justice minds. Our future jobs are not only about protecting the innocent and preventing more victims, but also helping people who are criminals or trying to prevent criminal behavior. It is useful to appeal to this in terms of a thought experiment. Imagine that a person had little control over what their life was becoming or external forces were so powerful they were overcome and misled. In a sense these people have a *their-life-was-determined type of innocence* as well. I personally cannot fault someone for being born to a certain family and growing up in a deprived area. I also think it is possible to forgive those whose life was up to a certain point, a life of crime. Or think about a person who simply made the wrong choices for various reasons. I think in both cases we, as people, should be able to forgive these people. The forgiveness I am talking about should reflect moving past their criminal acts and seeing potential in their ability to transform.

As a functioning society we must control what we have defined as criminals, but we should also feel an emotional pull on attempting to help them become better people. I would conceptualize better people as fitting in with society by following the laws that are in place. I am not attempting to push any moral standard in this perspective. My overall point by presenting this idea is to help us look past our negative thoughts of criminals. I feel it is necessary that I explain that the criminals I am talking about are the ones that I believe we can actually save. I understand there are some people who have done wicked incomprehensible crimes—and who don't subsequently change their lives—that may never be able to be brought back. I am stating that we should focus on the prisoners and people who can be influenced and taught about how to remain within society and have a comfortable degree of freedom. This is no easy task, but if we have the power to do so we should. Some of these prisoners need different kinds of help to transform, but it is up to us to provide it for them. Some prisoners if not helped will only return to prison.

These efforts should be collective and aimed at goals which reflect my agreement with Farrington and Welsh (2009) in their book *Saving Children from a Life of Crime.* They believe crime prevention should be a national plan that works together with several programs to solve the problems of crime.

Learning alongside a professor (Dr. Bill Tregea) over the course of a semester has given me the opportunity to go beyond the concepts in a textbook. Regarding *Prisoners on Criminology,* this books' author has supplied an insight that many of us cannot even imagine. He is sitting on a vast amount of information and data. In teaching prison classes the author has obtained many outlooks that can aid us in our abilities as criminal justice majors. With knowledge and passion we usually see goals nearby. If we are motivated to take on the task of preventing crime we must take prisoner voices seriously. Their words are pictures of the past describing the darkest times of their lives or providing thoughts on how they think the criminal justice apparatus can prevent crime. As students with the ability to go to college it may be extremely hard for us to grasp how difficult some people's lives have turned out to be. It is of my opinion that theory is most important when it is aimed at practical solutions.

In studying criminology it seems to me that the theories explaining crime have an incredible amount of utility when we look at what can come from them. If we can grasp what certain theories are arguing we may be able to better understand why crimes occur. If we imagine that the criminology theories that are prevalent within the discipline have some degree of truth then we must have some passion and hope for the implications that arise from this situation. With the knowledge of what causes crime it seems that we would have the ability to prevent it. Many criminologists have presented several theories, some similar and some very different. I have been convinced that it would behoove us to take these prevalent theories to heart and use them collectively to attempt the prevention and explanation of crime.

While considering determinism and free will, I believe there are ways to decrease the likelihood of criminal lifestyles. Families, neighborhoods, communities and the individual can be culpable when speaking about the causes of crime. Before learning about criminology and growing intellectually I believed that crime was always based on choice. To some degree choice may always play a role, but it is not always the main reason that crime occurs. As a criminal justice student helping with this book I have spoke with the author for numerous hours about criminology and he explained that he tends to follow community explanations for the causes of crime. I understand exactly why he leans to this conclusion and agree with his thoughts. When dealing with criminology human nature must be considered. It seems that people can have power over themselves no matter what neighborhood or community they grow up in. It also seems just as easy that the jaws of so called community norms can grasp whoever is in sight. Whether we are determined or make simple choices, we must ultimately understand what causes crime.

I believe people within the criminology discipline are working closer to explaining the causes of crime. Our beliefs will lead us to effectively saving at least some people. As criminal justice students it is our duty to learn as much as we can to fuel the passion for making a difference in the world. We must look past the paycheck and benefits to realize the true value in our jobs or fields of study. The criminals who speak to us in this book are people too and their words should be genuinely valued. We should feel an emotional pull when hearing about their childhood years and how they had life experiences that they think aided their criminal behavior.

I want to thank the author for making this an interesting and passionate semester. I learned many things; the impact the community and family can have on an individual, the degrees of determinism and freewill have on people's decision, numerous criminology theories, and the benefits of instituting early prevention programs. I also will never forget that the more I learn the more passion I have for not only life, but helping other people.

#####

EXERCISE 10.1

Describe figure 10.1. What is meant by justice reinvestment according to Jim Austin et al.? What policies could bring the U.S. rate of incarceration down? Elaborate.

DISCUSSION AND REVIEW QUESTIONS

1. Summarize former U.S. labor secretary Robert Reich's view on the implications of the city of Detroit, Michigan, declaring bankruptcy in the summer of 2013. What, in his view, is the "lesson of Detroit"?
2. Summarize U.S. attorney general Eric Holder's view that we "cannot incarcerate our way to safety." Explain. What does he recommend?
3. What evidence does chapter 10 give for believing that "the brakes have been put on" the prison build-up movement?
4. What does "effective crime control" require according to Travis Pratt? What, in his view, are the main causes of crime?
5. Summarize Karen Parker's argument that urban labor market conditions impact on family, leading to increased crime. Elaborate.
6. What is this book's author's main criticism of Shaw and McKay's "social disorganization" policies for crime prevention? What is missing? What is needed?
7. What are the solutions to crime according to Loic Wacquant and William Julius Wilson?
8. In thinking through chapter 10 and other parts of this book, do you think that the United States is reaching a "period immediately preceding a bifurcation" as described by Immanuel Wallerstein?

Appendix

SOCIAL SCIENCE AND WRITING

Special eight-week, post-GED class: Taught like a regular college "Crime Prevention and Criminology" class and examines what a (1) credit class is like if you enroll later in a college. Taught by: Adrian College professor, Bill Tregea, author of *The Prisoners' World: Portraits of Convicts Caught in the Incarceration Binge* (Lanham, MD: Lexington, 2010).

Sign up with Ms. Bates for this special class that meets eight times: class runs 6–8 p.m., Mondays, 10/18/2010 to 12/13/2010.

10/18—Creative Writing

(1) dropping out of high school, (2) recidivism in Michigan: nine offense categories, and (3) justice reinvestment and the criminology of reentry.

Orientation to this course: learn about writing, practice writing, read draft chapters from, and contribute short essays, to the author's second book: *Coming Up: Prisoners on Criminology* (Lanham, MD: Lexington) <u>Take in-class survey</u>: are you a parent? Education level? Job skills? Etc. Writing tips. <u>In-class reading #1</u>: *Coming Up*, Ch. 2 "Encountering High School and Dropping Out." Discuss. <u>In-class writing #1</u>: How does Ch. 2 relate to you? Tell a story. <u>In-class reading</u>: "Prison Blocks." Discuss. <u>In-class writing #2</u>: Start a story about your neighborhood. Share. <u>In-class reading</u>: *A Study of Prisoner Release and Recidivism in Michigan, August 2009*, Citizens Alliance on Prisons and Public Spending (capps-mi.org). In-class writing #3: connect CAPPS info to your own life or "someone you know." Tell a story. Share. Take-home writing assignment—Paper #1: "Recidivism, Reentry, and Me"—contribute to *Coming Up,* Ch. 15 "After Prison: Recidivism and Reentry Initiatives," tell a "story" about recidivism and reentry, due 10/25. We become a writing group, share stories.

10/25—Front End Criminology: Individual, Family, and Community Factors

Writing tips/share paper #1 "Recidivism and Reentry." Discuss. In-class reading: *Coming Up,* Ch. 3: "Growing Up Criminal: An Analysis of Criminology from Prisoner Views." Discuss; writing tips. In-class writing #1: Pick one topic generated out of this in-class reading and write for 20 minutes, discuss. Share. Handout: *Coming Up,* Ch. 4 "Individual Factors," Ch. 5 "Family Factors," and Ch. 6 "Community Factors." Review in class. Take-home writing assignment—Paper #2: "Influences Affecting My Life." Tell a "story" about *one* of the three levels: about the *individual,* the *family,* or the *community* factor(s) in your life, or "someone you know," and, how it relates to developing criminality. Due 11/1.

11/1—"Kinds of Places"/"Changing Places"—Social Disorganization Theory

Writing tips/share paper #2/discuss. In-class reading and writing: *Coming Up,* Ch. 7 "Prisoners Like Social Disorganization Theory: Why?" Discuss. Write for 20 minutes. Share. Take-home writing assignment—Paper #3: "Growing Up in My Community." Relate this "own story" paper to the reading. Due 11/8.

11/8—Social Structure and Community Level Variables—and Me: A Life Story

Writing tips/share paper #3/discuss. In-class reading and writing #1: *Coming Up,* Ch. 8 "Social Structure and Prisoners' Lives." Discuss. Write for 20 minutes. Share. In-class reading and writing #2: Read "The Community," by Robert Sampson (2002). Discuss in class, write for 20 minutes. Share. Discuss. Also review: In-class reading and writing: Read Ch. 12, "Social Structural Theories of Crime," from *Introduction to Criminology,* 9th ed., Kauzlarich and Barlow; discuss in class, write for 20 minutes. Read. Discuss. Take-home writing assignment—Paper #4: "Looking at Community Level Variables and Looking at Me." Relate this "own story" paper to the Sampson reading, to the Kauzlarich and Barlow reading, and to Todd Clear, from *Imprisoning Communities: How Mass Incarceration Makes Disadvantaged Neighborhoods Worse* (Oxford: Oxford University Press, 2007). Tell a "story" rather than an overly academic/analytic essay. Due 11/15.

11/15—Pathways to Prison: Social Process and Interaction

Writing tips/share paper #4/discuss. In-class reading and writing: *Coming Up*, Ch. 9, "Social Process and Interaction Theories." Discuss. Write for 20 minutes. Share. In-class reading and writing: Read *The Jackroller* (Shaw 1930), pgs. 50–57; and *The Prisoners' World* (Tregea and Larmour 2009), pgs. 95–98, 103–5, 109–121; and Ch. 13 "Social Process Theories of Crime," from *Introduction to Criminology*, 9th ed., Kauzlarich and Barlow; discuss in class, write for 20 minutes, read, and discuss. Take-home writing assignment—Paper #5: "Pathways to Prison and Me." Relate this "own story" paper to the readings—tell a story. Due 11/29.

[Optional but there would be great interest if: You could write a LONGER "Life Story." There will be a handout with some writing aids to help accomplish this.]

11/22   No Class

11/29—Conflict Theory, Critical and Anarchist Criminology

FEMINISM

Writing tips/share paper #5/discuss. In-class reading and writing: *Coming Up*, Ch. 10 "Alternatives? Conflict Theory, Anarchist Views, Critical Criminology, and Feminism." Discuss. Write for 20 minutes. Share. Take-home writing assignment—Paper #6: "Going to the Root: Then and Now." Write an "own story" paper that relates to one or more parts of the "Alternative Criminology" readings. Due 12/6.

12/6—Ending the Culture of Street Crime: Prisoner Leadership

Writing tips/share paper #6/discuss. In-class reading and writing: Read Ch. 6 "The Role of Education in Prison Reform," and Ch. 7 "The Difference Between 'Treatment/Remedial' and 'Restorative/Relational' Models of Reintegration to Society" from *Restorative Justice in a Prison Community*, Cheryl Swanson (Lanham, MD: Lexington, 2009); discuss in class, write for 20 minutes, read and discuss. Also, take-home handout: "The Redemptive Script," from *Making Good: How Ex-Convicts Reform and Rebuild Their Lives*, Shadd Maruna (Washington, D.C.: American Psychological Association, 2001). Take-home writing assignment—Paper #6: "Restorative Justice and Me." Relate this "own story" paper to the readings—tell a story. Due 12/20.

In-class reading and writing: *Coming Up*, Ch. 11 "In Prison Criminology Issues," and Ch. 2 "Ending the Culture of Street Crime." Discuss. Write 20 minutes. Share. Then handout. In-class reading and writing: Read "Ending the Culture of Street Crime: The Lifers Public Safety Steering Committee of the State Correctional Institution at Graterford, Pennsylvania," discuss in class, write for 20 minutes, read and discuss. Take-home writing assignment—Paper #7: "What do I think about ending the culture of street crime?" Tell "story" (or stories) about each factors or situations in your life, or the life of "someone you know," that relates to the ending of the culture of street crime. Read carefully the second half of the Graterford Prison Lifers essay and apply as a story how it relates to you. Due 12/13.

12/13—Criminology: A Tool Box for the Case at Hand, Rehabilitation and Transformation, and the Criminology of Reentry

Share papers #6 and #7. In-class reading and writing: *Coming Up*, Ch. 13 "Criminology: A Tool Box for the Case at Hand," and Ch. 14 "Life Stories: For Some—Rehabilitation, for Others—Transformation," and Ch. 16 "State Budgets, Downsizing, and Justice Reinvestment." Discuss, write for 20 minutes. Share. In-class: We re-read the last half of Graterford Prison Lifers essay in class and discuss. EXAM (in class short essay with three questions related to readings). Evaluate class. Handing out of CERTIFICATES of COMPLETION.

GOING TO COMMUNITY COLLEGE AFTER RELEASE

How to Get Money, What Education Programs Are Available: A Workshop
Special post-GED information workshop presents typical community college catalog information on skills sets, certificates and the "Associates of Arts in General Studies." Workshop includes a brief learning exercise—read, write, and report—taught like a regular college class to become familiar if you enroll later in a college. Taught by an Adrian College professor.
Sign up with Ms. Julia Cady. Workshop meets Saturday, December 7, 6–8 p.m., 2009
This Workshop Includes the Following Topics:

• Handouts of community college material, including:

  • What an "Associate of Arts in General Studies" looks like. General studies courses (English, social science, etc.). The ability to take some skills training courses.

- Facts: Like must enroll for 6 credits a semester to qualify for federal funding (Pell grants).
- 15-credit skills sets available in vocational areas (brakes, computers, etc.)
- 30-credit certificates available in areas like software, HVAC, Bus. Mgt.
- Information on community college services: tutoring, writing center, academic and career counseling

- Handout of FAFSA Form (federal application for <u>free</u> student aid), also known as "Pell grants" (approx. $1,500 tuition and $300 for books available each semester)

  - Going over form, instructions on how to fill it out online.

- Practice short class exercise: reading, writing, oral report, discussion.

References Cited

Abadinsky, Howard. 2008. *Drug Use and Abuse: A Comprehensives Introduction*. Belmont, CA: Thomson/Wadsworth.

———. 2006. *Probation and Parole: Theory and Practice*, 9th ed. Upper Saddle River, NJ: Parson/Prentice Hall.

Agnew, Robert. 2010. "Controlling Crime: Recommendations from General Strain Theory." Pp. 25–44 in Hugh D. Barlow and Scott H. Decker, eds., *Criminology and Public Policy: Putting Theory to Work*. Philadelphia, PA: Temple University Press.

———. 1999. "A General Strain Theory of Criminality Differences in Crime Rates." *Journal of Research in Crime and Delinquency* 36, no. 2 (May), in Henry J. Pontell. 2005. *Social Deviance: Readings, Theory and Research*, 5th ed. Upper Saddle River, NJ: Pearson/Prentice Hall.

Akers, Ronald L. and Christie S. Sellers. 2009. *Criminological Theories: Introduction, Evaluation, and Application*, 5th ed. New York: Oxford University Press.

Alexander, Michelle. 2012. *The New Jim Crow: Mass Incarceration in the Age of Colorblindness*. New York: The New Press.

Alperovitz, Gar. 2014. "Pluralist Commonwealth." www.pluralist commonwealth.org.

Alperovitz, Gar and Keane Bhatt. 2013. "What Then Can We Do? Ten Ways to Democratize the Economy." www.garalperovitz.com/what-then-can-I-do/.

Anderson, Elijah. 2008. "Against the Wall: Poor, Young, Black, and Male," in *Against the Wall: Poor, Young, Black, and Male: The City in the Twenty-First Century*. Philadelphia: University of Pennsylvania Press.

———. 1999. *The Code of the Streets: Decency, Violence, and the Moral Life of the Inner City*. New York: W. W. Norton & Company.

———. 1994. "The Code of the Streets." *Atlantic Monthly* 273, no. 5: 81–94.

———. 1990. *Streetwise: Race, Class, and Change in an Urban Community*. Chicago: University of Chicago Press.

Apollo Alliance. 2008. "Green Jobs for Inner City." www.appolloalliance.org.

Ashby, Gary. 1998. Criminal Justice Ministry—Lansing Catholic Diocese. Prisoner education support material. Personal communication.

Austin, James et al. 2013. "Ending Mass Incarceration: Charting a New Justice Reinvestment." JFA Institute, www.capps-mi.org.

———. 2007. "Unlocking America," JFA Institute, 4.

Austin, James and John Irwin. 1997/2001. *It's about Time: America's Imprisonment Binge*, 3rd ed. Belmont, CA: Wadsworth.

Bandura, Albert. 1977. *Social Learning*. Englewood Cliffs, NJ: Prentice Hall.

Barlow, Hugh D. and David Kauzlarich. 2010. *Explaining Crime: A Primer in Criminological Theory*. Lanham, MD: Rowman & Littlefield Publishers.

Beal, Calvin. 1998. "New Prisons in Rural and Small-town Areas," in CFECP 1998 conference materials.

Berger, Ronald J. 1985. "Organizing the Community for Delinquency Prevention." *Journal of Sociology and Social Welfare* 12, no. 1: 129–53. Pp. 261–81 in Ronald J. Berger, ed., *The Sociology of Juvenile Delinquency*, 2nd ed. Chicago: Nelson-Hall.

Bernstein, Leonard and Stephen Sondheim. 1956/1957/1958/1959. "Gee, Officer Krupke," *West Side Story*. Leonard Bernstein Music Publishing Company LLC, publisher.

Best, Joel and David F. Luckenbill. 1994. *Organizing Deviance*, 2nd ed. Englewood Cliffs, NJ: Prentice Hall.

Black, Donald. 1983/2010. "Crime as Social Control." Pp. 308–11 in Heith Copes and Volkan Topalli, eds., *Criminological Theory: Readings and Retrospectives*. New York: McGraw Hill.

Blau, Judith. 1995. "The Contingent Character of the American Middle Class," in Frederick C. Gamst, ed., *Meanings of Work: Considerations for the Twenty-First Century*. New York: State University of New York Press.

Blau, Peter. 1964. *Exchange and Power in Social Life*. New York: Wiley.

Blau, Peter and Judith Blau. 1982. "The Cost of Inequality: Metropolitan Structure and Violent Crime." *American Sociological Review* 47: 114–29.

Bluestone, Barry and Bennett Harrison. 1982. *The Deindustrialization of America*. New York: Basic Books.

Blumstein, Alfred. 2002. "Prisons: A Policy Challenge." Pp. 451–82 in James Q. Wilson and Joan Petersilia, eds., *Crime: Public Policies for Crime Control*. Oakland, CA: ICS Press.

Blumstein, Alfred and Jacquelin Cohen, "Characterizing Criminal Careers," *Science* 237 (August 28).

Braithwaite, John. 1989. *Crime, Shame and Reintegration*. New York: Cambridge University Press.

Brennan, Patricia A., Birgitte R. Mednick, and Sarnoff A. Mednick. 1993. "Parental Psychopathology, Congenital Factors, and Violence." Pp. 244–61 in *Mental Disorder and Crime*, Sheilagh Hodgins, ed., Newbury Park, CA: Sage.

Brofenbrenner, Urie. 1979. *Ecology of Human Development: Experiments by Nature and Design*. Cambridge, MA: Harvard University Press.

Bursik, Robert J. 1988. "Social Disorganization and Theories of Crime and Delinquency: Problems and Prospects," *Criminology* 26: 519–51.

Bursik, Robert J. and Harold G. Grasmick. 1993. *Neighborhoods and Crime: The Dimensions of Effective Community Control.* New York: Lexington.

CAPPS. 2013. "Safely Reducing Corrections Spending—Key Concepts and Myths," September, www.capps-mi.org.

———. 2013. "Sentencing Length Reforms." *Consensus* (fall). www.capps-mi.org.

———. 2009. "Recidivism Report: Reoffending of 76,000 Michigan Prisoners in Nine Offense Categories, Released 1986–1999." www.capps-mi.org.

———. 2008. Citizens Alliance on Prisons and Public Spending. Policy positions on reforms in sentence length for Michigan.

CEA. 2003. "Three State Recidivism Study: The Effect of Postsecondary Correctional Education." International Correctional Education Association.

CFECP. 1998. Campaign for Effective Crime Policy. "Crime and Politics in the 21st Century: Public Safety and the Quality of Justice," conference materials, November 12–14, Bethesda, MD.

Chiricos, Ted. 1995/2002. "The Media, Moral Panics and the Politics of Crime Control," in George F. Cole, Mark G. Gertz, and Amy Bunger, eds., *The Criminal Justice System: Politics and Policies.* Belmont, CA: Wadsworth/Thomson Learning.

Clear, Todd. 2007. *Imprisoning Communities: How Mass Incarceration Makes Disadvantaged Neighborhoods Worse.* New York: Oxford University Press.

Clear, Todd and Eric Cadora. 2003. *Community Justice.* Belmont, CA: Wadsworth.

Clear, Todd R., George E. Cole, and Michael D. Reisig. 2009. *American Corrections*, 8th ed. Belmont, CA: Thomson/Wadsworth.

Cloward, Richard and Lloyd Ohlin. 1960. "Illegitimate Means and Delinquent Subcultures." Pp. 45–49 in Henry Pontell, ed., *Social Deviance: Readings in Theory & Research*, 5th ed., Upper Saddle River, NJ: Pearson/Prentice Hall.

Cohen, Stanley. 1972/1980. *Folk Devils and Moral Panics: The Creation of Mods and Rockers.* New York: St. Martin's Press.

Conklin, John E. 2003. *Why Crime Rates Fell.* Boston: Allyn & Bacon.

Council of State Governments. 2008. "Corrections Budgets." www.csg.org.

Convict Criminology. 2008. www.convictcriminology.org.

CSG. 2012. "Justice Reinvestment Initiative." Council of State Governments. www.csg.org.

CRC. 2008a. Citizens Research Council. www.crc.org.

——— 2008b. "Michigan's Fiscal Future." Citizen Research Council. Report No. 349, June.

Cullen, Francis and Cheryl Jonson. 2012. *Correctional Theory: Context and Consequences.* Los Angeles: Sage.

Daily Telegram. 2011. "Governor's Pick for MDOC." April 21, A3.

———. 2010. "Detroit to Bulldoze 40 Square Miles." March 8, A3.

Darden, Joe T., Richard Child Hill, June Thomas, and Richard Thomas. 1987. *Detroit: Race and Uneven Development.* Philadelphia: Temple University Press.

Derber, Charles. 1998. *Corporation Nation.* New York: St. Martin's Griffin.

———. 2002. *People Before Profit.* New York: Picador.

DeRose, Julie. 2007 and 2010. MDOC director of correctional education. Personal communication.

Dicken, Peter. 2007. *Global Shift: Mapping the Changing Contours of the World Economy*, 5th ed. New York: Guilford Press.

Diulio, John J., Steven K. Smith, and Aaron J. Saiger. 1995. "The Federal Role in Crime Control," in James Q. Wilson and Joan Petersilia, eds., *Crime: Twenty-Eight Leading Experts Look at the Most Pressing Problems of Our Time*. San Francisco, CA: ICS Press.

Drum, Kevin. 2013. "America's Real Criminal Element: Lead." *Mother Jones* (January/February).

Dryfoos, Joy G. 1990. *Adolescents at Risk: Prevalence and Prevention*. New York: Oxford University Press.

Duguid, Stephen. 1992. "Becoming Interested in Other Things: The Impact of Education in Prison." *Journal of Correctional Education* 47, no. 2: 74–85.

Duguid, Stephen, Colleen Hawley, and Wayne Knights. 1998. "Measuring the Impact of Post-Secondary Education in Prison: A Report from British Columbia." *Journal of Offender Rehabilitation* 27, nos. 1/2: 87–106.

Duguid, Stephen and Ray Pawson. 1998. "Education, Change, and Transformation: The Prison Experience." *Evaluation Review* 22, no. 4: 470–95.

Duneier, Mitchell. 1999. *Sidewalk*. New York: FSG Books.

Durkheim, Emile. 1893/1964. *The Division of Labor*. New York: Free Press.

Einstadter, Werner J. and Stuart Henry. 2006. *Criminological Theory: An Analysis of Its Underlying Assumptions*, 2nd ed. Lanham, MD: Rowman & Littlefield Publishers.

Eitzen, D. Stanley and Maxine Baca Zinn. 2000. *Social Problems*, 8th ed. Boston: Allyn and Bacon

FAMM. 2008. Families Against Mandatory Minimums. "FAMMGram archives." www.famm.org/Resources/BrochuresandPublications/FAMMGramarchives.aspx.

Farrington, David. 2011. "Families and Crime." Pp. 130–57 in James Q. Wilson and Joan Petersilia, eds., *Crime and Public Policy*. New York: Oxford University Press.

Farrington, David P., Darrick Jolliffe, Rolf Loeber, Magda Stouthamer-Loeber, and Larry Kalb. 2001. "The Concentration of Offenders in Families, and Family Criminality in the Prediction of Boys' Delinquency." *Journal of Adolescence* 24: 579–96.

Farrington, David and Brandon C. Welsh. 2007. *Saving Children from a Life of Crime*. New York: Oxford University Press.

Feeley, Malcolm M. and Jonathan Simon. 1992. "The New Penology: Notes on the Emerging Strategy of Corrections and Its Implications." *Criminology* 30, no. 4 (November): 449–74.

Flack, J. C. and F. B. M. DeWaal. 2000. "Any Animal Whatever: Darwinian Building Blocks of Morality in Monkeys and Apes." Pp. 1–30 in Leonard D. Katz, ed., *The Evolution of Morality: Cross-Disciplinary Perspectives*. Bowling Green, OH: Imprint Academic.

Foucault, Michel. 1979. *Discipline and Punish: The Birth of the Prison*. New York: Vintage Books.

Garland, David. 2001a. *The Culture of Control: Crime and Social Order in Contemporary Society*. Chicago: University of Chicago Press.

————. 2001b/2004. "Crime Control and Social Order." Pp. 286–301 in Peter B. Kraska, ed., *Theorizing Criminal Justice: Eight Essential Orientations*. Long Grove, IL: Waveland Press.

Garreau, Joel. 1991. *Edge City: Life on the New Frontier*. New York: Anchor Books/ Doubleday.

Gillespie, Nolan. 2010. "Overcoming the Disconnect between Classroom and Streets." Personal communication, reprinted with permission.

Glaser, Daniel. 2005. "Differential Identification." Pp. 142–44 in *Social Deviance: Readings in Theory and Research*, 5th ed., Henry A. Pontell, ed., Upper Saddle River, NJ: Pearson/Prentice Hall.

Gopnik, Adam. 2012. "The Caging of America: Why Do We Lock Up so Many People?" *New Yorker* (January 30).

Goldstein, Herman. 1990. *Problem-Oriented Policing*. New York: McGraw-Hill Publishing.

Gouldner, Alvin. 1960. "The Norm of Reciprocity." *American Sociological Review* 25: 161–78.

Granholm, Jennifer, Governor. 2007. "Granholm Pushing to Change Sentencing Laws." *Daily Telegram*, Adrian, A1, July 16.

Green, J. R. and W. V. Pelfrey. 1997. "A Case Study of Police Practices in New York City." *Crime & Delinquency* 45, no. : 437–68.

Green, Michael. 1993. "Chronic Exposure to Violence and Poverty: Interventions that Work for Youth." *Crime & Delinquency* 39, no. 1 (January): 106–24.

Gusfield, Joseph P. 1967. "Moral Passage: The Symbolic Process in Public Designations of Deviance." Pp. 228–37 in Henry N. Pontell, ed., *Social Deviance: Readings in Theory and Research*, 5th ed. Upper Saddle River, NJ: Prentice Hall.

Hagan, Frank E. 1994. *Introduction to Criminology*, 4th ed. Chicago: Nelson-Hall Publishers.

Haley, Alex and Malcolm X. 1964. *The Autobiography of Malcolm X*. New York: Grove Press, Inc.

Haveman, Joe. 2013. "Review of state's criminal prison sentences is wise." *The Daily Telegram*, July 30, A6.

Hedges, Chris. 2010. "City in Ruins." *The Nation* (November 22).

Hegel, G. W. F. 1910/1967. *The Phenomenology of Mind*. New York: Harper Torchbooks.

Hernandez, Raymond. 1998. "Give Them the Maximum: Small Towns Clamor for the Boon a Big Prison Could Bring," in CFECP 1998 conference materials.

Heyman, Phillip B. and Mark H. Moore. 1996. "The Federal Role in Dealing with Violent Street Crime: Principles, Questions, and Cautions." *Annals of the American Academy of Political and Social Sciences*, January, in CFECP 1998 conference materials.

Higgins, Gina O'Connell. 1994. *Resilient Adults: Overcoming a Cruel Past*. San Francisco, CA: Jossey-Bass Publishers.

Holder, Eric. 2013. "Holder to map overhaul of drug-sentencing rules." *The Toledo Blade*. August 12, A1.

Holzer, Harry, Paul Offner, and Elaine Sorenson. 2005. "What Explains the Continuing Decline in Labor Force Activity among Youth Black Men?" *Labor History* 46, no. 1: 37–55.

Irwin, John. 2006. "Prisons in Turmoil." Pp. 112–37 in Edward J. Latessa and Alexander M. Holsinger, eds., *Correctional Contexts: Contemporary and Classical Readings*. Los Angeles: Roxbury Publishing Company.

———. 2005. *The Warehouse Prison: Disposal of the New Dangerous Class*. Los Angeles: Roxbury Publishing Company.

———. 1985a. *The Jail*. Berkeley: University of California Press.

———. 1985b. "The Return of the Bogeyman." Keynote Address at American Society of Criminology, San Diego.

———. 1980. *Prisons in Turmoil*. Boston: Little, Brown.

———. 1970. *The Felon*. Englewood Cliffs, NJ: Prentice Hall.

Irwin, John and James Austin. 1997. "It's About Time: America's Imprisonment Binge," in Edward J. Latessa and Alexander M. Holsinger, eds., 2006. *Correctional Contexts: Contemporary and Classical Readings*, 3rd ed. Los Angeles: Roxbury Publishing Company.

Jacobs, James B. 1977. *Stateville: The Penitentiary in Mass Society*. Chicago: University of Chicago Press.

Jacobson, Michael. 2005. *Downsizing Prisons: How to Reduce Crime*. New York: New York University Press.

Katz, Jack. 1988. *Seductions of Crime: A Chilling Exploration of the Criminal Mind—From Juvenile Delinquency to Cold-Blooded Murder*. New York: Basic Books.

Katz, Leonard. 2000. *Evolutionary Origins of Morality*. Exeter, UK: Imprint Academic.

Kraska, Peter. 2004. *Theorizing Criminal Justice: Eight Essential Orientations*. Long Grove, IL: Waveland Press.

Kraska, Peter B. and John J. Brent. 2011. *Theorizing Criminal Justice: Eight Essential Orientations*. Long Grove, IL: Waveland Press.

Kretzmann, John R. and John L. McKnight. 1993. *Building Communities from the Inside Out: A Path Toward Finding and Mobilizing a Community's Assets*. Chicago: ACTA Publication.

Kurbin, Charis E. 2012. Book Review of Ruth Peterson and Lauren Krivo, *Divergent Social Worlds* 2010, in *City & Community* 11, no. 1 (March): 119–21.

Lenski, Gerhardt. 1966. *Power and Privilege: A Theory of Social Stratification*. New York: McGraw-Hill.

Lerner, Steven E. 1980. "Phencyclidine Abuse in Perspective." Pp. 13–23 in *Phencyclidine Abuse Manual*, Mary Tuma McAdams, Ronald L. Linder, Steven E. Lerner, and Richard Stanley Burns, eds., Los Angeles: University of California Extension.

Leshner, Alan I. 1997. "Addiction Is a Brain Disease, and It Matters." *Science* (October 3): 45–47.

LIFERS Steering Committee. 2004. "The Culture of Street Crime." *Prison Journal* (December).

Lipsky, Michael. 1980. *Street-Level Bureaucracy*. New York: Russell Sage Foundation.

Lynch, James P. and William Alex Pridemore. 2011. "Crime in International Perspective," in James Q. Wilson and Joan Petersilia, eds., *Crime and Public Policy*. New York: Oxford University Press.

Lynch, James P. and William J. Sabol. 2001. "Prisoner Reentry in Perspective." *Prisoner Reentry and Community Justice*, National Institute of Justice Data Resources Program Workshop, ICPSR, Ann Arbor, MI, June 18–22.

MacLeod, Jay. 1987/2008. *Ain't No Makin' It: Aspirations and Attainment in a Low-Income Neighborhood*, 3rd ed. Boulder, CO: Westview Press.

Maruna, Shadd. 2001. *Making Good: How Ex-Convicts Reform and Rebuild Their Lives*. Washington, DC: American Psychological Association.

Marx, Karl. 1995. "Class Conflict Defines Society," in Lynn Barteck and Karen Mullin, eds., *Enduring Issues in Sociology: Opposing Viewpoints*. San Diego, CA: Greenhaven Press, Inc.

———. 1959/1970. *A Contribution to the Critique of Political Economy*. New York: International Publishers.

———. 1867/1967. *Capital: A Critique of Political Economy*, Vol. 1. New York: International Publishers.

Massey, Douglas S. and Nancy A. Denton. 1993. *American Apartheid: Segregation and the Making of the Underclass*. Cambridge, MA: Harvard University Press.

Matthews, Rick A. 2004. "Marxist Criminology," in *Controversies in Critical Criminology*, Martin D. Schwartz and Suzanne E. Hatty, eds., Cincinnati, OH: LexisNexis/Anderson.

Mauer, Marc. 1999. *Race to Incarcerate*. New York: The New Press.

Mauer, Marc and Meda Chesney-Lind, eds. 2002. *Invisible Punishment: The Collateral Consequences of Mass Imprisonment*. New York: The New Press.

McBarnet, Doreen. 2004. *Crime, Compliance and Control*. Burlington, VT: Ashgate Publishing.

McKibben, Bill. 2007. *Deep Economy: The Wealth of Communities and the Durable Future*. New York: Times Book/Henry Holt and Company.

MDOC. 1996. "Characteristics of Michigan Prisoners," Michigan Department of Corrections publication.

Merton, Robert. 1938. "Social Structure and Anomie." *American Sociological Review* 3: 672–82.

Michigan Department of Corrections (MDOC). www.michigan.gov.

Michigan STEPP 2008. "Michigan Skills Training and Education for Prisoners and Prevention Coalition/Consortium."

Miller, David. 1976/1989. *Social Justice*. Oxford: Claredon Press.

Miller, Gerald G. 1996. *Search and Destroy*. New York: Cambridge University Press.

Miller, Walter B. 1973/2004. "Ideology and Criminal Justice Policy: Some Current Issues." Pp. 110–20 in Peter B. Kraska, ed., *Theorizing Criminal Justice: Eight Essential Orientations*. Long Grove, IL: Waveland Press.

Milton, Trevor B. 2012. *Overcoming the Magnetism of Street Life: Crime-Engaged Youth and the Programs That Transform Them*. Lanham, MD: Lexington Press.

Mobley, Alan. 2003. "Convict Criminology: The Two-Legged Data Dilemma." Pp. 209–25 in Jeffrey Ian Ross and Stephen C. Richards, eds., *Convict Criminology*. Belmont, CA: Thomson/Wadsworth.

Moffit, Terrie F. 1997. "Adolescent-Limited and Life-Course Persistent Offending: A Complementary Pair of Developmental Theories." Pp. 11–54 in Terence P. Thornberry, ed., *Developmental Theories of Crime and Delinquency*. New Brunswick, NJ: Transaction.

MPRI. 2008. *Michigan Prisoner Reentry Initiative*. Newsletter at www.michpri.com.

Musto, Davis F. 1991. "Opium, Cocaine and Marijuana in American History." *Scientific American* (July): 40–47.

Newbold, Greg. 2003. "Rehabilitating Criminals: It Ain't That Easy." Pp. 150–69 in Jeffrey Ian Ross and Stephen C. Richards, eds., *Convict Criminology*. Belmont, CA: Thomson/Wadsworth.

Newbold, Greg and Jeffrey Ian Ross. 2012. "Convict Criminology at the Crossroads: Research Note," *Prison Journal* 93, no. 1: 3–10.

Newman, Annabel. 1993. "Prison Literacy: Implications for Program and Assessment Policy," Technical Report TR-93-1. Philadelphia: National Center on Adult Literacy.

Obermaier, Otto G. 1996. "Crime Isn't Always a Federal Case." *National Law Journal* (September 23), in CFECP 1998 conference materials.

Owen, Barbara. 1998. *In the Mix: Struggle and Survival in a Woman's Prison*. Albany: State University of New York Press.

Packer, Herbert. 1968/2004. "Two Models of the Criminal Justice Process." Pp. 85–100 in Peter B. Kraska, ed., *Theorizing Criminal Justice: Eight Essential Orientations*. Long Grove, IL: Waveland Press.

Page, Joshua. 2011. "Prison Officers Union and the Perpetuation of the Penal Status Quo." *Criminology & Public Policy* 10, no. 3: 735–70.

Parker, Karen. 2008. *Unequal Crime Decline: Theorizing Race, Urban Inequality, and Criminal Violence*. New York: New York University Press.

Perrone, Dina and Travis C. Pratt. 2006. "Comparing the Quality of Confinement and Cost-Effectiveness of Public versus Private Prisons: What We Know, Why We Do Not Know More, and Where to Go from Here." Pp. 474–86 in Edward J. Latessa and Alexander M. Holsinger, eds., *Correctional Contexts: Contemporary and Classical Readings*. Los Angeles: Roxbury Publishing Company.

Petersilia, Joan. 2003. *When Prisoners Come Home: Parole and Prisoner Reentry*, New York: Oxford University Press.

Peterson, Ruth D. and Lauren J. Krivo. 2010. *Divergent Social Worlds: Neighborhood Crime and the Racial-Spatial Divide*. New York: Russell Sage Foundation.

Polanyi, Karl. 1944. *The Great Transformation: The Political and Economic Origins of Our Time*. Boston: Beacon Press.

Pratt, Travis C. 2009. *Addicted to Incarceration: Corrections Policy and the Politics of Misinformation in the United States*. Thousand Oaks, CA: Sage Publications.

Radelet, Louis A. and David L. Carter. 1994. *The Police and the Community*, 5th ed. Englewood Cliffs, NJ: Prentice Hall.

Raine, Adrian. 1993. *The Psychopathology of Crime: Criminal Behavior as a Clinical Disorder*. San Diego, CA: Academic Press.

Reich, Robert. 2013. "Detroit and the American Social Contract." *The Toledo Blade*, July 26, A7.

———. 2010. *Aftershock: The Next Economy and America's Future*. New York: Vintage Books.

Reiman, Jeffrey. 2004. *The Rich Get Richer and the Poor Get Prison: Ideology, Class and Criminal Justice*. Boston: Pearson/Allyn and Bacon.

Reisig, Michael. 1998. Professor of criminal justice at Arizona State University. Personal communication.

Reiss, Albert J. 1986. "Why are Communities Important in Understanding Crime?" in *Communities and Crime*, Albert J. Reiss and Michael Tonry, eds. Chicago: University of Chicago Press.

Richards, Stephen C. 2003. "My Journey through the Federal Bureau of Prisons." Pp. 120–49 in Jeffrey Ian Ross and Stephen C. Richards, eds., *Convict Criminology*. Belmont, CA: Wadsworth/Thomson.

Richards, Stephen C. and Richard S. Jones. 1996. "Beating the Perpetual Incarceration Machine: Overcoming Structural Impediments to Re-entry." Pp. 201–32 in Shadd Maruna and Russ Immarigeon, eds., 2004. *After Crime and Punishment: Pathways to Offender Reintegration*. New York: Willan Publishing.

Richards, Stephen C. and Michael Lenza. 2012. "The First Dime and Nickel of Convict Criminology," *Journal of Prisoners and Prisons* 21, nos. 1 and 2, special issue commemorating the fifteenth anniversary of convict criminology.

Rifkin, Jeremy. 2006. *The European Dream*. New York: Basic Books.

Riley, Diane. n.d. "The Harm Reduction Model: Pragmatic Approaches to Drug Use from the Area between Intolerance and Neglect," Canadian Center on Substance Abuse. Internet. www.ccsa.ca.

Robbins, Ira. 1997. "The Case against the Prison-Industrial Complex," *Public Interest Law Review* (winter), in CFECP 1998 conference materials.

Rose, Dina and Todd Clear. 1998. "Incarceration, Social Capital and Crime: Examining the Unintended Consequences of Incarceration. *Criminology* 36, no. 3: 441–79.

Rosenbaum, Dennis P., Arthur J. Lurigo, and Robert C. Davis. 1998. *The Prevention of Crime: Social and Situational Strategies*. Belmont, CA: West/Wadsworth.

Rosenfeld, Richard, Kenna Quinet, and Crystal Garcia. 2010. *Contemporary Issues in Criminological Theory and Research: The Role of Social Institutions. Papers from the American Society of Criminology 2010 Conference*. Belmont, CA: Wadsworth.

Ross, Jeffrey Ian and Stephen C. Richards. 2003. *Convict Criminology*. Belmont, CA: Wadsworth/Thomson.

Rueschemeyer, Dietrich. 2009. *Useable Theory: Analytic Tools for Social and Political Research*. Princeton, NJ: Princeton University Press.

Sampson, Robert. 2011. "The Community." Pp. 210–36 in James Q. Wilson and Joan Petersilia, eds., *Crime and Public Policy*. New York: Oxford University Press.

———. 2002. "The Community." Pp. 225–52 in James Q. Wilson and Joan Petersilia, eds., *Crime: Public Policies for Crime Control*. Oakland, CA: Institute for Contemporary Studies.

Sampson, Robert J. 1987. "Communities and Crime." Pp. 91–114 in Michael R. Gottfredson and Travis Hirschi, eds., *Positive Criminology*. Beverly Hills, CA: Sage.

———. 1986. "Crime in Cities: The Effects of Formal and Informal Control," in *Communities and Crime*, Albert J. Reiss and Michael Tonry, eds.,. Chicago: University of Chicago Press.

Scammons, Richard, and Ben J. Wattenberg. 1969. *The Real Majority*. New York: Coward-McCann.

Schmalleger, Frank. 2001. *Criminal Justice Today: An Introductory Text for the 21st Century*, 6th ed. Upper Saddle River, NJ: Prentice Hall.

Schumpeter, Joseph A. 1950. *Capitalism, Socialism, and Democracy*, 3rd ed. New York: Harper & Row.

Scott, Richard W. 1992. *Organizations: Rational, Natural, and Open Systems*, 3rd ed. Englewood Cliffs, NJ: Prentice Hall.

Schwartz, John E. and Thomas J. Volgy. 1992. *The Forgotten Americans*. New York: W. W. Norton Company.

Sellin, Thorsten. 1938. *Culture, Conflict and Crime*. New York: Social Science Research Council.

Shaw, Clifford. 1930/1996. *The Jackroller: A Delinquent Boy's Own Story*. Chicago: University of Chicago Press.

Shelden, Randall G. 2008. *Controlling the Dangerous Classes: A History of Criminal Justice in America*, 2nd ed. Boston: Pearson/A&B.

Shelden, Randall G. and William B. Brown. 2000. "The Crime Control Industry and the Management of the Surplus Population." Pp. 217–32 in Peter B. Kraska and John J. Brent, *Theorizing Criminal Justice: Eight Essential Orientations*. Long Grove, IL: Waveland Press.

Shover, Neal and David Honaker. 1999. "The Socially Bounded Decision Making of Persistent Property Offenders," in Paul Cromwell, ed., *In Their Own Words: Criminals on Crime*. Los Angeles: Roxbury Publishers.

Simon, David and Edward Burns. 1997. *The Corner: A Year in the Life of an Inner City Neighborhood*. New York: Broadway Books.

Simon, Jonathan. 2007. *Governing Through Crime: How the War on Crime Transformed American Democracy and Created a Culture of Fear*. New York: Oxford University Press.

Stark, Rodney. 1987. "Deviant places: A theory of the ecology of crime," *Criminology* 25: 893–909.

Stenson, Kevin. 1991. "Making Sense of Crime Control." Pp. 1–32 in Kevin Stenson and David Crowell, eds., *The Politics of Crime*. London: Sage.

Strether, Lambert. 2013. "What Then Must We Do? Gar Alperovitz at the New Economy Summit." www.nakedcapitalism.com/2013/11/what-then-can-I-do.

Sullivan, Dennis and Larry Tifft. 2005. *Handbook of Restorative Justice*. New York: Routledge.

———. 2001. *Restorative Justice: Healing the Foundations of Our Everyday Lives*. Monsey, NY: Willow Tree Press.

Sullivan, Mercer L. 1989. *"Getting Paid": Youth Crime and Work in the Inner City*. Ithaca, NY: Cornell University Press.

Sutherland, Edwin. 1947. "Differential Association." Pp. 139–41 in Henry Pontell, ed., *Social Deviance: Readings in Theory & Research*, 5th ed. Upper Saddle River, NJ: Pearson/Prentice Hall.

Sutherland, Edwin H., and Donald R. Cressey. 1974. *Criminology*. 9th ed. Philadelphia: Lippincott.

Swanson, Cheryl. 2009. *Restorative Justice in a Prison Community: Or Everything I Didn't Learn in Kindergarten I Learned in Prison*. Lanham, MD: Lexington Books.

Sykes, Gresham. 1958. *The Society of Captives: A Study of a Maximum Security Prison*. Princeton, NJ: Princeton University Press.

Sykes, Gresham and David Matza. 1957. "Techniques of Neutralization: A Theory of Delinquency." Pp. 176–79 in Henry N. Pontell and Stephen M. Rosoff, eds., *Social Deviance: Readings in Theory and Research*. New York: McGraw-Hill.

Terry, Charles M. 2003. *The Fellas: Overcoming Prison and Addiction*. Belmont, CA: Wadsworth/Thomson Learning.

Thomas, Paulette. 1994. "Rural Regions Look to Prisons for Prosperity." *Wall Street Journal*, July 11, in CFECP 1998 conference materials.

Thompson, E. P. 1963. *The Making of the English Working Class*. New York: Vintage Books.

Tifft, Larry and Dennis Sullivan. 1980. *The Struggle to Be Human: Crime, Criminology, and Anarchism*. Sanday, Orkney, UK: Cienfuegos Press.

Tilly, Charles. 1998. *Durable Inequality*. Berkeley: University of California Press.

Tonry, Michael. 2007. "Crime and Human Rights—How Political Paranoia, Protestant Fundamentalism, and Constitutional Obsolescence Combined to Devastate Black America: The American Society of Criminology 2007 Presidential Address." *Criminology* 46, no. 1 (February 2008).

———. 1999. "Why Are U.S. Incarcerations Rates So High?" in *Crime and Delinquency* 45, no. 4 (October): 419–37.

———. 1995. *Malign Neglect: Race, Crime, and Punishment in America*. New York: Oxford University Press.

———. 1994. "Racial Disproportions in U.S. Prisons." *British Journal of Criminology* 34. Pp. 328–48 in George F. Cole, Marc G. Gertz, and Amy Bunger, eds., 2004. *The Criminal Justice System: Politics and Policies*, 9th ed. Belmont, CA: Wadsworth/Thomson Learning.

Travis, Jeremy. 2002. "Invisible Punishment: An Instrument of Social Exclusion." Pp. 15–36 in Marc Mauer and Meda Chesney-Lind, eds., *Invisible Punishment: The Collateral Consequences of Mass Imprisonment*. New York: The New Press.

Tregea, William S. 2003. "Twenty Years Teaching College in Prison." Pp. 309–332 in Jeffrey Ian Ross and Stephen C. Richards, eds., *Convict Criminology*. Belmont, CA: Wadsworth/Thomson.

———. 2002. "State Must Cut Prison Costs: Granholm Can Lead the Way to a Better Corrections Policy." *Lansing State Journal*, December 15, 15A.

———. 2001. "Prison Education and Skills Training in the Transition to Community," a presentation in collaboration with John Linton, U.S. Department of

Education at the "Prisoner Reentry and Community Justice," National Institute of Justice (NIJ) and ICPSR Data Resources Program Summer Program Workshop, June 18–22, 2001, Institute for Social Research, Ann Arbor, MI.

———. 1998. "Prison Post-Secondary, Recidivism, and the Current Political Climate," research report for Center on Crime, Communities, and Culture, Open Society Institute (Soros Foundation) (unpublished).

Tregea, William and Marjorie S. Larmour. 2009. *The Prisoners' World: Portraits of Convicts Caught in the Incarceration Binge*. Lanham, MD: Lexington Press.

Trojanowicz, Robert C. and Merry Morash. 1992. *Juvenile Delinquency: Concepts and Control*, 5th ed. Englewood Cliffs, NJ: Prentice Hall.

Trojanowicz, Robert C., Merry Morash, and Pamela J. Schram. 2000. *Juvenile Delinquency: Concepts and Controls*, 6th ed. Upper Saddle River, NJ: Prentice Hall.

Trout, Grafton, William Tregea, and Geoffry Simmons. 1968. "Youth Makes Itself Heard: Changing Participational Contexts." *AAUW Journal* (May).

Trout, Grafton and William S. Tregea. 1971. "The Social Problem Tradition: Crisis or Impasse?" Paper delivered Society of the Study of Social Problems, Denver, CO. August.

Tunnel, Kenneth D. 2000. *Living Off Crime*. Chicago: Burnham Publisher.

United Steel Workers News. 2012. "Worker Ownership for the 99%: The United Steelworkers, Mondragon, and the Ohio Employee Ownership Center Announce a New Union Cooperative Model to Reinsert Worker Equity Back in the U.S. Economy." March 26. www.usw.coop.

Useem, Bert and Anne Morrison Piehl. 2008. *The Prison State: The Challenge of Mass Incarceration*. New York: Cambridge University Press.

Useem, Bert, Raymond V. Liedka, and Anne Morrison Piehl. 2003. "Popular Support for the Prison Build-Up." *Punishment & Society* 5, no. 1 (January): 5–32.

Vera Institute. 2013. "Michigan Joins National Initiative to Expand Education in Prison and After Release." www.vera.org/news/michigan.

Vera Institute of Justice. 2006. "Dollars and Sentences: Legislators' Views on Prisons, Punishments, and the Budget Crisis." Pp. 474–86 in Edward J. Latessa and Alexander M. Holsinger, eds., *Correctional Contexts: Contemporary and Classical Readings*. Los Angeles: Roxbury Publishing Company.

Wacquant, Loic. 2008. *Urban Outcasts: A Comparative Sociology of Advanced Marginality*. Maldan, MA: Polity Press.

———. 2006. "Hyperghetto and Hyperincarceration." Presentation at the American Society of Criminology annual meeting, November 14, 2006, Los Angeles, CA.

———. 2002. "Deadly Symbiosis." *Boston Review* (April/May).

———. 1999. "Urban Marginality in the Coming Millennium." *Urban Studies* 36, no. 10.

Wallerstein, Immanuel. 1999. *The End of the World as We Know It*. Minneapolis: University of Minnesota Press.

Walsh, Edward. 1994. "Strapped Small Towns Try to Lock Up Prisons," *New York Times*, December 24, in CFECP 1998 conference materials.

Wanberg, Kenneth and Harvey Milkman. 1998. *Criminal Conduct and Substance Abuse Treatment: Strategies for Self-Improvement and Change—The Participant Workbook*. Thousand Oaks, CA: Sage Publishers.

Wenda, Walter. 1997. "The Relationship between Life-Skills Literacy and Vocational Education and Self-Perception of Eleven Domains and Global Self-Worth of Adult Incarcerated Males." *Journal of Correctional Education* 47, no. 2: 74–85.

Western, Bruce. 2006. *Punishment and Inequality in America*. New York: Russell Sage Foundation.

Williams, Corey. 2009. "Detroit Youth Charged in Violent Crimes in August." *The Daily Telegram*, September 1, A3.

Williamson, Thad, David Imbroscio, and Gar Alperovitz. 2002. *Making a Place for Community*. New York: Routledge.

Willis, Paul. 1977. *Learning to Labor: How Working Class Kids Get Working Class*. New York: Columbia University Press.

Wilson, James Q. and Joan Petersilia, Eds., 2011. *Rime and Public Policy*. New York: Oxford University Press.

Wilson, William Julius. 1996. *When Work Disappears: The World of the New Urban Poor*. New York: Vintage Books.

———. 1987/2012. *The Truly Disadvantaged: The Inner City, the Underclass, and Public Policy*, 2nd ed. Chicago: University of Chicago Press.

Wright, Kevin N. 1981/2004. "The Desirability of Goal Conflict Within the Criminal Justice System." Pp. 121–25 in Peter B. Kraska, ed., *Theorizing Criminal Justice: Eight Essential Orientations*. Long Grove, IL: Waveland Press,.

Wright, Richard T. and Scott Decker. 1994. *Burglars on the Job: Streetlife and Residential Break-Ins*. Boston: Northeastern University Press.

Wysong, Earl, Robert Perrucci, and David Wright. 2014. *The New Class Society: Goodbye American Dream?* 4th ed. Lanham, MD: Rowman & Littlefield.

Young, Jock. 1997. "Left Realism: The Basics." Pp. 28–36 in *Thinking Critically about Crime*, Brian MacLean and Dragan Milovanovic, eds., Vancouver, BC: The Collective Press.

———. 1986. "The Failure of Criminology: The Need for Radical Realism." Pp. 4–30 In *Confronting Crime*, Roger Matthews and Jock Young, eds., Beverly Hills, CA: Sage.

———. 1979. "Left Idealism, Reformism and Beyond." Pp. 13–28 in Bob Fine, Richard Kinsey, John Lea, Sol Picciotto, and Jock Young, eds., *Capitalism and the Rule of Law*. London: Hutchison.

Zakaria, Fareed. 2010 "Restoring the American Dream." *Time*, November 1, 30–35.

Zimring, Frank. 2007. *The Great American Crime Decline*. New York: Oxford University Press.

———. 2006. "Why the Incarceration Boom May Not End." Plenary Session, American Society of Criminology, November 3, Los Angeles, CA.

Zimring, Frank E. and Gordon Hawkins. 1997. *Crime Is Not the Problem: Lethal Violence in America*. New York: Oxford University Press.

Index

About the Author

William Tregea, who holds a PhD, MS, and an MA from Michigan State University, has helped to develop the bachelor and masters criminal justice programs at Adrian College, Michigan, and has taught criminal justice, criminology, sociology, management, and economics for more than thirty-six years. He has taught many hundreds of prisoners over thirty years in prison college programs (1981–2000) and volunteer classes in eleven prisons in Michigan and California (2001–2012), and is coauthor, with Marjorie Larmour, of *The Prisoners' World: Portraits of Convicts Caught in the Incarceration Binge* (Lexington, 2009). He founded the Michigan STEPP Consortium (Skills Training and Education for Prisoners and Prevention, wtregea@adrian.edu). From 1998 to 2003 he made organizing efforts to get accredited education back in Michigan prisons after the ending of Pell grant eligibility for prisoners and the collapse of the once lively 770 prisoner college education programs in the United States. He is a founding member and board member of the Michigan Citizens Alliance on Prisons and Public Spending (CAPPS 2008; www.capps-mi.org), is dedicated to evidence-based research and policy suggestions for capping prison growth and shifting resources to prevention in Michigan, and works with the CAPPS 2011 correctional programming group exploring possibilities for accredited prison postsecondary correctional education and the CAPPS 2013 justice reinvestment work group.

EARLY DRAFT COAUTHOR

Marjorie Larmour (deceased August 2007) helped to envision and create an early draft of this book (2005)—a draft that was used in criminology classes and social deviance classes at Adrian College. She held a masters degree (MA) in journalism and a BA in psychology, both from the University of California, Berkeley, and had been a radio and television scriptwriter, journalist, writer, and publications editor for many years. She had completed sixty credits of doctoral work in adult education, communications, and sociology at Michigan State University. For twenty years she taught college in prisons in Michigan. These included twelve minimum, medium, and maximum prisons, including two of the oldest prisons in the state: Jackson State Prison (maximum) (SPSM) and Michigan Reformatory (MR) for prisoners under twenty-five years of age, most of whom were from Detroit's tough inner city. During this time she wrote stories about her prison experiences and helped draft a book featuring prisoner views on the prison titled *The Prisoners World: Portraits of Convicts Caught in the Incarceration Binge* (Tregea and Larmour 2009).

THE PRISONERS

All of the prisoner essays in this book were obtained in the author's "Social Science and Personal Writing" classes from 2003 to 2012 at the Gus Harrison Correctional Facility, Adrian, Michigan, and the Parnall Correctional and Cooper Street Facilities, Jackson, Michigan. Many prisoner students have been released, paroled, and left the system. Some are currently assigned to a parole officer. Some are still in prison with outdates in the near future. Some are lifers, many of whom are transformed people awaiting a hope for commutation or a change to reviewable status. For a few, the outdate will never come, they will die in prison.